Feed Your Horse Like A Horse

Optimize your horse's nutrition for a lifetime of vibrant health

Juliet M. Getty, Ph.D.

First published by Dog Ear Publishing
4010 W. 86th Street, Ste H
Indianapolis, IN 46268
www.dogearpublishing.net

dog ear
PUBLISHING

ISBN: 978-160844-214-0

This book is printed on acid-free paper.

Printed in the United States of America

This book is dedicated to my cherished Belle. You came into my life pregnant and neglected. Years later, healthy and strong, you said goodbye, leaving behind a beautiful colt and an adoring family. You thanked me when I saved you from a harsh world, but I've thanked you every day since for all you taught me and the way you made me laugh with such abandon.

The horse is God's gift to mankind.
~ Arabian Proverb

Table of Contents

DISCLAIMER

I have made every effort when writing this book to present the most accurate and helpful information based on my expertise, and on the most reliable sources. I, my editor, and illustrator take no responsibility for any results or damages that might be obtained from the reliance on the information and recommendations made in this book. We further take no responsibility for the inherent risks of activities involving horses, including equine behavior changes that might result in personal injury.

Nutritional advice, especially in the case of illness, injury, disorders, or conditions requiring medical treatment, is not intended to take the place of proper veterinary care. It may be used in conjunction with such care to facilitate healing and maintain health. The information provided by Getty Equine Nutrition, LLC is presented for the purpose of educating horse owners. Suggested feeds, supplements, and procedures are administered voluntarily with the understanding that any adverse reaction is the responsibility of the owner. Furthermore, Getty Equine Nutrition, LLC cannot be held accountable for a horse's response, whether favorable or adverse, to nutritional intervention.

On occasion brand names have been used as examples. However, mention of a specific product or brand name is not intended to imply that other companies offer inferior products. I make no intent to violate any trademark laws.

Inspirational quotations at the beginning of each chapter were obtained from various sources and are meant to enhance this scholarly work. They comply with the fair use clause outlined by the U.S. Copyright Office and are in no way intended to infringe on copyright laws.

ACKNOWLEDGEMENTS

First and foremost, my deepest gratitude goes to my husband, Bob, for being the best cheerleader a gal could ever have. When fatigue would set in and my brain would feel like it was going to swell out of my head, he was there to offer pearls of wisdom that encouraged and inspired me. He reminded me that my work was a labor of love. And it was that passion for horses that kept me going.

I could not have accomplished this project without the love of my family. I thank my darling daughter, Alexandra, for all those nights she not only cooked dinner, but cleaned up — that's usually against the rules in my house! And for all the goodnight hugs and back rubs she so lovingly gave. I thank my precious son, Roy, living in Texas, who would entertain me over the phone with his marvelous sense of humor, stirring me into a therapeutic belly laugh.

Knowing that my friends were quietly supporting me on the sidelines, giving me time and space to write, while checking in on me every once in a while, made my work so much easier. I want to mention each and every one of them by name, but lest I leave out someone very important, I'll rely on each of you knowing who you are, and how much I love and value your friendship. There is one special friend I need to thank personally: Cathi, who kept me motivated with the funny and endearing emails she faithfully sent me each morning, is the one who got me back on track. If it weren't for her, a few more years might have passed before finishing this book. It was she who told me one cold morning in January when I was complaining how hard it was to find time to sit down and write that the only way I was ever going to get this book completed was to get up every morning, that's *every* morning, at 5:00 am. And she was right. 200 cups of coffee later and here it is!

I was blessed to have found my editor, Elizabeth Testa, who brought skill and insight into making my book the best it could be. I appreciate her perspective as a horseman as well as the care she gave the manuscript. And I especially thank her for all the times she gently nudged me into presenting the material in a way that would flow more easily, so it would be enjoyable for every reader, from the novice horse owner to the professional.

My illustrator, Robin Peterson, DVM, is a gifted artist. You may have already seen her work highlighted in many popular equine magazines. Her drawings throughout this book add professionalism and style. I appreciate her patience and attention to detail as I tried to convey what I needed, and she has my heartfelt thanks. Her company, FernWood Studio, in Washington State, has a wonderful website that shows her vast artistic skill: www.fernwoodstudio.com.

At the beginning of each chapter, I chose a personally meaningful quotation from various authors. I wish to thank these horsemen for their inspiration and wisdom.

And finally, *Feed Your Horse Like A Horse* would not have been possible without the outpouring of support I received from my clients. They're the ones who entrusted me with their horses' care. They're the ones who asked me to write this book. Over the years, I've celebrated with them as I watched their horses heal and thrive and I've cried a few tears as well, when a precious equine friend passed on. It is you, dear friends, who started me on this adventure.

~ Juliet M. Getty, Ph.D.

INTRODUCTION

Horses, always, coming and going, hoofprints across my heart.
~ Jo-Ann Mapson

Picture, for a moment, a group of wild horses. A sense of calm comes over you as you watch them graze peacefully, standing head to toe with a favorite friend, or just resting. A gust of wind bursts forth and they gallop away, only to settle down again, lowering their heads to the ground to enjoy the lush prairie. This is all they know.

They walk along without a care, foraging for the next delicious morsel. And they eat all kinds of things — flowers, fruits and berries, nuts and seeds, leaves and tree bark, and of course, plenty of grass. Eating is a way of life, the way they were designed to exist. They sleep in spurts, no more than 20 minutes at a time, and while they need to lie down part of that time, most of their rest is accomplished standing up so they can flee at a moment's notice.

Now picture the domesticated horse. A very different setting, indeed. Not a bad setting, just different. And in many ways, much better. We protect them, feed them, vaccinate them against diseases, take care of their feet, float their teeth, and may even cover them with a warm blanket when it gets cold. In short, we love them. We more than love them, we're *nourished* by them — the way they nicker when they hear us coming, the warmth of their soft breath and velvet noses, the countless times they make us laugh. Their magnificent strength and beauty is beyond comparison. They teach us so much. There's nothing like a horse.

That's why you're reading this book — because you care about your horse's wellbeing. You can't give him the wild setting his ancestors enjoyed, but you can come awfully close. The best way we can show respect for our equine friends is to honor how they're made. To feed them — like a horse.

I'm here to show you how to do exactly that. That's why I've written this book. As an equine nutritionist, I'm a scientist at heart. By combining this knowledge with my love for horses, I'm able to make a better life, a longer, healthier life, for these animals we call our friends.

I named this book *Feed Your Horse Like A Horse* because horses and other equines are different from most any other creature on this planet. Though they eat hay, they don't do it as efficiently as cows and therefore require much more to get the same level of nourishment. Though they eat oats, they're not like pigs that can eat a lot and just get fat — overfeed oats to a horse and it can damage his feet. They're not like dogs or cats, or even people, who can eat a few meals each day and not suffer any damaging consequences if a few hours separate them. Instead, horses are unique creatures that need a steady supply of grass or hay all day long. That's right: all day long, because that is the way they are designed.

And while we can't feed them the daily variety of foods they'd find in the wild, we can mix our feedstuffs to create a balanced diet that fulfills their nutrient needs. Sometimes we need to fill in the nutritional holes that are created when feeding the same thing day in and day out, along with dead grass (hay) that can't possibly be as nutritious as fresh, lush pasture. Fortunately, there are many ways to do this.

Your horse's needs are influenced by his physiology but they are also affected by his mental state. For this reason, my approach is holistic; I take into account his environment and level of stress, as well as his nutritional status, to optimize his overall health and have it last a lifetime.

How to Use This Book

My goal in writing this book is to help horse owners like you decide the best feeding method for your horse. I make recommendations on *what* to feed, but I also want you to know *why* a specific feedstuff or nutrient is important, so I include some of the scientific aspects of nutrition, too. I also discuss various medical conditions that can be prevented or treated through nutritional intervention, but please understand that there are medical situations that go beyond the scope of this book; it is not intended to be a medical guide.

I base my chapters on the types of queries and concerns I receive from folks each day. They range from basic questions about hay, commercial feeds, or which vitamin supplement is best, to serious concerns about colic, laminitis, ulcers, and joint problems. Sometimes the concern is about a pregnant mare or her growing foal, or an old horse who needs some support to gracefully grow even older. And every now and then, I'll hear from a new horse owner who simply needs to know where to start.

Everyone should read Chapter 1 — Ground Rules for Feeding a Horse. This will give you an overview of all the basics. It's not just for the inexperienced horse owner; this chapter is for everyone regardless of how long you've been around horses. It may teach you something new, or at the very least, affirm what you already know.

The remainder of this book is meant to serve as a reference. You have the freedom to pick and choose which sections to read; you may wish to review a particular nutrient, help your horse overcome a problem, or discover ways to ease your horse from one life stage to the next. Because each chapter is meant to stand on its own, you'll find some redundancy between chapters when I feel the need to emphasize important concepts or recommend certain feeds that benefit more than one situation. There are times when it's not possible to isolate a discussion of one disorder without bringing up another that's examined in a different chapter. When that's the case, I refer you to relevant chapters for expanded discussion or review.

There are many calculations throughout the book and rather than go through the details in each chapter, I offer you step-by-step instructions for each computation in an appendix called Crunching Numbers. It also includes conversions between the U.S. and metric measuring systems.

You'll notice that I use the generic "he" throughout this book when referring to your horse. Don't get me wrong — I love mares, so it has nothing to do with that. I just find the use of "he/she" to be somewhat awkward. Some authors prefer to say "he" in one paragraph, and "she" in another. I find that mentally distracting.

The book is divided into two main sections. Part I offers fundamentals of each nutrient classification, along with details on forages, concentrates, and even which treats are safe to feed. Part II describes specific conditions and circumstances your horse may be experiencing. I offer insight into the causes, treatment, and prevention of diseases such as laminitis and equine metabolic syndrome, digestive problems such as ulcers and colic, weight management for both the overweight and underweight horse, and conditions such as arthritis, allergies, and much more. This section helps you feed a pregnant mare and support her newborn foal as he grows into adulthood. And as more and more horses are living incredibly long lives, their nutritional needs change along the way — this, too, is discussed in Part II. The last chapter deals with the special needs of athletes, to keep them in top shape to work and perform.

One thing about learning, it brings up more questions. I expect you'll have many that are unanswered within these pages. Or perhaps you need assistance deciding on which supplement to choose. That's when you go to your computer or pick up the phone and contact me. Unlike most equine nutritionists, I do not work for any particular company, so I'm free to make unbiased suggestions. I also have a helpful "Ask the Nutritionist" forum on my website where I address horse owners' concerns. Feel free to call, email, or write; My contact information can be found below. I truly welcome hearing from you.

I'll close here by sincerely thanking you for choosing my book. Your interest tells me that your horse is very important to you. As you read on, I hope you feel, as I do, that we're having a conversation between people of like minds, both of whom love and admire horses.

                                          ~ Juliet M. Getty, Ph.D.

Juliet M. Getty, Ph.D.
Getty Equine Nutrition, LLC
Email: GettyEquineNutrition@gmail.com
Website: www.GettyEquineNutrition.com

PART I

THE FUNDAMENTALS

CHAPTER 1 —
GROUND RULES FOR FEEDING A HORSE

A horse is the projection of peoples' dreams about themselves — strong,
powerful, beautiful, graceful, spirited — he gives us escape from our
mundane world.
~ Pam Brown

The Basics

Is there one correct way to feed a horse? The short answer is "Yes." You can
keep your horse at his healthiest if (1) he's allowed to be turned out 24
hours a day along with a shelter for protection against nasty weather, (2)
has hay/pasture available at all times, and (3) has small, frequent meals to
provide additional calories for exercise or to serve as a carrier for supplements. But, in general, all horses need to have the following:

- **Forage.** Most of the diet should come from forage — approximately
  1.5 to 3.0% of body weight depending on energy requirements.

- **Water.** A clean, fresh water supply, free from algae, insects, and bird
  droppings, should be available and convenient at all times. To ensure
  adequate intake, water should be temperature-controlled in the winter if the outside temperature falls below 50° F. Eating snow will not
  provide enough water.

- **Salt.** Horses require sodium and chloride, from salt. Always provide
  a white salt block. Mineralized blocks are only important for horses
  that are not receiving any fortified feed or supplements containing
  minerals. Blue blocks contain cobalt and iodine, which here again,
  may not be necessary if the diet already contains these minerals from
  other sources. If horses ignore the salt block, add 2 tablespoons of
  plain, white table salt per day (divided between meals). Chapter 7 —
  Fundamentals of Water and Electrolytes provides more detail.

To these basics, you may want to add the following, depending on your
horse's particular needs:

- **Concentrates.** These are feeds that are not high in fiber, but are high
  in calories from carbohydrates, protein, or fat. They include cereal

grains (oats, corn, barley, wheat, etc.), soybean meal, seeds and seed meals (such as flaxseed meal), and fats (oils).

- **Digestible fibrous feeds**. These offer more calories than hay and pasture, without the sugar and starch levels of cereal grains. They include such things as beet pulp, bran, and grain by-products (such as distiller's grains, hulls, and middlings).

- **Legumes.** The most popular legume is alfalfa. Alfalfa hay (cubes and/or pellets), when fed with grass hay or pasture, helps improve overall protein quality. High-quality protein is necessary for the production of body tissues (e.g., muscle, skin, hooves, hair, bone, tendons, blood proteins, antibodies, enzymes, and more).

- **Supplements.** To fill in nutrient gaps, assist with medical disorders or injuries, and aid in optimizing overall health, it is helpful to improve the diet with appropriate nutritional supplements. When feeding more than one supplement, avoid overlapping nutrients by paying close attention to the ingredients of each product.

GETTING BY WITH ONLY HAY

You do not need to add any concentrates to your horse's diet unless he needs more calories. However, when fresh grass is dried and stored as hay, it loses many essential nutrients, so supplements are necessary to fill in the nutritional gaps if hay is the only food source. Supplements are easy to feed when added to a "carrier" meal such as a small meal of grain, beet pulp, or commercial feed. For the grass hay-only diet, consider adding the following:

- **Vitamin E.** Add a minimum of 1 IU per pound of body weight. For the 1100 lb horse this translates to 1100 IU of vitamin E.

- **Essential fatty acids.** Feed 1/2 cup of flaxseed meal per 400 lbs of body weight per day to provide essential fatty acids. Obtain a commercial stabilized product that has added calcium to correct the inverted calcium to phosphorus ratio naturally found in flax.

- **Minerals.** Add a multiple vitamin/mineral supplement that complements the mineral content of your hay.

- **Beta carotene.** To provide what has been lost in hay, add a daily dose of 72 mg of beta carotene per kg of body weight or 30 IU of vitamin

A per kg of body weight (beta carotene is converted to vitamin A). See Appendix — Crunching Numbers for the conversion factor between kg and lbs.

Pasture provides nutrients that are lost in hay. If your horse grazes on good quality pasture at least 8 hours each day, additional supplementation (except salt) should not be required (unless specific health or stress levels warrant more nutrient intake). If you remove your horse from pasture at night, be sure to provide enough hay so that your horse does not run out. Read on… I'll explain the reason for this.

Understanding the Digestive Tract of a Horse

The digestive tract of a horse is different from that of most other animals. Humans, cats, dogs, pigs, and other predators are able to digest meat and plant foods, but are not able to digest the fiber found in plants. This is because the digestive system does not produce the enzymes necessary to break down fiber molecules into small pieces. The result? The fiber leaves the body undigested as fecal waste.

But many animals have a four-compartment stomach that includes a "fermentation vat" where billions of beneficial bacteria live. These bacterial flora are quite capable of producing the enzymes needed to digest (break down into small pieces) the fiber found in plants. Ruminant herbivores, such as cows, sheep, deer, and goats, have this complex digestive system that is capable of efficiently digesting fibrous materials. They can take cellulose (one of the fibers found in hay, for example) and break it down into small molecules of simple sugar (known as glucose). In fact, if your goat gets hold of your cotton t-shirt, he can get glucose from it because cotton is the purest form of cellulose. Glucose is absorbed from the digestive system into the bloodstream, where it is transported to the animal's cells to be metabolized for calories that keep the nervous system working, the heart beating, and the lungs breathing, as well as produce body heat and provide energy to do exercise.

I still haven't told you about horses — that's because horses are not like either one of these groups. They belong to a category known as "non-ruminant herbivores." They are herbivores because they only eat plants. And they are non-ruminant because they do not have the four-chamber stomach that ruminants have. Instead, horses and all other equines, such as ponies, minis, donkeys, zebras, as well as the hippopotamus and the rhinoceros, have a digestive system that is a combination of ruminant and non-ruminant. They have a fermentation vat, called the cecum, that provides a home for fiber-digesting bacteria. But the cecum is toward the end of the digestive tract, and therefore not as efficient as the ruminant's, whose fermentation vat (rumen) is toward the beginning. Therefore, horses need to consume much greater amounts of forages (hay and pasture) than cattle do to get the same number of calories.

HORSES NEED TO EAT HAY AND/OR PASTURE AT ALL TIMES

The most basic approach toward keeping your horse healthy is realizing that horses are "trickle feeders." This means that they require a continuous supply of small amounts of forage. Horses in their natural setting will graze virtually all day, while taking approximately 2 hours each day to rest (though not at all one time). This is a very important concept to understand because a horse's digestive system needs to have food in it most of the time, in order to avoid digestive problems. Horses' stomachs, unlike our own, produce acid continually and if a horse consistently goes for more than 3 hours without anything to graze on, the excess acid can produce ulcers, as well as diarrhea, behavioral problems (because the horse is in pain), and even colic. Chewing produces saliva, which acts as a natural antacid, so if a horse has no hay or pasture, he will chew on anything he can to create saliva; some horses will start to eat their own manure. Furthermore, not eating is very stressful for horses, which results in the secretion of stress-related hormones. These hormones promote fat storage. So, putting an overweight horse on a "diet" by reducing hay consumption actually works in reverse — it promotes more weight gain. In addition, the reduced forage availability will make his metabolic rate slow down, causing calories to be burned at a slower rate. This, too, results in weight gain.

Horses are capable of self-regulating their intake when given the chance. If they are only offered a set amount of hay at a time, they will likely eat it very quickly and will be anxious for more. But if given all they want, they will overeat at first (for a week or less) and then, once they see that they can walk away and relax and the hay will still be there when they return, they will calm down and eat only what they need to maintain a healthy weight. If your horse is stalled at night, the only way to know whether he has enough hay for this self-regulation to take place is for some hay to be left over in the morning.

Pasture and/or hay offered free choice will affect how your horse behaves. The more you treat your horse like a horse in the wild, the calmer and more cooperative he will be. He needs to graze continuously, and he also needs to be able to interact with other horses. Negative behaviors such as cribbing, pawing, and irritability are often alleviated by feeding more hay and providing turnout with his buddies.

Digestive system

Let's break this information further down and examine the different parts of your horse's digestive system. It is essential for you to understand how a horse is built on the inside if you are to make good decisions about feeding. Take a look at the figure below:

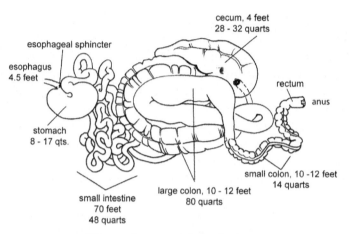

The equine gastrointestinal tract

When a horse eats, the following events happen:

Chewing

Food is chewed and moistened with saliva so it can be easily swallowed. Saliva contains two very important substances – bicarbonate, which acts as a buffer (neutralizer) of stomach acid, and an enzyme known as salivary amylase that starts breaking down (digesting) starch into small pieces.

Traveling down the esophagus

After your horse swallows, food travels down the esophagus. At the base of the esophagus is a circular muscle known as the lower esophageal sphincter. This sphincter acts as a "door" to the stomach that relaxes open to allow food to enter. But once food enters the stomach, the lower esophageal sphincter closes very tightly — so tightly in fact, that food cannot come back up from the stomach. Hence, horses cannot normally vomit. It's interesting to note, horses do not need to vomit in their natural state because they are herbivores. Animals that consume other animals need to regurgitate in order to remove diseased or spoiled meat from their systems. Unless they are very hungry, herbivores tend to be more selective and will avoid bad or poisonous plants.

The stomach

The stomach's volume is small in relation to the rest of the digestive tract. This is because horses are designed to eat small amounts of forage throughout the day, and not fill up the stomach. Unfortunately, feeding large concentrated meals (not hay or other forage) that overfill the stomach can lead to rupturing, colic, and inadequate digestion of carbohydrates, which can result in laminitis (see Chapter 11 — Laminitis). Therefore, limit meal size to no more than 4 lbs for the average 1100 lb horse. This means that *you need to weigh your feed*. Feeding "scoops" or "coffee cans" is not acceptable unless you know how much the feed weighs. A two-quart scoop that is filled with oats, for example, will weigh approximately 2 1/2 lbs. Fill it with beet pulp and it will only weigh 1 pound. Fill it with a commercial feed and it will weigh something completely different. So weigh your feed, then mark your scoop or can for that particular feed, so you know exactly how much your horse is being fed.

Inside the stomach, food is mixed with acid and pulverized by very powerful muscles into a semi-liquid mass. Stomach acid (hydrochloric acid) is necessary for three important functions. First, it starts protein digestion by activating an enzyme called pepsin. Next, hydrochloric acid (HCl) loosens the bonds between amino acids, making protein digestion easier. And finally, HCl destroys the multitude of microorganisms that your horse consumes by eating off the ground. Therefore, HCl is an important component of the immune system. Long term usage of antacids or ulcer medications disrupts this immunity component and makes your horse more susceptible to infections. In Chapter 14 — Digestive Problems, I go into this subject in more detail.

Once HCl has finished its function, it needs to be neutralized in order to prevent damage to the stomach lining and to allow for continued digestion as food flows into the small intestine. The lower glandular portion of your horse's stomach has a thick mucous layer to protect against acid corrosion. The upper, squamous portion, however, does not have this protection, and is where ulcers are most common. Most performance horses, especially those that perform in speed events, have ulcers because the squamous area is bathed in acid. This will also be discussed further in Chapter 14 — Digestive Problems.

So, let's get back to digestion… The pulverized feed is mixed with HCl as well as pepsin to start protein digestion. This mass enters the small intestine.

The small intestine

Your horse's small intestine produces enzymes that can digest proteins, fats, and carbohydrates such as starch and sugars (also known as non-structural carbohydrates — NSC). Fiber, on the other hand, cannot be digested in the small intestine. Digestion results in molecules that are small enough to be absorbed into the bloodstream. These units are amino acids (from protein digestion), fatty acids (from fat digestion), and glucose (from carbohydrate digestion).

Once these smaller components are absorbed into the bloodstream, they are transported to the tissues that need them, where they are either burned for energy, stored for later use, or used as building blocks to make body tissues such as muscle, enzymes, antibodies, hair, skin, hooves, and much, much, more.

A note about carbohydrates... Most starches and sugars are digested down to glucose molecules in the small intestine, providing much-needed energy to the cells. As blood glucose levels start to rise, the pancreas responds by producing the hormone insulin. Insulin allows glucose to enter the cells, where it can be metabolized for energy to meet exercise needs, keep the heart beating, lungs breathing, and nervous system functioning, and maintain life.

If too much starch and sugar is fed, blood glucose levels will have peaks and valleys as the horse tries to maintain a normal status. This can produce behavioral problems in some horses and is discussed further in Chapter 17 — Stress and Behavior.

Some horses suffer from insulin resistance. When blood glucose rises, insulin also rises above normal levels because it is not able to effectively remove glucose from the bloodstream. This condition, also known as metabolic syndrome, can lead to laminitis. A full discussion is provided in Chapters 11 — Laminitis, and 13 — Metabolic and Endocrine Disorders.

Furthermore, large amounts of starch and sugar fed at one time will overwhelm the small intestine, ending up in the hindgut, where bacteria ferment it. Laminitis can result. This can also happen when hay and pastures are high in starch, sugars, and fructan (a type of carbohydrate, consisting of fructose chains, that gets digested in the hindgut). Ways to evaluate hay and pasture, as well as carbohydrates in feeds are discussed in Chapters 2 — Fundamentals of Carbohydrates and 8 — Fundamentals of Forages.

So, by now you might be wondering about all that undigested fiber. Well, now we enter...

The cecum

As you can see, in between the small intestine and the large colon, there is the cecum, a relatively large fermentation vat. The cecum (along with the colon) is referred to as the "hindgut." This is where hay and pasture and other fibrous components of feeds (e.g., bran, hulls, etc.) are digested. The cecum, however, contains most of the live microbes, able to produce digestive enzymes that break down fibrous materials into smaller components that are converted to volatile fatty acids, providing your horse with energy (calories).

Non-structural carbohydrates (sugars and starch) can also be fermented in the cecum, but as I mentioned earlier, this is not good for your horse. Bacterial fermentation results in lactic acid production, which significantly reduces the pH (acidity level) of the hindgut, killing the microbial population, and increasing the potential for laminitis. For this reason, feeds high in sugar and starch (those that contain cereal grains and molasses) should only be fed in moderation so that they get digested in the foregut (in the small intestine), and not in the hindgut.

Notice that the cecum's entrance and exit are both at the top. So undigested fibrous material from the small intestine enters the cecum at the top, is digested by microbial enzymes, and then removed at the top. In order to do this gymnastic feat, it is imperative to have enough water. If too much dry matter is present, it can settle and compact at the bottom of the cecum, leading to colic. Also, when changing feeds, keep in mind that these microbes need time to adjust in order to prevent compaction colic. Please refer to Chapter 14 — Digestive Problems for more discussion.

But the microbes in the cecum play another important role in your horse's health. They are responsible for producing vitamin K and all eight B vitamins: B_1 (thiamin), B_2 (riboflavin), niacin, B_6 (pyridoxine), B_{12} (cobalamin), biotin, folic acid, and pantothenic acid. These vitamins have varying functions, revealed in Chapter 6 — Fundamentals of Vitamins.

One last stop along the digestive tract...

The colon

What remains undigested at this phase continues on its travels into the colon. This includes the large colon and the small colon — together known as the "large intestine." Undigested feedstuffs can remain here for as long as 2 to 2 1/2 days before being excreted. There are microbes living in the large intestine that actually continue the digestive process. The main function of the large intestine, however, is to absorb vitamins, volatile fatty acids, minerals, and water into the bloodstream. What remains is the fecal waste. Within the small colon, this manure is compacted into fecal balls and enters the rectum for excretion.

Types of Feed

FORAGES

Forages are high fiber feeds, typically containing at least 18% fiber. Hay and pasture fall into this group. Commonly available hay can be divided into two main groups: grasses and legumes. Within the grasses, there are cool-season and warm-season varieties. Cool-season grasses include timothy, orchard, and fescue. These grasses grow best in areas where the summer season is not very hot. They have a slightly higher sugar level than warm-season grasses and are therefore preferred by horses because of their better taste. Warm-season grasses include brome and Bermuda.

Nutritional value of hay

Grass hays have a medium to low protein content. They are low in the essential amino acid called lysine. Therefore, they are best fed as part of a feeding plan that includes a legume to balance out the amino acid profile. Alfalfa is the most commonly fed legume hay. It is energy (calorie) rich and contains approximately 0.94 Mcal per pound (compared to 0.80 Mcal/lb for grass hay). The protein content of alfalfa is high (averaging between 17 and 20 percent). This is not harmful, as many people have come to believe. Protein has been blamed for colic, hot temperaments, kidney failure, foal deformities, and more, but there is no scientific evidence to support these claims. *The key is to feed high-quality protein.* When low-quality protein is fed (as in grass hay, or grains that are not supplemented with lysine), a large amount of excess amino acids becomes available. These "left over" amino acids are destroyed and their byproducts can lead to insulin responses, blood pH imbalances, kidney stones, and calcium losses from the bones. The protein found in alfalfa, on the other hand, enriches the diet by adding the correct proportion of amino acids (including lysine) to the grass hay. This is why it is best to feed a mixture of grass and legume hays.

Grain hay such as oat, rye, wheat, and barley tend to be higher in starch, especially if seed heads have formed. Their protein quality is not as high as in grass hay and they are not appropriate for horses that need to reduce their starch and sugar intake.

Alfalfa is also blamed for promoting laminitis due to its *supposedly* high sugar content. But, in actuality, sugar and starch levels of alfalfa can be comparable to those of grass hay. For horses that are overweight, suffer from equine Cushing's disease, are insulin resistant (metabolic syndrome), or are prone toward laminitis, knowing the starch and sugar levels, as well as the fructan levels, is of particular importance. The combination of starch, sugar, and fructan levels is indicated by the percent non-structural carbohydrates (%NSC). Refer to Chapter 2 — Fundamentals of Carbohydrates for more on this topic.

Table 1-1 shows how hay varies in nutrient content. High-quality hay will be balanced in calcium, phosphorus, and magnesium. Ideally, the calcium to phosphorus and the calcium to magnesium ratios should be 2:1. It is essential that phosphorus levels should never exceed calcium; fortunately most grass hay will have more calcium than phosphorus. Magnesium from hay is poorly absorbed. Consequently, magnesium is often undersupplied. A full discussion of these and other minerals can be found in Chapter 5 — Fundamentals of Minerals.

Table 1-1 Nutrient Content of Hay[1]

Hay	Digestible Energy (Mcal/lb)	Crude Protein (%)	Ca (%)	P %)	Mg (%)
Bermuda	0.85	10.4	0.49	0.27	0.19
Timothy	0.81	8.6	0.43	0.20	0.12
Orchard	0.78	7.6	0.24	0.27	0.10
Brome	0.85	12.6	0.25	0.25	0.09
Fescue	0.86	11.8	0.40	0.29	0.16
Alfalfa	0.94	17.5	1.24	0.24	0.32

CONCENTRATES

Concentrates refer to feeds that are high in calories (mainly from carbohydrates and fat) and low in fiber. These generally include cereal grains (oats, corn, barley, wheat, etc.) and commercial feeds that are grain-based. These rations are designed for horses that are exercised regularly and therefore have a higher energy (caloric) need. Chapter 20 — Athletes provides specific guidelines on how to feed for this group.

Underweight horses are often fed excessive amounts of cereal grains for added calories. But fat provides more than twice the calories of carbohydrates and is therefore a much better way to promote weight gain (see Chapter 12 — Weight Management).

BEET PULP

Beet pulp does not fit in either the forage or concentrate categories. It is high in fiber like forage, but is also high in calories, like concentrates. However, it doesn't have the dangers of grain (e.g., elevated insulin, cecal acidosis, and laminitis) and provides fewer calories than oats — beet pulp has 1.3 Mcal/lb; oats provide 1.5 Mcal/lb.

GMO

Beet pulp is a dependable, nutritious feed. It is the by-product of table sugar production from sugar beets but it has little to no sugar of its own. Since beet pulp is digested by the bacterial flora in the hindgut, there is little insulin response and so it is safe to feed. If grain were to reach the hindgut, in comparison, it would be fermented, leading to acidosis and laminitis. Beet pulp is often sweetened with molasses, but the amount is minimal, at only 96 grams of sugar per 10 lbs of beet pulp (that's 1/2 cup of sugar in 20 quarts of beet pulp!). However, horses that need to avoid sugar should be fed unsweetened beet pulp or the sweetened version should be soaked and the water drained off.

Speaking of soaking... beet pulp is best fed moistened. It comes it two varieties: pellets and shreds. The pellets need to be soaked longer than the shredded version. But don't leave beet pulp soaking overnight. Bacteria will multiply and you can make your horse ill. If you have hot water in your barn, shredded beet pulp doesn't need more than two to five minutes to get fluffy. Don't worry about beet pulp expanding inside the stomach. This is a myth. But soaking does provide protection against choke.

A NOTE ABOUT THE GLYCEMIC INDEX OF FEEDS

There is valid concern about feeding horses that have metabolic disorders such as insulin resistance, pituitary pars intermedia dysfunction — PPID (commonly referred to as equine Cushing's disease), and laminitis as it relates to circulating insulin and cortisol levels. Therefore, the degree to which blood glucose levels respond to a particular feed will influence and even aggravate these metabolic disorders. How a feed influences blood glucose levels is referred to as its "glycemic index." In order for a feed to affect the blood glucose level, it must first be digested in the small intestine (foregut). In a recent study[2], several common horse feeds were evaluated for their blood glucose response and each was assigned a glycemic index (GI). The lower the GI the better the feed is for horses that need to have their starch and sugar intake reduced. The lower the percent starch in the feed, the lower the blood glucose level, since starch yields glucose once it has been digested. Table 1-2 is adapted from that study that indicates both the GI and the percent starch in each feed.

Table 1-2 Glycemic Index (GI) and Percent Starch for Common Horse Feeds

Feed	GI	Starch %
Sweet feed	129	62.3
Corn	113	78.1
Oats	100	54.0
Barley	81	62.6
Wheat bran	63	27.3
Beet pulp (unsweetened)	24	0.1
Alfalfa	21	1.2
Rice bran	13	16.3
Soybean hulls	7	1.0

Corn and barley

These two cereal grains are not as well digested in the small intestine as oats, and therefore can lead to laminitis due to fermentation in the hindgut. Keep in mind that laminitis can also be caused by too much indigestible grain or high fructan levels in pasture forage reaching the hindgut, and the *GI is not relevant for this type of laminitic cause.* Please see Chapter 11 — Laminitis for further discussion.

Supplementation

Supplements are indispensable in filling nutritional gaps. Complete, commercial feeds are fortified in varying degrees and generally speaking, if fed according to directions, provide all of the basic vitamin and minerals necessary for health. But if less than the recommended amount is fed, a comprehensive vitamin/mineral supplement is necessary. Vitamin E and omega-3 fatty acids are typically under-supplemented in commercial feeds. *In addition, it is critically important to calculate the overall selenium content in the entire diet because selenium is potentially toxic.* This means you ought to have your hay and pasture analyzed for selenium levels so you can evaluate how your feed and supplements fit into the overall program. Specific supplements will be discussed throughout this book as they apply to individual conditions.

How to Read a Feed Label

There are a few things that you should notice when examining a feed label. First, take a look at the list of ingredients. Table 1-3 shows a generic feed label. Most people assume that the ingredients are listed in order of concentration (as with human food ingredient lists) with the most highly concentrated ingredient mentioned first. Unfortunately, this is not the case with animal feeds.

The ingredients are analyzed in a laboratory for their overall protein, fat, fiber, vitamins, and mineral levels. Let's take a closer look at each of these indicators:

- **Crude protein.** This is a measure of nitrogen. It tells you nothing about protein quality. Look for the addition of two essential amino acids, lysine and methionine. Or see if soybean and alfalfa meals are added to provide these amino acids. Refer to Chapter 4 — Fundamentals of Protein and Amino Acids.

- **Crude fat.** Fat can be added from any fat source. Soybean oil, written often as "vegetable oil," is added to boost the fat content. However, too much soybean oil can increase inflammation because of its high omega-6 fatty acid content. Look for a balance between omega-3 fatty acids and omega-6 fatty acids. A 3:1 to 4:1 ratio of omega-3 to omega-6 fatty acids is ideal. Omega-3 fatty acids are generally supplied by flax. Refer to Chapter 3 — Fundamentals of Fats.

Table 1-3 Generic Feed Label	
XYZ 10% Horse Feed	**Ingredients**
Guaranteed Analysis	Grain Products, Plant Protein Products, Processed Grain By-Products, Molasses Products, Roughage Products, Vitamin A Supplement, Vitamin D3 Supplement, Vitamin E Supplement, Vitamin B12 Supplement, Riboflavin Supplement, Pyridoxine Hydrochloride, Folic Acid, Biotin, Thiamine, Calcium Carbonate, Salt, Dicalcium Phosphate, Manganese Oxide, Ferrous Sulfate, Copper Sulfate, Magnesium Oxide, Cobalt Carbonate, Potassium Chloride, Sodium Selenite, dl-alpha Tocopheryl Acetate.
Crude Protein 10.0% Crude Fat 4.0% Crude Fiber 10.0% Calcium (min) 0.9% Calcium (max) 1.2% Phosphorus (min) 0.9% Copper (min) 20.0 ppm Selenium (min) 0.30 ppm Zinc (min) 50.0 ppm Vitamin A 3000 IU/lb Vitamin E 100 IU/lb	

- **Vitamin A.** This exists as the actual vitamin or as beta carotene. Beta carotene is a much safer approach since too much vitamin A can be toxic. Beta carotene is the precursor to vitamin A and is only converted to vitamin A to the extent that your horse requires it. But beta carotene is destroyed by heat and air exposure so dried hay products (such as alfalfa and hay cubes or pellets) have lost much of their beta carotene content. Refer to Chapter 6 — Fundamentals of Vitamins.

- **Iron.** There is plenty of iron in hay and pasture so deficiencies are rare; therefore, supplementation is not necessary. This particular label does not give you any idea how much iron is actually in the feed since it is not listed in the guaranteed analysis. It is listed in the ingredients as ferrous sulfate, which is confusing. Refer to Chapter 5 — Fundamentals of Minerals.

- **Selenium.** This mineral has a small range of safety (also discussed at length in Chapter 5). Typically horses require between 1 and 5 mg per day. To calculate how much selenium is in your horse's diet, take a look at Appendix — Crunching Numbers.

Hay Analysis

One of the best ways to evaluate your horse's diet is to know what is in your hay. Since forage should be the foundation of any diet, knowing its nutritive value can provide invaluable information. If you purchase at least two or more months' worth of hay at a time, it is worth having it analyzed. Pasture can also be evaluated, though the values vary with the season, time of day, temperature, amount of rainfall, etc. To check your pasture for sugar, starch and fructan levels, it is best to pull a sample in the late afternoon on a sunny day (see Chapter 8 — Fundamentals of Forages for more information).

Check for selenium content, especially if your hay comes from the upper western U.S., including Washington State, Oregon, and northern California, the Ohio valley, and the eastern coastal states. These areas are typically low in this mineral. The remaining areas can vary in selenium levels; some may be adequate and others may be too high. Your local county extension service may offer analysis services, or consider Equi-Analytical Laboratories for assistance (www.equi-analytical.com).

Before describing the terms you are likely to see when having your hay analyzed, let me provide a review of the process of forage digestion.

Forage digestion takes place in two places – first in the small intestine (foregut) by the digestive enzymes that your horse produces, and next, in the hindgut by the digestive enzymes that the microbes produce.

In the small intestine, carbohydrates, proteins, and fats are digested down to their individual molecular components — glucose, amino acids, and fatty acids, respectively — which are absorbed into the bloodstream directly from the small intestine, to be delivered to the body tissues that need them.

What remains is mainly fiber, which moves further down the intestinal tract to the cecum. Bacterial enzymes digest fibers and ferment the digestive products into volatile fatty acids, which are absorbed into the bloodstream and used for energy (calories).

There are four main types of fiber: cellulose, hemicellulose, lignin, and pectin. Lignin is not digestible, meaning the cecal microbes cannot break it down into small molecules. The older the plant, the more lignin it will produce. Ever eat green beans and there's one on your plate that's so tough and stringy that you just cannot eat it? That's a very old green bean! Younger plants, on the other hand, are more tender because they haven't laid down much lignin. So, what does this mean in terms of hay? More mature cuts of hay will have more lignin, making them less digestible and more like straw.

The hay analysis results indicate lignin content in two measurements, acid detergent fiber (ADF) and neutral detergent fiber (NDF). The higher these numbers, the more lignin the hay contains. The more lignin the hay contains, the less digestible it is and your horse will not get as much feed value.

COMMON TERMS IN A HAY ANALYSIS REPORT

Crude protein (CP)

CP is an estimation of total protein based on the amount of nitrogen in the hay. It does not tell you anything about the amino acid composition or the protein quality. Most grass hay contains 8% to 10% CP whereas legumes (e.g., alfalfa, clover, perennial peanut) can range from 17-20%. Grain hay is generally lower than grass hay in CP.

Acid detergent fiber (ADF)

ADF is a measure of how indigestible the hay is. The higher the value, the lower the amount of digestible fibers it contains. ADF contains the fibrous components of the cell wall, including cellulose and lignin. The ideal value is less than 31%; however, ADF value is often higher than this and the hay can still be acceptable. Keep in mind that hay also has carbohydrates, proteins, and fats (not part of this ADF number) that are first digested in the foregut. The higher the ADF, the more fiber it contains. Digestibility will depend on the overall health of the cecal microbes.

Neutral detergent fiber (NDF)

NDF represents the total amount of cell wall content. *NDF gives the best estimate of the total fiber content of the feed.* This value includes all of the cell wall carbohydrates, including ADF and hemicellulose. Ideally NDF should be less than 45% but most hay has more. However, if the level is above 55%, the hay will not provide sufficient feed value. To compensate, more hay needs to be consumed. *The higher the NDF and ADF values, the less digestible the feed.*

Relative feed value (RFV)

RFV is an indication of the hay's overall quality in terms of its digestibility and available nutrients. A value over 150 is ideal; however, most hay doesn't meet this level. Strive for an RFV of at least 100. This is an average score based on approximately 40% ADF and 50% NDF on a dry matter basis.

Non-fibrous carbohydrates (NFC)

NFC includes starches, sugars, fructan, and rapidly fermentable pectin. Pectin, though technically considered a fiber, has different physical properties than cellulose and hemicellulose. Pectin does not make a large contribution to NFC values in most cases. For horses with insulin resistance, or equine Cushing's disease, an NFC value of less than 18% is favorable.

Non-structural carbohydrates (NSC)

NSC is not the best measurement of carbohydrate content because it doesn't distinguish between sugar, starch, and fructan. Instead, NSC measures all three, combined. But starches and sugars are digested in the foregut and fructan is digested in the hindgut, making the total confusing and difficult to interpret. There are better measurements; read about WSC, ESC, and starch in the following pages.

Nevertheless, NSC is still a commonly used indicator; look for a value below 12% if your horse needs to have a low sugar/low starch diet.

Water-soluble carbohydrates (WSC)

WSC measures both simple sugars and fructan levels — sometimes referred to as "sugar" on test results. Reducing simple sugars is important for overweight, insulin resistant, or cushingoid horses. Low fructan is important for horses prone toward laminitis. Since this value includes sugar and fructan, it is not as valuable an indicator as ESC.

Ethanol-soluble carbohydrates (ESC)

ESC is a subset of WSC and gives you a better idea of the simple sugar level (sugars that are digested in the small intestine). ESC also includes some starch. *The significant factor about ESC is that it includes only a small amount, if any, of fructan.* Therefore, this value provides a clearer assessment of the glycemic index of the feed or forage (how much it affects insulin levels). WSC minus ESC gives us a fair measurement of fructan levels.

Starch

To review, starch is normally digested in the foregut of the digestive tract down to individual glucose (blood sugar) molecules; therefore, it has a strong effect on blood insulin levels. Starch that reaches the hindgut, however, is fermented by cecal microbes, creating an increased risk of laminitis.

Calculating NSC

As I mentioned earlier, NSC combines sugar, fructan, and starch into one measurement. Since WSC equals sugar plus fructan, you can simply add it to the percent starch to determine percent NSC: WSC + Starch = NSC.

Calcium to phosphorus ratio

There needs to be more calcium than phosphorus in hay. Most hay will have this balance. The ideal ratio is 2:1, but the level of calcium can be as high as six times the level of phosphorus, and still be considered safe. Phosphorus concentration must never be higher than calcium levels.

Calcium to magnesium ratio

Ideally, calcium content should not be more than twice that of magnesium. Most hays have a magnesium level that is lower than what horses ideally require.

Salt and Water

Your horse needs salt — plain, white salt. Adding salt is one the simplest things you can do. Use salt blocks, add salt to meals, or provide a bucket with free choice table salt. Electrolytes can be appropriate for work during hot, humid weather (discussed in Chapter 7 — Fundamentals of Water and Electrolytes). But it is the sodium from salt that your horse needs on a daily basis to be healthy.

Sodium is the main electrolyte found in the blood and the fluid that surrounds cells (extracellular fluid). If sodium levels are low, the blood will not hold enough water. This causes the adrenal gland to release the hormone aldosterone. Aldosterone tells the kidney to hold on to sodium, and allows potassium, instead, to leave via the urine. Therefore more sodium needs to be added to the diet to stop the excretion of potassium.

Once the sodium concentration has been corrected, potassium levels can be easily managed by feeding hay or by allowing grazing on pasture. One pound of grass hay, for example, provides approximately 10% of the potassium requirement for a horse that is worked intensively. So it's easy to see that only 10 lbs of hay (much less than normal consumption for a full-size horse) will meet the potassium needs for most horses.

When your horse is not working, he requires at least 10 grams of sodium per day. That's provided by nearly one ounce of salt (two tablespoons). Increase the work, increase the salt. Two ounces (4 tablespoons) per day, divided between meals, is the minimum need while working. On hot, humid days, working horses can require as much as one ounce of salt per hour!

A plain white salt block should be within easy reach. It is usually all that you'll need for a horse at maintenance or light work, as long as your horse is consuming one ounce per day in cold weather, and four times as much during hot weather. Constant licking can irritate the tongue, however, so your horse may not get enough salt from a salt block. If you are not sure how much your horse is consuming, add loose salt to the diet. Go to your local grocery store and pick up table salt. It comes in iodized and non-iodized versions. Which you choose depends on how much iodine your horse is already consuming. Generally speaking, if you are providing iodine from another source (such as a commercial feed or vitamin/mineral supplement), avoid the iodized version.

A *mineralized* block is not advisable if you are already feeding minerals from a commercial feed or vitamin/mineral supplement. Furthermore, horses that rely on them for plain salt may not get enough due to their bitter taste. Molasses-sweetened licks are often eaten like candy, so they, too, should be avoided.

Fresh, clean water needs to be available at all times. Do not make the mistake of adding salt to the only water supply, since this will interfere with water intake.

Special Case: Feeding Donkeys and Mules

Donkeys should be fed differently than horses, since their needs are a reflection of their past environment. They originated genetically in the hot, dry climate of northeastern Africa and therefore their systems are accustomed to consuming plants that are able to withstand high temperatures and low moisture — typically high in fiber and low in quality.

Having a digestive tract similar to the horse's, they are trickle feeders, requiring a consistent source of forage for grazing. However, donkeys have a narrower muzzle allowing them to be highly selective in the morsels of food they consume. When presented with a pasture that has a variety of forages, they can target high-quality bites. When offered nutritious hay, however, they will eat freely without making an effort to be selective.

Donkeys have more efficient microbial digestion of forage in the hindgut than horses. Therefore, they are better able to digest fiber, resulting in less consumption that horses when presented with free choice hay. This natural adaptation is favorable for donkeys because they do not need as many calories as a horse to maintain a normal body weight. When offered starchy concentrates (cereal grains), they will generally moderate their intake, but don't risk giving them starchy or sweet feed because they are prone toward developing insulin resistance, and hence laminitis (founder).

Donkeys do well on much less water than horses, since they perspire less and excrete less water in their manure. They are less likely to suffer from dehydration since they easily recover from a water shortage. When offered water, they tend not to over drink, as horses may.

THE BASIC DIET FOR DONKEYS AND MULES

Mules should be fed the same way as donkeys. Bermuda, timothy, and brome grasses are best. Avoid alfalfa due to its high protein and calorie content, unless the donkey is growing, pregnant, or lactating, in which case a 50/50 combination of timothy/alfalfa hay is suitable. This grass/alfalfa mixture can also be fed during harsh winters. Adult donkeys can be fed hay that is low in protein. If they are being worked, offer them a meal to meet their caloric needs that is low in starch and sugar (low in non-structural carbohydrates — NSC) and contains no more than 10 to 12 percent protein. Avoid feeding cereal grains (oats, corn, barley, and wheat).

A feeding guideline for maintenance would be to feed 2% of body weight, with 90% of the total ration from forage. The remaining 10% can come from a low starch/low sugar feed. If the donkey is working, increase the total amount of feed to approximately 2.7% of body weight. For example, a 450 lb donkey that's being worked can be fed 12 lbs of total feed (2.7% of 450). Therefore, 90% of this total ration should come from hay (approximately 10 lbs) and the remainder (approximately 2 lbs) should consist of a pelleted, low starch/low sugar feed. The same 450 lb donkey at maintenance would receive a total intake of 9 lbs (2% of 450 lbs). Since 90% needs to be from forage, give him approximately 8 lbs of grass hay. The remaining 1 lb would be fed as a pelleted, low starch/low sugar feed. It is important to weigh the total feed intake rather than relying on the volume of the feed provided by a scoop or coffee can.

Offer free choice water, just as you would with horses, but don't expect them to drink as much. They will drink more if the temperature and humidity are high or if they are working.

As with horses, donkeys need access to salt at all times. If kept strictly on pasture, a mineralized salt block (without molasses) should be available. If a comprehensive vitamin/mineral supplement is offered, then a plain, white salt block is appropriate.

Donkeys and mules require less protein than horses, since they are able to reabsorb and recycle up to 80% of the urea that is created during protein metabolism. This accounts for their ability to subsist in areas where the forage is low in protein.

They can be offered free choice pasture and/or hay. It is best to have your pasture and hay tested, since lush forage may be too high in protein, sugar, fructan, and starch which can lead to obesity and its related disorders — insulin resistance and laminitis. Excess fat in the blood (known as hyperlipemia), caused by overgrazing in lush pastures, is particularly problematic for donkeys and can be fatal. Many owners tend to feed donkeys the same as horses. A normal diet for a horse will make a donkey overweight. Watch for a thick roll of fat along the crest of the neck, and/or fat accumulation along the cheeks and around the buttocks.

If a donkey does become obese, weight loss should be very gradual. Hyperlipemia can result if body fat is lost at too fast a rate. This medical condition is one of the main causes of death in donkeys.

Endnotes

[1] *Nutrient Requirements of Horses,* Sixth Revised Edition, 2007. Washington, D.C.: National Research Council, National Academy Press.

[2] Rodiek, A.V., and Stull, C.L., 2007. Glycemic index of ten common horse feeds. *Journal of Equine Veterinary Science, 27* (5): 205-211.

CHAPTER 2 —
FUNDAMENTALS OF CARBOHYDRATES

When I first fell in love with horses I did not want to ride them, I simply wanted to be one.
~ Jane Hirshfield

Carbohydrates exist in several forms: sugars, starch, fructan, and fibers. Sugars are simple, small molecules made up of single units called monosaccharides or double units called disaccharides. Molasses, commonly used to sweeten feeds, is a disaccharide: two monosaccharides, glucose and fructose, linked together. Starch and fructan are much longer molecules, known as polysaccharides, where hundreds of monosaccharides are connected in long strands. Starch is a branched chain of glucose molecules and is easily broken apart in the foregut into individual glucose units. Fructan consists of fructose molecules linked together that cannot be digested in the foregut. Instead, fructan is digested in the hindgut by microbial enzymes. Most fibers are found in the plant's cell wall and provide structure. They, too, are digestible in the hindgut.

Carbohydrates in the form of starch and sugars provide glucose for your horse, which is metabolized by cells for energy (calories). Fructan and fiber also yield calories but are first fermented by bacterial flora into volatile fatty acids (VFAs). All of the carbohydrate forms are found in commonly fed forages, cereal grains, beet pulp, legumes, and fruits and vegetables such as apples and carrots.

Fiber Digestion

In Chapter 1 — Ground Rules for Feeding a Horse, I explained how fiber is digested. But let's review:

Though forages do contain sugars, starch, and fructan, they are predominantly made up of fiber. Fibers include cellulose, hemicellulose, and pectin, which are digested by the microbial population in the hindgut.

Fibers are not digested in the foregut (small intestine) because horses cannot produce the necessary digestive enzymes. Instead, your horse relies on the microbes living in the hindgut to produce these enzymes. The hindgut consists of the cecum, large colon, and small colon, but most fiber digestion occurs in the cecum. This explains why these microbes are so critical to your horse's overall health and ability to obtain calories from hay and pasture. Cecal microorganisms rely on fiber for their own health as well, making it essential that we feed fibrous feedstuffs to horses.

Lignin, also found in forages, is characterized as an indigestible fiber; even the bacterial flora living in the hindgut cannot digest it. Therefore lignin is useless as a feed source. Straw is mostly lignin. As a plant ages, it produces more lignin to provide structure and rigidity. Young plants (which come from newly grown pasture and from first cuttings of hay) have less lignin and are therefore more digestible than more mature grasses.

Pectin is a water-soluble fiber that forms a highly digestible gel in the hindgut. Beet pulp is an excellent source of pectin and since it is not digested in the foregut down to glucose, there is minimal insulin response, making it a favorable feed for horses prone toward insulin resistance (see Chapter 13 — Metabolic and Endocrine Disorders).

Rice and wheat bran are commonly fed to provide fiber. Bran is the cereal grain's outer hull and provides a variety of fiber types, all digested by the bacteria in the hindgut. Feeding a bran mash for laxative purposes, however, is not only ineffective, it is dangerous because the bacterial flora need to adjust to the presence of a new feed. Consistency in feeding is the best approach to prevent colic. Bran is also very high in phosphorus and must be balanced with calcium. This is discussed further in Chapter 9 — Fundamentals of Concentrates and By-Products.

The products of microbial digestion are fermented into volatile fatty acids (VFAs) — acetate, propionate, and butyrate. VFAs enter the bloodstream and are metabolized within the cells to provide energy. Acetate and butyrate are immediately available for energy metabolism whereas propionate must first be converted to glucose before it can be metabolized for energy. This is how your horse derives calories from hay and pasture.

It's interesting to note that a natural byproduct of fiber digestion is gas. Gas production is certainly normal and healthy. It says that your horse's hindgut is functioning properly. But gas causes the abdomen to swell a bit, creating what is commonly referred to as a "hay belly." *A hay belly is not fat.* It is gas! And it is very normal. Horse owners who deliberately limit hay consumption and replace it with cereal grain to avoid a hay belly are doing their horses a disservice. Forage is vital for the health of the microbes, and hence, the health of your horse. And a constant supply is essential for the overall functioning of the digestive system (see Chapter 14 — Digestive Problems).

Heat is also a normal by-product of forage digestion in the hindgut. This is why hay is so helpful during the cold season (though forage should be provided in ample quantity year round). Contrary to popular thought, sweet feeds and high protein feeds do not increase body heat like forage digestion will.

Anatomy of a Cereal Grain

Cereal grains, such as oats, corn, barley, and wheat, are commonly added to horse diets. Take a look at the structure of a cereal grain.

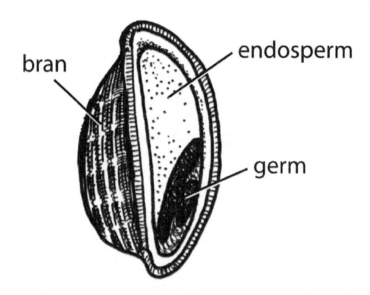

The kernel has three main components: the outer hull known as bran, the germ, and the inner endosperm. The bran contains most of the grain's fiber content — water-insoluble cellulose and hemicellulose, water-soluble pectin, and indigestible lignin. It also contains minerals, mainly calcium and phosphorus, though phosphorus levels are much higher than calcium.

There is some fat in the bran portion; rice bran, in particular, is high in fat. Foregut-digestible carbohydrates (sugars and starch) are also found in bran, though at relatively low levels.

The germ is what I like to refer to as the "power-house" of nutrients. This area is concentrated not only in carbohydrates, but also in fat, protein, vitamins, and minerals. The germ provides vital nutrients for a planted seed so it can germinate into foliage. The leaves help the plant, via photosynthesis from sunlight, put down roots that can ultimately receive nutrients from the soil.

So think of germ as a nutrient-rich source of calories. Wheat germ is the most common type of germ added to feeds. Wheat germ oil, by the way, does not contain any of these nutrients except fat and is mostly omega-6 fatty acids. See Chapter 3 — Fundamentals of Fats for a comparison between oils.

The endosperm makes up the majority of the grain kernel and is where most of the starch is found. When you eat white flour, for example, you are eating ground endosperm. Whole wheat flour on the other hand, contains the entire grain — bran, germ, and endosperm. Horse feeds generally contain the whole grain. If you feed oats, in any variety, you're feeding a whole grain.

Non-Structural Carbohydrates

Sugars, fructan, and starch found in grains and forages do not offer any structural component to the cells, hence they are named "non-structural carbohydrates" (NSC). Fructan is not digested in the foregut, but is fermented like fibers in the hindgut. Too much fructan can be problematic for horses prone toward laminitis. Discussion of fructan can be found a little further on in this section.

Foregut digestion of starch and disaccharides (sugars) results in glucose, which is easily absorbed into the bloodstream. Insulin, from the pancreas, responds to this glucose elevation, resulting in glucose leaving the blood and entering the cells. Inside the cells, it is metabolized for energy (calories). Sugars and starch provide more energy, gram for gram, than fiber, which is why they are often added to the diets of horses requiring more calories for activity. However, some horses are particularly sensitive to highs and lows of blood glucose levels and exhibit mood and behavioral changes. And as we will see in Part II of this book, elevations in glucose and/or insulin levels can be problematic for horses that are prone toward obesity, insulin resistance, laminitis, equine Cushing's, and other diseases.

SUGARS

There are many sugars; however, fructose, lactose, and sucrose are the most prevalent in your horse's diet. Fructose is a monosaccharide (one sugar molecule). You know it as fruit sugar. It sweetens carrots, apples, and other fruits and vegetables. It is also found in grasses and hay and gives them a sweet taste.

Lactose is a disaccharide (double sugar) and is called "milk sugar." It is the main carbohydrate found in milk. Foals are born with the ability to digest the lactose found in their dam's milk. However, as they are weaned, they stop producing the digestive enzyme (lactase) necessary for digesting lactose. Adult horses are lactose intolerant. So if you were to give your grown horse a milk product, such as yogurt, he would likely develop diarrhea and excess gas since he can no longer produce lactase. Many horse owners feed yogurt to provide live microbes (as a probiotic) but this is not advisable. There are far more reliable probiotic sources that won't give your horse a case of indigestion.

Sucrose is also a disaccharide, commonly referred to as "table sugar." This is the white, granular sweetener that you put in your coffee or tea. As a disaccharide, it is made up of two monosaccharides — glucose and fructose. Honey, interestingly, is made of glucose and fructose but as separate units, not linked together as in sucrose. Molasses, on the other hand, contains sucrose and is a byproduct of table sugar production. Molasses is also a source of calcium and iron, two minerals that other sweeteners lack. Most sweet feeds are sweetened with molasses. This is not a problem for the healthy, active horse who is not prone toward metabolic diseases (such as insulin resistance and equine Cushing's disease). However, many horses need to avoid sugar, as well as starchy diets, since starch is digested down to sugar.

POLYSACCHARIDES

Polysaccharides are long chains of monosaccharides linked together. They include starch, fructan, and digestible fibers.

Starch

Cereal grains are mostly starch. This polysaccharide is easily digested in the small intestine down to glucose molecules. Since starch digestion results in more energy (calories) than fiber digestion, grains are often supplemented in horses who work and therefore have more energy needs. *The key is to keep the digestion of starch within the foregut.* If there is too much starch in one meal, it will not be completely digested and will travel to the hindgut, where the bacterial flora will ferment it. Starch fermentation results in acid production which will kill these bacteria, leading to colic and even laminitis. For more discussion of this, please read Chapters 11 — Laminitis and 14 — Digestive Problems.

Fructan

Fructan is mainly found in hay and pasture, not in cereal grains. Hays can vary significantly is the amount of fructan they contain; alfalfa and clover, for example, contain very little, if any, fructan. These legumes tend to be highest in pectin, a safer carbohydrate in terms of laminitis risk. Cool-season grasses, such as orchard, timothy, brome, and crested wheatgrass, can contain significantly higher fructan levels than the warm-season grasses such as Bermuda and tropical grasses, including summer prairie grasses. Refer to www.safergrass.org as an excellent resource on forage safety. This topic is also discussed in Chapters 8 — Fundamentals of Forages and 11 — Laminitis.

The importance of understanding fructan is that your horse cannot produce the digestive enzymes necessary to break apart the bonds that hold the fructose molecules together. So fructan is not digestible within the foregut. It travels to the hindgut, where the bacterial flora will ferment it. The pH of the hindgut decreases (becomes more acidic), resulting in laminitis.

Fibers

The guaranteed analysis section found on feed tags will list the percentage of crude fiber. This is an estimate of cellulose, hemicellulose, pectin, and lignin levels. Since the lignin portion is not digestible, it is more informative to study the ingredient list to get an idea of the feed's hindgut digestibility. Ingredients such as soybean and alfalfa meal are excellent protein sources that are low in indigestible fiber. Beet pulp is another ingredient to look for since its fiber content is mainly pectin. Bran and other grain by-products are higher in water insoluble fibers (cellulose and hemicellulose) and their lignin component is not as high as that found in grasses. Timothy is a commonly used grass in high-fiber feeds.

Analysis Measurements

FIBROUS MEASURES

There are three indicators used to measure fibrous components: acid detergent fiber (ADF), neutral detergent fiber (NDF), and non-fibrous carbohydrates (NFC). ADF measures cellulose and lignin; NDF is a better measurement because it includes all of the fiber in the plant's cell wall which contains not only cellulose and lignin, but also hindgut digestible hemicellulose.

NFC can be confusing at first. It stands for *non-fibrous* carbohydrates so how can it include fiber? That's because in addition to sugar, starch, and fructan, NFC contains pectin. Pectin is not found in the cell wall, but is still considered a fiber since your horse cannot digest it in the foregut. Instead, it is highly digestible by the bacterial flora in the hindgut, providing calories for your horse to perform work. Consequently, it is safe to feed to the insulin resistant and laminitis-prone horse.

A comparison of these three indicators is shown in Chapter 1 — Ground Rules for Feeding a Horse. Table 2-1 shows the average levels of NDF, NFC, and starch for several common feeds. Remember, the NDF is a measure of all the cell wall contents (fibers including lignin, but not including pectin). The NFC is similar to NSC but it also includes pectin. Starch is included to show how this component relates to the others.

There are a few items worth pointing out from Table 2-1. Notice that since molasses is mostly sugar, its NFC level is very high, reflecting this high sugar content. Grains such as barley, corn, and oats are mostly starch. When comparing forages, there is little difference between grass pasture and grass hay, except that the hay sampled for this analysis is likely older than the fresh pasture, thereby having more lignin. Alfalfa hay is more digestible than the cubes simply because more stems exist in the cubes and hence, more lignin. Beet pulp is low in starch, and considered comparable to other forages. The majority of its NFC is from pectin, which as you know, is a safe feed for insulin resistant, laminitic horses, and others that need to avoid sugars and starches. The fructan levels, however, are not discernable from these measurements. Measurement of fructan, as well as sugars and starch, is discussed next.

Table 2-1 Average Fiber and Starch Levels of Common Feed Ingredients on a Dry Matter Basis[1]

Feed Ingredient	%NDF	%NFC	%Starch
Grass pasture	58.8	19.6	3.5
Grass hay	63.8	19.5	2.8
Alfalfa hay	38.5	30.8	2.4
Alfalfa cubes	43.3	26.6	2.0
Beet pulp	41.9	44.4	1.3
Distiller's dried grains	33.9	24.9	5.7
Rice bran	30.2	14.3	18.4
Soybean meal	13.1	28.3	2.0
Soybean hulls	61.7	19.7	1.7
Barley	19.6	63.9	53.9
Corn	9.1	78.4	72.3
Oats	27.9	50.9	44.3
Molasses	0.7	76.7	1.1

SUGARS, FRUCTAN, AND STARCH MEASURES

NSC includes these three carbohydrate forms. It does not include water-insoluble fibers cellulose, hemicelluloses and lignin found in the cell wall. Nor does it include the water-soluble fiber, pectin. The problem with using NSC as a measurement is that it does not differentiate between levels of each carbohydrate, so there is no way to tell which substance predominates. Generally speaking, NSC should not exceed 12% for overweight, cushing-oid, or laminitis-prone horses. This is also true for horses suffering from equine polysaccharide myopathy (EPSM).

If the majority of NSC's content is from fructan, it can lead to laminitis because of fructan fermentation in the hindgut. On the other hand, if NSC's main components are sugar and starch, it can be an issue for insulin resistant horses because blood insulin levels increase in response to glucose production. However, laminitis can also be caused by elevated insulin. So, all three fractions of NSC can be problematic. Insulin resistance is sometimes called equine metabolic syndrome and is discussed at length in Chapter 13 — Metabolic and Endocrine Disorders.

Water soluble carbohydrates, ethanol soluble carbohydrates, and starch

There are three better indicators than NSC: water soluble carbohydrates (WSC), ethanol soluble carbohydrates (ESC), and percent starch. WSC includes both sugars and fructan. ESC includes mostly sugars. And percent starch measures only starch. *NSC equals WSC plus starch.*

To approximate the fructan level, calculate the difference between WSC and ESC. Table 2-2 compares the WSC, ESC, and starch levels of several common feeds. Remember that if your horse needs to reduce sugar and starch intake, look for low ESC and starch levels. However, if your horse is prone toward laminitis, you also need to need reduce his fructan intake.

Notice that fructan levels in grass hay and cubes tend to be higher than levels found in alfalfa (both hay and cubes). There is a common misconception that alfalfa causes laminitis. But in fact, alfalfa is often lower than grasses in laminitis-causing fructan. Alfalfa and grasses also have comparable sugar levels (ESC). Furthermore, alfalfa, when fed with grass, boosts protein quality by providing enough amino acids needed to produce healthy tissue. This is important to consider for the horse that is healing from laminitis or any other injury.

Grain hays such as oat, wheat, and rye are not recommended for horses that need to reduce the sugar, starch, and fructan levels in the diet. The percent starch in these hays is higher than grasses or alfalfa, mainly because grain seed heads can be found throughout the hay.

Beet pulp is comparable to grass and legume hays in terms of its sugar and starch levels, but has trace amounts of fructan. This makes it a valuable feed for laminitis-prone horses. And it works very nicely as a low starch/low sugar carrier for supplements. To prevent choke, be sure to soak beet pulp for a few minutes before feeding. The warmer the water, the less soaking time required. Avoid soaking for more than an hour, especially in warm weather, to reduce bacterial growth. Beet pulp comes in pellets (requires longer soaking time) or shreds. The shredded variety is often sweetened with molasses. However, the amount of sugar added is minimal

Table 2-2 Sugar, Starch and Fructan: Common Feed Ingredients on a Dry Matter Basis Shown as %WSC, %ESC, Fructan, and %Starch[2]

Feed	Average %WSC	Average %ESC	Approximate %Fructan (WSC – ESC)	Average %Starch
Alfalfa hay	9.0	7.3	1.7	2.1
Alfalfa cubes	7.9	6.2	1.7	2.0
Alfalfa pellets	7.3	6.5	0.8	2.1
Grass hay	10.7	7.8	2.9	2.4
Grass cubes	8.8	5.3	3.5	2.3
Oat hay	17.1	12.8	4.3	5.2
Straw	6.5	3.8	2.7	2.4
Beet pulp (unsweetened)	10.2	10.6	--	1.4
Rice bran	7.2	7.1	0.1	19.4
Wheat bran	8.2	5.7	2.5	22.3
Barley	7.1	2.1	5.0	54.6
Corn	3.2	2.9	0.3	70.5
Oats	3.2	3.0	0.2	44.3
Carrots	34.1	21.8	12.3	5.1
Flaxseed meal	6.1	0	6.1	3.9

and can be well tolerated by most horses. Nevertheless, when trying to reduce sugar intake, the beet pulp can be soaked for a few minutes and the water drained, which will remove the majority of the molasses.

When bran is fed by itself it is referred to as a "grain by-product." This term has a negative connotation for most people, but it really shouldn't. It simply means that the whole grain is not used, just part of it. Rice or wheat bran, often thought to be a low starch feed because it is the "hull" of the cereal grain as opposed to the starchy endosperm center, turns out to contain a fair amount of starch. Rice bran is a good source of fat and can be fed to underweight horses, but the amount of starch should be taken into consideration when feeding to a horse that needs to reduce his starch intake.

Grains such as barley, corn, and oats are very high in starch. High starch equates to high sugar, since sugar is the result of starch digestion. Remember that carrots, apples, and other fruits are high in simple sugars (ESC).

Flaxseed meal is commonly fed to horses for its omega-3 fatty acid content, and has virtually no sugar content, some starch, and some fructan. Though fed at very small quantities relative to forages and even grains, flaxseed meal is not a major contributor of these carbohydrates and is exceedingly beneficial to your horse's health.

Keeping NSC low

If you are concerned about starch, fructan, and sugars in your hay or pasture, have your forage analyzed. This is the only way to know the levels you're feeding. Remember, percent WSC added to percent starch gives you percent NSC. NSC should be less than 12% to be considered safe to feed free choice to a sensitive horse. If your hay is higher than this, you can soak the hay and drain the water to significantly lessen NSC. If your pasture has a high NSC, turnout needs to be limited to those times when sugar and fructan levels are safer.

Summary

Forages (hay and/or pasture) should make up the foundation of your horse's diet. For many horses, especially those that are not exercised on a daily basis, this is all they require, along with a comprehensive vitamin/mineral supplement to fill in the gaps. Horses that work require more calories. This can be provided by adding grain or a grain-based commercial feed. But keep in mind that grain would only be appropriate for the healthy, adult horse that is of normal weight. Growing horses should not have high starch feeds. This is reviewed in Chapter 19 — Growth and Growing Old.

The horse that is exercised regularly but has health issues revolving around sugar and starch consumption (e.g., insulin resistance, equine Cushing's disease, equine polysaccharide myopathy) should be given a low starch/low sugar diet that contains feedstuffs such as beet pulp, soybean meal or hulls, flaxseed meal, and alfalfa meal. Rather than mixing your own ingredients, you can use a commercial low starch/low sugar feed. If your horse requires even more energy than these feeds can provide, consider adding fat to the diet. This is discussed at length in the next chapter — Fundamentals of Fats.

Endnotes

[1] Adapted from: *Nutrient Requirements of Horses*, Sixth Revised Edition, 2007. Washington, D.C.: National Research Council, National Academy Press: 36-37.

[2] Adapted from: Equi-Analytical Laboratories, 2008. Accumulated Crops 5/01/00 to 4/30/08. www.equi-analytical.com

CHAPTER 3 —
FUNDAMENTALS OF FATS

*I was now beginning to grow handsome; my coat had grown fine and
soft, and was bright black.*
~ Black Beauty by Anna Sewell

Fats are an excellent source of calories. They don't create insulin highs and
lows, they don't create negative behavior, they don't increase laminitis risk,
and they don't destroy the microbial population in the hindgut. In fact, fats
supply more than twice the calories of equivalent amounts of carbohydrates or
proteins. Therefore, fatty feeds provide far more energy with much less bulk,
so they are an efficient way to add calories. And beyond their role as a concentrated energy (calorie) source, fat offers other benefits.

Benefits of Fat

Fat:
- enhances overall body condition

- provides structure to cell membranes

- acts as precursor to prostaglandins and eicosanoids, which are important for many cellular functions

- serves as a carrier for fat soluble nutrients such as vitamins A, D, E,
  and K, and other antioxidants found in plants

- supplies essential fatty acids — those that your horse cannot produce
  on his own, and therefore, must be in the diet

- produces a more moderate blood glucose (sugar) and insulin
  response, creating more even temperament and energy levels

- reduces circulating cortisol levels associated with stress and exercise

- delays the onset of fatigue

- limits anaerobic carbohydrate metabolism during exercise, resulting
  in less lactic acid production and better muscle glycogen utilization

Adding Fat to the Diet

When fats are added to the diet to replace carbohydrates, they should be added gradually. If oil is added too quickly, much of it will not be digested and will end up in the manure. The manure will look greasy and will be more copious in volume. This is not dangerous but it does indicate that the fat you're adding is not being utilized.

It takes a while for your horse to become accustomed to using more fat for energy, and therefore, fat augmentation should begin 4 to 6 weeks before any intense physical activity occurs. This is discussed further in Chapter 20 — Athletes.

SPECIAL CASES

A serious word of caution: Ponies, minis, donkeys, and mules metabolize fat more economically than horses and are prone toward weight gain and the insulin resistance that results from obesity. Therefore, it is best to avoid adding large amounts of fat to their diets.

THE FORM MATTERS

Fats exist as solids or liquids (oils). Solid fats are chemically saturated (more on this later) and are typically found in animal fats and coconut "oil." *Horses are herbivores and do not eat large amounts of saturated fat or animal fat unless we give it to them. Please avoid giving your horse fat that his body is not designed to metabolize.* Atherosclerosis (plaque buildup in the arteries) is rare in horses but if we were to feed hamburgers and hotdogs (or coconut oil) to horses on a regular basis, I suspect we'd start to see some changes in the research literature.

Coconut oil: no innocent fat source!

Coconut oil is actually not a liquid, so why it is called oil is somewhat of a mystery. Though derived from a plant, coconut oil is more saturated than the fat you trim off your steak. You wouldn't pour hamburger grease on your horse's feed, yet there is a popular product that combines coconut oil with soybean oil in a tasty supplement that's designed to add more calories. No doubt the flavor appeals to horses, but in reality, coconut oil in any form is simply not good for your horse.

Liquid fats

Liquid fats are referred to as oils. They are mostly unsaturated in structure and plant-based foods contain them in high concentrations. Horses are used to eating this type of fat. There are many oils from which to choose if you want to add fat to your horse's meal: soybean, corn, wheat germ, peanut, olive, canola, and rice bran oils. All of these oils have the same number of calories — 9 kcal per gram — but that's where the similarity ends. They each have their own specific fatty acid content, making some beneficial to health and others less so. They taste different, too. I have never seen a horse that likes olive oil, though I suppose there is always an exception.

How Fats Differ Chemically

What differentiates one fat source from another is its fatty acid profile. All fatty acids fall into one of three categories — saturated, monounsaturated, or polyunsaturated. Within these types there are individual fatty acids, each with its own unique structure.

> What differentiates one fat source from another is its fatty acid profile.

All fatty feeds and oils contain all three fatty acids forms. However, what makes one fat source better than another depends on which type predominates. Let's take a closer look at how they differ and what this means to your horse's health.

SATURATED FATTY ACIDS

The chemical structure of a saturated fatty acid makes it rigid and quite stable when exposed to air, heat, or moisture. Animal fats and coconut oil mainly consist of saturated fatty acids. Since only a small amount of these fatty acids are needed to maintain cellular structure, it is neither necessary nor advisable to feed large amounts. Your horse gets all the saturated fat he needs from the small amount found in grasses, legumes, and hay. When selecting a feed or supplement, avoid those that show animal fat or coconut oil on the list of ingredients.

Unsaturated fatty acids

Unsaturated fatty acids exist in several varieties and are classified as either monounsaturated or polyunsaturated. These fatty acids have areas within their structure that bend and are extremely vulnerable to oxygen, heat, and moisture. When exposed to these environmental elements, they can become rancid. Rancid oil will taste and smell spoiled and should not be eaten. The fatty acids are no longer whole and have turned into molecules called free radicals. Free radicals are highly volatile, destructive molecules that can cause damage to your horse's tissues.

Monounsaturated fatty acids

Monounsaturated fatty acids are healthful for the heart and blood vessels. These are primarily found in olive oil, nuts, and avocados (all not typically fed to horses), rice bran, rice bran oil, and (to a lesser extent) canola oil. Rice bran oil contains another fatty substance known as gamma oryzanol, discussed later in this chapter. Canola oil offers a sizeable amount of monounsaturated fatty acids, as well, but it also has omega-6 and omega-3 fatty acids in significant quantities.

Omega-9 family: The omega system refers to the chemical structure of the molecule. Unsaturated fatty acids have places along their long carbon chains that can bend, providing structure to cell membranes and metabolic compounds. Monounsaturated fatty acids belong to the omega-9 family.

Polyunsaturated fatty acids

These fatty acids exist in many forms. There are two that your horse cannot produce and that need to be offered in the diet, referred to as *essential fatty acids*. They are named linoleic acid and alpha-linolenic acid (ALA). Together, they support your horse's brain function, vision, skin and hair growth, bone health, reproductive capacity, as well as promote normal growth and development in young horses. They also promote wound healing, prevent dermatitis, and fight infections.

Omega-6 fatty acids: Linoleic acid is the most prevalent omega-6 fatty acid. Though essential, *too much linoleic acid can increase inflammation* (through excess eicosanoid and prostaglandin production). This is of particular importance for the horse that experiences inflammation and pain from joint, muscle, and ligament strain. The respiratory system can also become inflamed during intense exercise. Omega-6 fatty acids increase exercise-induced bronchial constriction as well as the respiratory system's response to allergens.

Soybean oil, usually labeled "vegetable oil," is the oil most commonly added to commercial feeds. Unfortunately, it is very high in omega-6 fatty acids. It does contain some omega-3 fatty acids, but 50 percent is from linoleic acid. Remember, *omega-6 fatty acids are essential, so some are necessary.* But excessive supplementation contributes to poor recovery from injuries or surgery. While inflammation has a role in healing, too much can create further damage, lengthen healing time, and cause excess pain.

Corn oil and wheat germ oil, also commonly fed to horses, are very high in omega-6 fatty acids. Table 3-1 compares the fatty acid content of these oils and others.

Cereal grains such as oats, corn, and barley offer omega-6 fatty acids. In contrast, the fat found in fresh grass, alfalfa, and clover is primarily in the omega-3 form.

There is considerable speculation on the optimal omega-6 to omega-3 ratio. Commercial weight builder supplements generally provide between 3:1 and 5:1 omega-6 to omega-3 fatty acids. Much research still remains to be done on this topic. But my advice is to mix your fat sources so the diet doesn't become overwhelmingly high in omega-6s.

Omega-3 fatty acids: Alpha linolenic acid (ALA) is the most prevalent omega-3 fatty acid in plant foods. Like linoleic acid, ALA is essential, but it has the *opposite effect* on pain and inflammation — it *reduces* inflammation. ALA naturally exists in fresh pasture (containing four times more omega-3s than omega-6s), though not in hay. When grass is cut, dried, and stored, most of the ALA is oxidized and hence, destroyed. Therefore, during the cold seasons when your horse relies on hay, it is best to supplement this fatty acid.

OMEGA-3 FATTY ACID FUNCTION AND SOURCES

Omega-3s:
- balance the immune system
- protect joints and ligaments
- decrease nervousness
- improve heart and blood vessel health
- reduce skin allergies
- diminish airway inflammation
- support normal gastrointestinal function
- maintain hair and hoof health
- improve sperm motility and speed

Fish oils

Fish oils are high in two polyunsaturated fatty acids called docosa-hexaenoic acid (DHA) and eicosapentaenoic acid (EPA) and they contain the highest concentration of omega-3 fatty acids in the form of DHA and EPA. But it is not common to feed fish oils to horses. Feeding them is controversial because horses are not fish-eaters. Most fish oil research is directed toward increasing sperm production in stallions since sperm naturally contains these two fatty acids. I discuss this further in Chapter 18 — Breeding, Pregnancy, and Lactation.

However, ALA is converted to EPA and DHA within the horse's body. Consequently, it is not necessary to give your horse fish oil as long as adequate levels of the essential fatty acid, ALA, are provided. Nevertheless, I have found short-term fish oil supplementation helpful in severe cases of pain and inflammation, especially where horses suffer from laminitis-induced abscesses. But since we do not know the long term effects of DHA and EPA, it is a better normal practice for your horse to have a plant-based diet, the way nature intended.

Flaxseed

Flaxseed oil or meal is the best source of ALA. Small amounts are also found in soybean oil and canola oil, but as mentioned earlier, soybean oil is mostly omega-6 fatty acids. Canola oil contains some ALA as well, but is higher in monounsaturated fatty acids (omega-9).

Flaxseeds should not be fed whole since most of them will pass through the digestive system with the outer hull intact. The benefit of flax is found in the seed portion (inside the hard hull). Many horse owners soak flaxseeds to soften these hulls, but this is not sufficient. In addition, and more important, soaking results in free radical formation (from moisture-related rancidity) so you would be adding these damaging molecules to your horse's diet.

Grinding flaxseeds is a common practice. If you do this, please be aware that fresh flaxseed meal is highly vulnerable to the oxygen in the air and will easily spoil, making it necessary to grind a fresh batch each day. I generally avoid freshly ground flax for another reason, too — its calcium to phosphorus ratio is inverted (more phosphorus than calcium). To protect your horse against rancidity and too much phosphorus, consider feeding a commercial flaxseed meal product that is stabilized against rancidity and has added calcium.

Flaxseed meal provides high quality protein, vitamins, and minerals in addition to valuable fatty acids. Its omega-3 fatty acid concentration is four times higher than its omega-6 (one ounce of weight contains approximately 6 grams of omega-3s and 1.5 grams of omega-6s). Since the fatty acid content of fresh grass is largely omega-3, flaxseed meal is an ideal supplement for horses that cannot graze on pasture.

When supplementing flaxseed meal, it is useful to understand how it is measured. In general, 1/2 cup of flaxseed meal (4 ounces by volume) weighs 2 ounces by weight (which is 1/8th of a pound). It's easy to confuse volume with weight; refer to Appendix — Crunching Numbers for a clarification between measurements. Most horses should have 1/2 cup (2 ounces by weight) per 400 lbs of body weight per day to provide adequate omega-3 fatty acids.

Commonly Fed Fat Sources

Table 3-1 shows the percentage of each type of fatty acid in common fat sources. Keep in mind that all fats and oils contain most fatty acid types in varying amounts. Notice that the most commonly fed oils, corn and soybean, are the most likely to cause inflammation due to their high linoleic acid (omega-6) content.

Table 3-1 Approximate Fatty Acid Content of Fats/Oils Typically Added Horse Diets: Percentage of Saturated, Monounsaturated, Omega-6, and Omega-3 Fatty Acids[1]

Fat/Oil	Saturated Fatty Acids (%)	Mono-unsaturated Fatty Acids (%) (Omega-9)	Linoleic Acid (%) (Omega-6)	Alpha Linolenic Acid (%) (Omega-3)
Beef fat	51	41	3	0.7
Hog fat (lard)	51	41	10	1
Fish oils	37	15	2	2
Coconut oil	91	6	3	0
Canola oil	7	54	30	7
Corn oil	17	24	59	0
Flaxseed oil	9	19	14	58
Rice bran oil	17	48	35	1
Olive oil	16	75	8	8
Wheat germ oil	18	25	50	5
Soybean oil	15	26	50	7
Sunflower oil	12	16	71	1

VEGETABLE OILS

The average horse's diet has 10 times more linoleic acid than ALA. This is largely due to the addition of vegetable oil to commercial feeds. Vegetable oil is a confusing label because it can be extracted from any plant; it doesn't tell you which one. On most ingredient lists, however, it usually refers to soybean oil.

Notice in Table 3-1 that the ratio of omega-6 to omega-3 in soybean oil is more than 7:1. Yes, it's true — soybean oil does contain *some* omega-3s, but using this oil to any large extent adds more omega-6 fatty acids than is healthful. As mentioned earlier, high levels of omega-6s in the diet aggravate inflammation and hence, pain. This is helpful to know if you have a horse that suffers from arthritis or any other inflammatory condition; you would be exacerbating the problem by feeding oil with high omega-6 content.

Sunflower seeds

The fat found in sunflower seeds is very high in omega-6 fatty acids. Horses love them and they are nutritious in many ways, but keep in mind that they are inflammatory, leading to free radical production. Free radicals produce even more inflammation, so it is a vicious cycle. The way to break this cycle is to cut back on feeding omega-6 sources.

Adding vitamin E

Vitamin E naturally exists in vegetable oils to protect fatty acids against rancidity. Its level is sufficient to protect the oil, but more needs to be in the diet to protect your horse — 1000 to 1500 IU of vitamin E is best (minimum of 1 IU per pound of body weight). Vitamin E is an antioxidant and therefore neutralizes free radicals. Free radicals end up in the horse's system in two ways. First, feeding fat sources that have been improperly stored will add free radicals to the diet. Second, mental stress and pain lead to increased free radical production.

Wheat germ and corn oils

Wheat germ oil is a good source of vitamin E. However, in terms of its omega-6 to omega-3 ratio, it mimics soybean oil, making it just as inflammatory.

Corn oil is also widely used in horse diets. Though more palatable than soybean oil, it is worse for the horse's health. Unlike soybean oil, corn oil has no omega-3s. And its omega-6 percentage is higher than soybean oil's.

Animal fat and coconut oil

Animal fats (e.g., beef fat and lard, from pigs) and coconut oil are sometimes added to commercial feeds. As I mentioned earlier, these fat sources are very high in saturated fat. Horses are not accustomed to consuming large amounts of these fat sources. Therefore feeding them should be kept to a minimum and better yet, not at all. Fish oils are also, of course, from animals. However, their chemical composition is dramatically different from mammal's fat.

Fresh pasture and cereal grains

Fresh pasture typically contains 2 to 4 percent fat and its omega-3 content varies from as little as 25 percent to as much as 75 percent of the total fat content. Cereal grains have little to no omega-3s, and nearly half of the fat found in grains comes from omega-6s. So it's plain to see that allowing your horse to graze on healthy, fresh pasture for the majority of the day will provide him with most, if not all, of the omega-3 fatty acids he needs.

Gamma oryzanol

Rice bran oil contains gamma oryzanol, a fatty substance that has several benefits. Though rice bran's gamma oryzanol content is diluted, there are rice bran extract supplements that are more concentrated. The advantages of gamma oryzanol include:

- Reduction of post-exercise soreness
- Antioxidant capability that reduces inflammation
- Enhanced muscle production
- Improved mood and behavior

Chapter 20 — Athletes offers more discussion on gamma oryzanol.

The best fat to choose

Which fatty feed or oil you choose depends on your goal. If you are look-ing to increase omega-3 fatty acids, add flaxseed meal or flaxseed oil. Thirty-six percent of flaxseed meal is in the form of fat. That translates into 1/3 cup of oil for every cup of flaxseed meal.

If your goal is to add a more concentrated source of calories, you can use rice bran, unless your horse needs to cut down on starchy feeds (as is the case with insulin resistant or cushingoid horses). Rice bran is 15% fat but it also has nearly 20% non-structural carbohydrates (NSC). Chapter 2 — Fundamentals of Carbohydrates goes into more detail about rice bran and other starchy feeds.

When adding oil for additional calories, I recommend rice bran oil or canola oil. Rice bran oil contains only fat and no carbohydrates. Its high monounsaturated, omega-9 fatty acids are safe to feed and do not promote inflammation. Canola oil is mostly omega-9s, has less than a third omega-6, and some omega-3 fatty acids, making it more balanced than corn or soybean oils. Corn or soybean oil should only be fed in small amounts to provide omega-6s as long as you are not feeding cereal grain and you are feeding flaxseed meal.

Volatile Fatty Acids

Volatile fatty acids (VFA) are not found in any feed. Instead, they are the result of microbial forage fermentation in the hindgut. Stomach bacteria also produce VFAs from starch fermentation, which can lead to ulcers. Refer to Chapter 14 — Digestive Problems, for a discussion of this issue.

There are three VFAs — acetic acid (yes, you're right — acetic acid is found in vinegar), butyric acid, and propionic acid. When acetic and butyric acids are absorbed into the bloodstream, they can be metabolized quickly for energy or even converted to fat for later energy use. Propionic acid must first be converted to glucose before it can be used by the cells for energy. It, too, can be converted to fat if too much is available and needs to be stored.

Summary

In summary, fat needs to be in your horse's diet, but not all fats are the same. They all provide the same number of calories per gram, but each fat source has its own individual fatty acid profile. There are two essential fatty acids that must be in the diet: linoleic acid (omega-6) and alpha linolenic acid (omega-3). Most horse diets, especially those that are high in grain and commercial feeds, have too many omega-6 fatty acids in relation to omega-3s, leading to increased inflammation.

Depending on the health status and condition of your horse, supplementation of fat may be beneficial. Horses that are exercised regularly benefit from additional fat to provide a concentrated source of calories that is metabolized aerobically. Carbohydrates are metabolized anaerobically (without oxygen), and therefore contribute to fatigue and lactic acid production. Pregnant and lactating mares also have additional calorie needs which are best met by adding fat to the diet. Aging horses that have trouble maintaining their weight can benefit from fat calories. Other equines such as ponies, minis, donkeys, and mules need fat, as well, but cannot tolerate the high levels horses can.

To be at their best, horses require energy from three sources: carbohydrates, fats, and proteins. Though proteins provide calories, they have many other roles in the horse body. And this is the subject of the next chapter... Fundamentals of Protein and Amino Acids.

Endnotes

[1] Values do not necessarily add to 100% due to other fatty acids found in these fats/oils. This table was adapted from two sources: (1) *Nutrient Requirements of Horses*, Sixth Revised Edition, 2007. Washington, D.C.: National Research Council, National Academy Press: 163.
(2) Erasmus, U., 1993. Fat content and fatty acid composition of seed oils. http://curezone.com/foods/fatspercent.asp.

Chapter 4 —
Fundamentals of Protein
and Amino Acids

The city horse is a different breed, so to speak, than his rural
cousin... dressed up and ready to go out on the town.
~ Michael Plank

Protein is the third nutrient classification (following carbohydrates and
fats) that provides calories to the diet. All proteins provide 4 kcal (a kcal is
1000 calories) per gram, and like the other two classes of nutrients, they
vary in their structure, role, and efficacy. But unlike carbohydrates and fat,
protein should not be fed to provide energy. Instead, protein should be used
to create body proteins.

There are literally hundreds of different proteins in your horse's body. Here
is a short list of where proteins are found:

- Vital organs such as the heart, lungs, kidneys, pancreas, glands,
  spleen, and liver

- Skeletal muscles (the largest storage form of protein in the body)

- Blood proteins (to carry substances throughout the body and create
  the ability for blood to clot, as well as to provide water balance)

- Skin, hair, and hooves

- Bones (made up of a protein matrix onto which minerals such as calcium and phosphorus can lodge)

- Eyes (to provide night vision)

- Connective tissue (contains collagen, the main protein for blood vessel integrity and healthy joints)

- Enzymes (virtually all are proteins involved in digestion and every
  chemical reaction in the body)

- Immune function (antibodies are proteins)

- Red blood cells (contain protein to transport oxygen to tissues)

Protein *quality* is the main concern when planning diets. All proteins are not the same. Just as a house is only as strong as the materials you build it with, a protein is only as nutritious as the building blocks it contains. These building blocks are known as amino acids. While many amino acids can be produced by your horse, there are 10 that must be in his diet, since they cannot be produced either at all or in adequate quantity to meet his needs. These ten are referred to as essential amino acids. A high-quality protein is defined as having all ten essential amino acids in proper proportion to one another. If one or more essential amino acids are not available, protein synthesis cannot occur; this emphasizes the need for high-quality (balanced) protein in the diet.

> Protein quality is the main concern when planning diets. All proteins are not the same.

Lysine and methionine are two essential amino acids that are typically out of balance in horse feeds. Grains and grasses tend to be low in lysine; legumes such as alfalfa and soy tend to be low in methionine, but have plenty of lysine. By combining different feeds, they complement each other, resulting in a high-quality protein.

Lysine is the only essential amino acid that has a designated National Research Council (NRC) requirement, but others should be in proportion to one another so your horse has all the building blocks he needs to synthesize body proteins.

Protein Digestion

Protein digestion starts in the stomach. Hydrochloric acid (HCl) unravels protein's complex structure in order for enzymes to reach the interior of the molecule. HCl also activates the first digestive enzyme protein will encounter, known as pepsin. Pepsin starts the process of breaking large protein molecules into smaller fragments of amino acid chains.

Upon leaving the stomach, partially digested proteins enter the small intestine (foregut) where other digestive enzymes are available to completely digest protein fragments down to individual amino acids. These amino acids are capable of being absorbed into the bloodstream and contribute to the amino acid pool — a supply of amino acids that cells can use to make whatever protein they need. Inside each cell, amino acids are strung together in specific sequences to construct specific proteins needed to build new or repair damaged tissues.

Protein is extracted from concentrates and forages early in the digestive process (stomach and small intestine) and is completed in the foregut. However, if a very large meal is fed, some of the protein may not be digested because the feed will continue moving along the digestive tract at a faster rate than your horse can digest it. Consequently, protein will end up in the hindgut, where cecal microbes will ferment it. Unlike excess carbohydrates, protein fermentation in the cecum is not a problem, but it is wasteful since your horse will not have access to those amino acids.

Protein Deficiency

Amino acids are used according to priority. Your horse's primary concern is to stay alive. His brain and nervous system require glucose for energy, which is normally provided by carbohydrates. But if there are not enough carbohydrates in the diet, amino acids will first be used for glucose or energy production. Once this need is met, then they can be used to build body proteins.

This situation is fortunately uncommon since forages contain carbohydrates. But in cases where horses are placed on sparse, overgrazed pasture with nothing else to eat, they are essentially starving. Any protein content in the pasture will be used to make glucose or burned for energy. Body proteins will not be made, leading to muscle wasting, low immune function, liver problems, hormonal imbalances, and poor skin, hooves, and hair. Unfortunately, I see this type of situation all too often, especially during the winter when the grass is dead and horses are left on large pastures to dig through snow to get whatever morsels they can find. They may receive some hay each day, but because they are so deprived, the amino acids never get incorporated into body protein structures.

The bottom line is this… Protein needs to be fed in large enough quantity and at a decent level of quality to provide the amino acid pool necessary to keep body tissues healthy.

Poor-Quality Protein

If a poor-quality protein is fed, then the horse must make choices on how to utilize the available amino acids. Naturally, the vital organs such as the heart, liver, kidneys, and lungs must receive amino acids to support life. Other organs such as the pancreas, spleen, digestive tract, bone marrow, adrenal and pituitary glands (to name a few) are also on the priority list. But the skin, hooves, and hair are low on the totem pole when it comes to getting the amino acids they need for tissue synthesis and repair. Therefore, these areas are a window to the inside of the horse because if these tissues are in good health, there's a good chance the horse is doing well on the inside.

A horse who consumes poor-quality protein will urinate excessively and the urine will have a stronger-than-usual odor. That's because he is getting rid of excess nitrogen from the unusable amino acids. Since the amino acids are out of proportion in a low-quality protein, they cannot be utilized by the cells. Unused amino acids are destroyed in the liver, resulting in nitrogenous compounds that must be removed from the body. The kidneys can become overworked in this situation.

Determining Protein Quality

How do you know if your horse's diet has enough essential amino acids in the right proportion? To get this information, the first place you're likely to look is the percentage of crude protein (CP) written on the feed label. Well, I'm sorry to tell you this, but CP tells you *virtually nothing* about the protein's quality. It does tell you the amount of nitrogen found in the feed; amino acids contain nitrogen, so the more amino acids in the feed, the higher the percent CP. It says nothing about which amino acids are present or whether they are in the correct ratio to one another.

A better approach is to look at the list of ingredients on the label. This will give you a clue as to which protein *sources* are included. Now you have some valuable information to help you determine if the ingredients complement each other in their amino acid profiles. Most feed companies will give you an accurate list of ingredients. However, there are some companies that consider their formulations proprietary and give you vague ingredients such as "plant products" or "forages." Stay away from these. I don't care if the front of the bag tells you how wonderful this feed is, how nutritionally complete it is, or how gorgeous your horse will look. If they don't want you to know what's in the bag, you have no interest in buying their product!

Unlike ingredient lists used for our own foods, the ingredient lists for animal feeds are not necessarily presented in order of concentration. There is a federal regulation requiring ingredients to be listed in descending order of predominance according to weight, and while most reputable companies comply, if you have any doubt, I highly recommend contacting the feed manufacturer to confirm their observance of this rule.

So, the *only* way to make an intelligent decision about the protein quality in your horse's diet is to have a good idea which ingredients supply which amino acids and in what ratio. To do this, the essential amino acid lysine is given a value of 100. Then all other essential amino acids are compared to this value. Let's take a look at how amino acids exist in the body. Table 4-1 compares the essential amino acid proportions of muscle (the largest storage form of protein in the horse's body) with milk.

Table 4-1 Essential Amino Acid Proportion of Muscle and Milk[1] Relating to Lysine (given a value of 100)

Essential Amino Acid	Muscle	Milk
Lysine	100	100
Methionine	27	29 to 35
Threonine	61	53 to 68
Isoleucine	55	53 to 79
Leucine	107	127 to 147
Histidine	58	29 to 37
Phenylalanine	60	53 to 59
Valine	62	64 to 97
Arginine	76	70 to 82
Tryptophan	Not recorded	Not recorded

Though not related, these two tissues share similar amino acid profiles. Therefore feed profiles should closely match these proportions. Common feeds tend to fall short of these proportions with two essential amino acids: lysine and methionine. We refer to them as "limiting amino acids" because they limit the extent to which the others can be utilized in building body proteins. They are like the weakest link of the chain and therefore, the protein quality is only as high as the level of these two essential amino acids. If lysine and methionine are low, the overall usage of the other 8 essential amino acids will be reduced, leading to their inability to become part of body proteins. To give you an idea of the lysine and methionine levels in common feeds, take a look at Table 4-2.

Notice a few items shown on Table 4-2. First, if your horse receives a forage-based diet consisting of fresh grass and grass hay, the supply of lysine and methionine is minimal. Therefore, a legume (mainly alfalfa, though clover is also a legume) should be added to the grass diet to provide additional essential amino acids.

For example, let's consider an 1100 lb adult horse who is not exercised regularly and basically lives on hay and pasture. His lysine requirement, based on the NRC, is 27 grams per day. And though methionine has no published requirement, I like to see a 3:1 ratio of lysine to methionine. So in this case, we would want the diet to contain 9 grams of methionine.

If our horse in this example were to consume 30 lbs (dry matter) of a warm weather grass (.04% lysine), he would get 5.45 grams of lysine. And methionine in this grass (.01%) would amount to 1.36 grams. (The calculations for this are shown in Appendix — Crunching Numbers.) This diet is obviously inadequate when trying to meet lysine requirements.

Let's change his diet by replacing 8 lbs of the warm weather grass hay with alfalfa. Alfalfa provides .21% lysine and .06% methionine. Now the total amount of lysine in 30 lbs of mixed hay is up to 11.6 grams, and the total methionine level is 3.18 grams — still not reaching the 27 gram requirement for lysine and the 9 gram requirement for methionine.

So in this situation, there are two things you can do. First, have your hay analyzed. Hays vary in their lysine content and yours may have a much higher level than the values shown. Though you won't get the methionine level included in the analysis, you can estimate that it will be approximately 1/4th to 1/3rd of the lysine level. You can have your hay analyzed by

Table 4-2 Percentage (on a Dry Matter Basis) of the Most Common Limiting Essential Amino Acids, Lysine and Methionine, Found in Popular Feedstuffs[2]

Feedstuff	% Lysine	% Methionine
Legumes		
• Alfalfa Meal (pellets)	0.77	0.27
• Alfalfa Hay	0.21	0.06
Mixed hays		
• Predominantly Grass	0.12	0.04
• Predominantly Legume	0.17	0.06
Grass hays		
• Warm Weather	0.04	0.01
• Cool Weather	0.03	0.01
Other forages		
• Oat Hay	0.32	0.17
• Wheat Straw	0.16	0.06
Cereal grains		
• Barley	0.44	0.22
• Corn	0.33	0.19
• Oats	0.44	0.24
• Sorghum	0.22	0.19
Brans		
• Wheat bran	0.66	0.27
• Rice bran	0.66	0.29
By-products		
• Brewer's Grains	1.31	0.49
• Distiller's Corn	0.77	0.47
• Wheat Middlings	0.66	0.28
Other		
• Beet Pulp	0.55	0.08
• Flaxseed (Linseed) Meal	1.32	0.65
• Soybean Meal	3.08	0.67
• Brewer's Yeast	3.52	0.81

your county extension service or feed store, or contact a reputable lab such as Equi-Analytical Laboratories — www.equi-analytical.com.

Next, after having your hay analyzed, you may find that you need to feed one or two meals each day that offer more lysine and methionine. Let's go back to specific ingredients to see which ones would work for your horse. Cereal grains, if your horse can tolerate them, are a good source of essential amino acids. But so are beet pulp, flaxseed meal, soybean meal, and bran. Any of these feeds make useful meals. Soybean meal, in particular, is well balanced for lysine and methionine. It is a legume (like alfalfa) and has the highest protein quality among plant feeds. Be careful when feeding bran since it has too much phosphorus in relation to calcium; buy a commercial version with added calcium to correct this ratio.

If you have a pregnant mare or a growing horse, their higher need for lysine is best met through supplementation. Individual lysine requirements can be found in the NRC's newly revised edition of *Nutrient Requirements of Horses*[3].

Once you've determined that your feed provides high-quality protein, you can then look at the CP percentage to see if you're feeding enough protein. Growth, pregnancy, lactation, weight, age, and exercise level all influence how much protein is required. This is discussed further in three relevant chapters: 18 — Breeding, Pregnancy, and Lactation, 19 — Growth and Growing Old, and 20 — Athletes.

Feeding Too Much Protein

Healthy horses can tolerate protein levels that slightly exceed the requirements. Any excess amino acids, beyond the horse's need for body proteins, will be burned for energy or made into fat (for later energy usage). When this happens, nitrogen must be excreted in the urine as urea. For the most part this is not a concern; however, in aging horses or those that have kidney problems, excess protein puts a strain on the kidneys. Furthermore, too much protein can lead to dehydration due to excess urine output.

If a blood test reveals high protein levels, it is not an indication that you are feeding too much protein. Elevated blood proteins (such as globulin or fibrinogen) indicate underlying disorders such as inflammation, infection, or too much fat in the blood (hyperlipemia, generally a threat to ponies and donkeys).

CALCIUM LOSS

The kidney loses its ability to retain calcium when protein intake is high, resulting in urinary calcium losses. This can create an imbalance with other minerals such as phosphorus and magnesium. See Chapter 5 — Fundamentals of Minerals for more information.

Growing horses and those that are exercised intensively need to maintain normal blood calcium levels not only for muscle function, but also for healthy bones. Excess protein can cause the blood pH to become more acidic, leading to calcium depletion from the bones.

Protein Requirements

The NRC publishes protein requirements for horses in all life stages and exercise levels. These requirements are indicated by grams of protein per day, not by a percentage. Knowing the CP percentage in your hay will help you balance out the protein requirement from other sources.

For example, an 1100 lb adult horse at maintenance requires an average of 630 grams of protein each day (protein requirements for varying levels of activity are discussed in Chapter 20 —Athletes). If this horse consumes 18 lbs of 8% CP hay, he will get all the protein grams he needs. This calculation is illustrated in Appendix — Crunching Numbers. But if he only eats 16 lbs of this hay, he will be short 49 grams and a protein source must be added to his diet.

Other circumstances such as work, growth, pregnancy, recovery from injury, laminitis, immune deficiency, muscle loss from neglect or equine Cushing's disease, sustained illness, surgery, etc., will increase the protein requirement in order to rebuild healthy tissue.

Please note… The above example looks at grams of total protein, but does not address quality. As I discussed earlier in this chapter, it is best to combine grasses and legumes not only to meet protein requirements but to ensure the proper amino acid balance.

Rather than go through individual calculations each time you feed your horse, you can make life easier for yourself by providing 1.5 to 3% of your horse's weight in mixed forages. For additional calorie needs, add a commercial feed that has 12% protein. This is appropriate for most horses. Higher protein levels are necessary for conditions such as growth, pregnancy, lactation, performance, and illness. Look for a combination of ingredients including soybean meal, alfalfa meal, beet pulp, flax, bran, and distiller's grains (these are low in starch) to create high-quality protein.

Laminitis and Protein

Contrary to popular opinion, *protein does not cause laminitis*. Laminitis has several causes, the most common being either too much fructan reaching the hindgut or elevated insulin levels caused by high starch/high sugar diets. These causes and others are discussed in detail in Chapter 11 — Laminitis.

Alfalfa is higher in protein that grass hays, but in moderate quantity it boosts the overall protein quality, is low in sugar, and supplies additional minerals. However, I do not recommend feeding alfalfa as the only forage source; it should be mixed with grasses to keep protein levels in check and prevent intestinal enterolith formation.

For more on alfalfa, in particular its starch and sugar levels, go back to Chapter 2 — Fundamentals of Carbohydrates. You'll be pleasantly surprised to see how it compares with grasses.

Summary

In summary, protein is a necessary dietary component that is often ignored. It has a multitude of benefits for your horse:

- Balancing immune function
- Tissue and blood vessel integrity
- Injury repair
- Efficient digestion
- Water balance
- Health during pregnancy and lactation
- Proper growth
- Hair, hooves, and skin health
- Vision
- Healthy red blood cells
- Muscle development and repair from exercise
- Joint health
- Favorable attitude and behavior

To meet your horse's specific protein needs, consider his stage of life and his overall condition. During pregnancy, lactation, growth, exercise, and illness, high-protein feeds are advisable if the protein quality of your hay is not adequate.

Avoid the mistake of relying on crude protein to judge your feed or hay. Instead, evaluate the actual ingredients in order to make certain that you're giving your horse a variety of protein sources; this will ensure a balanced amino acid profile.

Too little protein makes it impossible to maintain health. Conversely, too much protein taxes the liver and kidneys, and creates mineral imbalances, especially between calcium, phosphorus, and magnesium. The next chapter, Fundamentals of Minerals, elaborates on these as well as other essential minerals.

Endnotes

[1] *Nutrient Requirements of Horses*, Sixth Revised Edition, 2007. Washington, D.C.: National Research Council, National Academy Press: 65.

[2] Adapted from: *Nutrient Requirements of Horses*, Sixth Revised Edition, 2007. Washington, D.C.: National Research Council, National Academy Press: Table 8-8, p. 166.

[3] *Nutrient Requirements of Horses*, Sixth Revised Edition, 2007. Washington, D.C.: National Research Council, National Academy Press.

CHAPTER 5 —
FUNDAMENTALS OF MINERALS

But he does have funny ways. It is terribly hard to gallop him
with a grey pony because when he was a three-year-old he fell
in love with a grey pony and still remembers it.
~ Robert Strauss
Go Man Go — American Quarter Horse Hall of Fame

Functions

The mineral concentration in your horse's diet is small in relation to other nutrients but don't let that fool you — minerals are just as essential to health. They are involved in hundreds of important functions. Here are a few:

- Acid-base balance
- Bone and joint structure
- Enzymatic reactions
- Energy metabolism
- Antioxidant support
- Red blood cell health
- Hormonal functions
- Pregnancy — uterine fluid and fetal growth
- Muscle contraction
- Nerve cell health

Individual Minerals

Minerals are classified according to two categories: macrominerals and microminerals. Macrominerals are fed in concentrations expressed most often as grams per pound (g/lb) or as a percentage. Microminerals are present in smaller levels and are therefore expressed as milligrams per kg (mg/kg), which is the same as parts per million (ppm). An illustration of how to manipulate these numbers in your feed or forage is provided in Appendix — Crunching Numbers.

Below is an alphabetical list of individual minerals that have been researched in horses' diets. Please refer to Part II of this book. It contains chapters that describe conditions and diseases that may respond to specific minerals.

MACROMINERALS

Calcium

Nearly 99% of calcium in your horse's body is found in the bones and teeth; the remaining one percent exists in the blood. Calcium concentration in the blood may be small, but it is critical to your horse's health. Calcium is needed for skeletal muscle contraction and relaxation, heart muscle pumping, digestive tract motility, and nerve conduction. Blood calcium levels also control cellular activity including blood clotting, cell membrane function, glandular secretion, enzymatic functions, and temperature regulation. The level of calcium in the blood is controlled by vitamin D (discussed in the next chapter — Fundamentals of Vitamins) and hormones from the parathyroid gland.

No discussion of calcium is complete without including phosphorus. The calcium content in the diet needs to be at least equal to phosphorus, and preferably two or more times higher. Mature, healthy horses can safely tolerate up to six times more calcium than phosphorus in the diet as long as phosphorus content is adequate. Grass hay generally contains calcium and phosphorus in correct amounts and in proper proportion to one another. Alfalfa hay not only adds essential amino acids that boost protein quality when added to grasses, but it also contributes additional calcium. This is good to know because there are times when more calcium is needed: growth, pregnancy, and lactation, as well as to balance out high phosphorus intake from other sources.

Cereal grains (oats, corn, barley, wheat, etc.), grain by-products, flaxseed meal, sunflower seeds, rice bran, and wheat bran all have more phosphorus than calcium. Wheat bran, for example, contains ten times more phosphorus than calcium; the phosphorus content in oats is five times higher than its calcium concentration.

Feeding these items separately or as part of a commercial feed necessitates adding enough calcium so it exceeds phosphorus levels. Feed companies generally do this for you; all you need to do is check the guaranteed analysis shown on the label to make sure there is a higher concentration of calcium than phosphorus. But if you choose, for example, to add flaxseed meal or bran to your horse's diet, you can do one of two things to add more calcium. You can balance it with a high-calcium feedstuff such as alfalfa or beet pulp. Or better yet, purchase name-brand commercial versions that have already corrected this inverted ratio.

Remember, simple grains are very high in phosphorus. If you feed your horse oats, you need to calculate the total amount of calcium and phosphorus in the diet, including levels found in your hay and/or pasture. Hopefully the grass will bring the total calcium level up to meet the high phosphorus content of grain. If not, the easiest approach is to add alfalfa, which varies between 1.3 and 1.5 percent calcium. There are calcium supplements available such as ground limestone (34% calcium) or calcium carbonate (39% calcium) but if you choose this route you must be especially diligent about calculating the mineral content in the entire diet since too much calcium can interfere with absorption of many other minerals.

Inadequate calcium intake: Your horse's priority usage of calcium is to maintain a normal blood level. Diets low in calcium will cause calcium to be removed from the bones in order to elevate blood levels, leading to porous bones that can fracture easily, abnormal bone development, or reduced healing capacity after a bone or joint injury. In addition, low blood calcium levels (hypocalcaemia) can lead to stress tetany, exhibited by excess sweating, muscle twitching, and stiff limbs. Your horse can also become exhausted and easily succumb to colic. In Appendix — Crunching Numbers, I give you an example of how you can determine the calcium to phosphorus ratio in your feeding plan.

Chloride

Chloride goes hand-in-hand with sodium as part of salt (sodium chloride). It is an electrolyte, meaning it has the ability to balance blood pH and regulate water flow in and out of cells (osmotic pressure). Chloride is also a component of bile (necessary for fat digestion) and hydrochloric acid (HCl), the acid found in the stomach that starts protein digestion.

Up until recently, it has been assumed that salt would provide enough chloride. However, we now know that this is not the case. Any horse that sweats for two hours or longer will lose significant amounts of this electrolyte. And sweat replacement products cannot provide enough. The key is to give your horse a head start on chloride blood levels before exercise begins. Fortunately, this is easy to do since grass hay is high in chloride. As little as 9 lbs will provide enough chloride to get your horse through his exercise session. Fresh grass also contains chloride, but your horse would have to graze for a several hours to get the same amount found in hay because pasture is mostly water.

Magnesium

Most of the magnesium found in your horse's body is located in the bones, but a large percentage (30%) is found in the blood and muscle tissue. Blood magnesium is necessary for enzymatic reactions and regulates muscle contraction. It works with calcium to promote muscle function and the two minerals should be balanced. A magnesium deficiency can result in soreness, muscle tremors, and ataxia (wobbliness and lack of coordination). If left unattended, it can lead to collapse and death. Even borderline deficiencies in magnesium can produce marked behavioral changes including irritability, reluctance to work, nervousness, inattention, and aloofness. Many horses do not receive enough magnesium because it is not well absorbed from pasture and hay. For this reason, magnesium supplementation may be beneficial.

If your horse suffers from any deficiency signs, give magnesium supplementation a try. I recommend 5,000 mg of magnesium for every 500 lbs of body weight, given daily over a three-week period. If a magnesium deficiency exists, your horse's behavior and muscle condition will improve. If there is no change, the problem was not due to low magnesium intake.

Be sure there is at least an equal amount of calcium in the diet. The ideal calcium to magnesium ratio is 2:1, though a 1:1 ratio is acceptable *as long as the magnesium level does not exceed calcium's*. If your horse is getting adequate pasture and/or hay, the calcium requirement is likely sufficient for adding magnesium safely.

Magnesium also lowers circulating insulin levels in the blood. When insulin levels are high, fat storage is increased, leading to even higher insulin secretion. Magnesium supplementation is, therefore, extremely valuable in stopping this vicious cycle of insulin resistance. This is examined further in Chapter 13 — Metabolic and Endocrine Disorders.

When supplementing magnesium, there are several forms from which to choose. Magnesium sulfate (Epsom salts) is commonly fed; however, it has a strong laxative effect. Better sources which are easier on the digestive tract and are more readily absorbed include, in order of their absorption ability (bioavailability): magnesium citrate, magnesium oxide, and magnesium carbonate.

Enteroliths: Though magnesium toxicities have not been reported, there is concern that too much magnesium in relation to calcium could lead to intestinal stone formations called enteroliths. Diets containing 50% or more alfalfa have also been blamed because legumes are higher in magnesium than grasses. However, not all horses on alfalfa-based diets develop enteroliths. So there may be a genetic component. Magnesium is well accepted with a maximum tolerable level set at 0.8%[1]. That means if your horse consumes 20 lbs of hay containing 0.8% magnesium (which is not possible), it would provide 72,000 mg of magnesium. To put this in perspective, the average alfalfa hay has 0.3% magnesium, translating into 27 grams of magnesium in 20 lbs — not even close to being a problem. The keys to intestinal stone prevention are enough turnout, exercise, water, and forage. Enteroliths are discussed further in Chapter 14 — Digestive Problems.

Phosphorus

As discussed above, phosphorus needs to be balanced with calcium and its level should never surpass calcium's. In fact, the phosphorus content really should be 50% or less than calcium's quantity in the diet. Too much phosphorus can lead to growth difficulties as well as bone deterioration. One potential problem in growing horses is a condition called nutritional secondary hyperparathyroidism, or more commonly referred to as "big head" which reflects a weakened skeleton. Bones become weak, leading to growth abnormalities. Since grain-based diets are higher in phosphorus than calcium, particular attention needs to be paid toward balancing grains with forages to improve this ratio. And better yet, feeding grain should be restricted and even eliminated for growing horses because of other osteopathic disorders. See Chapter 19 — Growth and Growing Old for more information on big head syndrome and healthy joint development.

Like calcium, phosphorus is a major component of bones. But, unlike calcium, it plays a central role in energy transfer reactions; it is part of energy "currency" called ATP. Phosphorus is also part of several structural compounds in the body including cell membranes, muscle tissue, and blood proteins.

Supplementation is very rarely needed unless your hay, upon analysis, reveals that the phosphorus level is inadequate. If this is the only feed source for your horse, consider adding unfortified bran to bring phosphorus levels up to par.

Potassium

Considered an electrolyte, potassium is mainly located within the skeletal muscles. A small percentage is found in the fluid surrounding the cells (known as extracellular fluid) and is therefore involved in maintaining acid-base balance, water balance and osmotic pressure.

Forages and seed meals (flaxseed meal, sunflower seed meal, etc.) contain high quantities of potassium. Since forage makes up the majority of the diet for most horses, deficiencies are rare. But cereal grains (oats, corn, barley, wheat, rye, etc.) are relatively low in potassium; if fed individually, deficiencies can develop. Fortunately, commercially available feeds, even if grain-based, are usually fortified with potassium so feeding them shouldn't be a concern. But it's always wise to check the feed label to make certain this mineral has been added.

A potassium deficiency leads to weight loss, failure to thrive, and an unhealthy appearance. Low potassium levels can also occur during excessive sweating. A hard working horse that lives in a hot, humid climate will benefit from an electrolyte supplement that contains potassium, as long as he is in good sodium (salt) standing to being with. Please refer to Chapters 1 — Ground Rules for Feeding a Horse and 7 — Fundamentals of Water and Electrolytes for guidelines on using electrolyte supplements.

Hyperkalemic periodic paralysis: HYPP is a devastating genetic disease passed down from the 1969 Quarter Horse sire Impressive. Horses with this condition can vary in their response to potassium intake depending on whether they inherited one or two genes. They require very close dietary monitoring of potassium. This disease is discussed in detail in Chapter 13 — Metabolic and Endocrine Disorders.

Sodium

Combined with chloride in salt (sodium chloride), the electrolyte sodium has a major role in your horse's health. Like potassium, it is involved in water balance, acid-base balance, and osmotic pressure. Sodium is excreted in the sweat and in the urine.

Horses can easily become deficient in this electrolyte because *grasses and legumes are extremely low in sodium.* If your horse does not consume enough sodium, he will attempt to conserve it by decreasing his water intake and urine output. His appetite will become depressed and, in extreme cases, his muscles will not contract properly, leading to tying up. Tying up, medically known as rhabdomyolysis, is a serious condition that has several triggers including a sodium deficit. See Chapter 13 — Metabolic and Endocrine Disorders for a full discussion its causes.

Salt supplementation: A salt block is a must. A good rule of thumb for judging adequate consumption is this: a 5 lb salt block should be used up within 2 months to meet maintenance sodium needs. But some horses will not touch salt blocks — they may be bullied away by more aggressive horses, they may find it unappetizing if covered with dirt, or their tongues may become sore from too much licking. If this is the case for your horse, add salt to his meals every day, not just when it's hot or when he's exercising. This will ensure proper sodium balance. Electrolyte supplements contain sodium, that's true, but they are designed to replace what has been lost in sweat, not what is needed throughout the body. You can supplement electrolytes after exercise or profuse sweating, but *they should only be added in addition to his daily salt intake.* Exact instructions on using electrolyte supplements can be found in Chapter 7 — Fundamentals of Water and Electrolytes.

> But some horses will not touch salt blocks — they may be bullied away by more aggressive horses, they may find it unappetizing if covered with dirt, or their tongues may become sore from too much licking.

Horses instinctively crave salt, so they will enjoy having salt added to their feed. This will also encourage adequate water intake, preventing dehydration. To add salt to the diet, choose plain, white, table salt, the kind you can get from your grocery store. Choose the iodized version unless your horse is already getting iodine from his feed or other supplements. Give him one ounce (two level tablespoons) per day, divided between meals, for maintenance conditions, including during cold weather. Excess sweating, exercise, and hot, humid conditions double his requirement.

Sulfur

Common substances such cysteine and methionine (amino acids), thiamin and biotin (B vitamins), insulin (hormone involved in carbohydrate regulation), and chondroitin sulfate (part of joint tissue), contain sulfur as part of their structure. Sulfur requirements are easily met by consuming protein, generally provided by forages, seeds, and cereal grains.

Hydrogen sulfide is often present in well water and at elevated concentrations can give the water a rotten-egg smell. The Environmental Protection Agency sets the safe limit for humans at 250 mg/liter (ppm) which is well below the maximum tolerable level of 5000 ppm for horses established by the National Research Council (NRC). Therefore you would be bothered by the extreme odor long before your horse would be affected.

MICROMINERALS (TRACE)

Cobalt

Cobalt has one function — it is needed by the microbes living in your horse's hindgut to produce vitamin B_{12}. Vitamin B_{12} is not found in any plant material and since horses are herbivorous (plant-eating), they must rely on the hindgut bacterial flora for its production. Horses that are experiencing stress or illness, or that are taking antibiotics can experience a B_{12} deficiency due to a reduction in the microbial population under these circumstances.

Commercial feeds generally add cobalt to assist with vitamin B_{12} production because many geographical areas are cobalt-deficient. In particular, forages from the New England states and coastal plains, as well as parts of Australia and New Zealand, tend to be low in cobalt.

In addition to fortified feeds, many multiple vitamin/mineral supplements contain cobalt. This is fine as long as your horse is healthy. But cobalt supplementation will be useless if the bacterial numbers in the hindgut are at all compromised. That's when it is better to add vitamin B_{12} individually or a B complex supplement to your horse's diet. The functions of vitamin B_{12} are described in the next chapter — Fundamentals of Vitamins.

Chromium

Chromium is involved in carbohydrate and fat metabolism, making it of particular benefit to the insulin resistant horse. It works with insulin to increase the amount of glucose entering the cells, thereby reducing the need for extra insulin. Chapter 13 — Metabolic and Endocrine Disorders contains more information on this mineral.

Copper

Copper is found in most feedstuffs, so a deficiency is unlikely unless there is too much iron and zinc in the diet, leading to inadequate copper absorption. High intake of iron or zinc generally arises from too much supplementation. Be careful when mixing more than one supplement — iron and zinc may be included in several products, leading to overlaps.

Deficiency signs: A copper-deficient horse will have poor stress tolerance, cannot exercise at potential, and will be more susceptible toward developing infections. He can also become anemic because copper is responsible for carrying iron from the intestinal lining to the bone marrow, where iron is used to make hemoglobin. Osteochondritis, physitis, and limb deformities can occur in foals born with inadequate copper stores, making supplementation during pregnancy a must. This is described in Chapters 18 — Breeding, Pregnancy, and Lactation and 19 — Growth and Growing Old.

Copper is required for melanin production, the pigment found in skin and hair. If copper is underprovided, the first place you'll notice it is in your horse's hair coat. Its color will not be as intense as it once was and will appear faded. Once your horse receives enough copper, his system will take care of his insides first, and then you'll notice a change in his hair color. This is only true if copper is deficient; *don't add copper to an already sufficient diet in hopes of improving your horse's hair color.* Though horses can tolerate relatively high levels of copper, too much can interfere with absorption of other minerals.

Fluoride

Though necessary for normal bone and teeth development, fluoride does not need to be supplemented. It is found in adequate quantity in forages and cereal grains. On the flip side, toxicities can develop if your horse drinks city water that has been fluoridated. Excess intake can lead to bone lesions, changes in hoof growth, lameness, and poor appearance. If your horse has any of these conditions and you've ruled out other medical/nutritional problems, consider having the fluoride in your water tested. The NRC has set the upper limit of fluoride at 40 mg/kg (ppm)[2].

Iodine

Most iodine is found in the thyroid gland in order to produce two hormones: thyroxin (T4) and triiodothyronine (T3). A shortage in either hormone is referred to as hypothyroidism. To diagnose this disorder, it is best to test for thyroid stimulating hormone (TSH). High TSH indicates hypothyroidism because the thyroid gland is struggling to produce thyroxin. The thyroid gland will increase in size (known as goiter). Testing for TSH, though ideal, is not typically available for veterinarians to use.

True hypothyroidism is rare in horses. However, thyroid medication is often administered to horses that are suspected of having equine Cushing's disease. I do not advocate this treatment, as a rule, because of the potential for thyroid dysfunction. This is addressed in Chapter 13 — Metabolic and Endocrine Disorders.

Goiter can also result from too much iodine. Toxic levels have been seen in newborn foals whose dams are supplemented with 40 mg per day. This level of supplementation is highly unlikely though it is always best to check the guaranteed analysis of any product before feeding it. I recommend avoiding products with added kelp (sea salt) since some strains are excessively high in iodine.

Iodine should be balanced with selenium. If the diet contains too much iodine combined with too little selenium, the thyroid gland will become damaged. Therefore, a commercial feed or vitamin/mineral supplement should have its iodine range between 0.1 and 0.6 ppm, and the total diet should never contain more than 5 ppm[3] of iodine. Selenium is discussed later in this section.

Iron

Iron is found in four areas of your horse's body. Sixty percent is found in hemoglobin's structure. Hemoglobin is the protein found in red blood cells and is responsible for delivering oxygen to tissues to allow for aerobic energy metabolism throughout the body. Twenty percent of his iron supply is part of another protein called myoglobin. Inside muscle tissue, myoglobin is responsible for storing oxygen, also used for energy metabolism but confined to muscle cells. The remaining twenty percent is located in the blood, bound to two proteins, ferritin (for iron storage) and transferrin (for iron transport).

Forages are high in iron, so most horses get more than enough. Consider that the maximum tolerable level for iron, according to the NRC[4], is 500 mg/kg of feed (also known as ppm). The minimum iron requirement for an 1100 lb adult horse that is not exercised, for example, is 400 mg. Let's make this your horse for the moment to show how easily iron needs are met. Consider a diet where he consumes 30 lbs of hay each day. And let's assume that this amount of hay provides 2000 mg of iron (not uncommon for a forage-based diet). This translates into 147 ppm, considerably lower than the 500 ppm maximum but higher than the 400 mg minimum requirement (Appendix — Crunching Numbers shows how this was calculated.)

Iron-deficiency: Because forage is so high in iron, I rarely recommend iron supplementation unless a horse suffers from iron-deficiency anemia. When we hear the word anemia, it's easy to think of an iron deficiency. But that is not necessarily the case. Anemia can also be caused by inadequate B vitamins, in particular a deficiency in folic acid, B_{12} or B_6. These B vitamins can be supplied by feeding a supplement which does not contain iron.

Because iron-deficiency is often the first thing that comes to mind when horse owners are told their horse is anemic, they'll typically reach for the iron-containing "blood builders" that are a common sight on feed store shelves. If this describes you and your horse, please resist the urge to buy this type of product. An iron deficiency is highly unlikely and too much of this mineral can be toxic, leading to depression, dehydration, diarrhea, insulin resistance (which can cause laminitis), and an increased risk of bacterial infections. Too much iron also interferes with copper absorption.

The only time I recommend an iron supplement is when I suspect internal bleeding, as in the case of ulcers. Many ulcers, though not all, bleed enough for there to be a significant blood loss and hence, loss of iron. This regrettable situation is all too common and iron status is best assessed through blood tests. I discuss it at length in Chapter 14 — Digestive Problems.

Iron status: Before supplementing iron, have your horse's blood tested. The best measurement is the total iron binding capacity (TIBC) test combined with the transferrin saturation index (TSI). Give your horse hay before drawing blood since fasting may cause a false low reading.

Testing ferritin levels is also a good way to assess iron status. If this storage protein is very low, it generally indicates anemia. During pregnancy, however, a low result can occur instead because the mare is pulling iron out of storage for the growing foal's use. On the other hand, infections or cancer can produce high ferritin readings; bacteria and cancer cells rely on iron to multiply, so the body is trying to protect itself by removing freely-circulating iron from the bloodstream and putting it into storage. This is discussed in the following section.

Iron and immune function: Bacteria thrive on iron. If your horse has a bacterial infection, his body will protect itself by sequestering iron within ferritin and transferrin forms, making iron unavailable for bacterial growth, a process known as nutritional immunity. However, this protective mechanism is not fool-proof[5]. Many bacteria have developed methods, predominantly the production of iron-chelators called siderophores[6], that can remove iron from transferrin, ferritin, and other iron-containing proteins, making their numbers increase beyond the immune system's ability to destroy them.

Too much[7] and even too little iron[8] can negatively impact the immune function. However, iron deficiency, as I mentioned earlier, is uncommon in horses. In the case of an iron overload, horses can block most iron from being absorbed. But it's that in-between stage where iron levels are not overly high but high enough to sustain an existing bacterial infection that is of concern. Laminitis, for example, tends to result in hoof abscesses; though not studied extensively in horses, I suspect that high iron intake may interfere with abscess healing[9].

Iron and insulin: Too much iron has been shown to increase insulin resistance in humans[10]. Elevated insulin results in increased iron absorption, creating a cycle of insulin resistance that can only be stopped by removing supplemental iron from the diet. Though not studied in horses, it is worth considering the possibility that excess iron can also interfere with their insulin levels, which can lead to laminitis. I have personally encountered cases where chronic laminitis attacks were alleviated by removing excess iron supplementation from the diet. Take a look at your feed tag or any mineral-containing supplements that you're feeding — they likely contain iron. If your horse is overweight, insulin resistant, has suffered from laminitis, or has equine Cushing's disease, change your feeding regimen to one that is very low in iron or, better yet, does not have any at all beyond what forage provides. Choose a vitamin/mineral supplement that does not include iron. If you cannot avoid adding iron to your horse's diet, limit his total iron intake to 500 ppm. See Appendix — Crunching Numbers for an explanation of how to calculate mg from ppm.

Manganese

Manganese is one of those minerals that few people know about; they may only learn of its existence when seeing it listed on a feed tag or supplement label. But manganese is very important for your horse's joints. It is needed for the chondroitin sulfate synthesis, found in cartilage; therefore, a manganese deficiency can result in abnormal bone development and enlarged joints in growing horses. A foal can be born with malformed limbs if his dam does not receive enough manganese during pregnancy.

Selenium

Selenium and vitamin E work together as an "antioxidant team." Selenium is part of the enzyme glutathione peroxidase, protecting the inside of the cell, while vitamin E guards the exterior cell membrane. Together, they neutralize damaging free radicals and therefore improve immune function. A secondary function of selenium is thyroid hormone metabolism, since it is necessary for T3 synthesis.

Selenium content in soils varies according to region, alkalinity, and moisture conditions. In areas of drought, when the roots search deeper into the soil for water, they encounter more selenium. However, toxic levels are rare when horses consume naturally-occurring sources of selenium. Supplementation, however, can be problematic if the forage is already adequate in selenium and commercial feed or supplements contain additional amounts of this mineral.

Selenium toxicity: Twenty polo horses died during an event where they were given a formulation that contained nearly ten times the safe amount of selenium. Too much selenium given at one time causes an acute toxicity condition known as blind staggers. This deadly situation is characterized by colic, diarrhea, increased heart and respiration rate, and apparent blindness.

The correct selenium dosage for equine athletes such as these polo ponies is between 3 and 5 mg. Most horses, even those receiving a commercial feed, get less than this. Feed companies typically add between 0.5 to 0.6 ppm of selenium. Five pounds, for example, provides between 1.14 and 1.36 mg of this mineral, which is well within the safe range. To assess your horse's intake, selenium levels should be calculated from all sources. Have your hay and/or pasture analyzed to eliminate guesswork. In general, *the total amount of selenium in the daily diet should not exceed 0.6 mg/kg of feed.* When adding selenium amounts from all sources, total intake should be between 1 to 3 mg for the horse at maintenance and up to 5 mg per day for the working horse weighing approximately 1100 lbs. Larger horses can tolerate slightly more.

If selenium is consumed at a slightly high level for a period of time, the chronic condition known as alkali disease can occur. Alkali disease is characterized by hair loss along the mane and tail and the hooves will crack around the coronary band. This occurs because selenium replaces the naturally existing sulfur found in keratin, resulting in poor hair growth and hoof tissue breakdown.

According to the NRC's 2007 recommendations, the maximum tolerance level for selenium is 5 ppm, but please do not feed anywhere near this amount. Let's suppose your horse consumes 30 lbs of feed each day (forage and concentrates combined). If the diet were to contain this ridiculously high concentration of 5 ppm, your horse would be consuming a whopping 68 mg of selenium! Whereas, to prevent a deficiency, only 0.1 ppm is sufficient; this calculates to 1.26 mg of selenium. So to play it safe, compute just how much selenium your horse is getting. This example is shown in Appendix — Crunching Numbers.

Vitamin E needs to be included with selenium since they work together. Be careful of vitamin E supplements that have added selenium, especially if your horse is already getting enough selenium from other sources. If you want to add more vitamin E to the diet, choose a supplement that only contains vitamin E.

Regional selenium levels: Low selenium levels exist in some regions of the country, particularly the northeast, the Ohio valley, Florida, the northwestern portions of the U.S., and parts of Canada. The map that follows gives you an idea of the selenium concentration in your area. But pockets of high-selenium soils can exist throughout the country's midsection. Therefore, it is always advisable to have your hay and pasture tested, especially if there is anecdotal evidence of high concentrations in your area.

> The total amount of selenium in the daily diet should not exceed 0.6 mg/kg of feed. Be careful of vitamin E supplements that have added selenium, especially if your horse is already getting enough selenium from other sources.

Selenium deficiency: Horses that consume low selenium hay and/or pasture can develop white muscle disease. Symptoms include muscle weakness, difficulty moving, and respiratory distress. To see if your horse is at risk, evaluate the selenium content from all feed sources. If the overall selenium intake is too

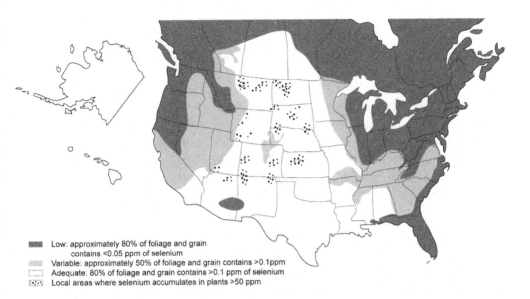

Low: approximately 80% of foliage and grain
     contains <0.05 ppm of selenium
Variable: approximately 50% of foliage and grain contains >0.1ppm
Adequate: 80% of foliage and grain contains >0.1 ppm of selenium
Local areas where selenium accumulates in plants >50 ppm

Soil concentrations of selenium throughout the U.S. and Canada

low, consider adding additional selenium to the diet. Selenium yeast is better absorbed than the traditionally supplemented sodium selenite. *But be
sure to do your calculations first before adding selenium.*

Silicon

This mineral has received much attention in recent years, mainly because
it is an important component of connective tissue, bone, and hyaluronic
acid (found in joints and blood vessels). Silicon is naturally found in the
environment as silica (SeO_2), which is poorly absorbed. When hydrated,
silica is converted to orthosilicic $[Si(OH)_4]$, which is very highly absorbed
and may be useful for performing and endurance horses (See Chapter 20
— Athletes). Deficiencies are rare and supplementation limits have been
designated at 0.2 percent for ruminants; however, a limit for horses has not
been established.

Zinc

Zinc works closely with copper to produce healthy bones, cartilage, and
connective tissue. It is also necessary for fighting infections and reducing
inflammation. Correct proportions between zinc and copper are critical,
since too much of one can cause a deficiency in another. Ideally, zinc

levels should be three times greater than copper levels. A deficiency in zinc can result in an increased susceptibility toward developing infection, poor wound healing, and reduced physical performance.

Excess amounts of zinc in the diet are well tolerated and the NRC's 2007 recommended maximum tolerance has been set at 500 ppm. The recommended level for the average 1100 lb adult horse is between 400 and 500 mg per day, which is only 37 ppm for a 30 lb diet. So, as you can see, there is a large degree of tolerance. No matter what the zinc level, it should be provided with similar iron levels, and should be higher than copper intake to maintain a balance between these three minerals.

Mineral Content Can Vary

The mineral content of forages can vary dramatically depending on the soil, plant species, stage of maturity, and harvesting conditions. For this reason, I continue to encourage you to have your hay or pasture evaluated. I understand that this is not always feasible when your hay supplier varies from week to week or your horses move from one pasture to another on a regular basis. However, if your horse's forage intake is mainly from one source, for at least three months at a time, I highly recommend that you have it analyzed. Your local county extension agency, feed store, or an online company such as Equi-Analytical Laboratories (www.equi-analytical.com), can offer this service.

Minerals are Indestructible!

Unlike vitamins, which are easily destroyed by moisture, heat, and even light, minerals are indestructible. This is because minerals are elements, not complex molecules like vitamins (which we'll discuss in the next chapter), and will stay intact through any environmental influence (unless you have an atom splitter!). This is good news since they remain in hay even after it has been stored for a length of time. If you soak your hay or it gets rained upon, the minerals will *leave* the hay and dissolve in the water, but they themselves will not be destroyed.

Though it's encouraging to know that minerals last forever, you are not likely to have a plain mineral supplement in your tack room. Carriers such as alfalfa, flax, and rice bran can spoil. Their fat content will go rancid over time, so check the label for an expiration date or limit storage length to six months.

Mineral Interactions and Supplementation

Minerals interact with each other, making their supplementation a bit tricky. As we've seen in the previous sections of this chapter, one mineral can influence the absorption, metabolism, or excretion of another; therefore proper ratios between minerals need to be maintained to prevent toxicities or deficiencies. For example, if you add too much iron to the diet, it will inhibit the absorption of copper and zinc. Conversely, too much copper, cobalt, manganese and zinc can interfere with iron absorption. Too much calcium can reduce the absorption of copper, manganese, zinc, and iron. And excess zinc interferes with calcium absorption.

Confused? I don't blame you. The easiest way to manage this situation is to use a fortified feed or comprehensive supplement that contains a mixture of minerals. Commercial feeds need to be fed according to directions to meet your horse's mineral needs. If you're feeding less than recommended, mixing your own unfortified ingredients, or if your horse is on an all-forage diet, you can fill in most minerals gaps by using a commercial, multiple vitamin/mineral preparation. This method is preferable to combining individual minerals because of their interaction potential.

There are cases when supplementing an individual mineral is beneficial, but extra care should be taken to keep it in balance with others.

FREE CHOICE MINERALS

I do not recommend free choice supplementation of minerals. There are products on the market that are designed to be fed at will, making the assumption that horses will consume what they need. Unfortunately, horses are not able to discern their need for most minerals with the exception of a few electrolytes (sodium, potassium and magnesium). When offered free choice, there is the danger of either over-consumption or not eating them at all (they tend to taste bitter), leading to imbalances, toxicities, and deficiencies.

Mineralized salt blocks are also not advisable. Most horses lick them to get sodium, since sodium is their main need. And there is no way to tell whether they are getting an adequate amount of other minerals. Worse yet, many mineralized blocks are sweetened with molasses, making them like candy to horses, creating a very real risk of over-supplementation (not to mention too much sugar). Blue salt blocks contain added iodine and cobalt, two minerals that may already be supplied in the diet if your horse is fed a fortified feed or supplement. To meet sodium needs, let me reiterate that your best bet is to provide a *plain, white salt block*, clean from mud and debris. Electrolyte preparations can be added for horses that are heavily exercised. A complete discussion of how to feed electrolyte supplements is provided in Chapters 1 — Ground Rules for Feeding a Horse and 7 — Fundamentals of Water and Electrolytes.

TESTING YOUR HORSE'S MINERAL STATUS

Blood tests are useful in determining whether your horse is receiving adequate levels of minerals. Some minerals, however, are not measured individually, but either as part of another compound or indirectly through hormone status. For example, iron can be measured using a serum ferritin test rather than simply measuring the iron concentration in the blood. Calcium status is typically measured by evaluating parathyroid hormone levels. Cobalt is part of vitamin B_{12}. And hormones secreted by the thyroid gland are evaluated to determine iodine status. Such test results, combined with the overall diet evaluation, are the best way to evaluate your horse's status.

Hair analysis

Hair analysis results are questionable since the mineral levels in hair are not related to the nutritional status of your horse. Hair grows very slowly so even the hair closest to the skin is several weeks old, too old to reflect current body status. Weather changes, standing in the rain, rolling in the mud, and other environmental conditions can influence what is in the hair. Even hair coat color can cause variations. Plus, a normal hair mineral content in horses has not been established. So save your money and rely on blood analysis techniques.

Endnotes

[1] *Nutrient Requirements of Horses,* Sixth Revised Edition, 2007. Washington, D.C.: National Research Council, National Academy Press: 80.

[2] Ibid. p. 99.

[3] Ibid. p. 92.

[4] Ibid. p. 93.

[5] Brownlee, C., 2004. Staph bacteria are choosy about their iron source. *Science News, September 14.*

[6] Bacterial siderophore production and bacterial proliferation have been extensively researched in humans and animals. Below are a few such studies:

> Courcol, R.J., Trivier, D., Bissinger, M.C., Martin, G.R., and Brown, M.R.W., 1997. Siderophore production by *Staphylococcus aureus* and identification of iron-regulated proteins. *Infect. Immun., 65*: 1944-1948.

> Crosa, J.H., 1999. Molecular genetics of iron transport as a component of bacterial virulence. Chapter in: Bullen, J.J. and Griffiths, E. eds. *Iron and Infection: Molecular Physiological and Clinical Aspects.* Chichester, UK: John Wiley & Sons: 255-288.

> Rattledeg, C., 2000. Iron metabolism in pathogenic bacteria. *Annual Review of Microbiology, January 1.*

[7] Mencacci, A., Cenci, E., Boelaert, J.R., Bucci, P., Mosci, P., Fe d'Ostiani, C., Bistoni, F., and Romani, L., 1997. Iron overload alters innate and T helper cell responses to *Candida albicans* in mice. *Journal of Infectious Diseases, 175*: 1467-1476.

[8] Hoen, B, Paul-Dauphin, A., Hestin, D, and Kessler, M., 1998. EPIBAC-DIAL: A multicenter prospective study of risk factors for bacteremia in chronic hemodialysis patients. *Journal of the American Society of Nephrology, 9*: 869-876.

[9] Ciere, E., 2001. Does iron cause bacterial infections in patients with end stage renal disease? *ANNA Journal, December 1.*

[10] There are many studies in human metabolism that show the relationship between iron and insulin resistance. An example: Green, A, Basile, R. and Rumberger, J.M., 2006. Transferrin and iron reduce insulin resistance of glucose transport in adipocytes. *Metabolism, 55* (8): 1042-1045.

[11] This map is compiled from several maps of selenium concentration across the U.S. and Canada, including: (1) Cornell University, Department of Animal Science. *Map of Selenium Status in the U.S.:* http://www.ansci. cornell.edu/plants/toxicagents/selenium_map.html (2) National Surveys

and Analysis Projects: http://minerals.usgs.gov/projects/surveys and analysis/images/se aa all sm.jpg (3) Sepp Hasslberger, News Media Explorer: http://www.newmediaexplorer.org/sepp/USselen.jpg

CHAPTER 6 —
FUNDAMENTALS OF VITAMINS

When I circle my arms around his massive, swan-shaped neck and
bury my face in his silver coat, breathing in gulps of his unmistakable
heavenly smell, I can't imagine my life without his alongside it.
~ Jo-Ann Mapson

Vitamins are organic molecules, involved in a multitude of chemical reactions throughout your horse's body. They are broadly classified by their water solubility. Water-soluble vitamins include vitamin C and the B vitamins. Fat-soluble (which are water-insoluble) vitamins comprise vitamins A, D, E, and K.

Fresh pasture contains lots of vitamins, many of which are subsequently eliminated during hay production because they are so sensitive to the environment — heat, air, sunlight, humidity, and rain can start destroying vitamins within hours after grass is cut. (Notice I didn't include cold — vitamins like cold weather. Unfortunately, there's no grass to be cut during the winter.) That's why an exclusively-hay diet will leave gaping holes in your horse's nutrient intake. Grazing on pasture will certainly make a difference, but even these horses will need supplementation to fill in gaps that are likely to exist if the grass is of poor quality, over-grazed, or suffers from heat or drought stress.

Now that I've convinced you (or so I hope) that you need to pay attention to your horse's vitamin intake, let's discuss each vitamin individually. I've divided them according to their water solubility, since each group has its own characteristics.

Water-Soluble Vitamins

It comes as no surprise that water-soluble vitamins dissolve in water. Therefore, when hay is rained on, or is soaked for a period of time, the vitamins will dissipate into the water, where they are ultimately destroyed.

But let's assume that the vitamins in grass or hay actually make it to the inside of your horse's body. Once there, they can perform specific duties. And the good news is, if water-soluble vitamins are fed in excess, your horse will not build up toxic levels — he will instead excrete what he doesn't use in the urine (which is mostly water, so that makes sense). There is an exception to this, and I'll mention it later in the section.

Conversely, since what isn't needed right then and there is excreted in the urine, there are very few water-soluble vitamins that get stored for later use, creating a very real potential for deficiencies to occur. If your horse receives enough to eat, you'll rarely see "textbook" deficiency symptoms, but borderline deficiencies can definitely occur — they are much less apparent and difficult to assess.

Free radicals — bad guys meet their match in antioxidants

A free radical is a very unhappy molecule. Although it was once stable, it is now missing an electron. Determined to become whole, it sets out in search of another vulnerable molecule and steals its electron. The original bad guy is now neutral and can relax. But in its wake, it has created another free radical that is just as desperate to steal and destroy.

A small number of free radicals is normal, but factors such as stress, nutritional imbalances, illness or injury can cause these outlaws to multiply beyond the body's ability to cope. Most commonly, we see the result as inflammation and pain. The only way to stop this destructive rampage is to call on a nearby "free-radical neutralizer."

This hero sacrifices itself by giving the free radical the electron it needs, thereby protecting defenseless cells from harm. Since he doesn't need that electron to be stable, his demise is without consequence and he quietly slips away without notice. Without these noble molecules, free radicals would be free to devastate healthy tissue. These selfless champions are known as antioxidants.

Vitamin C

Functions of vitamin C

Antioxidant: Vitamin C is a potent antioxidant and as such, it neutralizes damaging free radicals that are caused by pain, stress, and inflammation. There are many things that lead to free radical formation. Here are a few:

- Muscle soreness
- Overworked joints
- Intense exercise
- Weather extremes
- Arthritis
- Allergies
- Heaves
- Insect bites
- Injuries
- Surgery
- Pain
- Mental Stress
- Stalling
- Grazing deprivation
- Loneliness or boredom
- Pollution
- Infections
- Ulcers
- Colic
- Poor teeth
- Disease

All of these conditions trigger your horse's immune system into high gear. Free radicals are a normal part of that immune function, but when the system gets overwhelmed, your horse depends on antioxidants to calm things down. There are many such antioxidants — vitamin C is just one of them.

All antioxidants, by definition, are destroyed by oxygen. In fact, I've given vitamin C the title "The Most Unstable Vitamin" because not only is it destroyed by exposure by oxygen in the air, which you'd expect, but it also seems to disappear within minutes when you add heat, moisture, light, or anything alkali to the mix. Here's something you may not know... If you were to cut a grapefruit in half and leave it open to the air for 30 minutes, half of its vitamin C would be gone by the time you got back to it! Orange juice, too — once you open the container and let air inside, it starts losing vitamin C. Ok, enough of the vitamin C trivia. To continue...

Collagen: Vitamin C is necessary for collagen synthesis. Collagen is a protein that creates a matrix within bones and joints to which minerals and other substances can attach. It is also part of connective tissue. Therefore enough vitamin C is important for keeping bones and joints healthy. This is especially critical in the aging horse, since horses produce less and less of their own vitamin C as they get older.

Collagen also serves as the glue that holds blood vessels together. Capillaries close to the skin are one cell layer thick, relying on collagen to hold those cells together. If collagen levels are compromised, your horse will bruise easily whenever he so much as bumps into something. Skin that is covered with hair conceals bruising, as do dark hooves; bruises are more easily seen in light skin and white hooves. Regardless of visibility, ruptured capillaries can lead to abscesses and even internal hemorrhaging.

Antihistamine: Vitamin C is a natural antihistamine. This is especially helpful to know if your horse suffers from allergies that produce respiratory problems, hives, or itching. Exposure to allergens in the environment (generally from seasonal pollens or insect stings) leads to increased histamine production. Vitamin C, as an antihistamine, reduces this response, thereby making your horse more tolerant to allergens and hence, more comfortable.

Horses produce their own vitamin C

Horses, in fact most animals, are able to make all the vitamin C they need for every-day health. We humans, however, cannot produce vitamin C and we share this inability with only three other creatures — the ape, guinea pig and some fruit bats. How's that for a piece of trivia to impress your friends?! Have a dog or cat? Take a look at their feed's ingredients — it's very unlikely that you'll see vitamin C mentioned. That's because they don't need it — that is until they get older or if they're injured.

Circumstances when vitamin C intake is a concern

Since horses produce vitamin C, they do not normally require additional amounts in the diet. This is fortunate because while living grass (pasture) contains plenty, hay is virtually devoid of this nutrient.

But as your horse gets older, he is less able to make all the vitamin C he needs to stay healthy. He may start losing teeth, his joints will become stiff, his bones will become porous, and he may be more susceptible to infections. I discuss more on aging horses later in Chapter 19 — Growth and Growing Old.

Even your youngster may need more than he normally produces if he has to counteract an illness, repair a surgical wound, or recover from an injury.

Here is a list of possible circumstances that increase your horse's need for vitamin C:

- Wounds or surgery
- Bacterial, viral, or parasite infections
- Fatigue due to performance insufficiency
- Joint strain or bone injuries
- Recurrent airway obstruction (heaves)
- Endurance exercise and speed events
- Old age
- Transport stress
- Changes in environment or companionship
- Mentally or physically stressful conditions

Supplements

Vitamin C is known as ascorbic acid. It can be derived from food or flowers (e.g., rose hips) or can be made in a laboratory. Regardless of the source, they are chemically identical so don't waste your money on natural vitamin C. There's also ester-C, which contains ascorbic acid chemically esterified (attached) to calcium. It also contains vitamin C metabolites that may be better absorbed, though there is little scientific basis for this. I recommend you stick to plain ascorbic acid.

Vitamin C complex is another type of supplement that combines ascorbic acid with bioflavonoids. Bioflavonoids are found in the pulp of fruits and vegetables and work together with vitamin C. This complex is generally marketed to humans because we are notorious for not eating our fruits and veggies, unlike horses who eat plant foods all day long.

Dosage: If you've decided that your horse can benefit from extra vitamin C, how much should you give him? I pointed out at the beginning of this chapter that water-soluble vitamins that are not immediately used are excreted. If you give your horse a large dose at one time, he'll have very expensive urine. So smaller, frequent dosing is better. Plus he'll enjoy his feed more if you don't add too much because vitamin C typically tastes bitter.

An appropriate daily dose for an aging horse is 3 to 10 mg per pound of body weight per day, divided between at least two meals (see Chapter 19 — Growth and Growing Old). This amount will protect his joints, bones, blood vessels, and immune system. If you have a horse that is recovering from an injury or surgery, has allergies, or is experiencing an exceptionally stressful situation, double this dosage.

The National Research Council (NRC) does suggest an upper safe limit: 20 grams (that's 20,000 mg) per day for a 1000 lb horse (nearly 44 mg of vitamin C per kg of body weight)[1]. See Appendix — Crunching Numbers, for an illustration of how this is calculated.

Protect your supplement: If you have a container of vitamin C sitting in your hot barn, protect it from a cruel fate — keep it in a cool, dry place where the container is sealed shut. Refrigeration is fine. Purchase small sizes unless you are feeding it to several horses. Your supply should be finished within six months.

Weaning off of vitamin C: Once you start feeding vitamin C, you need to continue adding it to your horse's diet on a daily basis. He will become accustomed to what you provide so if you were to stop feeding it suddenly your horse would respond as though he were experiencing a deficiency. Therefore, when supplementing vitamin C to a young horse to treat a temporary situation, you need to wean him off of it — take three to four weeks. An older horse that is on vitamin C to replace what he no longer produces on his own should be supplemented indefinitely, for the remainder of his life.

B VITAMINS

There are eight B vitamins that all work in concert with one another:

- B_1 (Thiamin)
- B_2 (Riboflavin)
- Niacin (sometimes called B_3)
- B_6 (Pyridoxine)

- B_{12} (Cobalamin)
- Biotin
- Folic acid
- Pantothenic acid

They are involved in the following areas of your horse's body:

- Digestive tract
- Skin, hair, and hooves
- Red blood cells
- Nervous system including mental function
- Exercise
- Body protein synthesis
- Fat metabolism
- Pregnancy and lactation

Microbes residing in the hindgut produce much of the B vitamins your horse needs; however, specific situations warrant supplementation. Fresh grass is your best source, but don't fret about hay — unlike vitamin C, the B vitamins are far more stable and remain active to a greater extent. Nevertheless, they don't last forever, so last year's hay will not be as nutritious. If you have any supplements still on the shelf, be mindful of their expiration dates. To help you assess your horse's individual needs, I've divided my discussion of the B vitamins into groups according to common function.

Energy production

Vitamins B_1, B_2, niacin, and pantothenic acid are necessary for metabolizing carbohydrates, fats, and protein into useable energy. Much of this energy (calories) is used to do work. The more your horse exercises, the higher his requirement for these vitamins. It is best to provide a B complex preparation rather than administer an individual B vitamin (thiamin is the most common) because they work together to support your horse during work and performance.

These four vitamins are predominately found in cereal grains (oats, corn, wheat, barley, etc.), cereal middlings, bran, and brewer's yeast. Legumes such as alfalfa, clover, and soy offer high amounts of vitamin B_2 and niacin. Since many horses should avoid cereal grains (see Chapter 13 — Metabolic and Endocrine Disorders for a discussion), it may be important to supplement B vitamins. One thing you should know about riboflavin... it is vulnerable to sunlight. Therefore, if your hay is sitting out in the sun, the outermost layers will lose most of their vitamin B_2 content.

The bacterial flora living in your horse's hindgut can synthesize all of the B vitamins. However, they need to be in good numbers. Stress, illness, and antibiotic use can negatively impact their population, revealing symptoms such as reduced appetite, weight loss, ataxia, fatigue, and behavioral changes.

Body proteins

Your horse uses amino acids (from protein in the diet) to create body proteins needed to replace and repair hundreds of tissues, including skin, hair, hooves, muscle, red blood cells, antibodies, enzymes, hormones, and vital organs. Vitamin B_6 is a structural component of the enzymes involved in making these proteins. Therefore, enough B_6 is particularly important if your horse is recovering from a wound or repairing joints, is pregnant or lactating, anemic, growing, or in need of immune system support (for the production of antibodies, which are proteins). Fortunately, pyridoxine is produced by the hindgut's microbial population, so supplementation is generally unnecessary. B_6 is easily obtained by eating forage and concentrates, making a deficiency a rare occurrence.

I don't recommend adding large amounts of B_6, because this water-soluble vitamin can build up to toxic levels, instead of being excreted in the urine. Unlike the others, too much can cause nerve damage, so if you choose to supplement pyridoxine to your horse, limit the dosage to 200 mg/day. Most B complex preparations have far less than this amount, so don't be concerned about adding a complete supplement when conditions call for extra B vitamins (e.g., stress, illness, appetite loss, nervousness, antibiotic usage).

Skin, hooves, and hair

Biotin and vitamin B_6 are needed to produce keratin, the protein found in hair and hooves. These two are also essential to synthesize the proteins collagen and elastin, which keep the skin healthy and impart its elasticity.

There are ample sources of these B vitamins. Alfalfa is the best source of biotin; grasses offer both. Oats and soybeans contain some of these two as well, but in lesser quantity. And let's not forget production by cecal and intestinal microbes.

If you've ever used a hoof supplement, you're probably familiar with biotin. Some folks give their horses plain biotin for hoof support, which is beneficial, but biotin is more effective at promoting hoof growth when combined with other nutrients such as calcium, vitamin B_6, zinc, copper, and essential amino acids lysine and methionine. Omega-3 fatty acids, from flaxseed meal or oil, as well as orthosilicic acid (silicon), are also helpful. If your horse needs a hoof supplement, choose one that contains at least 20 mg of biotin per serving. A word of caution when adding a hoof product: Watch for nutrient overlaps, especially minerals, if you are also feeding other supplements.

Red blood cells

Red blood cells deliver oxygen to all of your horse's tissues for energy metabolism. If his red blood cells are not in peak form, he will be tired, his gums will be pale, and he just won't be his normal, happy self. There are three B vitamins responsible for healthy red blood cells: pyridoxine, folic acid, and vitamin B_{12}. In fact you may be surprised to learn that anemia in horses is usually due to a deficiency of one or more of these three vitamins, rather than insufficient iron. Iron deficiencies are uncommon but have been seen in horses with internal bleeding from ulcers. You may find reviewing iron helpful in Chapter 5 — Fundamentals of Minerals.

Vitamin B_{12} is of particular interest in red blood cell health because it is *not found in plants*. And since your horse is herbivorous, his diet does not contain this vitamin, unless he is fed a fortified commercial feed. Instead your horse must rely on his bacterial population to produce vitamin B_{12}. These microbes use the mineral cobalt since it is part of B_{12}'s structure. That explains why cobalt is added to most commercial feeds.

A nice aspect of vitamin B_{12} is that it can be stored, rather than excreted in the urine like most other B vitamins. So if your horse is feeling under the weather for a few days, he will likely have enough stored in his liver to sustain him. Of course, as with all the B vitamins, B_{12} production depends on microbial health.

Nervous system

Vitamin B_{12} has another important role — it is needed by nerve cells to produce their protective fatty covering called the myelin sheath. Horses suffering from a B_{12} deficiency, even if it's only slight, will develop a specific type of blood disorder called pernicious anemia that not only affects red blood cells, but also the nervous system. Signs of pernicious anemia mainly include fatigue, poor endurance, pale gums, and eating dirt and manure (see Chapter 17 — Stress and Behavior for more on this behavior). But your horse may also experience a tense attitude and startle easily.

Because B_{12} is so helpful for nerve cells, I have been successful in helping horses that have endured injury-related nerve damage by supplementing large dosages (5 to 10 mg per day, which is the same as 5,000 to 10,000 micrograms).

Vitamin B_1 (thiamin) is considered a worthwhile calming agent. To have this effect, large dosages (more than 500 mg) are needed. There are many thiamin supplements available, but frankly, when I hear about a nervous horse, I like to first try supplementing all of the B vitamins, even if the thiamin level is more moderate in a B complex preparation. If this doesn't give the desired results, I then add more thiamin. Magnesium is also beneficial for behavioral problems. See Chapter 5 — Fundamentals of Minerals for more on magnesium.

Fat-Soluble Vitamins

Given that fat-soluble vitamins cannot dissolve in water, they require some fat in the meal to facilitate absorption. Most commercial feeds add fat, generally in the form of soybean oil. While I'm not fond of soybean oil (which you may recall from reading Chapter 3 — Fundamentals of Fats), it does serve its purpose for this situation. Grass also has some fat, offering a nice balance between omega-3 and omega-6 fatty acids. Hay, on the other hand, no longer has most of its unsaturated fat content.

Once inside your horse's bloodstream, fat-soluble vitamins A, D, E, and K travel to the tissues that need them to be used right away, or they can be stored for later use. They are not, however, excreted in the urine. This can be a good thing because we rarely see deficiencies. But it can also be a bad thing because your horse cannot get rid of excesses, leading to potential toxicities.

Fat-soluble vitamins operate independently, each with its own functions. They're discussed below in alphabetical order.

VITAMIN A

Trick question — what vegetable is high in vitamin A? Did I hear you say, "carrots?" Sorry, you're wrong. Well, mostly wrong. You see carrots, or any other plant for that matter, do not contain vitamin A per se. They contain beta carotene which is *converted* to vitamin A. So ultimately your horse gets vitamin A by eating carrots. Fresh pasture is also high in beta carotene. Hay — you guessed it — loses beta carotene the longer it is stored. In fact, hay that has been stored longer than 6 months has nearly no vitamin A activity (no beta carotene).

Actual vitamin A is *only found in animal sources*. Nevertheless, it is often added to commercial feeds, which can present problems because vitamin A is toxic in high dosages. I wish all feed companies would add beta carotene instead. Some do, so check labels carefully. The nice thing about beta carotene is that it is converted to vitamin A only to the extent that your horse needs it. Any excess is used elsewhere as an antioxidant or stored. And because beta carotene is an antioxidant, it destroys inflammatory free-radicals, keeping your horse's immune function healthy.

What does vitamin A do?

Night vision: You know how keen your horse's vision is at night. He uses vitamin A, located his eye's retina, to produce a substance called rhodopsin which enhances his ability to see in dim light. Horses that do not get to graze on fresh grass, eat hay that is either too old or cut from very mature grass, or are fed high grain diets, are more likely to develop a vitamin A deficiency.

Bone growth: Youngsters depend on vitamin A for bone development. Mature horses also need it to continually produce new bone tissue. Bones are not static; they are dynamic, meaning they break down and build up throughout the day.

Mucous linings: Vitamin A improves your horse's ability to counteract illnesses by producing mucus that lines his airways, digestive tract, and urinary tract. This mucus is the first line of defense against infections.

Vitamin A deficiency

During the winter when your horse is fed hay, vitamin A shortages are likely to develop, especially if he hasn't had a chance to build up enough in storage. If you're not feeding anything but hay, it's a good idea to feed a comprehensive vitamin/mineral supplement that contains either beta carotene or vitamin A.

Some deficiency signs include:

- Impaired red blood cells
- Reduced immune function
- Infertility
- Respiratory infections
- Joint pain

Vitamin A toxicity

Truthfully, I'm more concerned about your horse getting too much vitamin A than too little because so much gets added in commercial feeds. Let me remind you that a vitamin overdose can only result from too much supplementation of the actual vitamin. Beta carotene, from forage and even when supplemented as such, cannot produce a vitamin A toxicity.

Too much vitamin A intake can lead to:

- Fragile bones
- Bone overgrowth (hyperostosis)
- Peeling skin (known as exfoliated epithelium)
- Birth defects (teratogenesis)
- Poor muscle tone
- Rough hair coat
- Hair loss
- Dandruff
- Muscle soreness

Meeting your horse's requirement

Vitamin A is measured in international units (IU) which relate to the activity of the vitamin. Beta carotene, on the other hand, is measured in mg and the conversion rate to vitamin A can vary with your horse's health status. The requirement for an adult horse at maintenance is 30 IU of vitamin A per kg of body weight, or 72 mg of beta carotene per kg of body weight. This translates into 12,000 IU per day for a 400 kg horse (see Appendix — Crunching Numbers, for the calculation). However, exercise, growth, and pregnancy all increase the requirement to as much as 60 IU/kg body weight and beyond (race horses, for example have been given much higher amounts — approximately 120 IU/kg BW[2]). As I pointed out, commercial feeds are often supplemented with vitamin A, necessitating care on your part when adding any other supplement since toxic symptoms can easily occur, especially if you feed more than 10 times the requirement.

Vitamin D

Vitamin D's metabolic pathway begins with the oils that naturally exist in your horse's skin. When these oils are exposed to sunlight, a series of chemical reactions takes place, resulting in the production of vitamin D in the kidney. Therefore horses can make their own vitamin D just by soaking up the sun. But enough is not always produced. Factors that lessen vitamin D production include:

- Excessive bathing
- Coat sprays
- Fly sprays
- Stalling indoors
- Cloudy days
- Shorter days
- The lower angle of the sun in the upper one-third of the U.S. as well as throughout Canada

Function of vitamin D

Vitamin D has one important role — to increase the level of calcium in the blood. It does this in one of three ways:

- It increases the absorption of calcium from your horse's food.
- It removes and reassigns calcium from his bones (only if the diet is low in calcium).
- It reduces the amount of calcium lost in the urine.

If there is not enough vitamin D produced or the diet is too low, your horse can develop poor muscle contraction, bone deformities, and even fractures.

Forms of vitamin D

Vitamin D exists in both plants and animals. The plant form is called ergo-calciferol and is commonly referred to as vitamin D_2. Vitamin D found in animals is called cholecalciferol, identified as vitamin D_3. D_3 is the version normally used in fortified feeds.

Requirement

Horses that do not produce enough vitamin D on their own will benefit from supplementation. It is recommended that you provide at least 6.6 IU of vitamin D per kg of body weight[3]. For an 1100 lb (500 kg) horse, this translates into 3300 IU/day. However, there is no true minimum dietary requirement since so much variation in sunlight exists between horses' exposures.

Toxicity

Fortunately, toxic dosages of vitamin D are unusual. Even so, improper supplementation can cause excessively high intake. An upper limit of 44 IU/kg of body weight (22,000 IU for an 1100 lb horse) has been established[4]. Check all your supplements and fortified feeds to make certain you're feeding a safe amount. Too much vitamin D can cause calcification of soft tissues, including the heart, kidneys, and blood vessels. But don't worry about turnout time — sunlight exposure cannot lead to excessive vitamin D production.

VITAMIN E

Vitamin E is as a powerful antioxidant. As you know, antioxidants protect healthy tissues against the damaging effects of free radicals. Therefore, vitamin E is an important contributor to your horse's immune function. Additional vitamin E is helpful during physical and mental stress, such as those circumstances listed earlier in this chapter under the Vitamin C discussion.

Vitamin E works with the mineral selenium. However selenium can be toxic at relatively low levels. If your horse needs extra vitamin E and you go to your feed store to buy a supplement, you'll likely find vitamin E and selenium packaged together. Hold off on buying this until you have evaluated the total selenium content of his diet. He needs some selenium, but it's easy to give too much. I encourage you to read more about this in Chapter 5 — Fundamentals of Minerals.

Sources of vitamin E

Good sources of vitamin E include wheat germ oil, soybean oil, and stabilized rice bran. However, I do not recommend wheat germ oil or soybean oil in excess since both of these are high in omega-6 fatty acids, and therefore increase inflammation (see Chapter 3 — Fundamentals of Fats). When feeding stabilized rice bran, be sure it has enough calcium added to overcome the inverted calcium to phosphorus ratio that naturally exists in bran.

Actually, fresh pasture is your best source of vitamin E. When cut and baled to make hay, the level declines over time (I know you expected me to say that). Grains such as oats, corn and barley have very little vitamin E. Commercial feeds are generally fortified with 100 to 200 IU per pound, but check the label for the exact amount.

Forms of vitamin E

All forms of vitamin E are referred to as tocopherols. In forages and other sources in nature, there are many different tocopherols, but the one with the highest activity, and hence more commonly added to commercial feeds and supplements, is alpha-tocopherol. When added in its natural state, it is noted as d-alpha tocopherol; in its synthetic version, as dl-alpha tocopheryl acetate. Natural vitamin E is more effective than the man-made vitamin; however, the synthetic form is more stable and therefore has a longer shelf-life. If you choose to supplement dl-alpha tocopheryl acetate, increase the amount by one-third to make it comparable to d-alpha tocopherol's activity.

Requirement

The horse community is starting to pay closer attention to vitamin E. And the NRC has increased the requirement in its most recent reports. They list the requirement for maintenance at 1 IU per kg of body weight. An 1100 lb (500 kg) horse, therefore, has a minimum maintenance requirement of 500 IU/day. However, horses do better with at least 1 IU *per pound* which for the same horse translates into 1100 IU per day. The vitamin E content of fresh pasture varies tremendously depending on its maturity, the season, and amount of rainfall. Levels can range from 22 to 210 mg/kg of dry matter. Generally speaking, your horse will get most if not all of the vitamin E he needs if your pasture is lush and not overgrazed. If your pasture is not up to par, or your horse is strictly fed hay, without any other supplemental source of vitamin E, his minimum requirement will not be met. Health issues such as illness, injury, growth, performance, pregnancy, and lacta-tion, as well as training and performance, all create an increased need.

Not enough vitamin E

Several diseases can result when not enough vitamin E is supplied in the diet, including equine degenerative myeloencephalopathy (EDM) and equine motor neuron disease (EMND), a condition that resembles Lou Gehrig's disease in humans.

Treatment with large dosages of vitamin E

Large dosages (5 to 8 IU per pound of body weight) are beneficial for sev-eral disorders. Equine protozoal myeloencephalitis (EPM) is often treated with high dosages of vitamin E to boost immune function. Horses that tie up (exertional rhabdomyolysis) also benefit from extra vitamin E supple-mentation. And scar tissue, adhesions, and proud flesh resulting from injury or surgery may be significantly reduced with large amounts of vita-min E.

No problem with over-supplementation

Unlike vitamins A and D, which can be over-supplemented, vitamin E has not been shown to produce toxicity problems. Period.

VITAMIN K

Vitamin K has one main role in your horse's body — blood clotting. With-out enough vitamin K, an injured horse could bleed excessively. It works with calcium and amino acids to produce fibrin, the protein found in the blood that produces a crusty scab.

Racehorses often experience exercise-induced pulmonary hemorrhaging (EIPH) where there is bleeding from the lungs. This condition has been treated with vitamin K. However, such treatment is risky, having some-times led to kidney failure and even death. The best nutritional approach involves bioflavonoids and other antioxidants. See Chapter 20 — Athletes for more about EIPH.

Requirement and sources

There is no minimum daily requirement for vitamin K in horses but they can safely receive at least 20 mg per day. Horses will get sufficient amounts from pasture, hay (surprise!), and microbial synthesis. Beware of sweet clover in hay which may have turned moldy. It can contain a vitamin K-antagonist called dicumarol.

The healthy horse can rely on his bacterial flora in the hindgut to produce adequate levels of vitamin K. This is important to remember, because anything that compromises their numbers will lessen the production of this vitamin, as well as the B vitamins. Have a good probiotic on hand to replenish live microbes just in case your horse becomes ill and requires an antibiotic. Feed the probiotic at double doses throughout therapy and for one week following.

Endnotes

[1] *Nutrient Requirements of Horses*, Sixth Revised Edition, 2007. Washington, D.C.: National Research Council, National Academy Press: 123.

[2] Ibid., p. 112.

[3] Ibid., p. 113

[4] National Research Council,1987. *Vitamin Tolerance of Animals.* Washington, D.C.: The National Academies Press.

Chapter 7 —
Fundamentals of Water
and Electrolytes

A man maie well bring a horse to the water. But he cannot make
him drinke without he will.
~ John Heywood, 1546

Water, the stuff of life, taking up nearly 70 percent of your horse's weight. Think about it... Your horse has 700 pounds of water in his body. No wonder water is the most important of all six nutrient classes.

Deprived of water, a horse will die within two to three days. This level of neglect is a rarity, thank goodness. But I come across a variation of it all too often, as I believe you have — horses standing in a dry paddock for hours without anything to drink. Or a stalled horse whose water bucket has run dry, looking forlornly for someone to come fill it. Another common sight is the horse who's working on a hot, humid day for several hours without stopping for water. These guys are thirsty. I expect they eventually get the water they need, but fresh, clean water should be available at all times; horses that are working need to stop and drink every hour. Just writing about this makes me thirsty.

What makes water so essential is its complexity. Every cell within your horse's body is made of water. He needs it to see, to hear, to breathe, and to digest his food, lubricate his joints, cushion his nervous system, keep his body temperature steady, and remove waste. Blood and lymphatic fluid are made of water, bringing sustenance to every part of his body.

Water Balance

Balance: two sides being the same. Water intake must equal water output. Your horse has the amazing ability to keep his water level in balance. He ingests water directly by drinking water, but he also gets it from feed, hay, and pasture. Your horse can even make some of his own water by metabolizing carbohydrates, proteins, and fats.

WATER OUTPUT

Water leaves the body through several pathways: fecal, urinary, respiratory, skin, and milk, in the case of lactating mares.

Fecal losses

Surprisingly, most water is lost in the manure, not the urine. This is because the intestines are the main water reserve. Consequently, manure carries water with it. The amount of water depends on the diet. Grain-based diets produce drier feces than hay-based diets. By keeping an eye on your horse's manure consistency, you can determine his level of hydration.

Urine losses

The urinary system is controlled by the kidneys. They have the job of regulating what stays in the blood and what goes. High protein diets, for example, make your horse want to drink more to allow for the increased urine output necessary to get rid of nitrogen (in the form of urea). The more water your horse drinks, the more dilute the urine; the healthiest condition is urine that is pale yellow. But if less water is consumed, his urine will be concentrated, dark in color, and can even have a thick appearance. Even horses deprived of water will still produce some urine because they need to get rid of metabolic waste.

Losses from skin

Water is lost from the skin by means of heat and sweat. Heat losses involve water that is evaporating off the skin's surface, and can range from 0.5 to 1.5 quarts per hour, depending on the outside temperature.

Sweat losses average 6 to 7 quarts per day when the horse is resting at moderate temperatures. As outside temperatures rise from mild (68° F) to hot (95° F), water losses can quadruple[1]. Exercise creates far more sweating. Sweating is highest during the first 30 minutes of exercise and then it tapers off[2]. After one hour of work, your horse can lose 15 quarts of water (compared to humans, who typically lose only 2 quarts).

Respiratory and lactation losses

Horses lose water through respiration. Though difficult to measure, the levels can become significant during intense exercise, especially in hot, humid climates.

Milk production varies between breeds. Since milk is mostly water, a significant increase in water intake is expected. Lactating mares also eat more, which further increases their water requirements for digestion.

WATER INTAKE

Drinking water is the best way to meet your horse's need. Pasture does supply some water, but hay and feeds contain very little. And horses that consume mostly hay will need more water than those fed a combination of hay and grain. Measuring water intake will give you an idea if your horse is drinking enough. Unfortunately, automatic watering systems make it difficult to gauge your horse's consumption. If you have one of these, spend some time observing your horse's drinking pattern. The average horse will drink 8 to 20 times each day, depending on heat, humidity, and amount of exercise.

Table 7-1 is a guide to how much your horse needs to drink. This varies with exercise level, age, and outside temperature. You'd expect water intake to increase in hot weather, but notice how much it declines during cold temperatures. This is one of the main causes of dehydration. Your horse still needs to drink just as much during the winter, so adding salt to each meal will help increase consumption. If the water is frigid, horses will drink less. Heating your water to at least 50° F will encourage adequate drinking.

As you can see in Table 7-1, water intake significantly increases when the weather gets warmer. Though humidity conditions are not shown on this table, humidity interferes with sweat evaporation, making your horse less able to maintain a normal body temperature and he will drink more to compensate.

A lactating mare needs to replenish her water loss — she produces 4% of her body weight in milk per day during her first two months of lactation (for an 1100 lb mare, this translates into 5.5 gallons per day). Notice in Table 7-1 that her water intake requirement doubles from when she was pregnant.

Table 7-1 Estimated Water Needs of Horses[3]		
Class	**Outside Temperature (degrees F)**	**Range of Water Intake (Gallons/day)[4]**
Mature, Idle	68	5.5 to 10
	86	11 to 14
	-4	8 to 12.5
Pregnant	68	7 to 9.5
Lactating	68	14 to 21
Moderate Exercise	68	9.5 to 12
	95	19 to 24.5
Yearling	14	4 to 5.5
	68	4.5 to 5.5

Determining Optimal Hydration

Oddly, horses do not always know that they're thirsty. This has to do with the hormones that regulate sodium and water levels in the blood. If your horse does not drink enough water, his blood will become concentrated with sodium. The hormone that manages this problem is called antidiuretic hormone (ADH). A diuretic increases urine formation. An *anti*-diuretic causes less urination. Therefore ADH will tell the kidney that it needs to retain water in order to dilute the blood; your horse will urinate less and his urine will be more concentrated. His blood, on the other hand, will become more diluted due to water retention and he won't know that he's thirsty.

But there's a flip side to this situation. Let's say your horse is getting enough water, but not enough salt (sodium). Low sodium in the blood causes another hormone to come on the scene — aldosterone. This hormone delivers a different message to the kidney. It says, "Don't let any sodium leave!" When the kidney holds on to sodium, it excretes potassium in its place. This would lead one to think that the horse needs more potassium. But it's just the opposite — he needs more sodium; not enough sodium is what caused the potassium loss in the first place!

In both cases, the hormones make an effort to maintain balance between water and sodium, so your horse may not sense that he is dehydrated. He will not realize that he either needs more salt, or more water. Why, you ask? Well, this is a survival mechanism. But as caring horse owners, we do not want our horses to go into "survival mode." We want them to thrive.

The solution is to provide adequate sodium so your horse will drink enough water. Even mild dehydration can be harmful — muscles get tired and can tie-up, and colic risk increases due to depressed intestinal motility. To check for dehydration, most folks pinch a fold of skin on the horse's neck to see if it goes back into place. But frankly, the best barometer of hydration is to offer him a drink. You "cannot make him drink" as the old saying goes, but if he does drink, then you know he needed it. If his thirst mechanism is out of whack, feed him something he enjoys and add some salt to it, while keeping water nearby.

Here's bit of trivia for you… Ever wonder why you need to use the bathroom more frequently when it's cold outside? Well, cold weather turns off ADH, so you urinate more! Same is true for horses, by the way.

DRINKING ENOUGH WATER WHILE TRAVELING

If your horse is getting enough salt, this problem may resolve itself automatically. However, water from unfamiliar sources can taste different and some horses will refuse to drink enough to stay hydrated.

Try adding some flavoring to the water, such as apple juice, apple cider vinegar (oh, they love this and there's no sugar), or even a fruit punch. Also there are commercial flavoring products available that will encourage water intake.

If possible, get your horse accustomed to this flavoring a week or two before traveling so he will recognize the good taste when he gets to his destination. Watering at frequent stops along the way is also easier when flavoring is added. But I suggest you avoid adding sweet feed or other foods to the water supply because they are an invitation for bacterial growth.

This and other needs during travel are discussed at length in Chapter 17 — Stress and Behavior.

Electrolytes and Salt

Electrolytes are minerals that control blood volume, muscle and nerve function, and maintain blood pH. The main electrolytes are sodium and chloride (which are the components of table salt — sodium chloride). Other electrolytes include potassium, calcium, magnesium, phosphorus, zinc, iron, copper, and manganese. See Chapter 5 — Fundamentals of Minerals for a discussion of each mineral.

ELECTROLYTE SUPPLEMENTS

I am often asked whether or not it is appropriate to feed an electrolyte supplement. The concern is certainly appropriate. Your horse sweats more during the summer and drinks less during the winter, making electrolyte supplementation worth considering. But electrolytes alone will not stimulate your horse to drink more water. To do that, your horse needs to have enough sodium (salt). Electrolyte supplements should only be given to a horse that is already in good sodium balance. This can be accomplished by simply keeping a salt block in close proximity to where your horse lives. Keep it clean so he'll enjoy licking it and watch for bullying from other horses. To determine that he's getting enough, a good rule of thumb is: a 5 lb salt block should be consumed within two months. If he's not getting this much, add salt to his meals. Throughout the year, he'll need one ounce (two level tablespoons) of salt per day divided between meals. In hot, humid weather, add twice to four times this amount.

> Electrolyte supplements should only be given to a horse that is already in good sodium balance.

An electrolyte supplement is designed to replace what is lost from perspiration, or at least that's the premise. The sodium content of most electrolyte supplements is too low. If you choose to use a supplement, look for one that is not diluted. One way to determine this is to make certain it contains at least 13 grams of chloride, 6 grams of sodium, and 5 grams of potassium. The salt (sodium chloride) percentage needs to be at least 75%. And it need not be sweetened. Horses enjoy the flavor of salt and do not need the extra sugar that is often added.

Table 7-2 gives you an idea of how much sodium, potassium, and chloride are needed in various work intensities. It also shows how much is provided by hay and electrolyte supplements.

Table 7-2 Estimated Electrolyte Requirements (g/day) of an 1100 lb Horse[5] at Varying Work Intensities, and Amounts Provided by Hay and Electrolyte Supplements

Electrolyte	Light Work	Moderate Work	Heavy Work	Very Heavy Work	Provided by Hay	Provided by Typical Electrolyte Supplement
Sodium	13.9	17.8	25.5	41.0	< 2.0	2.5 to 5.0
Potassium	28.5	32.0	39.0	53.0	197.0	5.0 to 10.0
Chloride	46.6	53.3	66.5	93.0	66.0	2.25 to 4.5

Hay provides almost no sodium, but plenty of potassium and chloride. (Cereal grains, by the way, are low in all three electrolytes.) And electrolyte supplements do not come anywhere close to replenishing these levels. But before you get discouraged, understand that electrolyte supplements are not *supposed* to meet these needs. *The assumption is that your horse starts off with adequate electrolyte levels before he starts working.* The supplement, then, does just that — *supplements* the existing levels by replacing what was lost in the sweat.

Assuming your horse is in good sodium standing before the hot, humid condition sets in, you can supplement electrolytes on an as-needed basis. To use an electrolyte, follow the label instructions. You can add it to one or two gallons of water, followed by plenty of fresh water. You can also add electrolyte supplements to your horse's feed, but if you're already adding table salt, you'll make it unpalatable. Electrolytes also come in a paste version, which is fine, but don't forget to immediately follow it with fresh water.

Always allow your horse to eat something before giving him an electrolyte. The risk of developing ulcers is very real if electrolytes are given on an empty stomach. This is especially true for horses that are already at high risk for ulcers (those that race or do speed events).

A common mistake is adding electrolytes to a horse's only water supply — this will interfere with water intake. A white salt block should be within reach and is all that you'll need for a horse at maintenance or light work as long as your horse licks enough of it. A mineralized block or a iodine/cobalt block (typically blue) is not advisable if you are already feeding a commercial feed or a vitamin/mineral supplement. Also, many horses will not lick them because they are bitter. And the molasses-sweetened licks are often eaten like candy, so they, too, should be avoided.

Free choice supplements

Considering a free choice electrolyte supplement? I don't recommend them. Horses do not have the ability to discern their blood levels of most electrolytes (with the exception of sodium, chloride, potassium, and magnesium) and therefore may over-consume trace minerals (zinc, iron, copper, and manganese) in an effort to get the salt they need. It is safer to offer a plain white salt block and/or added table salt to the feed.

Summary

Let me go over the key points. The bottom line is this… *Give your horse salt* — plain, white salt. Potassium and chloride needs for the 1100 lb horse are met by feeding hay, but one ounce of salt will provide the sodium he requires for maintenance. One ounce is easily measured as two level tablespoons and provides 14,000 mg of sodium. Sodium requirements are based on weight and exercise intensity, so a mature 1100 lb horse at maintenance, in a comfortable climate, requires 10 grams (10,000 mg) per day. For heavier sweating and exercise, increase this amount to up to four ounces per day. Adding this much salt to your horse's meal may be difficult since it will be unpalatable. Salt blocks are a necessity. Have several available, keep them clean, and watch for bullying from competing horses. But salt blocks may not be sufficient to meet your horse's need. You can also offer free choice salt. Excessive sweating sometimes results in avoiding salt, even though his body desperately needs it. Syringing a salt dose may be necessary if this situation arises. Electrolytes can be given when there is excessive sweating or intense work, but only when your horse starts out in good sodium balance.

Water Safety

If you have an outside water trough, take a look inside. Run your fingers along the surface of the container. Is it slimy? That's algae buildup. It can also be rotting vegetation from feed and hay that dropped into the water.

And if the temperature is warm, bacteria multiply, causing the release of toxins in the water. Are there bird droppings or insects in the water? You're asking for trouble if your horse consumes these. And never let your horse drink from a water trough that has a dead rodent floating in it. Empty the container, scrub it clean with soapy water, and rinse first with a diluted bleach solution, followed by clean water. Botulism is a real issue in water where dead animals have been found.

City water is tested frequently and you should receive a report at least once each year, outlining its mineral content. If you have well water, have it tested yourself. Potentially toxic levels of key nutrients and contaminants are shown in the Table 7-3.

Table 7-3 Safe Upper Concentrations (mg/L) of Potentially Toxic Nutrients and Contaminants in Water for Horses

Element	Safe Upper Concentration (mg/L)[6]
Aluminum	5.0
Arsenic	0.025
Boron	5.0
Cadmium	0.08
Chromium	0.05
Cobalt	1.0
Copper	0.5
Fluoride	1.2
Iron	0.3
Lead	0.1
Mercury	0.03
Molybdenum	0.5
Nickel	1.0
Selenium	0.05
Vanadium	0.1
Zinc	50.0

POND WATER

Horses that rely on pond water are potentially exposed to a number of problems. Infections from *Leptospira, Listeria, Salmonella* and *E.coli* can be transmitted by wildlife that defecate in the pond. Opossums carry *Sarcocystis neurona*, the organism responsible for equine protozoal myeloencephalitis (EPM). Insects carrying *Neorickettsia risticii* can cause Potomac horse fever.

Fertilizer runoff from nearby farms can contribute toxic minerals as well as nitrates. Some forms of algae can be poisonous, causing illness as well as death. Not all algae is harmful, but certain blooms can be a problem. If the water turns deep green and thick, and has a muddy smell, it may be contaminated.

If you are going to rely on a pond for watering your horses, consider lining it with asphalt or other dark liner to discourage light absorption. Algae control products can be added but do so with caution and proper expert assistance. Your best bet, truly, is to use water tanks that are regularly cleaned.

Winter

Snow cannot provide enough water. Depending on the density, it generally takes two gallons (32 cups) of snow to make 3 cups of water. Eating snow can lead to hypothermia (low body temperature). Horses instinctively know this and will either not get enough water to drink or they will look for a flowing water source. Walking down an icy slope to a pond is dangerous, leading to injury and falls through the ice. A nearby automatic waterer or water trough will keep your horses hydrated and safe.

Endnotes

[1] Morgan, K., Ehrlemark, A., and Sallvik, K., 1997. Dissipation of heat from standing horses exposed to ambient temperature between -3 and 37 degrees Celsius. *Journal of Thermal Biology,* 22: 177-186.

[2] Kingston, J., Geor, R.J., and McCutcheon, L.J., 1997. Use of dew-point hygrometry, direct sweat collection and measurements of body water losses to determine sweating rates in exercising horses. *American Journal of Veterinary Research,* 58: 175-181.

[3] Adapted from: *Nutrient Requirements of Horses*, Sixth Revised Edition, 2007. Washington, D.C.: National Research Council, National Academy Press: 130.

[4] Values are averages and specific water intakes by individual horses may be lower or higher depending on the individual horse's baseline, his clinical health, and variations in environmental conditions.

[5] Horse Journal, 2008. *Water Requirements,* June: 6-8.

[6] CCME (Canadian Council of Ministers of the Environment), 2002. *Canadian Environmental Quality Guidelines.* Canadian Water Quality Guidelines for the Protection of Agricultural Water Uses: Chapter 5.

CHAPTER 8 —

FUNDAMENTALS OF FORAGES

She had galloped into the hearts of people across the nation in only
two short seasons and she would never be forgotten.
~Raelyn Mezger
Ruffian — National Museum Racing Hall of Fame

Your horse is designed to graze continuously throughout the day and night. You know this to be true if you've ever driven by a pasture where there are horses. They've all got their heads to the ground. Oh, they'll take a snooze every now and then, but their main goal in life is to eat! That's because a horse's digestive system is designed to have forage flowing through it constantly.

Forage may not be enough for some horses; concentrates, which we'll discuss in the next chapter, provide additional calories and nutrients. They can also serve as carriers for feeding supplements. But forage, from hay and pasture, is the foundation of your horse's diet and should be available at all times.

Overweight horses, for example, should never be placed on a diet that restricts hay. Certainly reducing concentrates is appropriate, but hay is necessary to keep your horse from developing ulcers, colic, and behavioral problems (such as chewing on fences, trees, wood, and even eating their own manure out of boredom). And ironically, the stress that results from dieting actually prevents your horse from losing weight. We will discuss this more in Chapter 12 — Weight Management. But as a horse owner, you owe it to him to *feed him like a horse*. Let him self-regulate his intake, which *he will do* if given the chance.

The non-structural carbohydrate (NSC) content of pasture and hay is of significant concern for horse owners with insulin resistant or laminitic horses. These two conditions are among several that call for careful monitoring of sugar, starch, and fructan levels. There's much to be said about this topic; to help you manage your horse's pasture and hay intake, I discuss facts and definitions in Chapters 11 — Laminitis and 13 — Metabolic and Endocrine Disorders. In addition, there is an excellent resource on the internet that I know you'll find informative: www.safergrass.org.

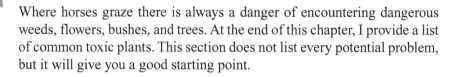

Where horses graze there is always a danger of encountering dangerous weeds, flowers, bushes, and trees. At the end of this chapter, I provide a list of common toxic plants. This section does not list every potential problem, but it will give you a good starting point.

Pasture vs Hay

Fresh grass — pasture — is living forage. It contains mostly water — approximately 80%, along with protein, carbohydrates, fats, and many vitamins and minerals. Once fresh grass is cut and dried to make hay, it dies. The longer it is exposed to air, heat, humidity, and rain, the more vitamins, antioxidants, and omega-3 fatty acids are destroyed. Hay has little, if any, beta carotene (needed for vitamin A synthesis) or vitamins C, D or E. Therefore, horses on hay-only diets need to have these nutrients replaced by supplementation.

Hay also loses water — averaging 90% dry matter, leaving only 10% percent water. So while water needs to be accessible at all times, no matter what your horse is eating, it's especially important that it be close by while he's eating hay to keep things moving along the digestive tract, thereby preventing colic. Some horses have an endearing routine of dunking each hay morsel in water before eating it — a wise habit!

Types of Hay

Commonly available types of hay can be divided into four groups: grasses, legumes, mixes, and grain grasses. Within the grasses, there are cool-season and warm-season varieties. Cool-season grasses include timothy, orchardgrass, brome, crested wheatgrass, and fescue. These grasses grow best in areas where the summer season is not very hot. They have a slightly higher sugar level than warm-season grasses, which is why they taste better. The most prevalent warm-season grasses are Bermuda, Tifton-9 bahiagrass, and prairie grass. Johnson grass, sudan, and sorghum grass are also considered warm-season grasses but they produce glycoside which is converted to cyanide in varying amounts and are too risky to be fed to horses.

NUTRITIONAL VALUE OF GRASS HAY

Grass hay has a medium to low protein content. It is low in the essential amino acid lysine. Therefore, grass hay is best fed as part of a plan *that includes a legume* to balance out the amino acid profile. (See Chapter 4 —

Fundamentals of Protein and Amino Acids for more on balancing amino acids.)

The fiber content of grass hay is relatively high compared to other types of hay. Orchardgrass, timothy, and Bermuda have more stalks, and hence more fiber, than leafier brome or fescue. This can affect their protein content as well as their digestible energy (calories) as shown in Table 8-1. Grass hay is typically low in calcium, zinc, and selenium. Timothy is some-

Table 8-1 Nutrient Content of Grass Hay[1]

Hay	Digestible Energy (Mcal/lb)	Crude Protein (%) (midbloom)	Ca[2] (%)	P (%)	Mg (%)
Timothy	0.81	8.6	0.43	0.20	0.12
Orchardgrass	0.78	7.6	0.24	0.27	0.10
Bermuda	0.89	10.9	0.30	0.19	0.11
Brome	0.85	12.6	0.25	0.25	0.09
Fescue	0.86	11.8	0.40	0.29	0.16

what higher in calcium than other grass hay. It also has a balanced calcium to phosphorus ratio. Orchardgrass, on the other hand, can have more phosphorus than calcium, which is potentially harmful if this is the only hay fed, leading to porous or malformed bones. This condition is called nutritional secondary hyperparathyroidism and is discussed at length in Chapter 13 — Metabolic and Endocrine Disorders.

Hay typically provides enough iron to meet your horse's need; have it analyzed to confirm this. As long as your horse is getting plenty of forage, there is no need to add iron; therefore I do not recommend iron-fortified feeds or supplements without first confirming that he suffers from iron-deficiency anemia. (See Chapter 5 — Fundamentals of Minerals for more on iron and anemia.)

Prairie grass, also known as wild native grass, has considerably less protein (6% on average) than other grass hay; its protein quality is also lower. Vitamins and minerals are scant, as well. It typically has a lot of weeds, which pull nutrients away from the grass plant, making it less nutritious.

NUTRITIONAL VALUE OF LEGUME HAY

Alfalfa mixed with or without clover is the most commonly fed legume hay. Soybeans are also a legume, but only the bean itself is used for horse feeds. Legumes do not require as much fertilization as grasses since they contain more nitrogen. Higher nitrogen level translates into higher protein content, especially in the leaves. The protein quality of legume hay (i.e., amino acid composition) is higher than in grasses. Legume hay is also very high in calcium and low in phosphorus. Feeding legumes with grasses helps balance the ratio between these two minerals.

Alfalfa is rich in digestible energy. It contains approximately 0.94 Mcal per pound (compared to 0.80 Mcal/lb for grass hay). The protein content of alfalfa is also high, averaging between 17% and 20%. *This is not harmful.* Protein has been blamed for colic, hot temperaments, kidney failure, foal deformities, and more, but there is no scientific evidence to support these claims. The quality of protein is what has an impact on your horse's health. When low-quality protein is fed (as in grass hay, or grains that are not sup-plemented with lysine), a large amount of excess amino acids become available. These "left over" amino acids are destroyed and their metabolic by-products lead to elevated insulin, blood pH imbalances, kidney stones, and calcium losses from the bones. The protein found in alfalfa, on the other hand, enriches the diet by adding the correct amount of amino acids (including lysine) to the grass hay to avoid a large amount of residual amino acids. This is why it is best to feed a mixture of grass and legume hays.

Table 8-2 shows the nutritional content of alfalfa, along with Ladino clover, another commonly found legume.

Perennial peanut hay is also a legume and is very similar to alfalfa. It is not the same as peanut hay. Peanut hay is what's left over after peanuts have been harvested. Perennial peanut hay is a high-quality legume forage that can be fed just as easily as alfalfa, and has comparable levels of crude pro-tein and digestible energy. It grows in southern states and is sometimes referred to as "Florida's alfalfa," because of its nutritional similarity.

Because legumes start out with high beta carotene levels when fresh, their hay also retains a good amount. The longer legume hay is stored and exposed to the elements, however, the less beta carotene it will contain.

Table 8-2 Nutrient Content of Legume Hay[1]

	Alfalfa	Ladino Clover
Vitamin A (IU/kg) as beta carotene	41,900	57,475
Vitamin D (IU/kg)	1,810	--
Vitamin E (IU/kg)	15	--
Digestible energy (Mcal/lb)	0.941	0.864
Crude protein (%)	17	20
Calcium[2] (%)	1.24	1.35
Phosphorus (%)	0.24	0.30
Magnesium (%)	0.32	0.42

Most multiple vitamin supplements add vitamin A which may not be necessary if your horse gets sufficient beta carotene from legume hay.

Vitamin E content will also be reduced the longer it is kept in storage. Alfalfa does contain some vitamin E; however, the level is quite low and supplementation is worth considering.

MIXTURES

Feeding alfalfa as your only hay source creates potential problems. It is too high in protein by itself, and has too much calcium in relation to phosphorus and magnesium, so it needs to be mixed with other forages to balance out the diet. I recommend a 30% alfalfa/70% grass mixture for many horses. Pregnant or lactating mares, as well as growing horses, will do well with 40% alfalfa.

Forages that are grown and harvested together as mixed hays are also an option. But there is less control over the amount of each type. You may find it helpful to know that the first cutting contains more grass and later cuttings will have more alfalfa because alfalfa regrows at a faster rate.

Timothy/orchardgrass/clover/brome mixtures, known as "4-Way" hay is another combination that provides three types of grass hay with a legume. The result is a nutritious hay that offers high-quality protein to your horse.

CEREAL GRAIN HAY

Cereal grain hay, mainly harvested from oats, rye, barley, wheat, and triticale, is not the best choice for your horse. There are two reasons for this. First, grain hay is often harvested late and you'll see grain kernels interspersed throughout the hay. These seed heads are mostly starch, making this hay inappropriate for horses that need to reduce starch (and sugar) intake. If your horse is overweight, prone toward insulin resistance, has suffered from laminitis, or has equine Cushing's syndrome, this type of hay should be avoided. These conditions, and other situations where diets low in starch are necessary, are discussed in Chapter 13 — Metabolic and Endocrine Disorders.

Second, even if the hay is harvested early enough to avoid seed heads so the starch level will be lower, the amount and quality of protein will still be poor. To compensate for this, oat hay, for example, is often grown with a legume to enhance the overall protein profile.

PROBLEM WITH FESCUE

Fescue is an abundant cool-season grass throughout the U.S. It's hardy and resistant to weeds, but it has one short-coming — its seeds can harbor a toxic endophyte fungus known as *Neotyphodium coenophialum*. While especially harmful for pregnant mares, all classes of horses can experience weight loss and reduced circulation in the feet, over time as the seeds are ingested.

Pregnant mares in their last trimester should not be allowed to graze on fescue pasture or hay. (Turf-type perennial ryegrass, not forage-type, can also harbor this fungus.) Fungal toxicity can delay foaling beyond 360 days. A thickened placenta may develop, leading to dummy foal syndrome caused by oxygen deprivation during delivery. Milk production will be diminished and may even cease. And stillbirths are common.

Since the exact last trimester is difficult to determine, especially if you have a maiden mare or you don't know the conception date, I suggest playing it safe and removing your mare from fescue closer to half-way through her pregnancy. Even determining halfway could be a guessing game. You could have my situation where I adopted a rescue mare and found out she was pregnant, so I had no idea when she was due. An ultrasound should have helped, but my veterinarian severely misjudged. He told me that she was due the end of November. Having only two weeks to go, I watched her every night. Two weeks came and went, *two months* came and went. She foaled on May 1st! Lesson learned — when in doubt, make sure your veterinarian has a great deal of experience interpreting ultrasounds and err on the side of caution.

Evaluating Hay Quality

The nutritional value of your hay can vary dramatically from the values published in feed charts. Variations due to the amount of fertilization, the life-stage of the plant, drying procedures, and length and conditions of storage can all influence the nutrient content. Therefore, the only way to truly assess your hay's quality is to have it analyzed. Many county extension agencies and land-grant universities, as well as commercial labs, provide this service. Equi-Analytical Laboratories is highly regarded throughout the country: www.equi-analytical.com.

MATURITY LEVEL

The quality of your hay depends upon the plant's growth stage when it was cut. Older, more mature hay loses nutrients and develops thick, tough stems. This has to do with the development of lignin. Lignin is a structural fiber that cannot be digested (even by the microbes in your horse's hindgut). Undigested fiber does not provide any calories. So feeding mature hay may not be sufficient to maintain your horse's condition.

There are two measurements used to describe the fiber content in hay: Neutral detergent fiber (NDF) and acid detergent fiber (ADF) (also discussed in Chapter 1 – Ground Rules for Feeding a Horse). NDF measures digestible fibers known as cellulose and hemicellulose, as well as the indigestible fiber, lignin. ADF is a lower number since it only includes cellulose and lignin. The difference between NDF and ADF is the hemicellulose content, which is more digestible than cellulose. Since both indicators measure indigestible lignin, the higher the number, the lower the quality. Ideally, high quality hay will have an NDF lower than 45 percent and an

ADF level less than 30 percent. These ideals are rarely met, so look for hay where the NDF is no more than 60%. If it's more than 65%, the fiber level is too high and can lead to impaction colic. This is especially hazardous if free access to clean water is not provided.

I'm often asked if you can tell just by looking at the hay if it is too high in fiber. To a degree, yes, you can. Take a look at the amount of stems in relation to leaves. Good quality hay will have more leaf content than stems.

Since the leaves are more digestible, they provide more calories. As you know, hay cut from older plants is less nutritious. But that doesn't mean you have to throw it away; you can simply feed more of it. A good rule of thumb is to add a third more than you would feed of a more nutritious hay. For example, if you normally feed 12 pounds of immature hay, you'll need to feed 16 pounds of a mature hay to get the same nutritional value. This is assuming, of course, that your horse will eat the older hay. If he won't, you're out of luck.

Growing or working horses have high energy needs, so an immature hay will be your best choice. A horse that is overweight, however, can benefit from a hay with higher fiber, and hence fewer calories. But don't forget the vitamin and omega-3 fatty acids supplements, regardless of the hay you feed. *Hay alone will not meet any horse's entire nutritional needs.*

CUTTING

The cutting does not determine hay quality as much as the maturity does. As I mentioned earlier, as a plant matures, its feed value decreases mainly because of lignin development. More mature hay may also contain weeds, further reducing its nutritional value. *The cutting, however, has nothing to do with maturity*; it has to do with the number of crops obtained from the same piece of land. An overly-mature first cutting will be less nutritious and not as tasty as a less mature second cutting.

First cuttings sound better in theory. Early cuttings tend to have a larger percentage of leaves. However, early cuttings have higher moisture content, making drying difficult. Mold is more likely to occur in this situation. Furthermore, first cuttings may be delayed due to seasonal rains, forcing harvesting at a more mature level than desired. Most folks prefer the second cutting because it is cut during the drier season and therefore has less risk of rain delays or damage.

So, regardless of the cutting, it is best to first visually assess the quality for color and good stem to leaf ratio. Your hay should be crisp and bright in color. Avoid any hay that is dark, browning, or is hot to the touch (an indication of fermentation). When separating a flake of hay, look for any signs of mold — a white cloud of dust with a moldy smell, white or gray fuzz, or blackened, dusty areas. Avoid it at all cost — it can lead to colic and the dust produced can lead to recurrent airway obstruction (RAO). Fortunately, when given a choice, horses will reject moldy hay. Symptoms of mold ingestion include increased photosensitivity and slobbering.

> The cutting has nothing to do with maturity. An overly-mature first cutting will be less nutritious and not as tasty as a less mature second cutting.

Legume hay is more prone to mold development than grass hay. Stalks and leaves should be clearly identifiable and not all packed together in a large mass. This is an indication that the hay was produced while the plant was wet, which virtually guarantees the presence of mold. Even if your hay is fine when purchased, clover and alfalfa tend to mildew in hot, humid environments. So check it frequently and remove the least signs of mold.

STORING HAY

To protect your hay for as long as possible, store it off the ground, away from direct sunlight, and covered to protect it from rain. Stack your hay in such a way that you use the oldest bales first. Air circulation is important to prevent mold, so avoid tight-fitting tarps. Small animals can spread diseases such as equine protozoal myeloencephalitis (EPM) or *Leptospirosis* and should be discouraged from making nests in stored hay. If you find any feces in your hay, do not use it.

BLISTER BEETLES

When purchasing alfalfa, make certain that it is of *horse quality* — this will provide some reassurance that it is not infested with deadly blister beetles. These insects produce a toxin that can destroy your horse's kidneys and intestines, induce colic, and kill a horse even in relatively small amounts.

Blister beetles populate all areas of the country. With more than 300 species, all alfalfa hay is suspect. Visually inspecting your hay will not help much because you're not likely to see small pieces of crushed insects in baled hay. Your best approach is to minimize risk:

- Blister beetles tend to be more prevalent in cuttings done in late summer — July and August, so stick with safer first or second cuttings harvested in May and June.

- Young, immature hay (nothing to do with cutting) is safer because beetles like to feed off of the blossoms found in more mature plants.

- If there are dead grasshoppers in the hay it is a danger sign since blister beetles eat grasshopper larvae.

A reputable alfalfa supplier will:

- Look for swarms of blister beetles before harvesting. Blister beetles stay for a few days and then move on.

- Scout field borders since blister beetles do not migrate far from the field. A conscientious hay grower separates bales from the field margins from the rest of the crop.

- Avoid using harvesting equipment that crushes beetles, such as mower-conditioners or sickle bar mowers.

- Avoid using insecticides because dead beetles are just as dangerous and will end up being baled in the hay.

How Hay Fits into Your Feeding Plan

You probably have to rely on local growers for your hay. It's comforting to know that the specific type of grass is not as important as the overall hay quality since all grasses are relatively similar in nutrient content.

Since grass hay cannot provide all of the nutrients your horse needs, feeding even the finest grass hay will still leave nutrient gaps to be filled by other sources. A legume, such as alfalfa, is a good place to start, but your horse may have higher energy needs than what forage can provide. And as you know, vitamins need to be supplemented.

When pasture is not available, grass hay acts as a dietary staple; it provides a continual source of roughage that keeps your horse's digestive tract healthy (see Chapter 14 — Digestive Problems for a complete discussion). Grazing all day reduces stress, preventing many problems — take a look at Chapter 17 — Stress and Behavior for a complete list.

Alfalfa, alfalfa-mixes, and clover-mixes are highly suitable for horses that require additional amino acids and calcium for growth and performance. Pregnant and lactating mares, youngsters, performance horses, those recovering from illness or injury, or horses with suppressed immune function will benefit from the additional nutritional value that legumes provide. If you're concerned about sugar content, you'll be pleased to know that alfalfa is not any higher than grass hay. In many cases, alfalfa is actually lower. Refer to Table 13-1 in Chapter 13 — Metabolic and Endocrine Disorders for a comparison between alfalfa and other types of forage.

ROUND BALES

Choose a reputable supplier when purchasing round bales. Though convenient for feeding large numbers of horses, there are real risks associated with lower quality bales. If they are not properly dried before baling, or if stored outside and exposed to rain, decaying vegetation can contain bacteria called *Clostridium botulinum*. These organisms thrive deep inside the bale where there is no oxygen and produce a deadly nerve toxin that causes a paralytic illness known as botulism.

C. botulinum is found in soil, streams, lakes, and the intestinal tracts of mammals. When small animals die in the field, they can become part of the bale. Do not use any hay that has rodent feces or dead animals.

GRASS CLIPPINGS

Grass clippings are not a problem as long as they stay on the pasture after mowing, where they can dry in small amounts. But never gather them into piles to feed them to your horse. This can be dangerous for several reasons:

- Eating large amounts at one time can lead to excess fermentation in the hindgut, potentially causing colic and laminitis (founder).

- Piles of clippings can become moldy. This is especially true in hot, humid environments. Clippings that are collected in plastic bags will develop mold very quickly.

- Botulism, caused by a deadly toxin, is a threat because there is no air deep inside the pile.

- Clippings can contain pieces of toxic ornamental plants.

Toxic Plants

A healthy pasture will have a minimal amount of weeds. But if your pasture is sparse, over-grazed, or has suffered from heat or drought stress, weeds will sprout first. Many weeds are toxic, but poisonous plants can also take other forms, such as bushes, trees, and ornamental plants.

Some toxic plants actually taste good, making them more of a potential risk. Fortunately, most are offensive, so your horse will usually avoid them in favor of tastier grass. But a horse that is thirsty, hungry, or just plain bored will give them a try. Even horses fed unpalatable hay will look elsewhere for something better to eat.

You may not realize your horse is eating something toxic until symptoms become apparent days or weeks later. And the signs, such as weight loss and general malaise, can be confused with other disorders. In some circumstances, however, your horse can become violently ill — demonstrating drooling and inability to swallow, convulsions, tremors, labored breathing, and weakness — all serious signs that can occur within hours after exposure.

I recommend having your pasture evaluated by an expert for potential problems. Your local county extension service can help you find a qualified individual. Also, there are plenty of toxic plant photos on the internet. But a good field manual with pictures of plants in your part of the country is an invaluable tool. Unlike having to refer to your computer screen, you can carry it with you, as you walk your pasture to identify problem plants.

COMMON PLANTS

The following list will get you started. However, this list is not complete and plants will vary depending on where you live.

- **Alsike clover.** Induces photosensitivity (looks like sunburn) and prolonged consumption leads to liver damage. It is generally found in cool climates where clay soils are poorly drained. If you see white clover flowers in your hay, be sure to determine whether or not they are alsike clover.

- **Dogbane.** Sometimes called Indian hemp, this plant is commonly found along streams as well as in open fields. Immediate medical attention is needed if your horse develops bloating, a rapid pulse, and starts to stagger.

- **False dandelion.** Causes stringhalt, a joint disorder characterized by a goose-stepping gait in the hind legs.

- **Garlic.** Garlic causes gastrointestinal distress. It is marketed to horse owners as an insect repellent. However there is no scientific evidence to support this. And garlic can cause Heinz body anemia. So please do not give your horse raw garlic.

- **Hoary alyssum.** Found in the northeastern and north central portions of the U.S. and Canada, hoary alyssum grows best in drought stressed, over-grazed pastures. The main concern with this weed is that horses like to nibble on it. Toxic symptoms include fluid retention in the lower legs (stocking up), diarrhea, and depression.

- **Locoweed.** Found throughout the western states, horses seem to become addicted to it. Over time, your horse can lose weight and exhibit unpredictable behavior, eventually leading to reduced vision and death.

- **Nightshade.** These plants include tomatoes, potatoes, peppers, and eggplant. Though not deadly, they can be very irritating to the mouth.

- **Oak leaves.** The leaves are mildly toxic, especially in the early spring when they are young and tasty. Acorns, produced later, are more dangerous and addictive, causing diarrhea and colic, and eventually leading to irreversible liver damage.

- **Ornamental plants.** These include azaleas, rhododendron, foxglove, gladiolas, oleander, hydrangea, ivy, lily-of-the-valley, yew, and larkspur, to name a few. They can be tasty, but deadly.

- **Poison hemlock.** This weed is easy to spot because it grows up to 10 feet tall. Eating it can lead to coma and death within a few hours, depending on how much is ingested.

- **Red maple trees.** Their leaves are highly toxic, but they are most troublesome later in the fall, when the leaves start to wilt. If you have neighbors with red maple trees, watch for leaves that may have blown into your horse's pasture. They can cause anemia and kidney damage, exhibited by urine that is red-brown in color.

- **Russian knapweed.** Ingesting this weed causes chewing disease, where horses lose their ability to chew and swallow food. The damage is irreversible and can lead to starvation. Horses need to consume it over a period of time, so one bite will not be damaging. However, if a horse is not getting enough to eat, he will try feeding on this weed.

- **St. John's Wort.** This herb is commonly used to treat mild depression in people but it should not be given to horses. It can damage the liver, leading to photosensitivity. Other plants that have the same effect include hound's tongue, creeping indigo, and bishop's weed. (See Chapter 16 — Immunity Issues for a discussion on sunlight sensitivity.)

- **Water hemlock.** Found in marshes and wet pastures, this plant is considered one of the most toxic plants in the U.S. Small amounts can cause paralysis of the central nervous system, killing a horse within minutes.

ANIMAL POISON CONTROL CENTER

Here's a good phone number to have on hand: 888-426-4435. It's the number for the Animal Poison Control Center offered by the American Society for the Prevention of Cruelty to Animals (ASPCA). This emergency hotline is staffed by veterinarians and toxicologists. They will provide you with immediate treatment recommendations and consult with your veterinarian about your horse's case. They charge a reasonable fee for this service, but it's well worth the peace of mind that comes from knowing you have accurate information.

PREVENTION

- Inspect your fence line for toxic plants. Be aware that horses can reach 3 to 4 feet beyond the fence to gain access.

- Watch for bald spots in your pasture. These areas are more likely to become weed-infested.

- Seed your pasture with lush grass.

- Rotate your pastures to prevent over-grazing. Also, since conditions can vary depending on irrigation, climate, and vegetation, I recommend consulting with reliable local sources on the optimal number of horses for your pasture.

Endnotes

[1] *Nutrient Requirements of Horses*, Sixth Revised Edition, 2007. Washington, D.C.: National Research Council, National Academy Press.

[2] The calcium to phosphorus ratio should ideally be 2:1, but can safely go as high as 6:1. The calcium to magnesium ratio should ideally be 1:1 to 2:1.

CHAPTER 9 —

FUNDAMENTALS OF CONCENTRATES AND BY-PRODUCTS

Foolish showed more expression in his face than most horses,
you could see his will to win.
~ Joanie Davison
Foolish Pleasure — National Museum Racing Hall of Fame

Concentrates are different that forages. They're high in calories, low in fiber, and concentrated (hence, the name) in starch, sugar, protein, and fat. There are many forms of concentrates. Cereal grains (e.g., oats, corn, and barley) mainly provide starch; soybean meal, flaxseed meal and sunflower seeds are high in protein and fat; oils such as corn, soybean, wheat germ, flax, rice bran, and canola are high in calories without added carbohydrates or protein. Not all oils are the same, however; different oils have varying effects on your horse's health. They're compared in detail in Chapter 3 — Fundamentals of Fats, and discussed further in Chapters 12 — Weight Management and 20 — Athletes.

By-products are a little different than concentrates — they are high in fiber, though not so high as forages, and also contain protein. The term "by-product" has a negative connotation stemming from the use of animal by-products typically added to dog or cat food — lungs, kidneys, and other body parts other than muscle — things we wouldn't want to eat. But *grain* by-products are good for your horse. They're especially useful for horses that need to decrease starch intake.

Take a look at the grain illustrated in Chapter 2 — Fundamentals of Carbohydrates, and you'll see that the endosperm is the starchy center of the grain, surrounded by the protein-rich germ and fibrous bran layer. Wheat middlings, a grain by-product, is the wheat kernel minus its endosperm — it consists of the nutritious wheat germ along with the outer bran layer, which is high in fiber and various minerals. Beet pulp is an example of a feed by-product that consists of the pulp of the sugar beet without the sugar, leaving a highly digestible fibrous feed that has as many calories as oats — a wonderful energy source that is especially beneficial for horses that should avoid starch.

Digestible Energy Requirements

Performance horses, those in training, and youngsters that are still growing need the additional calories that concentrates and by-products provide. If you have a pregnant mare, she needs plenty of extra calories and once her foal is born, she'll need even more for milk production.

Energy requirements are measured as Mcal of digestible energy (DE). A Mcal is a megacalorie. To give you a basis for comparison, the caloric value of human food is indicated as kilocalories (kcal). A Mcal is 1000 kcal. DE requirements vary with the horse's age, size, and level of activity, as shown in Table 9-1.

Table 9-1 Digestible Energy (DE) Requirements of Horses[1]		
Horse Classification	**Weight (lbs)**	**Mcal per day (DE)**
Adult — Maintenance	1100	16.7
Adult — Moderate exercise	1100	23.3
Pregnant Mare — less than 5 months pregnant	1100	16.7
Pregnant Mare — 10 months pregnant	1200	20.2
Lactating Mare — 1 month	1100	31.7
Lactating Mare — 5 months	1100	28.3
Growing — 6 months	475	15.5
Growing — 18 months	850	19.2
Growing — 24 months, moderate exercise	943	24.8

To use Table 9-1, let's look at an example:

You have an 1100 lb horse who is moderately exercised. He gets fed 22 lbs of grass hay each day (2% of his body weight) plus 4 lbs alfalfa hay. Will this meet his DE needs?

On average, grass hay provides 0.8 Mcal/lb. Alfalfa provides 1.0 Mcal/lb. Calculate the total Mcal provided by this hay mixture.

- 22 lbs Grass Hay X 0.8 Mcal/lb = 17.6 Mcal
- 4 lbs Alfalfa Hay X 1.0 Mcal/lb = 4.0 Mcal
- Total Mcal per day = 17.6 + 4.0 = 21.6 Mcal

According to Table 9-1, an adult horse, weighing 1100 lbs, who is moderately exercised, requires 23.3 Mcal/day. So, this amount of hay falls short of his requirement. You'd want to add more calories from concentrates or by-products. Notice that the maintenance horse's needs are exceeded, so concentrates would not need to be added in that case.

Take a look at Table 9-2. Many horse owners choose to feed cereal grains such as corn, oats, or barley to add more DE. Soybean meal (a legume, not a cereal grain) is also an option. I'll discuss the attributes of each of these concentrates later in this chapter.

Table 9-2 Digestible Energy (DE) in Common Concentrates

Concentrate	Mcal/lb
Corn	1.5
Oats	1.0
Barley	1.7
Soybean meal	1.4

But for now, let's go back to our example. We have an 1100 lb adult horse, exercised moderately, who requires 23.3 Mcal/day to maintain condition. The hay that we're providing falls short of this requirement by 1.7 Mcal/day.

Referring to Table 9-1, in order to obtain 1.7 additional Mcal, you could add 1.7 lbs of oats, or a little more than one lb of corn, or one lb of barley. Soybean meal could also be added — 1.2 lbs per day would fulfill the extra DE need.

But which one do you choose? Or should you choose a by-product instead, such as beet pulp? How about one of the many commercial feeds on the market? To help you make a decision, let's take a closer look at each feed-stuff.

Concentrates

CEREAL GRAINS

The word grain is often used to describe "feed that is added to forage." But not all feeds are cereal grains, so reserve the use of this word for oats, corn, barley, etc. Oats and corn are the mostly commonly used grains, followed by wheat and barley. Rye, rice, and millet are also grains but used less frequently.

All cereal grains have an inverted calcium to phosphorus ratio, meaning they contain more phosphorus than calcium. Feeding grain should not be a problem as long as the basis of your horse's diet is forage (typically higher in calcium). However, too much phosphorus in the diet can lead to a disorder known as nutritional secondary hyperparathyroidism (discussed in Chapters 13 — Metabolic and Endocrine Disorders and 19 — Growth and Growing Old).

Grains contain large amounts of carbohydrates (mostly in the form of starch), some protein, and even a little fat. They are digested early in the digestive tract — in the foregut (small intestine) — where your horse is able to produce digestive enzymes that break down starch to glucose, protein to amino acids, and fat to fatty acids. These digestive products are small enough to be absorbed from the small intestine into the blood stream, where they are transported throughout the body to be utilized by the tissues.

To digress for a moment... The foregut can digest only small amounts of grain at a time. If you were to feed your 1100 lb horse more than 3 to 4 lbs of oats, for example, the undigested grain would leave the small intestine and enter his cecum (hindgut). The microbes that live there would ferment it to lactic acid, leading to a condition known as cecal acidosis. This is not a good situation for your horse. The pH (acidity) of the hindgut becomes lower, destroying these important bacteria. As a result, your horse may colic or even develop laminitis (founder). In Chapter 1 — Ground Rules for Feeding a Horse, there is a diagram of the entire gastrointestinal tract. You'll notice that your horse has a relatively small stomach compared to the rest of his digestive system. This is what makes feeding a small meal so important. To avoid hindgut fermentation, play it safe and don't feed more than two pounds of cereal grain at a time. To learn more about this topic, please read Chapters 11 — Laminitis and 14 — Digestive Problems.

To get back on track, I was telling you about the different cereal grains. I'll start with the most commonly fed grain — oats.

Oats

Horses love the taste of oats. Table 9-3 shows several grains and you can see that the starch content of whole oats is lowest among the three most common grains. Oats are also the safest grain to feed because they are easily digested in the foregut, as long as the meal size is not too large, so there is less likelihood of undigested oats reaching the hindgut.

But remember that starch digestion results in glucose. And since whole oats contain 44% starch, a lot of glucose enters your horse's bloodstream. At first, your horse will experience a sugar-high, followed by a sugar-low as a surge of insulin (hormone from the pancreas) does its job to lower blood glucose levels. Some horses do not behave well when their blood sugar levels reach such sharp peaks and valleys. So for these horses, it is best to avoid high starch feeds.

Crimped, rolled, or steamed oats are better digested than whole oats because the inner pulp is exposed, making it easier for digestive enzymes to reach. They also have more available starch (approximately 50%) than whole oats. So you can feed less and get more calories. With whole oats, the outer hull remains intact. Your horse must chew them sufficiently to have the same benefit, otherwise you'll notice undigested whole grains in his manure. And getting back to the safety issue, since whole oats are less likely to be digested in the foregut, they will be fermented once they reach the microbes in the hindgut. So bottom line... Keep meal size two pounds or less and avoid whole oats.

Corn

I do not recommend feeding corn. It is not as balanced as oats, with far more starch, less fat and less protein, but the real problem is its poor digestibility. Regardless of the amount fed, corn is not adequately digested in the small intestine. This means that more of it will reach the hindgut, creating a very real risk of colic and laminitis. Corn is also more likely to contain mycotoxins, a potentially deadly substance which I'll discuss at the end of this chapter. So, do not feed corn to your horses. Save it for your chickens!

Table 9-3 Average Nutrient Content of Traditional Concentrates[2]

Feedstuff	Crude Protein %	Mcal/lb	Fat %	Starch %	Ca %	P %
Corn (cracked)	9.4	1.8	4.2	60.0	0.04	0.30
Oats (whole)[3]	13.6	1.5	5.2	44.0	0.07	0.30
Barley	12.0	1.7	2.2	54.0	0.06	0.39
Soybean meal	44.0	1.4	44.0	7.0	0.30	0.6
Sunflower seeds[4]	28.4	1.5	36.0	42.0	0.48	1.0
Flaxseed meal	21.0	1.3	40.0	--	0.25	0.6
Oil[5]	--	4.1	100.0	--	--	--

Barley

Barley is not commonly fed in the U.S. It is better digested than corn, but not as well as oats. Barley is typically steamed to soften the tough outer hull, making it more digestible, but here again, if you're going to feed grain, oats are your best choice.

HIGH FAT CONCENTRATES

Soybean meal

The outer hull of soybeans is removed and the inner pulp is ground to make soybean meal. As a legume, it complements the protein found in grass hay, improving the overall protein quality. When feeding soybean meal, it should be heat processed before feeding, especially to young horses. Raw soybeans contain a substance known as a trypsin inhibitor that interferes with normal growth.

Seed meals

Seeds, such as sunflower seeds and flaxseeds, can be ground up into a nutritious feed that is not only high in protein, but contains a substantial amount of fat. Fat provides more energy (calories) than carbohydrates or protein, so you don't have to feed as much. Be aware, however, that these feedstuffs have far more phosphorus than calcium; commercial products containing seed meals typically add calcium to correct this problem.

The fat content of sunflower seeds differs greatly from flaxseeds. Though they provide similar numbers of calories, sunflower seeds are high in omega-6 fatty acids whereas flaxseeds contain mostly omega-3 fatty acids, each with their own impact on your horse's health. There's a lot to be said about this subject, so I've devoted a whole chapter to it: Chapter 3 — Fundamentals of Fats.

Vegetable oils

Oils provide calories purely from fat — no protein, no carbohydrates. They can be safely added to most diets, especially if your horse needs to gain weight or requires high amounts of energy for intense exercise. You can safely add up two cups of oil per day for a full-sized horse, but I generally reserve this amount for racing or endurance horses.

If you choose to add oil to your horse's meal, add a little at a time; most horses do not like oily feed. And don't expect immediate changes — it takes several weeks for a horse to switch over to using fat as his main energy source.

I shy away from giving ponies, miniatures, donkeys, and mules added oil. They do not metabolize fat as efficiently as horses, so they are more likely to gain weight and develop insulin resistance.

COMMERCIAL FEEDS

Just open a bag, scoop out the feed, and you're done! That is the premise behind commercially produced, complete feeds. They are fortified with vitamins and minerals, making supplementation unnecessary. But there's a catch — you have to feed the recommended amount in order to be assured that your horse is getting the vitamin and mineral levels printed on the bag. This is often way too much to feed, unless your horse is heavily exercised.

Sure, you can feed less, but then you'll need to add a vitamin/mineral supplement to fill in the gaps.

The variety of commercial feeds is staggering. Some are cereal grain-based, others are low in starch, some are sweet feeds, and others are pelleted. Some are designed for growth, others for broodmares, and still others for performance horses. And let's not forget senior citizens — they have their own feed as well. There are even feeds for horses that need to lose weight! That's right — and on the label it recommends feeding 6 to 8 lbs per day. Don't believe it — fat horses need hay, water, salt, and a vitamin/mineral supplement. Period.

Confusing? Let's take a closer look...

Remember, *the majority of your horse's diet needs to be from hay and/or pasture*. A complete feed means that it supplies all the vitamins and minerals your horse needs if fed according to their recommendations, but it is not meant to replace forage.

Sweet feeds

Horses are born with a sweet tooth. So were you, but do you put sugar on nearly everything you eat? Of course not, and you shouldn't do this for your horse either. And not only are sweet feeds sweetened with sugar, they are grain-based — typically containing oats. Oats are mostly starch. And here's a quiz... What does starch become after it's been digested? Correct! Sugar. So, now we have sugar from molasses, and sugar from starch. What a nutritious meal.

Sweet feeds typically add 10% molasses. So, let's see... If you feed 5 lbs of sweet feed per day, that is equivalent to 0.5 lbs of molasses. Half a pound of sugar. Are you getting the picture?

> Horses are born with a sweet tooth. So were you, but do you put sugar on nearly everything you eat? Of course not, and you shouldn't do this for your horse either.

You know when I recommend sweet feeds? When you're trying to get your horse to eat something bitter, like medications or certain supplements. And this can only apply to a horse that is able to have sugar. If your horse has ulcers, is insulin resistant, has equine Cushing's disease, or is prone toward laminitis — sweet feeds are out of the question, even in small amounts.

Pelleted feeds

All types of feedstuffs can be processed into pellets. And this can provide more opportunity to feed your horse a mixture of ingredients. Legumes such as alfalfa meal and soybean meal can be made into a pellet, along with bran, beet pulp, flax, and more. Cereal grains can also be included, so not all pellets are low in starch.

Consistency can be an issue with pelleted feeds. Some feed companies have different feed recipes for different manufacturing plants. Some change their ingredients based on which suppliers bring the lowest bid. These changes will likely be reflected in the ingredient list, so check it carefully each time before buying, even if you purchase the same feed from the same store.

Look for a pelleted feed that provides at least 15% fiber since this will keep your horse's digestive tract moving properly. Digestible fiber is best. Straw will provide fiber, but it certainly isn't very digestible. Look for ingredients such as beet pulp, alfalfa meal, and soybean hulls.

The crude protein level should be 12-14% for the vast majority of horses. As I wrote about in Chapter 4 — Fundamentals of Protein and Amino Acids, the crude protein percentage tells you absolutely nothing about the protein's quality. It is strictly a measurement of nitrogen. So look for complementary protein sources such as alfalfa meal or soybean meal, combined with seed meals, beet pulp, and bran to know that the feed offers a complete, quality protein for your horse.

Extruded feeds

Since many older horses have worn or missing teeth, senior feeds offer a good option. Senior feeds are extruded — the ingredients are cooked, ground together, and forced through a die to produce uniformly sized nuggets, resembling dry dog food. These nuggets are easy to chew and are highly digestible. Extruded feeds are less dense that pellets; therefore they take up more volume. So, one scoop will weigh less than the same scoop filled with pelleted feed. To avoid confusion, it's best to weigh your feed rather than eye-balling a scoop or coffee can — that way you know exactly how much your horse is getting.

By-Products

By-products are often included in pelleted and extruded feeds, but the components are not always clearly listed on the ingredients label. You might see phrases such as "grain by-products" or "feed by-products," leaving you unsure about the true contents. Fortunately, more and more feed companies are divulging accurate lists in response to discerning customers like you.

Table 9-4 shows commonly used by-products and their nutrient content.

Table 9-4 Average Nutrient Content of By-Products[6]								
Feed	**CP %**	**Lysine %**	**Mcal/lb**	**Fat %**	**Starch %**	**Crude Fiber %**	**Ca %**	**P %**
Beet pulp	10	0.4	1.3	1.1	4	15	0.9	0.1
Brewers grains	22	0.8	1.3	9.0	10	15	0.2	0.6
Distillers grains	28	0.8	1.5	12.0	16	9	0.1	0.7
Wheat middlings	15	0.6	1.4	3.6	34	7	0.1	0.8
Cottonseed hulls	4	--	0.6	--	--	40	0.1	0.1
Soybean hulls	11	0.5	1.1	2.3	5	32	0.5	0.1
Sunflower hulls	5	--	0.8	3.9	--	44	0.3	0.1
Rice bran	13	--	1.4	18.0	22	12	--	1.6
Wheat bran	17	0.7	1.5	4.3	21	43	0.1	1.3
Corn gluten	21	0.6	1.3	3.2	23	8	0.2	0.7

Beet pulp

Beet pulp is one of my favorite things to feed. It is the pulp of the sugar beet plant, after the sugar has been removed. So the remaining pulp has virtually no sugar. If molasses is added to improve taste, it is low — slightly over 2%, that's approximately ½ cup of sugar in 10 lbs of beet pulp. And you likely wouldn't feed anywhere near that amount — it takes 2 quarts of beet pulp to equal 1 lb, so 10 lbs would be 20 quarts!

Beet pulp contains 15% crude fiber, a little less than the 18% fiber typically found in forage. But it is still a good source of fiber because this 15% is mostly *digestible fiber,* meaning it is easily digested by the bacterial flora in your horse's hindgut. And better yet, it doesn't get digested in the foregut, so blood glucose levels are not affected. So it has a low glycemic index, making it a wonderful feed for any horse that needs to reduce starch and sugar intake. And from a digestible energy perspective, beet pulp is right up there with the big cereal grains. It supplies 1.3 Mcal/lb compared to oats, with 1.5 Mcal/lb.

It comes in two forms — pellets and shreds. Pellets must be soaked to pre - vent choke. The shredded form can be fed dry, but soaking will ease your mind since it is very dry and some horses labor over chewing it. Soaking time depends on the water temperature. If you have hot water in your barn, the beet pulp shreds will soak this up almost immediately; pellets will require approximately 30 minutes. Cold water will take longer to soak up. But do not soak beet pulp overnight; bacteria and mold will accumulate.

Beet pulp is a good source of calcium, though not as high as alfalfa. Don't worry about feeding too much calcium when offering beet pulp because much of the calcium is bound to oxalates, making it less available. For the same reason, you cannot rely on beet pulp calcium to offset a high phosphorus intake (from bran, for example).

Finally, beet pulp makes an excellent carrier for supplements or medications. If your horse is on hay or pasture, and you want to add a vitamin/mineral supplement, you need to add it to something. The supplement will mix in well with soaked beet pulp, and you won't find it sifting to the bottom of the feed bucket. One more thing — be sure to add your supplement once you're ready to feed; don't soak it since prolonged water contact will destroy most vitamins.

BREWER'S AND DISTILLER'S GRAIN

Brewer's grain is a by-product of the brewing industry, hence the name. But it doesn't contain grain (they saved that for the beer). You see, the starchy portion of the grain is fermented into alcohol, leaving a by-product that is palatable and high in low-quality protein.

Distiller's grain is similar to brewer's grain, but is derived from the distilled liquor industry. Like brewer's grain, it is exceptionally high in protein, though not complete (low-quality) — its lysine level is low so lysine must be supplied by another feed source to create a high-quality protein. Both serve as good sources of B vitamins. They are highly digestible and a good source of fiber.

WHEAT MIDDLINGS

Don't let the name make you think you're feeding a cereal grain to your horse — it is not wheat, at least not completely. To understand this, please look at the picture of a cereal grain shown in Chapter 2 — Fundamentals of Carbohydrates.

The majority of the wheat kernel consists of the endosperm. This is where most of the starch is located. It is ground into what we know as white flour. To access the endosperm, the bran and the germ must be removed. Therefore, the bran and germ are considered by-products of the milling process. The bran is mostly fiber, but also contains vitamins and minerals. The germ, however, is where all the good stuff is — protein, fat, vitamins, and minerals.

Wheat middlings are the result of milled wheat kernels — the bran and germ — without the starchy endosperm. They are excellent for your horses. But you should be aware that while lower in starch than the endosperm, wheat middlings are not considered a low starch feed, just a *lower starch* feed because their starch content averages 26%.

SOYBEAN, SUNFLOWER, AND COTTONSEED HULLS

The outer hull of the soybean is high in fiber and low in starch. Soybean hulls also contain a fair amount of fat, making them a good energy source without the notorious blood glucose highs and lows created by feeding grain.

Remove the shell of a sunflower seed, and you have sunflower hulls. They are high in fiber, but not digestible, consisting largely of lignin (described in Chapter 8 — Fundamentals of Forages), which makes them more of a filler than anything else.

Cottonseed contains a mycotoxin known as gossypol. To destroy this toxin, cottonseed hulls are usually heated before being added to feed. But I consider them risky — this mycotoxin can lead to infertility, slow growth, and even death. And since cottonseed hulls are not highly nutritious, it is simply best to avoid them.

BRAN

Rice and wheat bran are commonly fed to horses to provide a highly digestible form of fiber. But like the seed meals discussed earlier, bran contains much more phosphorus than calcium — ten times more. Plus, the phosphorus is in the form of phytate, which inhibits calcium absorption from other sources. So only feed bran when you have adequate calcium in the diet to overcome the high phosphorus levels.

Also worth noting is the relatively high starch content of rice and wheat bran. Most starch is in the endosperm, that's true, but the bran layer also contains some, making bran a questionable feed source for insulin resistant or cushingoid horses.

Rice bran is particularly high in monounsaturated fatty acids (see Chapter 3 — Fundamentals of Fats), making it a good fat source for underweight horses. It can, however, easily become rancid, so it's best to obtain a commercially stabilized product. Not only will your rice bran last longer, but these products contain added calcium to correct for high phosphorus levels.

Bran mashes

Ever give your horse a warm bran mash on a cold winter night? Or perhaps you give your horse bran as a once-a-week laxative (not helpful, by the way, and the softer manure that results is an indication of an irritated intestinal lining). Either way, it is a dangerous practice. Here's why…

Consistently be consistent — that should be your motto when it comes to feeding your horse.

The hindgut microbes need time to adjust to any new feed, and bran is no exception. If you feed bran, add it gradually, over a period of two weeks, and then feed it every day. A once a week bran mash is asking for a case of colic. *Consistently be consistent* — that should be your motto when it comes to feeding your horse.

CORN GLUTEN

Corn gluten is basically shelled corn that has had most of the endosperm and germ removed. It is low in lysine, low in fiber, and low in calcium. It is poorly digested, can contain excessively high levels of sulfur, and is prone toward developing mycotoxins. Sounds like I don't have a very good opinion of this by-product, doesn't it? I don't.

Special Section — Protecting Your Horse From Mycotoxins

Mycotoxins are a result of mold — myco means fungus (mold is a fungal growth) and toxin means poison. There are several different mycotoxins, but aflatoxins are most commonly found in horse feeds. They are produced by the fungi strains *Aspergillus flavus* and *Aspergillus parasiticus*.

Mycotoxins are a fact of life in animal feeds because they can be present within the plant before it is even harvested. Drought and other stress can reduce the plant's ability to resist mold. But storage at high temperatures and humid conditions can lead to excessive mold growth. Corn and corn by-products are particularly susceptible to infestation.

At high enough concentrations, mycotoxins can cause severe damage. If the concentration exceeds 50 ppb (parts per billion), such symptoms as refusal to eat, weight loss, lethargy, and diarrhea can result. More serious effects include liver and kidney damage, jaundice, suppressed immune function, and birth defects.

Take a look at your feed when you open the bag. Signs of mold are dustiness, caking of feed, and a dark color. Feed should have separate pieces that flow easily through your fingers. It should have a fresh smell. Use the bag within two months, faster when the weather is hot and humid.

Several commercial feed manufacturers add mycotoxin adsorbents to remove potential dangers. If there is no indication on the packaging of an added adsorbent, it would be wise to contact the feed company before using it, especially if corn or corn by-products are included in the list of ingredients.

Endnotes

[1] *Nutrient Requirements of Horses*, Sixth Revised Edition, 2007. Washington, D.C.: National Research Council, National Academy Press: 298.

[2] Adapted from: *Nutrient Requirements of Horses*, Sixth Revised Edition, 2007. Washington, D.C.: National Research Council, National Academy Press: 304.

[3] Rolled or crimped oats have their hulls broken open, making them more digestible in the foregut. They therefore provide slightly more protein, fat, and starch, and hence, more Mcal.

[4] Sunflower seed meal generally has the fat extracted, leaving a product that only has 1.4% fat.

[5] All oils have the same number of Mcal. But they differ in their fatty acid content. Refer to Chapter 3 — Fundamentals of Fats to see how oils differ in their health benefits.

[6] Adapted from: *Nutrient Requirements of Horses*, Sixth Revised Edition, 2007. Washington, D.C.: National Research Council, National Academy Press.

CHAPTER 10 — FUNDAMENTALS OF TREATS

He usually knows when you're happy,
he usually knows when you're sad,
and he always knows when you have carrots.
~ Unknown

I have a forum on my website where I respond to a variety of questions from horse owners. There was this one question that I'll never forget. It went something like this: "I have two horses, and they are both very fat. I only feed them hay, but they are still terribly fat. I can't figure it out. Can you help? Oh, I should mention that I do give them treats since they're only getting hay. Are French fries ok for treats? I buy them each a large fries when I go to McDonalds most days."

Oh my goodness! How should I respond? My inclination was to say, "You're crazy!" But that would be far from diplomatic. So, I very kindly explained to this writer that French fries were not a good choice for horses, nor would they help them lose weight.

The next day, I found out that it was a practical joke from my son and his friend!

But you know, it got me thinking. Maybe I should write about treats. Who knows? There may be a reader or two out there who actually *does* feed French fries! And while one or two won't hurt, they certainly won't help.

Take hamburgers. I know a lady, who shall remain unnamed, who occasionally gives her horse a hamburger. "He loves it!" she shouts. Well, that's nice.

Feeding his emotions (He loves it!) while damaging his body does not make sense. You wouldn't offer a piece of chocolate layer cake to a friend who has diabetes, would you? Oh, your friend would enjoy it for the moment (He loves it!) but what about the lethal effect on your friend's body?

It's a known fact that too much of a good thing is a bad thing. I knew a gal who loved her horse very much, and it gave her great pleasure to watch him enjoy carrots. She asked me one day if I thought carrots were ok for her horse. I told her that as long as he was not overweight or had never had laminitis, it would be fine for him to enjoy a carrot or two every day. She became silent and then reluctantly told me that I probably wouldn't approve of how many she fed. When I prodded for the exact amount, she admitted to giving him 4 pounds each day!

Horses are our friends. They trust us to take care of them — both mind and body — allowing them to thrive physically and be mentally content. We like to give them treats, but please, keep in mind that treats are just that — treats. And they are for your horse, not for you. Understanding our motivations can help us make good decisions about the type and frequency of treating. Even the most nutritious treats are only meant to be fed once in a while.

Unconventional "Treats"

So, while we're on the subject, let's talk more about hamburgers and French fries. I'll start with hamburgers, since that's an easy one. Horses are herbivorous — they only eat plants. Their systems are designed this way. Hamburgers are made from cows. Don't feed your horse a cow!

Moving on to French fries… Potatoes, first of all, should never be fed raw — they contain a deadly toxin called solanine that can make your horse very ill. But cooked potatoes fall into the same category as bread. In other words, potatoes (and bread) are mostly starch. Starch is the same as sugar once it's been digested. Many horses should avoid starch for a variety of metabolic disorders (see Chapter 13 — Metabolic and Endocrine Disorders) but *any* horse can develop colic or laminitis if enough starch reaches the bacteria in the hindgut.

MORE THAN HAMBURGERS AND FRENCH FRIES!

As I delved into the subject further, I found a long list of so-called treats that folks give to their horses. I'll take a moment to list a few of the most common ones. But keep in mind, there really is no humor in offering your horse something that may be comical to you, but damaging to your equine friend.

Know anyone that feeds these: bacon, chicken McNuggets, fried catfish, pizza? Check out Chapter 3 — Fundamentals of Fats for why not to clog your horse's arteries.

Or how 'bout beer? I hear that one a lot. Or a glass of champagne?! Why give this to a horse? Please, please, do not give your horse alcohol.

Chocolate is another one. Chocolate contains a chemical called theobromine that is potentially toxic for horses, just as it is for your dog. No matter how much your horse likes it, it is not safe to feed. And stay away from milk products — milk shakes, ice cream, cheese, and even yogurt. I know — you've perhaps heard that yogurt is good for your horse because it's a probiotic (contains live microbes) but it also contains lactose and grown horses are lactose intolerant. Your horse will get diarrhea and he will not like you.

To Treat or Not to Treat

Enough of the craziness — let's talk about giving treats in general. It is a personal choice, strictly between you and your horse. Some folks offer them freely, some not at all, and others like to use them for rewarding specific behaviors. Methods vary — I know a trainer whom I respect greatly who never uses her hand to give a treat. Your relationship with your horse is unique and I am not here to change your philosophy. I am simply trying to keep your horse healthy, if you choose to offer him a treat.

Fruits and Vegetables

Speaking of keeping your horse healthy, let's talk about some sensible treats. We all know about carrots and apples. But there is a variety of fruits that your horse will also enjoy. On the vegetable side, there aren't very many items, except lettuce and celery, but I haven't come across many horses that like them. Here's a list of safe fruits and vegetables:

- Apples
- Apricots
- Bananas (including the peel)
- Beets
- Berries (boysenberry, raspberry, strawberry, blackberry, blueberries, etc.)
- Carrots
- Celery
- Cherries
- Coconut
- Dates
- Grapes (and raisins)
- Grapefruit
- Lettuce
- Lemons
- Limes
- Mango
- Melons (cantaloupe, honeydew)
- Oranges
- Peaches
- Pears
- Peanuts (roasted, never raw)
- Pineapple
- Plums
- Squash (pumpkin, zucchini, butternut, etc.)
- Sweet potatoes
- Tangerines
- Watermelon (including the rind)

Your horse's digestive system does have limits: It is not safe to feed cruciferous vegetables such as broccoli, cauliflower, cabbage, or kale. Tomatoes and peppers belong to the nightshade family, which is also harmful. And never give your horse a fruit pit.

Table 10-1 provides a list of hazardous fruits and vegetables.

Table 10-1 Hazardous Fruits and Vegetables		
Hazardous Fruits and Vegetables	**Those That Can Lead to Starch Overload**	**Fruit Pits**
Asparagus	Corn	Apricot pits
Avocados	Cooked potatoes	Avocado pits
Broccoli	Rice	Cherry pits
Brussel sprouts	Bread	Date pits
Cabbage		Peach pits
Chard		
Collard geens		
Eggplant		
Garlic (unheated)		
Kale		
Leeks		
Onions		
Peppers		
Potatoes (raw)		
Rhubarb		
Spinach		
Tomatoes		

Candy

An occasional sugar cube or peppermint candy is fine for most horses. I say most because sugary treats should never be given to horses suffering from:

- Insulin resistance (also known as metabolic syndrome)
- Laminitis (founder)
- Equine Cushing's disease (pituitary pars intermedia dysfunction)
- Polysaccharide storage myopathy (excessive accumulation of glycogen)
- Obesity or fat deposits along neck, back, and rump

Keep in mind that sugar is sugar; sugar from a peppermint candy ends up the same as sugar from an apple. So, sugary treats of any kind would not be appropriate for these horses. I'll discuss some alternatives later in this chapter.

Commercial Treats

Ever go down the treat aisle at your feed store or browse through page after page of treats offered in catalogs? Treat manufacturers work hard to entice you with pretty packaging, fancy claims, or the highest number of cookies for your buck. They even make them look good enough to serve to your guests. So how do you make a decision?

Truth is, the only way to tell what's in the bag is to look at the ingredient list. Commercial treats generally fall into one of two categories. The most common treats are cookies made from cereal grains such as oats, barley, corn, and wheat. They are likely sweetened with molasses. These can be offered to a healthy horse as an occasional treat. If your horse needs to stay away from sugar and starch, these treats are not for him.

Some treats come with added vitamins and minerals, making them a nutritional supplement. This is risky since you may already be feeding a fortified feed or another vitamin/mineral supplement. Conversely, you may not be feeding any other supplements, but the treat may fall short of providing all that your horse needs. So, I think it is best to provide a treat that is just that — an occasional reward — and leave the supplementing to products designed for that purpose.

Companies that produce probiotics are also getting on the treat bandwagon. To make probiotics easier to administer, why not just give your horse a treat? Two reasons. First, they may not be appropriate for your horse because they are typically high in starch. Second, and even more significant, is that their microbial concentration (referred to as CFUs on the label) is too low to make a difference, unless you were to feed the whole bag.

Treats that do not contain preservatives are an attractive option. Just be sure to take into account their limited shelf life, so finish them within a few days. Keeping them in a hot barn will make them spoil faster, making refrigeration your best option.

LOW SUGAR/LOW STARCH TREATS

As I mentioned earlier, apples and carrots are high in sugar, and should not be given to sensitive horses. Wanting to do the best for your horse, you stop feeding them, but it's painful to see their disappointment when you greet them empty-handed. However, there are alternatives you can feed.

I rarely make recommendations in this book (though I'll be delighted to help you if you'd like to contact me) but at this writing, there is only one company that I've found that has developed a full line of cookies and trail mixes that are low in starch and sugar. They're made by Skode's Horse Treats and are safe and nutritious for all horses.

Another choice is alfalfa cubes. Alfalfa makes a good treat for the insulin resistant horse since it is comparable in sugar levels to most grass hays. And horses love the taste. Be sure to break the cubes into small pieces and allow your horse to chew one piece carefully before offering another. They are very dry and some horses can choke on them if fed at too fast a rate.

Fruit rinds and peels are also good for your horse. Apple and banana peels, and cut-up watermelon rinds are tasty and low in sugar.

Concluding Part I

This chapter concludes Part I of this book. The information provided so far was intended to give you a firm understanding of each nutrient and feed type to help you better judge your horse's diet. In Part II, I address specific health conditions and life stages that benefit from nutritional intervention.

PART II

CONDITIONS, DISEASES, AND LIFE STAGES

CHAPTER 11 —
LAMINITIS

The hooves of horses!
-Oh! witching and sweet
is the music earth steals from the iron-shod feet;
no whisper of lover, no trilling of bird,
can stir me as much as hooves of horses
have stirred.
~ Will H. Ogilvie

No greater fear exists in the hearts of horse owners than to see their precious friend standing with the "laminitis stance" — stretching his front legs forward while leaning back on his hind legs to take the weight off his painful front feet.

Laminitis pain in front feet causes the horse to lean back

It's like needles piercing his flesh with each step. And as he tries to move, the coffin bone starts to sink, causing permanent changes to the foot. In many cases, this damage will make your horse lame and unfit for riding. And in extreme cases, it can kill him.

Founder and Laminitis

The term founder, in its technical sense, refers to a long-term, chronic condition resulting from a sudden painful attack of the laminae known as laminitis. The terms laminitis and founder, however, are often used interchangeably.

Laminitis means "inflammation of the laminae." The laminae secure the coffin bone (a wedge-shaped bone within the foot) to the hoof wall. In the initial phases of the disease, the enzyme matrix metalloproteinase (MMP) is released by the laminae, causing inflammation and reduction of blood flow. The resulting oxygen deprivation causes cellular death within the laminae. This loosens the connection between the laminae and the hoof wall, making the foot internally unstable.

The deep digital flexor tendon (DDFT) that runs along the back of the leg works with the laminae to provide support. However, during laminitis, the foot is out of balance, causing the DDFT to increase injury by pulling the coffin bone away from the hoof wall. When your horse puts pressure on his foot, the coffin bone can shift from its normal position and point down toward the sole. In severe cases, the coffin bone separates from the hoof wall, rotates, and sinks downward to eventually penetrate the sole, as in the famous cases of Secretariat and Barbaro, whose deaths resulted from severe laminitic attacks.

Fortunately, most cases are not that grave. Once the emergency has passed, changes in dietary management will give your horse an excellent chance of returning to a normal life.

ACUTE VS CHRONIC LAMINITIS

Acute laminitis

Acute laminitis flares up suddenly. There are many possible causes, and I list them for you a bit later in this chapter. What differentiates acute from chronic laminitis is the number of occurrences. Once the cause is removed and the symptoms wane, your horse may not experience the problem again unless confronted with the same set of circumstances.

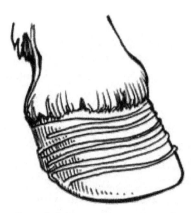

Laminitis produces ringed ridges

Chronic laminitis

In cases of chronic, ongoing laminitis, the foot suffers from repeated attacks. The soles will show bruising, seedy toe disease will develop (widening of the white line), and ringed ridges will appear on the hoof wall. This type of founder tends to have a hormonal basis such as insulin resistance (also known as metabolic syndrome) or pituitary pars intermedia dysfunction (PPID), more commonly referred to as equine Cushing's disease. Chronic laminitis can also result from prolonged medication usage, long-term stress, and even unresolved illness.

Even while your horse is not suffering from laminitis, per se, he may continue to have pain. Or he may be fine during warm weather and exhibit lameness once winter sets in. These chronic symptoms can be helped by two pain-relieving treatments.

Natural pain treatments[1] for unresolved pain: Ongoing pain can afflict your horse because of changes to the nerves in his feet. Such neuropathic pain has been alleviated by supplementing an amino acid metabolite called acetyl-L-carnitine. Feed 1 gram per 100 lbs of body weight.

Poor circulation can result from standing on snowy ground. You may find that lined boots or leg wraps are useful in keeping out the winter chill. To improve circulation, a helpful herbal treatment is 3/4 to 2 teaspoons twice daily of *Gynostemma pentaphyllum* (jiaogulan), given 15 minutes before feeding. Since horses like the taste, you can simply make a paste in a shallow bowl and your horse will lick it right up. This herb stimulates nitric oxide production inside the blood vessels, which has a dilating effect.

Common Causes of Laminitis

Though laminitis occurs in the feet, it often initiates elsewhere within the body. The biological mechanisms are complex and research continues to be done on the exact cause; however, the dietary recommendations have not changed.

There are many factors that can cause a laminitis attack, but *the prevalent opinion that protein brings about founder is not true.* Here's a list of what does cause laminitis:

- Hormonal disorders such as PPID and insulin resistance
- Elevated insulin
- Obesity
- Genetic prelaminitic syndrome
- Overfeeding of grain and sugar from sweet feeds (carbohydrate overload)
- Endotoxins released from the hindgut (leaky gut syndrome)
- Grazing on pasture that is high in sugar/starch/fructan
- Physical stress to the feet (concussion founder)
- Injury to one limb, leading to laminitis in another foot
- Retained placenta after foaling, resulting in a blood infection
- Colic
- Prolonged use of antibiotics or steroidal medications
- Bedding that contains black walnut shavings
- Selenosis (selenium toxicity)
- Iron overload (causes insulin resistance)
- Mental stress (leading to elevated cortisol levels)
- Forage restriction
- Rhabdomyolysis (tying up)
- Equine polysaccharide storage myopathy (EPSM)
- Thyroid disorders
- Toxic plants

HORMONAL DISORDERS

Any condition that disrupts hormonal function has the potential to affect your horse's feet. His immune system can also be impaired, leading to infections. In the sections that follow I offer basic descriptions of endocrine (hormonal) issues because they directly result in laminitis, but please refer to Chapter 13 — Metabolic and Endocrine Disorders to provide considerably more detail.

Insulin resistance and chronically elevated insulin levels

Recent research[2] has revealed that a chronic elevated circulating insulin level (even when blood glucose is normal) leads to laminitis. This is a result of the disorder known as insulin resistance, which simply means that cells do not respond to insulin. Insulin's job is to allow glucose (blood sugar) to leave the blood and enter the tissues, where it is metabolized for energy. If the cells do not permit insulin to do this, blood glucose levels are initially elevated. The pancreas reacts by secreting more insulin, in hopes of eventually getting the glucose into the cells, thereby lowering blood glucose levels back to normal. In the meantime, however, the high level of insulin causes laminitis.

Insulin resistance (also called metabolic syndrome) can be caused by several conditions, most notably obesity. However, while all obese horses have some degree of insulin resistance, not all insulin resistant horses are obese. The key factor is *where* fat exists. Fat deposits along the crest of the neck, back, tailhead, shoulders, chest, and over the eyes indicate that insulin resistance is a problem. Fat cells in these areas produce an enzyme that synthesizes the hormone known as cortisol. When cortisol levels are elevated, cells become resistant to insulin, which in turn causes insulin levels to rise, leading to laminitis.

Hoof tissue, unlike most other tissues in the body, does not require insulin for glucose entry. So, *lack of glucose is not the issue — insulin is.*

While obesity is discussed further in the next chapter on weight management, it is relevant to note here that *you can induce laminitis by restricting forage.* Horses are designed to be grazers and going without forage for any length of time is extremely stressful. Cortisol is a stress hormone, and your horse releases it when he has nothing to eat. And as I mentioned, elevated cortisol levels reduce cellular response to insulin, causing elevated blood insulin levels. I have seen many unfortunate cases where an overweight horse is allowed to go hungry for three, four, or more hours at a time, and has developed laminitis as a result. So if anyone tells you to restrict hay because your horse is overweight, ignore this advice! You can restrict concentrates, grain, and treats, but *never, never restrict forage.*

Equine Cushing's disease

As horses age they are more inclined to become cushingoid and develop an endocrine disorder known as pituitary pars intermedia dysfunction (PPID). This condition occurs when the pituitary gland produces too much adrenocorticotropic hormone (ACTH), which stimulates the adrenal gland to pump out more cortisol (stress hormone). Elevated cortisol levels make it difficult for insulin to do its job. So the pancreas pumps more insulin into the bloodstream, causing laminitis.

If your horse has equine Cushing's disease, he will exhibit certain signs. The most common is the condition of the coat: It will be kinky and very slow to shed. In addition, the increased cortisol level will make your horse very thirsty. He may lose muscle mass and become more susceptible to infections. All this and more is discussed in Chapter 13 — Metabolic and Endocrine Disorders.

GENETICS

There are horses born with a genetic tendency, linked to a dominant gene, that are more likely to develop insulin resistance. Known as prelaminitic syndrome, affected horses gain weight easily ("easy keepers") which explains why some horses can graze on sugar-rich pasture all day and night without ill effect, while others need to avoid pasture grazing. Ponies, Quarter Horses, Arabians, and Morgans, as well as gaited and draft breeds, are particularly prone toward inherent insulin resistance, but no breed is immune.

Allowing pasture turnout is a valid concern, which I discuss later in the chapter. But generally speaking, if a horse is of normal weight, has never had a laminitic attack, and is young (older horses tend to develop PPID), he can have free access to pasture. But continue to be diligent in your observations.

CARBOHYDRATE OVERLOAD (GRAIN FOUNDER)

Carbohydrate overload (feeding too much starch and sugar) is a common cause of laminitis, but can arise from two very different reasons. First, too much grain overwhelms the small intestine, resulting in microbial destruction within the hindgut. And second, starch and sugar cause insulin levels to rise suddenly. Let's look at each cause individually.

Overwhelming the small intestine

Feeding grains, especially oats, has always been a tradition. It stems from the days before the automobile when horses were required to work hard and could not maintain their weight on just hay. Oats provided an inexpensive and easy source of calories. And even today, they can be part of a balanced diet for a horse that is required to do intensive exercise. But to feed oats safely, meals need to be small and offered frequently.

Oats, corn, barley, and other cereal grains are high in starch. Sweet feeds contain cereal grains with added molasses and even pelleted feeds can be grain-based. When a large, starchy meal is fed, it starts a complex series of events. The size of the meal can overcome the small intestine's digestive capacity, leaving undigested starch to travel to the hindgut (cecum and large colon) where it is fermented by the microbes living there. More specifically, gram positive *Streptococcus* and *Lactobacillus* bacteria ferment starch into lactic acid, causing a rapid reduction in pH. This acidic environment causes the destruction of gram negative bacteria belonging to the *Enterobacteriaceae* family. Endotoxins result and are released from the hindgut into the bloodstream (called leaky gut syndrome). These endotoxins activate enzymes in the foot known as matrix metalloproteinases (MMPs), which destroy the laminae.

Oats are the safest grain to feed because they are more completely digested in the foregut (small intestine) than barley or corn. Therefore, feeding oats is far less likely to cause a problem, especially when fed in small amounts (no more than 2 lbs at a time). Rolled, crimped, or steamed oats have the outer hull broken open, exposing the inside to digestive enzymes. If you feed whole oats, they must be completely chewed for your horse to digest them. Unchewed whole oats are more inclined to reach the hindgut, leading to laminitis.

Corn is especially problematic for two reasons. First, if you feed the same size scoop of corn that you used for oats, you'll give your horse nearly twice the amount of starch. And second, corn is not as well digested in the foregut, making hindgut fermentation more likely. Barley falls in between oats and corn in terms of its digestibility. For more details on grains, turn to Chapters 2 — Fundamentals of Carbohydrates and 9 — Fundamentals of Concentrates and By-Products.

Sudden elevation of insulin levels

Starch and sugar are digested in the small intestine down to glucose molecules, which are absorbed into the bloodstream. Insulin levels will dramatically rise in response to glucose in the blood. This is perfectly normal. The more sugar and starch you feed, however, the more glucose there will be in the blood. Hence, insulin will rise to accommodate this additional glucose. It does not stay elevated as with insulin resistance, but *high levels of insulin can cause laminitis in susceptible horses.*

Molasses, used to sweeten grains in sweet feeds, will certainly cause insulin levels to rise. But what you may not realize is that fruits and carrots are also very high in sugar. I remember a client whose horse had foundered. We went over his diet very carefully and there was nothing to indicate a problem, until I asked her whether she was giving him any treats. "Oh yes!" she replied enthusiastically. "He gets two pounds of apples each day!" Now you may not feed that many apples, but even one can upset the hormonal response in a horse that already has too much insulin in his bloodstream.

PASTURE LAMINITIS

More than half of all laminitis cases are due to the over-consumption of tasty, early spring grasses. The common belief has been that grass founder occurs because such grasses are higher in protein. But as I stressed in the beginning of this chapter, protein is not the problem. Instead, it is due to one or both potentially harmful substances in pasture: the high sugar and starch content, or the elevated fructan levels.

Sugar and starch are digested in the foregut and produce a rise in blood glucose, followed by a concomitant rise in insulin. Too much insulin, as you know, causes laminitis. Fructan, on the other hand, cannot be digested in the foregut and therefore has no affect on insulin levels.

Fructan consists of fructose (a type of simple sugar) molecules linked together. But the small intestine does not produce the necessary digestive enzymes to break apart the bonds between fructose molecules. So, fructan travels past the small intestine into the hindgut, where the microbes produce enzymes to break apart its long fructose chain. Overconsumption, however, results in hindgut fermentation and leaky gut syndrome (just as described above with grain founder), leading to laminitis.

It is interesting to note that these three carbohydrates (sugar, starch, and fructan, together known as non-structural carbohydrates — NSC) are at their peak in the late afternoon when the plant has been exposed to sunlight all day and hence has produced these carbohydrates through the process of photosynthesis. Once the sun starts to set, the plant will consume NSC, only to start the process again the next day. So, the NSC concentration *is at its highest in the late afternoon.* The night and early morning hours are the safest time to let your horses graze since the NSC levels are at their lowest.

> Anything that stresses your pasture will result in higher levels of NSC. It could be cold nighttime temperatures, hot, dry weather with intermittent rainfall, and even overgrazing.

But spring pasture is not the only problem. A sunny day, *any time of year*, will trigger grass to continually store more NSC as the day progresses. And there's more — *anything that stresses your pasture will result in higher levels of NSC.* It could be cold nighttime temperatures (below 40° F), hot, dry weather with intermittent rainfall, and even overgrazing. In fact, when your horse eats the tops off the grass, the new growth will be concentrated at the base of the stems, which is why grass should be allowed to rest and grow a few inches before your horse is again allowed to graze.

If your horse exhibits normal insulin levels but foundered on pasture, it indicates that the grass is high in fructan. If insulin is high, sugar and starch are the culprits. *But regardless of the cause, you get the same result.* More discussion on forage and how it specifically relates to laminitis caused by insulin resistance is offered in Chapter 13 — Metabolic and Endocrine Disorders. The rest of this section focuses on laminitis caused by excess fructan ingestion.

To best evaluate your pasture and hay, you need to get it analyzed for sugar, starch, and fructan levels. Up until recently, fructan levels have been difficult to assess because the NSC content was the only measurement available. While it is still used, keep in mind that it includes fructan, along with starch and sugar. Since fructan is a significant laminitis-causing component, knowing the percent NSC is not adequate. Nutritionists are now able to review three other measurements: water-soluble carbohydrates (WSC), ethanol-soluble carbohydrates (ESC), and starch. WSC contains sugars and fructan; ESC is mostly sugar, so the difference between the two provides a good estimate of fructan levels. When you add starch (measured separately) to WSC, it gives the total NSC content. These measurements are also discussed in Chapter 1 — Ground Rules for Feeding a Horse.

So, my point is that NSC does not tell you anything about the fructan level. For example, if the NSC level is 18%, it could be 12% fructan and 6 % sugar and starch. This would be fine for the insulin resistant (IR) horse because he requires reduced sugar and starch intake, but it is potentially harmful for the laminitic horse since excess fructan is fermented in the hindgut. But what if the 18% NSC level equates to 15 % sugar and starch, and only 3% fructan? Then the opposite case is true — the laminitic horse will do great on this pasture, but the IR horse will do miserably because sugar and starch contribute to an increased insulin response. Starch percentage is provided as a separate statistic and is important to know for the IR horse because it, too, raises insulin levels after being digested in the foregut. WSC and ESC do not include starch.

I should note here that cool-season grasses, such as timothy, orchardgrass, brome, and fescue can accumulate high fructan levels when stressed, whereas alfalfa, clover, and warm weather grasses such as bahia, Bermuda, Tifton-85, and teff store carbohydrates as sugar and starch, not as fructan.

CONCUSSION FOUNDER

In the wild, the horse's foot is remarkably able to withstand stress and force. Domesticated horses, on the other hand, are ridden more and for greater lengths of time, resulting in concussive stress that would make a horse lame if he were in the wild. The fact is, as remarkable as his foot is, it is not designed to take consistent pounding on hard surfaces. Heavy horses are more susceptible to this problem, as are horses with small feet relative to their overall size. Also, if a horse sustains an injury to one leg, this can lead to laminitis due to sustained weight bearing on the healthy foot. This type of laminitis involves the mechanical detachment of the laminae from the coffin bone in response to physically stressing the foot.

Related to concussion founder is damage caused by contact with overly hot surfaces. During the summer months, the floor of a trailer, for example, can get too hot for your horse's hooves. Additional padding and bedding should be considered.

Also, be cautious of over-trimming your horse's hooves. I have witnessed this type of laminitis occurring shortly after a horse received excessive hoof trimming. It is not common, but definitely can occur.

First Aid

At the first sign of laminitis, contact your veterinarian. Do not wait.

By the time your horse exhibits symptoms, laminar degeneration is well underway, so the faster you get treatment, the better your horse's chance of recovery.

While you're waiting for your vet to arrive, make your horse as comfortable as possible by adding very thick bedding to his stall. Put his hay and water where it can be easily reached. *Do not walk him or make him move.* He is in a lot of pain. And unnecessary walking can cause the coffin bone to sink toward the sole of the foot.

COLD THERAPY

Ice-water baths for 48 to 72 hours are beneficial. (After 72 hours ice is no longer effective.) If your horse will not stand in buckets of ice water, add crushed ice to a rectal sleeve and tie it to the pastern, replacing it as the ice melts. Or use soaking boots, specifically designed to withstand the force of a horse's hoof. We now know that treatment with ice inhibits the damaging enzymatic action of MMP. Cold therapy also acts as an anti-inflammatory agent and slows the metabolic rate (enzyme activity) of inflamed tissues.

ACTIVATED CHARCOAL

If you think your horse got into the grain supply, act immediately by giving him a tube of activated charcoal gel to adsorb and neutralize toxins in the gut. You should always have this on hand since it needs to be administered as soon as you notice the problem. Do not overdose since it can be constipating and lead to colic.

REDUCING TENSION ON THE LAMINAE

To reduce tension on the laminae, it helps to lessen the weight on the heel. Elevation, *not lowering*, of the heel with an 18-degree wedge is often recommended. You can use Styrofoam as a temporary padding; your veterinarian and farrier will have more durable alternatives.

Bedding from straw or pine shavings should be provided to create one to two feet of depth. This will allow a toe-down stance, creating better blood flow, and taking pressure off of the DDFT to reduce its force toward separating the laminae from the hoof wall.

Your veterinarian may suggest stall rest. This is fine as long as your horse is accustomed to being confined to a stall. But if this adds additional stress, I do not recommend it. Instead, if at all possible, put him in a dry lot and make it easy for him to eat by supplying easy access to hay. Believe me, he won't be walking far — it is much too painful.

Medications

Your veterinarian will likely administer one or more medications to reduce inflammation and pain, as well as to promote circulation.

NON-STEROIDAL ANTI-INFLAMMATORY DRUGS (NSAIDS)

These medications include:

- Aspirin
- Phenylbutazone ("bute")
- Banamine (flunixin meglumine, made by Intervet Schering-Plough Animal Health)
- Equioxx (firocoxib, made by Merial) — slow acting; therefore not typically used for acute cases

An intravenous dose of bute or Banamine will likely be the first drug administered. But these pain killers can only be used for a short time. They are designed to reduce pain and inflammation but they do not cure the problem, and can actually make it worse. Some inflammation is important for healing and NSAIDs can create stagnant fluid retention in the foot, leading to abscesses.

If your horse must be on a pain killer for more than 3 days, consider adding an antacid that does not contain cereal grains, or oil to protect the stomach lining. Aspirin can also be used instead of stronger NSAIDs for a slightly longer period. I prefer aspirin because it reduces platelets better than other NSAIDs, making the blood less sticky and thereby preventing coagulation and blood clots.

Be careful of overdosing NSAIDs; toxicity can result. Here are the dosing guidelines[3]:

> Bute: 1.0 to 2.0 mg per lb of body weight every 12 hours. That's *milligrams*, so a 1000 lb horse would have 1000 to 2000 mg, or *1 to 2 grams*, every 12 hours.

Banamine: 0.5 mg per lb of body weight every 12 hours or 0.1 mg per lb of body weight every 8 hours. So a 1000 lb horse would have 500 mg or *0.5 grams* every 12 hours or 100 mg or *0.1 grams* every 8 hours.

Aspirin: 5.5 to 11.4 mg per lb of body weight every 12 to 48 hours. So a 1000 lb horse could have between 5500 and 11,400 mg (5.5 to 11.4 grams) of aspirin. To put this into perspective, one plain aspirin has 325 mg. So to reach 5500 mg, you would give your horse 17 pills; to reach 11,400 mg, you would need 35 pills. It's much easier to find an aspirin product designed for horses that offers a more concentrated dosage.

Buteless, herbal preparations can also be useful to reduce the dosage of NSAIDs or eliminate them all together. There are many on the market, so it may take some trial and error to see which one works best for your horse.

DRUGS THAT PROMOTE DIGITAL CIRCULATION

Drugs such as acetylpromazine, phenoxybenzamine, isoxsuprine, and prazosin are used to decrease vasoconstriction (increase circulation). Isoxsuprine use, however, has recently been questioned since it does not seem to increase laminar blood flow; many veterinarians do not find it effective and have discontinued its use. Acetylpromazine is also used as a sedative to encourage your horse to lie down. Heparin is sometimes administered to reduce the incidence of blood clots. I recommend that you discuss the pros and cons of each medication with your veterinarian.

ANTIBIOTICS

Antibiotics are sometimes administered to prevent infection. However, unless an infection is apparent, avoid their use. Antibiotics kill the beneficial microbes in the hindgut, and can induce colic. Therefore, do not use them as a preventive measure. And if you do end up using them, be sure to provide a potent probiotic with CFUs (colony forming units) in the billions (10^9).

Feeding and Management Objectives

Most cases of laminitis are due to the increase in insulin that arises from feeding too much starch and sugar (from grain or forage) or excess fermentation in the hindgut, compromising the bacterial flora. It's sometimes difficult to differentiate between the two causes, so your best approach is to immediately remove your horse from pasture and stop feeding any cereal grains (oats, corn, barley, etc.), pelleted feed that is grain-based, or sweet feed. Replace these with a commercial low starch feed that has 12-14% protein.

Offer free choice, *good-quality* grass hay (to provide nutrients for healing) along with fresh water and salt. Alfalfa hay can also be added to the diet because it is low in carbohydrates, low in fructan levels, and will provide additional protein to the diet to help your horse rebuild healthy foot tissue.

Never starve your horse. This will worsen the problem by setting the stage for a relapse; the stress created by this situation will lead to insulin resistance. Furthermore, starving causes fat to be mobilized into the bloodstream, leading to a condition called hyperlipemia, which causes damage to the liver. So, give your horse all the hay he wants. Once your horse knows that he has a constant hay supply, he will calm down and not eat as quickly, or as much, and will self-regulate his intake.

Knowing the NSC content in your hay will relieve your mind about offering it free choice. If you find that the NSC level is more than 12%, consider soaking the hay before feeding and draining the water to remove much of the sugar and fructan content.

In cases that are not related to carbohydrates, however, such as laminitis from toxic plants, infections, retained placenta, or concussion founder, your approach should be to remove the cause, treat the symptoms, and provide nutritional support to help ease inflammation, increase circulation, and promote healing.

BENEFICIAL SUPPLEMENTS

- **Omega-3 fatty acids.** These fatty acids will stabilize the immune system and reduce inflammation. Flaxseed meal or oil can be added to a low starch meal. Feed 1/2 cup of flaxseed meal or one ounce of oil per 400 lbs of body weight.

- **Coenzyme Q10.** This potent antioxidant is very helpful in reducing pain and neutralizing damaging free radicals caused by endotoxins. You may have to go to your local pharmacy or grocery store to purchase a human supplement. Give your horse a therapeutic dose for the first two weeks: 50 mg per 100 lbs of body weight. After two weeks, take an additional week to slowly wean your horse down to 20 mg per 100 lbs of body weight. He can remain on this dose for as long as he is experiencing discomfort.

- **Probiotics and prebiotics.** I suggest you use both. A *probiotic* replenishes the number of live microbes living in the hindgut (cecum). These bacteria are critical to the health of your horse and their destruction may be the very cause of the problem. So it is essential that you replenish them immediately. Choose a probiotic that has adequate numbers of CFUs (colony forming units) and also offers oligosaccharides to stabilize his immune system.

  A *prebiotic,* on the other hand, does not contain live bacteria. Instead, it contains fermentation products from many types of naturally-occurring bacteria that will feed the existing microbes and boost their numbers.

- **Vitamin C.** During a laminitis attack, vitamin C should be supplemented. Vitamin C (ascorbic acid) has antihistamine properties, which reduce blood vessel constriction. Furthermore, it promotes the formation of collagen, a necessary component of blood vessel integrity. And finally, vitamin C is a potent antioxidant, reducing damage from free radicals.

  In order for vitamin C to be effective, you will need to provide a large dose — 20 mg per pound of body weight each day, divided between meals. Build up to this level over a few days; if loose stools result, you can cut back a little.

  Once your horse has healed, you can wean him off of vitamin C, but do it slowly. The large dose has made his body accustomed to having more than he normally produces on his own. If you were to suddenly stop feeding vitamin C, he would react as though he were experiencing a deficiency. So, take your time — 3 to 4 weeks of slowly reducing the dosage. If your horse is over 16 years old, you can still cut back, but continue to give him vitamin C on a regular basis to compensate for what his body no longer produces. This is discussed further in Chapter 19 — Growth and Growing Old.

- **Vitamin E.** Vitamin E reduces the incidence of clots forming, is an antioxidant, and increases circulation to the area. Provide your horse with 5 IU of vitamin E per pound of body weight daily. Most vitamin E supplements come with added selenium. *Do not choose these unless you know for certain that your horse is not getting enough selenium.* Too much selenium is toxic and can induce laminitis.

- **Hoof supplement.** There are several excellent hoof supplements on the market. Depending on what else you're feeding, choose one that complements and does not overlap your existing diet.

- **Magnesium.** To reduce circulating insulin levels, provide 5,000 mg per 250 lbs of body weight. This is discussed further in Chapter 13 — Metabolic and Endocrine Disorders.

- *Gingko biloba.* This herb improves circulation and has an anticoagulation effect. You can purchase a human supplement and simply provide 10 times the human dose for the 1000 lb horse.

- **MSM (Methylsulfonylmethane).** Often included in joint preparations, MSM is a potent anti-inflammatory agent. Give your horse 1,000 mg per 100 lbs of body weight.

- **Comprehensive vitamin/mineral supplement.** If you are feeding a commercially fortified feed according to directions, you may not need to supplement anything else other than the above nutrients for therapeutic purposes. However, if you are feeding less than what is recommended or your horse is on a hay-only diet, you'll want to fill in the gaps with a comprehensive vitamin/mineral supplement. Choose one that is designed for laminitic horses because it will contain antioxidants and anti-inflammatory agents that are not typically found in the average preparation.

SOME THINGS TO AVOID

- **Straw or chaff.** These are virtually indigestible and therefore, they do not provide any significant nutritive value.

- **Rice bran.** While much lower in starch than cereal grains (18% compared to approximately 50%), it will still produce an undesirable insulin response. Therefore it is best to avoid rice bran for IR horses.

- **Grazing muzzles.** If a grazing muzzle stresses your horse, you will defeat your purpose and induce another laminitis attack. Instead of a

grazing muzzle, try to move your horse off of pasture during the most
dangerous times. On the other hand, if your horse doesn't seem to
mind it, choose one that has a large enough opening to allow for small
amounts of grazing as well as the ability to drink water. *Make sure
water can drain from muzzle.*

- **Iron.** Consider removing all supplemental sources of iron from the
  diet. Your horse gets plenty of iron from his forage. Too much interferes with copper absorption and also lowers your horse's ability to
  resist infection. In addition, iron has been proven to increase insulin
  resistance in humans. And while not studied extensively in horses, it
  is worth making this change in the diet. Please refer to Chapter 5 —
  Fundamentals of Minerals for a complete discussion.

PREVENTING ABSCESSES

Abscesses result from fluid, blood, and dead tissue accumulation in the
foot. Reducing inflammation will slow down this process and may even
prevent an abscess from forming in the first place. Several of the supplements I suggested earlier have an anti-inflammatory effect. To review, consider adding the following:

- Vitamin C
- Vitamin E
- Flaxseed meal or oil
- MSM

An abscess is not necessarily indicative of a bacterial infection. However,
an abscess can become infected, so antibiotics may be administered. As I
mentioned earlier, any time your horse is on antibiotics, it is important to
give him a probiotic to replace hindgut bacteria.

Instead of oral or injected antibiotics, I have seen excellent results by placing the drug directly into the draining abscess. In addition to this, consider
applying Manuka honey, which has natural anti-microbial properties.

A LITTLE MORE ABOUT ALFALFA...

Many people ask me, "Does alfalfa cause laminitis?"

The answer is simple: "No."

Throughout this chapter I've explained that when it comes to preventing laminitis, the concern should be about the sugar, starch, and fructan levels in the hay. Alfalfa is low in sugar and starch, and contains very little, if any, fructan. In fact, it typically has an even lower NSC percentage than grass hay. Alfalfa is blamed, however, for causing laminitis due to its high protein content. Protein does not cause laminitis; *protein is needed to heal laminitis.*

Alfalfa is an excellent feed to offer your horse with laminitis because *it is* such a good source of protein. Alfalfa is a legume, and unlike grass hays, legumes are high in the essential amino acid called lysine. Lysine is typically the limiting amino acid in your horse's diet, meaning its reduced quantity limits the extent to which all other amino acids can be utilized to make body proteins. It's like the weakest link in a chain influencing the strength of the entire chain. If the diet is low in lysine, it doesn't matter how many other amino acids are present.

But when lysine is available, your horse can not only produce new hoof tissue, but also repair blood vessels, produce muscle, build red blood cells, boost the immune system, have healthy eyes, hair, and skin, and so much more.

As much as I like alfalfa, though, I do not recommend feeding it exclusively. It should be combined with grass hay to balance out its high calcium content. For the average horse, it's beneficial to feed 20% of the entire forage ration as alfalfa. However, to help your laminitic horse heal, give more than that — a 2:1 ratio of grass to alfalfa is acceptable.

When adding a vitamin/mineral supplement, look for one that is designed for high-alfalfa diets. They have reduced calcium levels to compensate for feeding plans that contain 8 lbs or more of alfalfa.

And, finally, when purchasing alfalfa hay, choose a reputable supplier that takes precautions against blister beetles. I discuss this at length and give you suggestions on how to make the right choice in Chapter 8 — Fundamentals of Forages.

Summary

Prevention is always ideal, but even under the best of circumstances, laminitis can creep up on your horse without warning. Your first approach should be to figure out the cause so you can remedy the situation and prevent another attack. This is not always easy to do, especially if your horse foundered while grazing on pasture. Pasture laminitis can be caused by excess sugar and starch, leading to elevated insulin levels. Or it could be caused by high fructan levels which have nothing to do with insulin. But regardless of the exact cause, you'll want to take future precautions when allowing your horse to graze. Having your pasture analyzed is the best approach since it gives you an idea of the risk. However, this is tricky because NSC levels can not only vary with time of day, season, temperature, rainfall, and stress, but also with location in the pasture. The best you can do is to take precautions based on the most likely factors that increase NSC. Take a look at www.safergrass.org. This website provides a wealth of information about your particular grass.

More than any other health problem, insulin resistance predisposes your horse to laminitis. This endocrine disorder does not affect all horses that experience laminitis, but the horse community is seeing more and more insulin resistance cases caused by overeating, obesity, high starch diets, and inactivity. I offer a comprehensive discussion of insulin resistance in Chapter 13 — Metabolic and Endocrine Disorders. However, before we go there, the next chapter deals with weight management, both overweight as well as underweight horses, since these conditions can be affected by the problems discussed in Chapter 13.

Endnotes

[1] Kellon, E, DVM., 2009. Chronic laminitis care. *Horse Journal, 16* (4): 13-14.

[2] Research related to laminitis and its relation to elevated insulin levels is discussed in: Walsh, D.M., McGowan, C.M., McGowan, T., Lame, S.V., Schanbacher, B.J., and Place, N.J., 2009. Correlation of plasma insulin concentration with laminitis score in a field study of equine Cushing's disease and equine metabolic syndrome. *Journal of Equine Veterinary Science, 29* (2): 79-84.

[3] Obtained from *Large Animal Internal Medicine*, Chapter 32: Disease of the Alimentary Tract. St Louis, Missouri: Mosby Elsevier: 755.

CHAPTER 12 —
WEIGHT MANAGEMENT

A horse is a thing of such beauty…
None will tire of looking at him as long as he displays
himself in his splendor.
~ Xenophon

A healthy horse maintains a healthy weight. This certainly makes sense. But feeding your horse a nutritious diet may still make him heavy. A horse, just like a person, has his own metabolic rate and genetic tendencies, making a one-size-fits-all feeding plan inappropriate. Combined with lack of exercise, too many treats, and overfeeding, it's no wonder that horses are developing hormonal problems, arthritis, and laminitis at an alarming rate.

Underweight can be just as serious and is generally a result of poor dental care, old age, worm infestation, stress, various disease states, or just plain being underfed.

The first step in any weight management program is to have your horse thoroughly examined by your veterinarian, including a complete blood count and chemistry panel tests, to rule out any underlying medical disorders. This information will help you develop the best diet for your horse.

How Much Does Your Horse Weigh?

It's important to know how much your horse weighs for a variety of reasons, such as calculating feed requirements, administering dewormers, and deciding how much medication to provide. Furthermore, most commercial feed preparations base their directions on your horse's weight and activity level.

There are several ways to determine your horse's weight. Using a scale, of course, would be the most accurate, but most horse owners do not own one that's large enough. So, the next best thing is measuring your horse.

MEASURING YOUR HORSE

Using a simple tape measure, use one of the following methods:

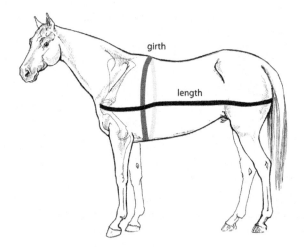

How to measure girth and length

Calculating weight in pounds, using inches

1.   Measure your horse's length in *inches* (measure in a straight line from the point of shoulder to the buttocks as shown above)

2.   Measure your horse's girth in *inches* (circumference of the horse's body about 4" behind his front legs)

3.   Use the following formula: Horse's Weight (in lbs) = (Girth X Girth X Length) ÷ 330

Calculating weight in kilograms (kg), using centimeters (cm)

1.   Measure your horse's length in *centimeters* (measure in a straight line from the point of shoulder to the buttocks)

2.   Measure your horse's girth in *centimeters* (circumference of the horse's body about 12.5 cm behind its front legs)

3.   Use the following formula: Horse's Weight (in kg) = (Girth X Girth X Length) ÷ 11900

   To change his weight to pounds, multiply your answer by 2.2.

USING A WEIGHT TAPE

Weight tapes are inexpensive and easy to use. They are not as accurate as using the above formulas, but they can give you a good estimation. To measure a foal less than 90 days old, use the formula found in Chapter 19 — Growth and Growing Old. Weight tapes are also useful in tracking trends over a period of time as you work on helping your horse gain or lose weight.

To use a weight tape, measure your horse by wrapping the tape around the girth, directly behind the elbow and behind the withers, as shown below:

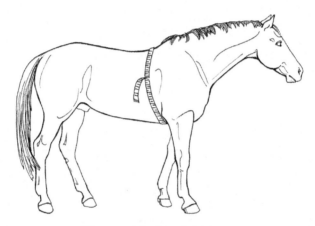

Placement of weight tape

If you do not have a weight tape, you can still estimate your horse's weight by measuring his girth using a tape measure. Use Table 12-1 to determine your horse's approximate weight.

Table 12-1 Estimating Horse's Weight Using a Tape Measure			
Girth Length		**Weight**	
inches	cm	lbs	kg
40.0	102	200	91
45.5	116	300	136.5
50.5	128	400	182
55.0	140	500	227
58.5	148	600	273
61.5	156	700	318
64.5	164	800	364
67.5	171	900	409
70.5	179	1000	455
73.0	185	1100	500
75.5	192	1200	545
77.5	197	1300	591
79.5	202	1400	636
81.5	207	1500	682
83.5	212	1600	727
85.5	217	1700	773
87.5	222	1800	818

Henneke Body Condition Scoring System

The Body Condition Scoring System, developed in 1984 by Don Henneke, Ph.D. at Texas A&M University, is still the mainstay for equine health professionals. This system uses the amount of stored fat on your horse's body. Horses tend to put on weight (fat) in specific areas, as shown in the following picture:

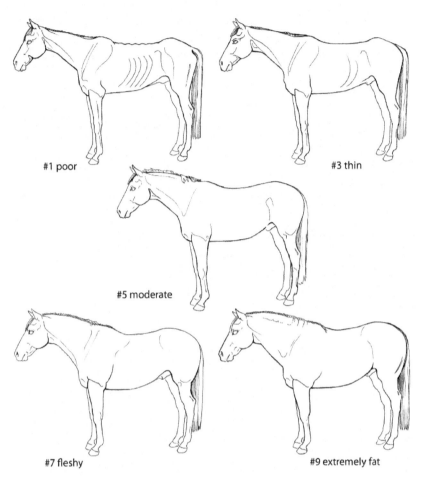

#1 poor   #3 thin

#5 moderate

#7 fleshy   #9 extremely fat

Body condition changes as Henneke scores progress from 1 to 9

Notice that fat does not accumulate extensively on the lower abdomen (belly). A distended abdomen is often referred to as a "hay belly" to describe a fat horse, even when the rest of his body is normal. He's not fat, he just has gas! In fact, gas production is perfectly natural and healthy; it indicates that your horse is getting enough hay for hindgut microbial fermentation to occur. Many horse owners try to eliminate a hay belly by overfeeding grain. This goes against your horse's natural bodily function, as well as increases his risk for colic and laminitis.

When figuring your horse's score, you will need to do a visual assessment, as well as palpating your horse for degrees of fatness in specific areas: neck, withers, back, ribs, and hind quarters shown in the illustration below.

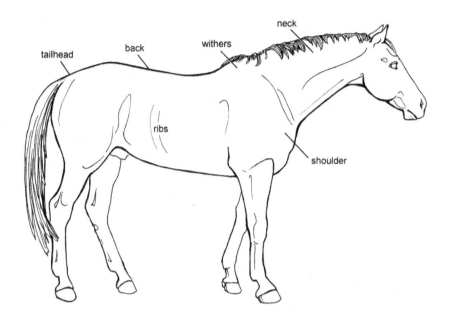

Henneke developed a scoring system that places all horses, regardless of breed, on a scale of 1 to 9, where 1 is the thinnest, and 9, the most obese. Even though there are breed conformation differences that affect where a horse naturally builds flesh (e.g., AQHA natural back crease vs Foxtrotter flat back), all six elements should be taken into consideration to determine your horse's score. Table 12-2 describes each score: 4 is very fit; 5 and 6 are acceptable; 6 and 7 are acceptable for broodmares.

Score	Neck	Withers	Back	Tailhead	Ribs	Shoulders
1 Poor	Extremely emaciated	Extremely emaciated	Spine projects	Tailhead projects	Easily noticeable	Easily noticeable
2 Very Thin	Faintly noticeable	Faintly noticeable	Slight fat over backbone	Tailhead prominent	Ribs are prominent	Faintly noticeable
3 Thin	Prominent	Prominent	Fat starting to build up	Tailhead less prominent	Slight fat over ribs	Shoulder prominent
4 Mod. Thin	Neck not obviously thin	Not obviously thin	Sunken crease along back	Fat can be felt	Faint outline noticeable	Shoulder not obviously thin
5 Mod.	Blends smoothly into body	Withers rounded	Back is level	Tailhead slightly spongy	Ribs felt but not seen	Blends smoothly into body
6 Mod. Fleshy	Fat beginning to be deposited	Fat beginning to be deposited	Slight crease down back	Fat around tailhead feels soft	Fat over ribs feels spongy	Fat beginning to be deposited
7 Fleshy	Fat deposited along neck	Fat along withers	Positive crease down back	Fat around tailhead is soft	Fat apparent between ribs	Fat behind shoulder
8 Fat	Thick, cresty neck	Fat along withers	Positive crease down back	Tailhead fat is very soft	Cannot feel ribs	Shoulder flush with body
9 Very Fat	Bulging fat	Bulging fat	Obvious crease on back	Building fat around tailhead	Patchy fat appearing over ribs	Bulging fat

Table 12-2 Henneke Body Condition Score[1]

Weigh Your Concentrates

Feed bags list how much to feed based on weight, level of activity, and sometimes age. Recommended amounts are usually expressed as so many pounds of feed per 100 lbs of body weight. However, many folks use a scoop to dish out their feed. Scoops measure *volume*, not weight. And they come in all sorts of sizes.

Our measurement system can be confusing, unlike the metric system that has separate units for volume (ml, liters) and weight (grams, kg). We use ounces for volume — such as 32 ounces in a quart. And we also use ounces for weight — such as 16 ounces in a pound.

If you use a 2 quart scoop, how much does 2 quarts of feed weigh? It depends. Two quarts equals 64 fluid ounces of volume, which says nothing about weight. So, since 16 ounces of weight is one pound, does that mean that 2 quarts (64 fluid ounces) is 4 lbs of feed? Not necessarily; it depends on the feed. Fill the scoop with marbles and you can't expect it to weigh the same as filling the scoop with cotton balls. Feeds vary in weight depending on their ingredients. I can tell you, however, that in general, a 2-quart scoop of the average pelleted feed weighs between 2.5 and 3.0 lbs, whereas a 2-quart scoop of dry beet pulp only weighs 1 lb.

> Scoops measure volume, not weight. Feeds vary in weight depending on their ingredients.

So what I'm getting at here is this… *Get a scale and weigh your feed*. Scoops, coffee cans, and "eye-balling" are not ways to properly measure your horse's feed. Once you weigh your feed, you can mark a container, if you like, but if you change your feed, you need to weigh the new feed and re-mark the container.

The Easy Keeper

Is it your horse's fault if he's an easy keeper? After all, he eats the same amount as everyone else, and he gains weight while his friends stay trim and svelte. Horses, just like people, can be genetically wired to store fat; some horses gain weight just *looking* at a carrot! But the way to take off pounds, whether the cause is genetic or just plain hanging out at the barn too much, is not a restrictive diet. Diets don't work; they don't work for you and they won't work for your horse. Reducing calories is fine, but taking away forage is not the way to help your horse lose weight. In fact, it does just the opposite (I'll explain later).

Keep in mind that too much fat leads to a hormonal disorder known as insulin resistance (also called metabolic syndrome), a disease very much like Type II diabetes in people. Watch for fat accumulation above your horse's eyes, on his rump, along his neck (called a cresty neck), or along either side of the spine, causing a crease to develop down his back. An insulin resistant horse is a strong candidate for laminitis; please read more about it in Chapters 11 — Laminitis and 13 — Metabolic and Endocrine Disorders.

FEEDING BASICS FOR THE OVERWEIGHT HORSE

Why is your horse chubby? Easy. He may eat too much, exercise too little, have bad genes, or he may just be getting older, which makes fat appear where it wasn't before. Another factor, one that you may not have thought of, is stress. Stressed horses often gain weight.

Avoid weight loss products

For the most part, healthy horses become obese because they are given concentrated feeds. Every year, feed companies come out with a product that horse owners *must try*. And they all have new features to tempt you. Crazy thing is, there are even feeds designed to help your horse lose weight, but that's impossible if you feed the amounts they recommend. There is nothing magical about these feeds; they do not help your horse burn more calories. Don't be like my aunt who decided to go on a diet. I caught her eating a big lunch and asked her what happened to her plan to have SlimFast instead. "Oh, I *do* have SlimFast," she replied. "After I finish my lunch, I drink it to take away the calories!" (She wasn't kidding.)

But all kidding aside, weight loss horse feed is a ridiculous concept. These products are meant to simulate what we do for our dogs and cats. An overweight pet needs to eat, so a low-calorie feed is a good idea. But an overweight horse already *does* eat. He gets hay and pasture. Why then give him more feed? The only use for these feeds is to provide a small meal so he doesn't feel deprived while other horses are eating. Or they can serve as a carrier meal for supplements. But feeding them according to directions would require that you reduce something else, specifically hay and pasture. That's not acceptable.

Avoid feeding cereal grain and sugary treats

The word grain is often used to describe any concentrated feed. But it really should only be used to describe *cereal* grains such as oats, corn, barley, wheat, etc. or pelleted feeds that contain cereal grains. Fortunately, there are many low starch feeds made from other ingredients, such as alfalfa, soybean meal, flax, and beet pulp, which are beneficial for horses that have hormonal disorders and need to reduce sugar and starch intake.

See Chapter 13 — Metabolic and Endocrine Disorders for more details.

So, getting back to actual cereal grains… Since all overweight horses have some degree of insulin resistance, the best advice I can give you is to stay away from starchy feeds. That means getting rid of anything that contains cereal grains, including sweet feeds or pelleted feeds that are grain-based. You really don't want to risk a laminitis attack. If you have an overweight horse, please read Chapter 11 — Laminitis to learn what it involves and how to prevent it.

Carrots and apples are very high in sugar and should be avoided because they also increase blood insulin levels. Most commercial treats are made from cereal grains and molasses, making them inappropriate to feed. Take a look at Chapter 10 — Fundamentals of Treats for a list of healthful and not-so-healthful choices for your horse.

Consider an all-forage diet

If your horse is not being exercised, *you may not need to feed any concentrate at all*. This of course depends on the growth cycle of the horse and his condition. But in many cases, an all-forage diet can be a very healthful way to feed. If hay is all your horse gets, however, you'll need to add a vitamin/mineral supplement to fill in the nutritional gaps.

Provide a "carrier" meal for supplements: Offer a small meal or two of a non-starchy feed such as alfalfa pellets, beet pulp, or a low starch commercial feed, to serve as a carrier for any supplements.

Alfalfa: Be careful when feeding high-calorie hay. These are typically grain hays (oat, crested wheatgrass, rye) and grass/legume combinations such as timothy/alfalfa mixes. Alfalfa is a wonderful feed, but because it's higher in calories than grass, you should limit it to no more than 20% of the total forage ration. I talk about alfalfa extensively throughout this book, especially in Chapters 4 — Fundamentals of Protein and Amino Acids, 8 — Fundamentals of Forages, and 11 — Laminitis, so I invite you to investigate this further.

I like feeding some alfalfa hay, cubes, or pellets. When added to a grass, it boosts the protein quality in the diet, making it easier for your horse to remain healthy. High-quality protein is needed for hundreds of areas within your horse's body. He uses it to maintain immune function, protect his heart, liver, kidneys, and lungs, keep his bones, muscles and joints strong, and build healthy hooves, skin, and hair. A low-quality protein is wasted and can end up being stored as fat, which defeats your purpose. Protein and its quality are often overlooked. Chapter 4 — Fundamentals of Protein and Amino Acids will give you a good understanding of its value in your horse's diet.

Provide hay free choice

All horses, regardless of their weight condition, should have access to pasture and/or hay at all times. Yes, you read that right — 24 hours a day. Your horse's digestive tract is designed to have forage flowing through it consistently throughout the day.

As you drive down the road, take a look at horses in a pasture. Their heads are to the ground as they are busy grazing. Horses are trickle feeders; it's what horses are meant to do. Sure, they rest — approximately 2 hours out of every 24, but not consecutively — a few minutes here and a few minutes there. Going for hours without anything to graze on will not only make it difficult for your horse to lose weight, but he'll likely develop an ulcer, and may even colic.

"But won't my horse get fat?" you ask. I *knew* you'd ask that excellent question. The short answer is, "No." Over time, he will learn to eat only what he needs. And ironically, restricting forage promotes weight gain.

Self-regulation of hay intake: *Give your horse a chance to tell you what he needs.* Horses will not overeat if they arc given the opportunity to self-regulate their intake. If your horse "inhales" his hay and eats every spec in sight, then looks for more, it's because he has endured hours of anxiety waiting for his next hay feeding. But if you give him all he wants, and he starts to get the message that he can walk away, take a nap, look at the scenery, chat with a friend, and the hay will still be there when he comes back, then and only then, can he relax and moderate his intake according to his need. Fretful horses, anxious for their morning meal, will relax when given enough to get them through the night. If you board your horse away from home, have your barn manager give enough hay so there is some left over in the morning; this is the *only* way to know if your horse is getting enough hay in his last feeding of the day.

Calmer behavior: An added bonus of feeding this way is the change in your horse's demeanor and behavior; it will amaze you. I can't count the number of times I've heard from clients that their horses act better, are calmer, easier to handle, more willing to learn, and generally nicer to be around when they are fed all the hay they want. And this makes perfect sense because you've removed a source of major stress in their lives.

This process takes about a week to occur, during which time he will overeat simply because he is not used to having all he wants. But once his intake becomes regulated, you can then weigh how much your horse is eating, if you like, to better judge his hay serving.

Starving your horse makes him fat! If you're ever told to stop feeding so much hay to your overweight horse, politely thank the person for the advice, walk away, and do what you know to be the right thing. This old-school thinking abounds, but more and more knowledgeable professionals are starting to understand that horses do best when they are permitted unlimited access to hay.

Restricting forage is counter-productive. There are two reasons for this. First, starving lowers your horse's metabolic rate, making him burn calories more slowly, so he tends to put on weight. Eating small amounts throughout the day does the opposite — it *stimulates* the metabolism, thereby *promoting weight loss.*

And second, *starving is extremely stressful.* Stress causes the release of cortisol, a stress hormone that increases insulin levels. Increased insulin leads to fat storage. Increased fat leads to even more insulin and the vicious cycle repeats itself, getting your horse fatter and fatter.

Stress can also harm your horse's liver due to a condition known as hyperlipemia caused by elevated insulin levels. Ponies, miniature horses, donkeys, and mules are particularly prone toward hyperlipemia, but no horse is immune.

Have your hay tested

It's always a good idea to have your hay tested for its sugar, fructan, and starch levels. Strive for a non-structural carbohydrate (NSC) level of less than 12%. The term NSC has been expanded to include water soluble carbohydrates (WSC), ethanol soluble carbohydrates (ESC), and starch, all measured separately. Chapters 1 — Ground Rules for Feeding a Horse and 11 — Laminitis will help you get familiar with these measurements.

Let your horse graze on pasture, within limits

Overweight horses are more prone toward developing laminitis. So pasture grazing may need to be limited to safer times of the day and year. Grass is safest to feed (has the lowest sugar, fructan, and starch levels) in the early morning after the grass has used up most of its carbohydrate content during the night. As grass is exposed to sunlight, it produces more NSC, making the late afternoon the most hazardous for your horse. Nighttime temperatures are also a factor; grass is more dangerous in the early spring and late fall when the thermometer dips below 40° F overnight. For a complete discussion of this issue, please refer to Chapter 11 — Laminitis.

Grazing muzzles: I'm often asked if a grazing muzzle is a good idea and I can certainly understand how it seems like the ideal solution. It gives your horse the opportunity to graze with his buddies while limiting the amount of grass he consumes. The goal is help your horse lose weight, and in many cases, prevent laminitis. But I caution you about their use for two reasons:

> 1. Muzzles can be stressful. And as you know, stress causes the horse's body to hold on to more fat, rather than lose it; muzzle use contradicts its own purpose.

> 2. Restricting feed slows down the metabolic rate, making it difficult to lose weight.

A grazing muzzle must always allow for water drinking. And there are designs that have a wider opening, thereby reducing frustration. If you choose to try one, watch your horse to see if he is making an attempt to take it off. If it's causing him stress, it's not helping.

BENEFICIAL SUPPLEMENTS

Multiple vitamin/mineral supplements

Grass is alive with an abundant supply of vitamins and minerals. Once cut and dried, you have hay; hay is dead grass. Its nutrient content depends on how well and how long it's been stored. Minerals such as calcium and phosphorus will stick around, but vitamins are very fragile and do not survive for long. Therefore, hay-only diets require supplementation of lost vitamins.

Most comprehensive products contain a mixture of vitamins and minerals. If your horse's diet contains more than 8 lbs of alfalfa, which is calcium rich, choose a supplement that is designed for alfalfa-based diets; it will be lower in calcium than general supplements.

I recommend avoiding supplements that have high levels of iron. Forage is already high in iron, giving most horses all that they need. Too much iron may increase insulin resistance, as well as depress immune function. See Chapter 5 — Fundamentals of Minerals for details on iron.

To improve palatability, many supplement manufacturers add molasses. This should be avoided if you are trying to reduce insulin resistance and body fat.

There are so many supplements from which to choose and often times, you'll need to supplement the supplement, especially when it comes to vitamin E and omega-3 fatty acids. Magnesium is also undersupplied by most products. So let me describe these three nutrients in more detail as they relate to weight management.

Magnesium

Most horses do not get enough of this mineral. Magnesium helps lower circulating insulin levels, which allows your horse to burn fat, rather than store it. This is discussed further in Chapter 13 — Metabolic and Endocrine Disorders. I recommend that you add enough magnesium to provide 5,000 mg per 250 lbs of body weight. If possible, have your hay analyzed first to see how much your horse is getting and then supplement the difference. Make sure the calcium level exceeds magnesium's.

Vitamin E

This antioxidant is generally undersupplied and horses do well with 1 IU per pound of body weight at maintenance; more if exercised. Chapter 6 — Fundamentals of Vitamins offers more detail. When supplementing vitamin E, be sure to evaluate the selenium content of the *total* diet. Vitamin E and selenium work together; however, don't make the mistake of choosing a vitamin E supplement that has added selenium, if your horse is already getting sufficient selenium from other sources. Chapter 5 — Fundamentals of Minerals discusses this further.

Omega-3 fatty acids

These unsaturated fatty acids are not only necessary for proper immune function, joint health, and hoof and hair condition, but they also regulate blood insulin levels, making them especially beneficial for an overweight horse. Flaxseed meal is your best choice. Yes, it's high in fat and therefore high in calories, but in small quantities it provides unparalleled support for your horse's health. See Chapter 3 — Fundamentals of Fats for more information.

EXERCISE

Calorie reduction, monitoring insulin resistance, and removing starch and sugar are all excellent means of helping your horse reach his weight-loss goals. But don't forget exercise. Exercise on a daily basis will help your horse overcome obesity for three reasons. The most obvious rationale behind increased activity is to burn more calories. But it also builds muscle mass. Since muscle is more metabolically active than fat, the more muscle your horse has, the more calories he'll expend. The third benefit of increased activity is reduced insulin resistance, leading to reduced fat storage.

If your horse has not moved much in months, give him a few minutes each day of activity. Use your judgment — advance him slowly from one level to the next.

If he's out in the paddock while you're at work, encourage him to move by placing hay in several places. If he's young enough to still have some spunk in him, he may like a toy or a ball. Your horse is naturally curious and will enjoy distractions and investigating new things.

THYROID HORMONE REPLACEMENT

Since we're discussing ways to help your horse lose weight, it's important to note that many veterinarians will prescribe a synthetic hormone supplement known as levothyroxine sodium, or more commonly referred to as Thyro-L (Vet-A-Mix). This approach is most appropriately used when a horse is consistently suffering from bouts of laminitis due to obesity and therefore cannot be exercised. However, long term usage of this hormone beyond 6 months is inappropriate and the horse should be gradually weaned off of it to allow for resumed thyroid gland function. I discuss the thyroid gland further in Chapter 13 — Metabolic and Endocrine Disorders.

The Hard Keeper

There is so much discussion these days about the overweight horse and health problems that arise from too much weight, the owner of an underweight horse almost feels fortunate! But any time a horse cannot maintain a healthy weight, there is reason for concern.

Horses vary in their ability to burn calories. This is referred to as their metabolic rate and it is influenced by genetics and body composition. We all know that Thoroughbreds have a genetic tendency to be on the lean side. And a highly muscular horse will have a faster metabolic rate than one who is out of shape.

But what about the true hard keeper who cannot seem to gain weight? Throwing more feed at him is not always the correct approach. You have to rule out a few things first.

CONDITIONS THAT CAUSE WEIGHT LOSS

Medical problems

If your horse has been healthy up until now and is suddenly starting to lose weight, he may be suffering from a serious medical disorder. Have your vet do a thorough examination, including blood work, to rule out disease. Here are a few things to ask your vet to do:

- **Blood proteins.** Run a serum biochemical analysis to assess hypoalbuminemia (low albumin levels) and globulin levels. The albumin/globulin ratio may be decreased when inflammation is present. It can also indicate internal abscesses, liver disease, kidney disease, and intestinal granulomatous bowel disease.

- **Anemia.** Calculate erythrocyte indices to look for evidence of anemia. Keep in mind that anemia can be caused by a deficiency in B vitamins (e.g., folic acid, B_{12}, and B_6); it is not caused only by an iron deficiency (which is rare).

- **Inflammation.** Measure fibrinogen levels to evaluate inflammation.

- **Hyperlipemia.** Measure serum triglycerides. High levels (known as hyperlipemia), especially in miniature horses, ponies, and donkeys, can indicate liver dysfunction. But this can also occur in horses enduring severe physical stress.

- **Malnutrition.** Assess unconjugated bilirubin levels. They will be elevated in a horse that is not eating or is malnourished. Also measure serum urea nitrogen; low levels indicate prolonged protein malnutrition.

- **Liver disease.** Evaluate the enzyme GGT (gamma-glutamyltransferase). It will be elevated during liver disease.

- **Cushing's disease.** Test for equine Cushing's disease, which can lead to liver failure, causing the horse to use more calories, and hence, lose weight (refer to Chapter 13 — Metabolic and Endocrine Disorders).

- **Ulcers.** A fecal blood test can be done first before considering an endoscopy. Ulcers are discussed at length in Chapter 14 — Digestive Problems.

- **Worm infestation.** Test a manure sample to evaluate the fecal egg count. Some veterinarians will perform an enzyme-linked immunosorbent assay (ELISA) to rule out tapeworms; however, most often your vet will simply treat your horse with praziquantel, a dewormer designed for tapeworms.

- **Sand.** Evaluate the hindgut for sand accumulation. Over time, this can interfere with forage digestion.

Dental health

The most common reason for underweight is poor teeth. Neglected teeth develop sharp, jagged points that dig into your horse's soft mouth tissues, making eating a painful experience. Your horse's teeth should be floated (points filed) at least once each year; some horses need their teeth floated every 6 months.

Older horses experience normal wear that creates dull surfaces, making it difficult to chew hay. Sometimes they lose teeth, necessitating a softer diet. I address this problem and ways to feed older horses in Chapter 19 — Growth and Growing Old.

Poor chewing, whether due to improper maintenance, loss of teeth, or hereditary deformities (such as parrot mouth), can often result in swallowing large amounts of unchewed feed which cannot be adequately digested. Undigested feed ends up in the manure and your horse is deprived of calories. So, if you notice that your horse is reluctant to eat, drops his feed, yawns as he eats, or spits out clumps of partially-chewed hay, your first phone call should be to an equine dentist or qualified veterinarian.

Stress

The next thing to look at is your horse's stress level. Many situations can affect a horse, but some of the major ones include excessive travel, moving to a new environment, loss of a buddy, addition of a new horse to the herd, illness, and temperature extremes. Stall confinement can lead to boredom, depression, and insecurity, all contributing to bad habits, pacing, and loss of appetite. You know your horse best, so if you see changes in his behavior that coincide with weight loss, his stress level needs to be evaluated. The effect of stress is discussed in depth in Chapter 17 — Stress and Behavior.

Pecking order

When a new horse is added to the herd, not only can it be stressful, it can actually interfere with how much a horse is allowed to eat. The hierarchy can change, leading to bullying, both of the new horse, and even those that has been around for a while. Access to hay may be challenged causing your horse to be deprived of his fair share. Spend some time studying how your horse interacts with others during feeding. The solution may be as simple as adding more piles of hay, or tying your horses during meals to protect the underdog in the group.

HELPING YOUR HORSE GAIN WEIGHT

Now that you've ruled out or dealt with underlying medical disease, ulcers, worm infestation, problems with his teeth, and stressful situations, you can concentrate of improving his digestive function and overall diet.

Attend to hindgut microbial population

Your horse's hindgut (cecum and large intestine) contains billions of beneficial bacteria that produce enzymes for digesting fiber found in forage (hay, grass, and other high-fiber feeds). If their numbers get disrupted, your horse will not be able to derive enough calories to maintain a normal weight.

There's an old saying, "no hoof, no horse." I want to add another one: "no hindgut microbes, no horse!" You can feed the best diet in the world, but if these little guys are not healthy, your horse will not be able to hold his weight. And they're more delicate that you think; they can be destroyed by illness, stress, over-consumption of cereal grains, ulcers, forage restriction, and antibiotic therapy.

Your horse needs these microbes in order to gain weight. There are a couple of ways you can help.

Prebiotics: One very effective way to improve the health of these microbes is to provide a prebiotic. This is not the same as a probiotic. A prebiotic boosts the health of the bacteria that naturally live in the hindgut. In other words, a prebiotic contains fermentation products that feed these bacteria so they can multiply in number. The result is better forage digestion. Furthermore, these bacteria are also responsible for producing necessary B vitamins, which are needed to obtain calories from other nutrients in his diet.

Probiotics: A probiotic refers to a product that contains live microbes, including bacteria and yeast (*Saccharomyces cerevisiae*), thereby adding to the general microbial population in the hindgut. Yeast is especially helpful in improving digestion efficiency of hay with a high NDF level (see Chapter 1 — Ground Rules for Feeding a Horse for a description of NDF and other indicators). If your horse has been taking antibiotics or has experienced laminitis, a probiotic is a must.

Understand the importance of B vitamins

B-vitamin deficiencies, even marginal ones, can reduce your horse's desire to eat. So that's the first step in getting him to gain weight — he has to eat.

Once food is inside his small intestine, it must be digested down to small enough pieces to be absorbed into the bloodstream. B vitamins keep the digestive tract in good working order.

Now we're at the final step; the critical moment when your horse's cells make calories. If glucose and fatty acids arrive at the cell's doorstep and there are no B vitamins to greet them, your horse is out of luck.

Malnutrition at the cellular level (even though he's getting enough to eat) will result in weight loss.

So how do you ensure that he's getting enough B vitamins? The first step is to keep his hindgut bacteria in good shape through the use of probiotics or prebiotics. These microbes produce B vitamins. But you may want to add more by giving him a B complex supplement. Take a look at Chapter 6 — Fundamentals of Vitamins for more information.

Give him more calories

There are many ways to add calories to your horse's diet. You could simply feed him more of what he normally eats or you could change his feed to one that will help him gain weight with less bulk. It's important not to overload your horse's stomach capacity; it can only hold so much at a time. That's why you should weigh his feed and limit his meal size to no more than 4 lbs (for an 1100 lb horse).

Adding fat: Commercial feeds vary in their fat content. Choose one that contains at least 8% fat. Adding more fat, rather than carbohydrates, is a good choice because it takes less bulk to get the same amount of increased calories. Fat offers more than double the energy (calories) than starch and sugar and is safer to feed. I'll talk more about carbs in a moment, but first I'd like to offer you ways to increase the fat level in your horse's diet.

You have several options. Flaxseed meal is my favorite because it is not only high in fat, but it is high in beneficial fat: omega-3 fatty acids. Omega-3 fatty acids will reduce inflammation, protect your horse's joints and hooves, keep the immune system healthy, and make him shine. Read Chapter 3 — Fundamentals of Fats for guidelines on the best way to use flaxseed meal.

Another good fat source is rice bran. Use only a commercial product that has added calcium to balance out its high phosphorus level. And when feeding bran, be consistent. Many folks like to give a warm bran mash, once a week, as a treat or a laxative. This is asking for an episode of colic since the bacteria in the hindgut do not have time to adjust to the new feed. And it doesn't work as a laxative, either — the loose manure you see is because his intestinal lining is irritated.

Oil is another option but avoid adding soybean oil or corn oil to the diet since they are too high in omega-6 fatty acids, which increase inflammation. If your horse has aging joints, these oils can increase his pain. Rice bran or canola oils are much more balanced. Add oil gradually since many horses do not like the texture. Start with only 1 tablespoon per meal. You can slowly build up to as much as 1 cup per 500 lbs of body weight. Flaxseed oil is also fine, but less needs to be fed (no more than 1/3 cup per 500 lbs) so combine it with another oil to get enough calories. And be patient — it takes four to six weeks for a horse's system to adjust to and begin to benefit from extra fat.

Weight-gaining supplements may be a good choice. They usually contain a variety of ingredients including soybean meal (which also boosts protein quality), flaxseed meal, rice bran, and alfalfa. Some contain animal fat, which I don't recommend.

Carbohydrates — high starch vs low starch: Excessive carbohydrates, mainly from cereal grains (oats, corn, barley), can destroy the bacteria population in the hindgut. That being said, you can still give your horse some starch, but I like to limit it to no more than 2 lbs at a time. You could feed rolled or crimped oats plus a supplement to add extra vitamins and minerals. Or you can choose from one of the many commercial feeds; even sweet feeds are acceptable in small amounts.

But you should not feed oats or sweet feeds if your horse is suffering from any hormonal imbalance that calls for a low starch/low sugar diet. Many older horses, for example, develop equine Cushing's disease, which makes them insulin resistant. Or your horse may be prone toward laminitis (founder), which calls for careful attention to carbohydrate levels in the diet. Your best choice in this case is to find a feed that is low in starch and sugar and high in fat. There are many from which to choose. Check the ingredients on the label — it should not contain any oats, corn, or barley. Grain by-products are ok, as well as beet pulp, soybean meal, alfalfa meal, and flax. Sometimes senior feeds are a good choice, but they can vary across brands, so check the label or call the manufacturer to find out the percent NSC (non-structural carbohydrates) — it should be less than 15% to ensure your horse's safety.

Feed your horse like a horse

Finally, allow him to graze at all times. Just like the easy keeper described earlier in this chapter, underweight horses also need to have free access to good-quality hay and/or pasture. Have your hay analyzed to make sure it has a high relative feed value (RFV) — at least a score of 100, but preferably higher, as well as a neutral detergent fiber (NDF) level of no more than 55 (see Chapter 1 — Ground Rules for Feeding a Horse for a description of this and other indicators). These measurements will tell you if your hay is providing enough calories to make a difference in his weight.

I recommend serving 20-30% of his hay ration as alfalfa. Because it is a legume, its protein content will complement the protein in grass hay, giving him the building blocks he needs to build body tissues. It is also higher in calories (but not in sugar and starch), contains beneficial minerals, and your horse loves the taste. So, allow him to enjoy this nutritious hay. If you cannot get alfalfa hay, there are always cubes or pellets; moisten them before feeding.

Keep in mind that hay is not as nutritious as fresh grass, so extra vitamin E, along with a comprehensive vitamin/mineral supplement, is always important to add unless he is getting enough of a fortified commercial feed.

SUMMARY OF MANAGING THE UNDERWEIGHT HORSE

Here are the key points to remember:

- **Restore the bacterial flora in the hindgut to normal levels.** Either feed a prebiotic (fermentation products) or a probiotic (where numbers have been significantly reduced, as with antibiotic usage).

- **Feed more fat instead of grain (starch).** Fat has more than twice as many calories per gram as carbohydrates. Some beneficial fat sources include:

  - flaxseed meal (stabilized against rancidity, with added calcium)
  - rice bran (stabilized against rancidity, with added calcium)
  - weight gain supplements
  - oils such as canola oil, rice bran oil, and flaxseed oil. Avoid soybean oil because it can increase inflammation. Coconut oil is too high in saturated fat, so avoid this one, as well. Corn oil is in the middle — not as bad as soybean oil, but not as good as canola oil. Your goal is to avoid overfeeding omega-6 fatty acids; your horse needs some but too much increases inflammation. A complete discussion of these oils is found in Chapter 3 — Fundamentals of Fats.

- **Don't overfeed!** A horse's stomach is relatively small. Limit meal size of concentrates (grains, grain-based commercial rations) to no more than 4 lbs for an 1100 lb horse. Weigh your feed; a scoop measures volume, not weight. Offer more meals, rather than larger ones.

- **Provide nutritious snacks.** These include carrots and apples (if your horse can tolerate the sugar), or alfalfa cubes. Chapter 10 — Fundamentals of Treats offers other fruit ideas that your horse will enjoy.

The Severely Underweight Rescue Horse

If you have recently adopted a rescue horse, let me first commend you for your actions. Saving a horse that is in desperate need of care and nursing him back to health can be one of the most gratifying experiences a horse owner can have. But you must be committed to giving him a lot of time and attention. He'll need to be moved in and out of pasture throughout the day, fed hay nearly every couple of hours and frequent meals until he gets to where he can hold his own.

If your horse is very thin due to starvation, you will want to proceed slowly and with caution, giving his body a chance to adjust to change with each step. Some horses are in such poor condition they are unable to eat. In this extreme situation, your veterinarian will use a stomach tube to feed the horse. This is a short term procedure with the goal of getting your horse interested in eating again.

Retired race horses almost invariably have ulcers. Your veterinarian may prescribe an ulcer medication, but this can only be used for a month or so. The three main components of healing an ulcer are: chewing on hay or pasture at all times, plenty of water, and reduction in stress. Please review Chapter 14 — Digestive Problems to go over ways to treat and prevent an ulcer; this will give you more specific ideas.

Your ultimate goal is to allow your rescued horse to graze freely, as much as he wants, on hay and/or pasture. You'll want his forage to include a legume such as clover or alfalfa. But take your time — you can't just put him out on pasture right away if he's been severely deprived. I know you want to, but his digestive tract isn't ready just yet. The microbial population in his hindgut is not adequate for fiber digestion; too much, too soon and he may colic or founder. Here is my recommendation for an 1100 lb horse (his normal weight):

- You should give him a probiotic, at a double dose, every day for approximately one month; then reduce the dosage to a maintenance level.

- Start with 1 lb of grass hay every two hours, or pasture grazing for 30 minutes with an hour break in between. At night, leave him with 4 lbs of hay, plenty of water, and a salt block.

- After 3 days, increase the amount of hay to 2 lbs per every two hours and give him 8 lbs of hay at night.

- By the end of two weeks, he should be able to have hay available free choice or graze on pasture 24/7. Be sure he has enough at night to last him throughout the night. There should be some hay left over in the morning.

- Starting at week three, add alfalfa to his hay ration. Start with 1 lb per day for 3 days, and add one more pound every three days, until you reach a total of 8 to 10 lbs per day. If you're not able to obtain alfalfa hay, get hay cubes. Break them into small pieces and let them soak for a few minutes. Feed them as a snack throughout the day.

- Also starting at week three, you'll want to begin feeding him 6 small meals each day. A good recipe for each meal that weighs approximately 1 lb:

  - 2 cups of crimped, rolled, or steamed oats
  - 1/4 cup of flaxseed meal (get a commercial product instead of grinding your own)
  - 1/2 cup stabilized rice bran (also a commercial product that adds calcium)
  - 1 cup of alfalfa pellets (if he is not getting fed alfalfa hay or cubes)

- 1 cup of shredded beet pulp (soaked for 30 minutes prior to feeding)
- 1/2 cup soybean meal
- Continue feeding the probiotic — use double the recommended amount and spread it out over 6 feedings. A powdered version can be used now since you have a meal to which it can be added.
- Vitamin E — pick up 200 IU capsules from your local pharmacy and give him one capsule per meal to create a total dosage of 1 to 1.5 IU per pound of body weight per day.
- A vitamin/mineral supplement designed for horses that is high in antioxidants, contains B vitamins, and has a full complement of minerals.

Or to make things easier than assembling this whole list, you can purchase a commercial feed that contains 14-16% protein, at least 18% fiber, and at least 8% fat. Give him 4 cups each meal (weighs approximately 1 lb). You'll still need to add the flaxseed meal, probiotic, and vitamin E.

- After two weeks, reduce his feedings to 3 to 4 meals per day, still feeding the same total amount (approximately 6 lbs) of feed, making sure he has hay and/or pasture in between meals and throughout the night.

- Two weeks later, start reducing the number of meals to 2 to 3 each day. You can increase his total feed concentrate consumption to 8 to 12 lbs per day, as long as each meal does not weigh more than 4 lbs.

Other things to consider:

- If you do not have healthy pasture and rely mostly on hay, give him 1 to 2 lbs of carrots each day; feed them throughout the day, not all at one time.

- If he's older than 16, give him 3-5 mg of vitamin C per lb of body weight each day. Past 20 years old, increase it to 10 mg per lb of body weight. He'll need vitamin C supplementation for the rest of his life. See Chapter 19 — Growth and Growing Old for more details.

- Provide a plain, white salt block. He needs to consume 1 ounce of salt each day, so if he is not doing this, add salt to his meals. Choose table salt that you buy in the grocery store. If his supplements or feed contain iodine, choose the non-iodized version of salt. One ounce is equal to 6 teaspoons or 2 tablespoons, so divide it between meals.

- Water should always be available. If it's winter, use heated water buckets. He should be drinking 8 to 12 gallons of water each day.

Endnotes

[1] Henneke, D.R., et. al., 1983. *Equine Veterinary Journal, 15* (4): 371-372.

CHAPTER 13 —
METABOLIC AND ENDOCRINE DISORDERS

The early morning sun was generous with its warmth.
All the sounds dear to a horseman were around me —
the snorts of the horses, the swish of their tails,
the tinkle of irons as we flung the saddles over their backs —
little sounds of no importance, but they stay in the
unconscious library of memory.
~ Wynford Vaughan-Thomas

Nutrients and hormones interact in a variety of ways, but when they get out of sync, diseases can develop that reduce your horse's ability to enjoy life and work alongside you; they may even lessen his lifespan. Serious problems can sometimes develop without warning, leaving very few options. But others can creep up slowly, giving you opportunity to make changes.

You see your horse more often than anyone else does, making you the best judge of what's normal. Subtle changes in his appearance and behavior give you clues, telling you to check into them further. If you suspect a problem, have your vet look at him and take blood tests. In fact, a yearly blood panel as a matter of course is an excellent way to get a snapshot of how your horse is doing on the inside. It gives you time to act.

This chapter covers several common disorders. I want to help you understand not only what is going on with your horse, but why it is problem and what you can do about it. Let's begin by talking about one the most common ailments seen in the domesticated horse — insulin resistance.

Insulin Resistance (Equine Metabolic Syndrome)

You're likely reading this section because your equine friend is an easy keeper or he may have suffered from laminitis. You're concerned because he has fat deposits along his neck, rump, and shoulders, and a crease going down his spine. Someone may have told you to read this chapter because it looks like your horse has insulin resistance. You've come to right place.

Perhaps your horse has equine Cushing's disease (more accurately called pituitary pars intermedia dysfunction — PPID) and isn't fat at all. Or he has elevated fat levels in his blood (known as hyperlipemia). Insulin resistance plays a role in these disorders, as well. Same problem, different reason. These conditions will be discussed later, but first, I want to give you a clear idea of what, exactly, insulin resistance is. To do that, let's first talk about what it is not…

Insulin resistance (IR), also known as metabolic syndrome, is sometimes, though incorrectly, called diabetes. It's similar to Type II diabetes in humans, with elevated blood glucose and insulin levels, but doesn't involve the presence of glucose in the urine, as is found in people suffering from this disease. Another form of diabetes in humans, Type I, is characterized by no insulin production, and has been recently documented in horses. It necessitates insulin injections and significantly decreases the lifespan of the horse. But this disease is not related to equine metabolic syndrome.

People can suffer from metabolic syndrome, which is often a precursor to Type II diabetes. They develop abdominal fat deposits and high blood pressure (which horses do not). These folks are generally overweight because excess fat causes cells to become insulin resistant. They also tend to sit on the couch a lot, which further exacerbates the problem, because lack of exercise promotes insulin resistance. Metabolic syndrome in horses is the same as in humans; it just doesn't lead to Type II diabetes.

What about your horse? Does he have excess fat along the crest of his neck? Does he hang out all day watching the scenery, visiting with friends, and taking naps? How 'bout genetics — that's also a factor. Is your horse a large draft breed, a Morgan, an Arabian, Paso Fino, Quarter Horse, or a warmblood? Do you have a pony or a mini, or perhaps a donkey or mule? These breeds show a genetic tendency toward IR, though the disorder can affect any equine. But if you know your horse is genetically predisposed toward developing IR, you can take steps to prevent it from becoming a serious problem. More on that later.

CRASH COURSE ON INSULIN

To begin discussing insulin resistance, let me give you a 5-minute lesson on insulin…

Insulin is a hormone that is secreted (released into the bloodstream) by the pancreas whenever blood sugar levels begin to rise. Blood sugar, known as glucose, is most often a product of non-structural carbohydrate (sugars and starch) digestion in the small intestine (foregut). When your horse eats something starchy, such as oats, the enzymes in the small intestine break down this large starch molecule into small glucose units. Glucose leaves the small intestine and enters the bloodstream. Its goal is to reach the tissues, where it can be metabolized (burned) for energy inside each and every cell.

But glucose needs assistance to get inside cells. It cannot simply "walk" inside the cell. There's a "door," if you will, on the outside of the cell that needs to be opened in order for glucose to enter. And glucose cannot open this door. It needs a "doorman." *Insulin is the doorman that opens the door and lets glucose enter the cell.*

But what if there is no door? This can happen when your horse gets too fat or sedentary. The cells become "door-deficient," leaving glucose out in the cold. Hundreds, thousands, of glucose molecules remain in the blood along with their doorman friends waiting for a door to appear.

And what does the pancreas think about this? Well, it says, "Gee, I just shipped out some insulin (doormen) and it doesn't seem to be able to do its job and get glucose into the cells. So, [shoulder shrug], I guess I'll ship out some more!"

Now think about this… insulin levels keep escalating because the pancreas thinks it needs to send out more so glucose can enter the cells. But the cells are not responding to it — they can't. There aren't enough doors. This situation is called insulin resistance; the cells are resistant to insulin. And the "doors" are called insulin receptors. Too few insulin receptors force blood levels of glucose and insulin to go higher and higher.

Remember, I didn't say there weren't *any* insulin receptors, just too few. So eventually, glucose will enter the cells, but it takes a while, and eventually blood glucose levels will return to normal. This situation is referred to as *compensated* insulin resistance. However, if the pancreatic beta cells (cells that produce insulin) work too hard, for too long, they can fail, and blood glucose levels will not return to normal. This is referred to as *uncompensated* insulin resistance. This condition is not as common but can be indicative of more serious problems.

Regional fat deposits

Elevated insulin causes your horse's body to store more fat, and excess fat causes a reduction in insulin receptors (doors), leading to still more insulin; it's a vicious cycle. This is why your horse develops fat along various parts of his body. And the more fat he produces, the higher his insulin levels become because his cells have become resistant to insulin. He'll tend to get fat in specific places: typically along the neck, tailhead, and the spine. This regional adiposity is the key to visually identifying insulin resistance; your horse may not be overweight in general but still be insulin resistant. Even underweight horses with a high metabolic rate can be insulin resistant and will eventually develop these fat deposits.

More than just fat storage

Elevated insulin does more than lead to fat deposits — it causes laminitis (founder). The exact mechanism of this action has not been determined but it may be due to glucose deprivation in hoof cells known as keratinocytes, leading to weakened laminae attachment. And the fat itself is not benign; it produces substances called cytokines, which promote inflammation throughout your horse's body, including his feet. Therefore, the goal is to maintain normal insulin levels (less than 20 microunits per milliliter) to prevent your horse from developing laminitis. Ways to do this are discussed later in this section as well as in Chapter 11 — Laminitis.

A note about iron

In human-based studies, it has been shown that insulin resistance is enhanced when there is too much iron in the diet. This may also be the case for horses. But until the research catches up, I recommend avoiding feeds and supplements that contain iron. Your horse certainly needs this mineral, but forage (pasture and hay) supplies plenty. There really isn't a need for additional iron unless your horse is not getting enough forage or is suffering from a bleeding ulcer. Please read the section on iron in Chapter 5 — Fundamentals of Minerals for more discussion on this important topic.

DIAGNOSING INSULIN RESISTANCE

The best and most common way to diagnose insulin resistance is by measuring resting blood insulin levels. To perform this test properly, it is important that your horse not be allowed to graze on fresh pasture or eat any concentrates for at least 24 hours prior to the test. However, horses should be allowed to graze on hay during the testing. Feed deprivation is stressful for horses and stress will influence the test results by raising insulin levels.

Some horses get stressed when they see the vet's truck roll up. This, too, can create a false positive result. Stress from pain, as well, causes spikes in blood insulin. If your horse is suffering from laminitis, for example, it is best to wait until he heals before testing for insulin resistance.

Ideally, your veterinarian should perform tests that help distinguish between compensated and uncompensated insulin resistance. Remember, with compensated insulin resistance, the pancreas is functioning normally — *insulin will be elevated* and blood glucose levels will be normal or near normal. Compensated insulin resistance puts your horse at risk for laminitis.

With uncompensated insulin resistance, the pancreas is worn out from producing so much insulin. This leads to *decreased insulin output* and elevated blood glucose (hyperglycemia). Uncompensated IR is not as common but can accompany advanced stages of equine Cushing's disease, making an accurate diagnosis important for developing treatment options.

The following indicators are used to make this differentiation:

- **Reciprocal of the square root of insulin (RISQI).** It is calculated by the equation 1/square root of insulin. This value measures the resting serum insulin concentration and insulin sensitivity. *The lower the RISQI value, the higher the insulin level.* A low RISQI value, therefore, indicates compensated insulin resistance (functioning pancreas).

- **Glucose to insulin ratio (G:I).** Here, glucose (measured in mg/dL — milligrams per deciliter) is divided by insulin (measured in uIU/ml — microunits per milliliter). If the insulin concentration is reported in pmol/L (picomoles per liter), it can be converted to uIU/ml by dividing by 7.1. *The higher the insulin level, the lower the measurement.* A G:I ratio below 4.5 indicates compensated insulin resistance and your horse's risk of laminitis is high.

- **Modified insulin-to-glucose ratio (MIRG).** Its formula is complicated[1] but fortunately the lab or your vet does it for you. MIRG measures blood concentrations of both glucose and insulin, thereby giving a good indication of how well the pancreas is functioning. Notice that the ratio is reversed from the G:I ratio. This ratio has insulin in the numerator (the top number of the fraction) so *the higher the insulin level, the higher the MIRG value.* A high MIRG results from high insulin levels, indicating compensated insulin resistance.

However, if the level is low, it means that insulin is low and glucose is high (an indication of a failing pancreas) which described uncompensated insulin resistance.

I should note that many veterinarians will not test blood glucose levels because it is not an accurate assessment of your horse's status. A normal blood glucose level can co-exist with an elevated insulin level simply because the glucose has finally caught up with increased insulin output and entered the cells. Also, there are challenges in getting the sample to the lab in time to be centrifuged; delays can create lower glucose results.

If your horse is hospitalized, another test called the combined glucose-insulin test (GGIT) may be used. Its reliability in diagnosing insulin resistance is questionable due to the stress caused by the horse being away from home but your veterinarian may decide to try it on a calm horse. The GGIT requires taking your horse off-site because it is cumbersome to perform. A glucose solution is administered intravenously, followed by taking blood samples every five to 15 minutes over a period of 2 1/2 hours.

TREATING INSULIN RESISTANCE

Once a horse is diagnosed with insulin resistance, he will have this tendency for the rest of his life. But the good news is, when properly managed, the symptoms can disappear. For example, if your horse has a cresty neck and a crease going down his spine, a change in his diet can cause those fatty deposits to recede. And once they're gone, his risk of developing laminitis is significantly reduced — even removed. But keeping tabs on his diet and exercise is a lifelong commitment. If you become lax regarding your horse's care, he will return to an insulin resistant state.

You'll notice that I talk about laminitis in this chapter, but I also have a chapter devoted entirely to laminitis. That's because laminitis can have many causes, insulin resistance being one of them. So there is some repetition between this chapter and Chapter 11 — Laminitis. However, this chapter offers more detail on insulin resistance.

Non-structural carbohydrates (NSC)

Your goal is to reduce insulin output from the pancreas. Since insulin is released when glucose is elevated, starchy and sugary feeds should be avoided. Some feeds are higher in starch and sugar than others and therefore affect blood glucose levels differently.

The glycemic index of a feed has been used a great deal in human nutrition and to some extent in equine nutrition, but it has been replaced with more accurate measurements. However, it is still interesting to see how some feeds affect blood glucose more than others. Table 1-2 found in Chapter 1 — Ground Rules for Feeding a Horse compares the glycemic index values of common horse feeds.

Non-structural carbohydrates (NSC) is more commonly used among equine nutritionists but even this measurement is not as accurate as the following indicators:

- Water soluble carbohydrates (WSC)
- Ethanol soluble carbohydrates (ESC)
- Starch

NSC includes WSC and starch. A full discussion of these measurements is found in Chapters 1 — Ground Rules for Feeding a Horse and 2 — Fundamentals of Carbohydrates. But to give you a general idea, WSC comprises sugar and fructan, ESC is mainly sugar, and starch is a large chain of sugar molecules linked together. Blood glucose levels, and hence, insulin levels, tend to rise when feeds high in ESC and starch are fed. Fructan, a component of WSC, does not cause insulin to increase, but can lead to laminitis because of its effect on the hindgut bacteria. This is discussed in Chapter 11 — Laminitis.

It is best to have your hay analyzed so you know how much sugar and starch your horse is eating. To calculate NSC, add together the starch and WSC percentages. Basically, you're looking for forage that has an NSC value (on a dry matter basis) less than 12%. If your hay is higher than this, soaking it for 30 to 60 minutes (the colder the water, the more soaking time is necessary) will remove some of the sugar (remember to discard the water).

Let's take a look at how common feeds compare. You'll notice in Table 13-1 that the sugar and starch amounts do not add up to NSC. That's because NSC includes fructan, which is not shown in this table. Fructan is an issue for laminitis, but not insulin resistance.

Cereal grains, such as oats, corn, and barley, are very high in starch. Starch digestion results in glucose, and consequently, elevated insulin. Notice that among the different types of hay, alfalfa has the lowest %NSC (surprise!), making it an excellent choice for the insulin resistant horse. I express my

Table 13-1 Average Sugar, Starch, and Non-Structural Carbohydrate (NSC) Values of Selected Feedstuffs[2]

Feedstuff	% Sugar	% Starch	% NSC
Oat hay	16.0	6.3	22.1
Barley hay	14.9	5.8	20.8
Alfalfa hay	8.9	2.5	11.5
Bermuda hay	7.5	6.1	13.6
Cool-season grass hay (timothy, orchardgrass, brome)	11.1	2.9	18.8
Alfalfa pellets	7.2	2.3	9.5
Alfalfa cubes	8.3	2.0	10.3
Rice bran	6.2	17.7	24.2
Oats	4.8	44.4	54.1
Corn	3.7	70.3	75.3
Barley	6.0	53.7	61.7
Beet pulp	10.7	1.4	12.3
Wheat bran	8.7	23.0	31.8
Soybean hulls	4.3	1.9	6.3
Wheat middlings	10.1	26.2	38.0
Soybean meal	14.3	2.1	16.4

approval for alfalfa throughout this book, but I realize that some horses appear to be sensitive to it. The reason for this is unknown, but if your horse cannot tolerate alfalfa, it is best to avoid it.

Grain hay, such as oat and barley hay, have relatively high NSC levels at 22.1 and 20.8%, respectively. So they are not appropriate to feed to an insulin resistant horse. Rice and wheat bran, though not as high as a cereal grains, are still too high to feed to a horse in this situation since their NSC levels are 24.2% and 31.8.0%, respectively. Unsweetened beet pulp is an excellent feed with only 12.3% NSC.

Pasture grazing

The WSC and starch content in grasses can vary significantly according to the season, temperature, rainfall, time of day, amount of sunlight, mowing, geographic location, and even the area grazed within the same pasture. I highly recommend reviewing the articles at Safergrass.org: www.safergrass.org. This website offers a wealth of information on every possible situation and type of grass. But I'd like to describe some common circumstances to get you started.

The safest time to graze is during the early morning hours when the night temperatures are mild (above 40° F). Sugar and starch levels increase as the grass is exposed to sunlight. And the levels reach a peak in the late afternoon after a sunny day. The grass uses this fuel for itself during the dark hours and by morning, the levels are at their lowest.

Anything that stresses your grass will make it hold on to its sugar and starch. Things like mowing the grass too short, inadequate rainfall, cold weather, and over-grazing will increase NSC levels. Don't be fooled by the brown grass you see in the late fall. It may be dead at the top, but spread it apart and you'll likely see some green at the base, which is high in sugar and starch. If it hasn't rained in a while, your grass will look dried out; but be careful — *dry grass can actually have higher NSC levels than long, lush-looking grass.*

If your horse has suffered from laminitis resulting from insulin resistance, he may have to be completely removed from pasture turnout. A grazing muzzle can be considered, but only if your horse is not bothered by it. *Stress can trigger laminitis.*

Return to pasture grazing: If your horse has a history of laminitis, but the insulin resistance issue has been resolved through weight loss, diet, and exercise, you can consider pasture grazing. Start out small — 30 minutes the first day, 1 hour the next, and then build up to 1-2 hours, twice a day. I hesitate a bit while saying this because every horse is different. But I have had many clients whose horses have been laminitis-free for years and have allowed their horses to graze without consequence. Only you and your veterinarian can make the best choice.

Exercise

Since excess body fat is the main cause of insulin resistance, reducing weight is the best way to avoid laminitis. A sedentary horse doesn't burn very many calories so getting him to move a little more each day (assuming he's not in pain) will slowly but surely take the pounds off.

An added benefit of exercise is an increase in insulin receptors within cell membranes, allowing for improved glucose entry. This reduces the need for more insulin and less insulin results in less fat storage. So, even if your horse does not lose weight at first, the exercise itself will improve insulin sensitivity.

Keep the hay!

If your horse is overweight, avoid the temptation to put him on a diet. You can remove concentrates, but restricting hay is the worst thing you can do. As I've mentioned several times before, hay should be provided free choice. I realize that this is not always practical, especially in boarding settings; however, do whatever you can improve your horse's situation. The only way for you to know that he's getting enough hay at night, for example, is for there to be some left over in the morning. Running out of hay is stressful and one of your main objectives in managing insulin resistance is to reduce stress. Stress causes the secretion of the stress hormone cortisol, which increases insulin resistance. I've seen many horses founder (laminitis) due to the stress of going without anything to graze on for several hours.

The tension of being deprived of hay will not only increase laminitis risk or trigger a relapse, but will make your horse get fatter, not thinner. This complex issue is discussed throughout this book, but predominantly in two main chapters: Chapter 12 — Weight Management and Chapter 17 — Stress and Behavior. Trust me… I see this time and time again. Feed a horse the way he was meant to be fed, and he will eat only what he needs and lose weight.

Magnesium/chromium supplementation

Not all insulin resistant horses are overweight but they all have fat deposits that need to be reduced. Magnesium and chromium will help that cresty neck diminish by reducing circulating insulin levels. This is good to know since many horses do not consume enough magnesium. Marginal deficiencies can be easily corrected by adding some to the diet. But before you do, evaluate your horse's overall diet.

Calcium to magnesium ratio: Too much magnesium, in relation to calcium, can result in diarrhea, urinary tract stones, and changes to the bone structure. So before supplementing magnesium, have your hay analyzed for its calcium and magnesium content. Most hay, however, does not have enough magnesium — the ideal ratio being 2:1 calcium to magnesium. With insulin resistant cases, I like to get closer to a 1:1 ratio. But magnesium content should not exceed calcium levels.

Let's take a look at a sample hay mixture and evaluate its calcium and magnesium content. Table 13-2 shows an example of 15 lbs of the average cool-season grass and 5 lbs of a legume hay[3].

Table 13-2 Calcium and Magnesium Content of Sample Grass/Legume Hay Diet		
	Calcium content (grams)	Magnesium content (grams)
Grass hay: 15 pounds 0.47% Ca and 0.18% Mg	32	12
Legume hay: 5 pounds 1.22% Ca and 0.27% Mg	28	6
Totals	60	18

This hypothetical hay mixture has more than three times the amount of calcium than of magnesium — the calcium to magnesium ratio is 3.3:1 (60 divided by 18). We'd like to have 30 grams of magnesium to create a 2:1 ratio. To do this, you would need to supplement 12 grams (that's 12,000 mg) of magnesium per day. And this is a minimum level since insulin resistance is best treated with enough magnesium to bring the total closer to the calcium level. In general, magnesium should be provided at a rate of 5 grams per 250 lbs of body weight as long as it doesn't exceed calcium levels.

Chromium is involved in carbohydrate and fat metabolism. It works with insulin to increase the amount of glucose that gets into the cells, thereby reducing the need for extra insulin. Supplementation in horses, however, has not been conclusive. It is likely that that grasses have enough chromium to meet most horses' needs. However, poor chromium uptake from alkaline soils can lead to reduced grass levels. And since the maximum tolerable level is very high (300 ppm), it is worthwhile considering chromium supplementation for insulin resistant horses. I recommend adding 1.25 grams per 250 lbs of body weight.

Omega-3 fatty acids

No doubt you've noticed me mention omega-3 fatty acids again and again throughout this book. I talk about how they keep your horse healthy inside and out and I encourage you to look at Chapter 3 — Fundamentals of Fats for details. But what I want to let you know in this chapter is that these gems regulate insulin levels. You'll need to add flaxseed meal or flaxseed oil to provide enough, and I can understand your concern about that because these sources are high in fat (oil is 100% fat) and fat is very high in calories. But you can give your horse a modified dosage. Consider giving him 1/4 cup of meal or 1 tablespoon oil per 400 lbs of body weight.

Joint supplements containing glucosamine

Glucosamine is a common ingredient in most joint preparations and many horse owners are reluctant to give it to their insulin resistant horse that has joint pain. This is a valid concern. Insulin resistant people have experienced adverse effects when given high dosages of glucosamine. However, glucosamine is not digested down to glucose, so it should not cause a rise in insulin. So what causes the glucose and hence, insulin to rise? Evidently, glucosamine confuses the cells into thinking that *they have enough* glucose. So, glucose from other sources cannot enter the cells. The result is increased blood glucose, not from glucosamine, but from the diet in general, leading to elevated insulin.

That's what happens in people; we really do not know if the same thing happens in horses. So, use your judgment. If your insulin resistant horse has been taking glucosamine without any problem, continue using it. But if your horse is battling laminitis or equine Cushing's disease, consider getting a joint supplement that does not contain glucosamine. Other joint nutraceuticals are discussed in Chapter 15 — Joints, Hair, Hooves, and Skin.

Medications

Thyro-L: Levothyroxine sodium, commonly sold as Thyro-L (Vet-A-Mix), is a thyroid medication that is often prescribed for insulin resistant horses when their blood test results reveal low levels of thyroxin (T4). Low T4 levels, or hypothyroidism, would create weight gain and associated insulin resistance. But I need you to understand that *low T4 levels are not necessarily indicative of sustained hypothyroidism.* True hypothyroidism is rare in horses. People often conclude that an overweight horse must have an underactive thyroid gland because humans and dogs become obese with this condition. But in horses, there are many reasons why T4 levels can be below normal. For example, the pain reliever bute (phenylbutazone) is commonly given to horses with laminitis and it lowers circulating thyroxin levels, resulting in a false assumption that your horse's thyroid gland is not functioning properly.

Nevertheless, Thyro-L can help accelerate weight loss for the horse that is not responding to exercise or who cannot exercise due to lameness. This drug increases the metabolic rate, the rate at which your horse burns calories. And when weight loss is accomplished, insulin receptors return in greater numbers, leading to a decrease in insulin resistance. But be cautious about how long you administer this drug. *It is not intended for long term use*, only for a specified period of time to help induce weight loss, usually 3 to 6 months. Long term use can lead to suppressed thyroid function.

Metformin: This drug, known as Glucophage (Bristol-Myers Squibb), is used to control type II diabetes mellitus in humans where diet and exercise have not been effective. It is available for horses to improve insulin sensitivity. It does not appear, however, to be readily absorbed (bioavailable) into the bloodstream. And its safety is questionable; it may have dangerous side effects including tying up, colic, and respiratory failure. Talk to your veterinarian about the risks before using this drug.

Overview of how to feed the insulin resistant horse

Though most insulin resistant horses are overweight, your horse may be of normal weight, except for regional fat deposits. If he is suffering from equine Cushing's disease (which I'll be discussing in the next section) his weight can vary; some horses are overweight and others get very thin. But regardless of the reason for IR or how it affects your horse's body weight, there are feeding guidelines that will help treat and even prevent the disorder:

- **Eliminate any cereal grains.** Grains such as oats, corn, barley, wheat, etc. or any commercial feeds that are made from cereal grains will cause an elevated insulin response.

- **Avoid molasses or sweet treats.** Sweet feeds, cookies made from grain, and candy, as well as carrots, apples, and other fruits are not appropriate for your horse. See Chapter 10 — Fundamentals of Treats for suggestions.

- **Use a low starch feed.** Alfalfa pellets or cubes, unsweetened beet pulp, or a commercial low starch/low sugar product can be fed according to your horse's weight and exercise needs. Fat levels in commercial feeds can vary so choose one that contains 3% or less fat if your horse is overweight; 6% or higher if he is underweight. If he is overweight and sedentary, do not feed a full-sized meal; offer a small amount to serve as a carrier for supplements. If he can use the extra calories, give him two to three meals per day, limiting the meal size to no more than 4 lbs (for an 1100 lb horse).

- **Add fat if he needs extra calories.** Instead of starch, use oil to provide additional calories if your horse needs to gain weight. Rice bran or canola oils are fine. You'll want to avoid oils that are too high in omega-6 fatty acids. Chapter 3 — Fundamentals of Fats will help you make comparisons.

- **Feed hay that has less than 12% NSC.** Feed hay free choice to allow your horse to self-regulate his intake. Hay with a high NDF (neutral detergent fiber) level (55 to 65) is less digestible, and therefore provides fewer calories. If you cannot feed free choice, feed 1.5 to 2.5% of his current body weight, depending on his activity. But if he goes for hours without anything to eat, he will likely stay heavy.

- **Include alfalfa.** Make this between 10% and 20% of the total hay ration depending on your horse's weight condition. Alfalfa has a low %NSC and boosts protein quality.

- **Exercise decreases insulin resistance.** As long as your horse is not in pain, you can slowly exercise him each day to build up his endurance and assist in weight loss.

- **Supplement magnesium.** Be sure it is balanced with the calcium content of your hay. Magnesium should never exceed calcium. Add enough to equal at least half the calcium content in the diet.

- **Omega-3 fatty acids regulate insulin.** Flaxseed meal or oil is your best choice for adding omega-3s. Even a small amount, if your horse is overweight, will provide more benefits than any harm done by the extra calories. If your horse needs additional calories, however, give him 1/2 cup of flaxseed meal or 2 tablespoons of flaxseed oil per 400 lbs of body weight.

- **Fill in nutritional gaps.** If your horse is on a hay-only diet, and you're not feeding full servings of commercially fortified feed, you'll want to give him a comprehensive vitamin/mineral supplement that provides 1 IU of vitamin E per pound of body weight. Avoid supplements that contain more than 500 ppm of iron since too much creates insulin resistance.

Case Study: Insulin Resistance

Dymond, before treatment

Meet Dymond, a 3 year old Belgian filly. She had a weak muscle on her neck, causing it to flop over, or so her owner was told. She was also told that there was nothing she could do about it. No cure, sorry.

Dymond was not overweight. She just had this extremely fat crest along her neck that flopped over. But I just wasn't convinced that it was due to a weak muscle. It looked like a case of insulin resistance to me. I knew she was awfully young but insulin resistance can occur at any age.

Those of you who know me know that I am not discouraged by gloomy predictions; I am challenged by them. Here was a young horse, who from all indications had a wonderful future

and was loved by a large family. Because of a dead end prognosis — *nothing you can do about it* — her owner was resigned to
the fact that her precious gal would be misshapen for life.

I told her owner that I wanted to give her case a try; it might not
work, but then again, it might. And that's what I was shooting
toward. My approach was two-fold. First, just in case there was
a muscular injury (which I didn't believe, but just in case), I
would work on ways to provide a nutrient-rich blood supply that
would feed the area and promote healing. But while doing so, I
would meet my second, and more important goal — to treat
Dymond's situation as an insulin resistance issue.

She wasn't getting much hay, so the first change I made was to
give her all the grass hay she wanted. We had it analyzed and we
were lucky — it had 10.7% NSC, below the 12% cap. And since
she was still growing, I gave her alfalfa (approximately 4 lbs per
day). Her total hay ration provided 60 grams of lysine, so there
was no need to add more. Growing horses need enough lysine to
build healthy tissue and utilize all the protein that the diet provides.

She needed extra calories since she was an active lady, so she
received three meals each day. I started with a base of unsweetened beet pulp. Beet pulp is a great feed — with as many calories as oats, but without the insulin response.

She needed extra fat to fuel her activity needs, so I wanted to
add a fatty feed to the beet pulp. I had to choose something that
would not further aggravate the inflammation she was experiencing. No, not from the supposed muscle injury (though that
would cause inflammation) but from the body fat — fat releases
inflammatory cytokines which create damage throughout the
body. Soybean oil or corn oil was not an option since these oils
are high in inflammatory omega-6 fatty acids. Instead I chose
flaxseed meal, high in anti-inflammatory omega-3 fatty acids.
Plus, they help regulate insulin levels. I chose a commercially
ground product that was stabilized against rancidity and contained added calcium to correct the high phosphorus content
naturally found in flaxseeds.

My supplementation approach was aggressive. To neutralize the damaging free radicals caused by inflammation, I added a potent commercial antioxidant preparation that was high in vitamin E, vitamin C, beta carotene, and grape seed extract. I wanted her to have 5,000 IU of vitamin E so I had to add a separate supplement; I chose one without added selenium because she was already getting selenium from the antioxidant formula. In addition, I gave her 10,000 mg of vitamin C each day, even though she was young enough to produce her own.

So, let's review… We met her energy (calorie) needs with hay, beet pulp and flaxseed meal, her anti-inflammatory agents were provided from flaxseed meal and antioxidants, and her protein needs were rounded out by adding alfalfa to the mix. Only one thing left — magnesium. Magnesium helps lower circulating insulin levels.

The magnesium and calcium content of her diet was evaluated, revealing that she could benefit from an additional 10,000 mg of magnesium. I also gave her chromium to further increase her insulin sensitivity.

Well, 6 months later, here she is again! She was originally thought to be a lost cause. Amazing.

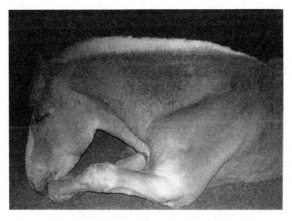

Dymond, after treatment

Equine Cushing's Disease
Known as Pituitary Pars Intermedia Dysfunction (PPID)

As horses age, they are more inclined to develop equine Cushing's disease. Young horses, however, can also develop this condition. And it can affect any breed. Its name is based on its similarity to Cushing's disease in dogs and humans. However, it is more correctly referred to as pituitary pars intermedia dysfunction (PPID).

Here's some physiology to help you understand how its mechanism is different in horses. In dogs and humans, the anterior portion of the pituitary gland (called the pars distalis) develops a hormone-secreting tumor. In horses, however, a different portion of the pituitary gland is affected — the intermediate portion, called the pars intermedia, hence the name "pituitary *pars intermedia* dysfunction." The tumor that develops in this area exerts pressure on the brain (specifically, the hypothalamus), resulting in a reduction in function. The pars intermedia remains active, however, and releases excessive amounts of adrenocorticotropic hormone (ACTH) as well as other hormones. ACTH is the most researched and understood hormone secreted by the pars intermedia and is typically measured to diagnose PPID. ACTH stimulates the adrenal gland (that sits next to the kidney) to produce cortisol. Since ACTH levels are high in the cushingoid horse, the level of cortisol is also high. Cortisol can cause tissues to become resistant to insulin, causing insulin to rise in the blood stream. The result is often laminitis.

> ACTH is the most researched and understood hormone secreted by the pars intermedia and is typically measured to diagnose PPID.

Insulin resistance and PPID often occur together, with a resulting misdiagnosis since abnormal fat deposits (cresty neck, crease along back, etc.) become apparent before other symptoms of PPID occur. And laminitis is a common result of both disorders. Though not confirmed, there seems to be a connection between insulin resistance and the eventual occurrence of PPID, especially as the animal ages.

Signs of PPID

The signs are numerous:

- Long, wavy hair coat that fails to shed or shed completely
- Excessive thirst and urination
- Excessive sweating
- Increased appetite
- Muscle wasting, especially along the back leading to a swayed back, pot-bellied appearance
- Abnormal fat deposits, same as those found in insulin resistance
- Depressed immune function, leading to increased susceptibility to infections, delayed wound healing, and abscesses
- Rotation of the coffin bone within the foot, which can occur before outward laminitis signs appear
- Heaves
- Infertility or lack of estrus cycles
- Swollen sheath

Testing for PPID

Most veterinarians can correctly diagnose PPID simply by examining the outward signs. A curly hair coat that does not shed, excessive thirst and urination, and muscle wasting are common indications that the disease exists. Blood tests are useful, but not 100% accurate. Below are a few commonly used tests. Discuss these with your veterinarian to determine the course of action for your horse.

Dexamethasone suppression test (DST)

This is an overnight test. The blood is first evaluated for cortisol concentration. Then your horse receives an injection of dexamethasone (a steroid). Another blood sample is taken 19 hours later to test again for his cortisol level. PPID is confirmed when the second cortisol level is too high. There are disadvantages to this test: It requires a second visit from your veterinarian, but the real problem is that it may increase the risk of laminitis. Laminitis can start developing before your horse exhibits symptoms, so there is no way of truly knowing if he is at an increased risk level before starting this test. Therefore, I prefer to measure ACTH.

ACTH measurement

This test is simple to perform. It involves one blood test that measures ACTH, along with insulin levels. It can also distinguish between PPID and insulin resistance since the insulin resistant horse will have normal ACTH levels.

However, there are two problems. First, if performed during the fall, the test results may not be accurate. As the temperatures and daylight hours start to decline, the pituitary gland pumps out more ACTH, even in healthy horses. However, if you have this test done in the fall, and it turns out to be negative (low ACTH), you can make a strong assumption that your horse does not have PPID.

Second, ACTH levels can vary throughout the day. Therefore, repeated testing (along with insulin tests) should be done in order to make comparisons. Testing should be at the same time of day each time, and while feeding low NSC hay to minimize stress.

Other tests

Your veterinarian may choose to perform other tests such as checking for white blood cells (lymphocytes and neutrophils), or measuring thyrotropin releasing hormone (TRH).

Treating PPID

There is no cure for PPID, but it can be managed through diet, exercise, and medications (including herbal preparations).

Diet

Horses with PPID can be overweight or underweight. They will exhibit regional adiposity (fat deposits along the specific parts of the body mentioned earlier) due to the insulin resistance that accompanies PPID. So reducing circulating insulin levels is the key to managing the diet.

A low starch/low sugar diet is important. However, not all low starch feeds are the same. Some are higher in calories (generally from fat) than others. So the overweight, easy keeper, needs to have calories restricted. Reducing or even avoiding concentrated feeds is best for these horses, while allowing free choice grass hay (with some alfalfa). You'll need to provide a small, low starch meal to serve as a carrier for supplementation, but it should be minimal.

Underweight cushingoid horses, however, need additional calories, but still need to keep their insulin levels in check. So, a low starch feed that contains more fat is worth considering. Or you can add fat supplements such as rice bran oil. Actual rice bran, however, is not the best source of fat for these horses since its percent NSC is too high (approximately 20%).

Follow the feeding guidelines shown earlier for insulin resistance when feeding a horse with PPID. Since cushingoid horses have depressed immune function, they need even more nutritional support. I highly recommend adding a potent antioxidant preparation. You'll likely need to add vitamin E and C. Vitamin E intake should be high: 5 IU of vitamin E per pound of body weight. Supplement vitamin C at 10 mg per lb of body weight.

Grazing

Horses with PPID are at an increased risk of developing laminitis, so the same precautions that you would take for an insulin resistant horse apply in this situation. If your horse, however, has lost fat deposits, is receiving the proper nutrients, is on pergolide (commonly used medication for PPID), and has never shown any signs of laminitis, then you can consider allowing your horse to graze for short periods of time, during the safest times.

Care

Since the cushingoid horse sweats excessively and has a long hair coat, you can make him more comfortable by keeping him outdoors or changing his bedding frequently (due to excess urination). Also, body clipping and frequent bathing in hot weather will be helpful.

Stress, as you'll recall, increases cortisol secretion and cushingoid horses already have too much cortisol flowing through their veins. So anything you can do to reduce stress for your horse would be beneficial. Otherwise, you can exacerbate the chances of his developing laminitis.

Infections are common with PPID since excess cortisol depresses the immune function. So, check your horse each day for skin infections, abscesses, or respiratory problems.

Even if your horse shows no signs of laminitis, it's best to have his feet x-rayed for changes. These changes can occur early, before outward signs appear. Being proactive is best.

Medications

There is a limited number of medications used to treat PPID. Some herbal preparations may also be effective.

- **Pergolide.** This is the drug of choice for PPID. The hypothalamus is not able to produce enough dopamine on its own, but pergolide stimulates dopamine receptors in the brain, making dopamine more plentiful. This calms down the pituitary gland and less ACTH is released, resulting in lower cortisol secretion. Side effects include loss of appetite, lethargy, and depression. And not all horses respond to pergolide.

- **Other drugs.** Cyproheptadine and trilostane are options for horses that do not respond to pergolide. Your veterinarian is the best source for discussing these drugs, their effectiveness, and side effects.

- **Herbs.** Herbs are listed as medications because they contain drugs in diluted amounts. They need to be administered with care due to the potential for side effects and interactions, just as with any other medication. Chasteberry (*Vitex agnus castus*) and jiaogulan (*Gynostemma pentaphyllum*) may be helpful for horses with PPID. However, their benefits are anecdotal and not scientifically proven. Cinnamon may also be promising in reducing circulating insulin levels. One teaspoon per 250 lbs of body weight is a safe dosage.

Muscle Disorders

EXERTIONAL RHABDOMYOLYSIS (ER)

Exertional rhabdomyolysis (ER), otherwise known as tying up, is a generalized term that describes painful cramping of muscles during and after exercise that damages muscle cells. It can affect a horse once in a while or can be a chronic condition. Intermittent, sporadic attacks of ER result from overworking an out of shape horse, or can be due to a nutritional deficiency. However, genetic disorders such as recurrent exertional rhabdomyolysis (commonly found in Thoroughbreds and Arabians) and PSSM —

polysaccharide storage myopathy — can become chronic. I elaborate further on PSSM a bit later in this section.

Signs of exertional rhabdomyolysis

- Refusal to move
- Short strides
- Hind feet stabbing the ground
- Excessive sweating
- Appears to be in pain
- Hardening and cramping of muscles, in particular large muscles of the hind quarters, and thighs
- Reddish or dark brown urine (to remove cellular toxins from dying muscle cells)

Causes of ER

- Dehydration
- Electrolyte imbalance
- High protein diets
- High starch/sugar diets
- Estrogen levels in clover-based hay may have an effect, though not proven

What you should do for your horse

- Contact your veterinarian.
- Do not walk your horse to work out the cramp.
- Keep your horse still and calm.
- Blanket his hind quarters if the weather is cold.
- Encourage water drinking to help his kidneys flush out the toxins.
- Avoid giving him pain relievers, unless instructed by your veterinarian. Bute and Banamine can cause kidney damage if your horse is severely dehydrated.

Prevention and dietary treatment

Vitamin E and selenium: Your horse relies on vitamin E and selenium while exercising to prevent oxidative damage to his muscles and other tissues throughout his body. Heavily exercised horses should have 5,000 IU of vitamin E per day or 5 IU per pound of body weight of body weight. Selenium should also be supplied and for heavily exercised horses, you can supplement up to 5 mg per day for the 1100 lb horse, or slightly more for heavier horses. In general, the selenium concentration in the entire diet should not be more than 0.6 mg per kg of feed (ppm). However, because of its low toxicity threshold, before supplementing selenium it is best to have your hay and/or pasture analyzed as well as calculate selenium from other feed and supplemental sources.

Salt: Salt is a critical factor in preventing ER. Make sure your horse is getting enough. One to four ounces (depending on the amount of sweating or exercise) should be provided each day. A five-pound salt block will last between 20 and 80 days if consumed at that rate, but it is not likely that your horse will lick enough each day to get 4 ounces. Some horses may avoid salt blocks because of tongue irritation or mouth sores from a bit. You can also put some salt in a bucket and offer it free choice. Table salt from your grocery store will work, but see if you can find kosher salt, since it is coarser. Your horse will likely dab his tongue on it to get what he needs. But one thing you should know… salt, sodium chloride, does not provide enough chloride. Hay does. So give your horse some hay before exercising.

Electrolyte supplements are intended to replace what has been lost through perspiration; however, your horse must be in good sodium balance to begin with in order for electrolytes to be effective. This means that you will probably have to add salt to his meals if his needs are high. Take a look at two other places in this book for more information: Chapter 1 — Ground Rules for Feeding a Horse and Chapter 7 — Fundamentals of Water and Electrolytes.

Salt will encourage him to drink more and that is essential toward preventing dehydration. He should always have water nearby. It should be clean (free of algae, insects, and bird droppings) and not too cold (heat your water during the winter so it does not go below 50° F) or hot (as it would become by standing in the sun).

Calcium, phosphorus, and magnesium: These three minerals should be in balance. Calcium levels always need to exceed phosphorus, and your horse can tolerate up to six times more calcium than phosphorus. Have your hay analyzed to be certain the ratios are proportionate. Most hay has more calcium but occasionally I'll come across an analysis that has an equal amount of phosphorus or slightly more. If other high-calcium sources are not added to the diet, this inverted ratio can create bone loss. I discuss this condition, known as hyperparathyroidism, later in this chapter.

Magnesium should be approximately half the level of calcium. Many horses suffer from borderline magnesium deficiencies because this mineral is not well absorbed from forage. The result can be muscle spasms, as well as irritable behavior, poor attention span, and being easily startled. If your horse is experiencing ER, I recommend adding 5,000 mg of magnesium per 500 lbs of body weight.

B vitamins: All eight B vitamins are necessary to protect muscle and nerve function. Choose a B complex rather than individual B vitamins since they work in concert with one another. And when looking for a supplement, avoid blood builders that add iron. Your horse gets plenty of iron as long as he is eating all the hay and pasture he needs.

POLYSACCHARIDE STORAGE MYOPATHY (PSSM)
ALSO KNOWN AS EQUINE POLYSACCHARIDE MYOPATHY (EPSM)

Polysaccharide storage myopathy (PSSM) can have one of two causes. Up until recently, we thought that PSSM was strictly due to insulin *sensitivity*, which may still be what happens to Quarter Horses. Instead of insulin resistance, as in the case of equine metabolic syndrome and PPID, the insulin situation is reversed. Horses with PSSM may have an *increased* sensitivity to insulin. In other words, glucose enters cells at a very high rate.

But we now know that PSSM has a very strong genetic component. In draft horses, the problem is an inherited abnormality where the enzyme glycogen synthase is overactive, resulting in too much glycogen accumulation within muscle cells. Regardless of the cause (insulin sensitivity or abnormal glycogen synthase) the result is the same — elevated glycogen formation.

Glycogen is the storage form of glucose in the muscles (and liver); it is a long, branched chain of glucose molecules linked together, like a beaded necklace. I like to think of glycogen as a "glucose pantry" that your horse accesses when he exercises. When his muscles need energy, they go to the glucose stash and break off a few glucose molecules. But this doesn't happen in the case of PSSM. Instead, glucose is stuck in the form of glycogen. Consequently, your horse's muscles cannot get the energy they need, resulting in painful cramping known as tying up (rhabdomyolysis). PSSM can also cause shivers, an abnormal hind step gait affecting warmbloods and drafts, often confused with stringhalt. Stringhalt is described in Chapter 15 — Joints, Hair, Hooves, and Skin.

PSSM is most prevalent in specific breeds

As I mentioned, PSSM can be a hereditary disease, occurring most frequently in Quarter Horses, drafts, draft crosses, and warmbloods. Other breeds such as Arabians, Thoroughbreds, Standardbreds, Appaloosas, Morgans, and Tennessee Walking Horses have been shown to develop this disorder but not to the same extent.

Quarter Horses can show signs of PSSM early in life, generally between 1 and 5 years of age, whereas draft breeds, draft crosses, and warmbloods typically do not show signs until 8 years of age.

Diagnosis

A genetic blood test is now available to diagnose PSSM in nearly 90% of cases. It tests for the glycogen synthase 1 gene (GYS1), a mutation responsible for the overproduction of glycogen within muscle tissue. The GYS1 gene is dominant, meaning if either the mare or sire carry the gene, there is a 50% chance that the foal will be affected. If both parents have the gene, there is a 75% chance that the foal will have PSSM and a 25% chance that he will be born with two copies of the gene, leading to severe, and often deadly, symptoms.

Performing a muscle biopsy to test for elevated glycogen is worthwhile because some horses will test negative for the genetic GYS1 mutation and still have PSSM. Serum enzymes such as creatine kinase (CK) and aspartate aminotransferase (AST) are also important indicators, though not conclusive for many breeds. This information, along with clinical signs such as exercise intolerance, muscle loss, and weakness, allows for a correct diagnosis.

Treatment and exercise

There is no cure for PSSM; however, with proper diet and adequate exercise, the clinical signs can be diminished. In fact, many cases go undiagnosed in horses with complete pasture turnout and low concentrated diets. When they're brought indoors, have reduced exercise capability, or fed starchy diets, we then start to see signs of the disorder.

Keeping your horse fit is essential to prevent PSSM symptoms. He should not be confined to a stall. If your horse is very stiff, start exercise slowly. Even hand walking for five to ten minutes can trigger another episode.

Offer less than 10 minutes a day, gradually increasing the time on the ground each day. After three weeks of ground work, exercise under saddle can be considered.

Diet

Reduce starch and sugar: The most important approach for feeding PSSM horses is to totally eliminate cereal grains and other high starch feeds from the diet. This includes oats, corn, barley, wheat, wheat middlings, sweet feeds, and pelleted feeds that include cereal grains in their ingredients. Rice bran also contains too much starch and should be avoided. Sugary treats such as cookies, fruits, and carrots also need to be removed. If you like to offer treats, you can offer alfalfa cubes (broken in small pieces) or a handful of pellets.

There are many commercial feeds that claim to be low in starch, but that doesn't mean they are low enough. Contact the manufacturer and choose one that has less than 12% NSC, at least 6% fat, and at least 14% protein.

Fiber: Adequate fiber is critical and can best be achieved by total pasture turnout or free choice hay. It is advisable, however, to have your forage tested for ethanol soluble carbohydrates (ESC) and starch. ESC will give you the level of sugar in the diet. ESC plus starch should be than 10%. If NSC is your only available measurement, it should be less than 12%. For this reason, pasture may not be appropriate since sugar and starch levels can vary.

Protein: To prevent muscle loss, enough protein, between 14 and 18%, is important. Alfalfa or soybean meal will meet this need. Don't worry about alfalfa. It is as low in sugar and starch as most grass hay and provides the protein your horse needs. Since he cannot get glucose from glycogen in his muscles, he will break down muscle tissue to produce glucose if the diet does not contain extra protein for that pupose.

Additional calories: To provide additional calories for exercise, fat is your best source. Flaxseed meal is high in fat, but more important, it provides essential omega-3 fatty acids to reduce inflammation. Additional oil can be fed, up to 1 cup per 500 lbs of body weight. See Chapter 3 — Fundamentals of Fats for a comparison between oils.

Supplementation and salt: The same suggestions outlined earlier for ER also apply for PSSM.

Multiple acyl-coA dehydrogenase deficiency (MADD)

MADD is another documented version of tying up that is caused by an interference in fat metabolism. Horses with this genetic disorder cannot burn fat for energy and must rely on carbohydrates (glucose); therefore, they will break down muscle tissue to provide glucose. MADD has similar symptoms to other cases of rhabdomyolysis — severe muscle cramping and degeneration. Myoglobin can spill into the urine, causing it to be a dark reddish color. Blood tests will reveal high levels of glucose and lactic acid, increased muscle enzymes (AST, LDH, CK) and increased urea and creatinine, revealing impaired kidney function and muscle atrophy.

Hyperkalemic periodic paralysis (HYPP)

Hyperkalemic periodic paralysis (HYPP) is a genetic disease going back to the 1969 Quarter Horse sire, Impressive. The gene for HYPP is dominant so even horses that are heterozygous for the gene (H/N) can exhibit symptoms of muscle tremors and severe cramping. For this reason, HYPP horses should not be bred. The American Quarter Horse Association estimates that 4% of Quarter Horses are affected; those testing homozygous for HYPP (H/H) cannot be registered with their organization. Four percent is a lot of horses. And these horses must be managed with the correct diet, exercise, and even medication.

HYPP involves abnormal potassium movement between the blood and cells. To help you get a feel for what goes wrong, let me first describe the normal situation. For muscles to work, potassium is inside the cell, causing sodium to remain in the blood. This creates an electrical gradient that stimulates nerve impulses when the muscle is being exercised. Calcium joins the picture by binding to muscle fibers called myosin, resulting in muscle contraction. Relaxation occurs when the calcium pump gets the calcium back into muscle storage sites.

However, with HYPP, sodium is not able to stay in the blood and is constantly leaking into the cell; therefore, potassium is forced into the blood. And calcium is released from muscle storage, binds to myosin and causes the muscles to repeatedly contract. Muscle fasciculation occurs throughout the body, especially over the rib cage and flank area. The eyes can start to twitch and the horse may appear to be suffering from colic. In severe cases, the horse may sit down like a dog and eventually lie down. This situation can lead to respiratory failure and death. Your veterinarian may prescribe acetazolamide or administer calcium carbonate to promote potassium excretion by the kidneys.

Nutritional management

Maintaining normal serum potassium levels is the goal when managing HYPP. To do this, the total potassium level in the diet should be less than 1.5% and each individual meal should not contain more than 33 grams of potassium.

Hay is the basis for most horses' diet but in this case, hay may be too high in potassium to control symptoms. Some hay, depending on fertilization, rainfall, and maturity level, can have potassium levels as high as 3%. Hay cut at an immature stage is higher in potassium than more mature cuts. Legume hay, such as alfalfa or clover, is much higher in potassium than grass hay. And brome or orchardgrass tends to be higher than timothy or Bermuda. So, to avoid confusion, it is best to have your hay analyzed — that is the *only* way you are going to know how much potassium your horse is eating.

Cereal grains are low in potassium, generally below 0.5%. Another advantage of grain is its high starch content, which stimulates insulin production; insulin increases potassium uptake in muscle cells, causing serum potassium levels to decline. But be careful of commercial feeds that contain molasses — molasses is much too high in potassium to be safe. And commercial feeds may contain alfalfa or soybean meals, which are also too high in potassium.

The following feeds are low in potassium:

- **Cereal grains.** Oats contain 0.6% potassium. Other cereal grains such as wheat, corn and barley are also low, but I do not recommend them because of their relatively poor digestibility.

- **Beet pulp.** Contains 0.7% potassium. Make sure to find an unsweetened beet pulp since many products add molasses.

- **Flaxseed meal.** Contains 0.9% potassium. Slightly higher than grain or beet pulp, flaxseed meal can be used in a small quantity to boost the nutritional value of the diet.

- **Fresh pasture.** Because of its high moisture content, the potassium concentration is diluted. So while hay can be too high in potassium, fresh pasture is an excellent source of forage.

- **Lower-potassium hay.** All hay should be analyzed, just to be safe. But in general, timothy, Bermuda, fescue, Kentucky bluegrass, and oat hay tend to be lower in potassium than other hay.

- **Salt.** Plain salt is fine. Avoid mineralized salt blocks or sea salt.

- **Oils.** All oils are safe; they do not contain any potassium.

- **Soybean hulls and distiller's grain.** These by-products are low in potassium and tend to be of similar concentration as oats.

- **Fruits and vegetables.** These do contain potassium, some more than others, but apples have one of the lowest potassium concentrations (approximately 70 mg). Carrots are higher with 200 mg, and even bananas, noted for their high potassium level, have 450 mg of potassium. One serving each day is not going to make a significant dent in your horse's overall potassium level.

Wheat bran and rice bran are borderline with 1.4% potassium. They can be fed as long as the total meal is not high in potassium (no more than 33 grams — that's 33,000 mg).

The following feeds should be avoided due to their high potassium content:

- Alfalfa hay (approximately 2.4% potassium)
- Brome and orchardgrass hay (approximately 2.3% potassium)
- Soybean meal (2.2% potassium)
- Kelp-based salt (plain salt is fine)
- Molasses (4.1% potassium)
- Sweet feed (due to molasses content)
- Electrolyte supplements that contain potassium
- Vitamin/mineral supplements that contain potassium
- Commercial feeds that have added potassium at levels more than 1.5%

Additional guidelines

Turnout on grass pasture (no alfalfa or clover) is the best approach in managing a horse with HYPP. Not only is it low in potassium but it provides a stress-free environment.

Stress can lead to an HYPP episode. Trailer rides can be especially taxing so it's best to keep your horse close to home. If your horse is experiencing stressful situations, it is best to remove the source rather than feeding calming agents, which only put a band-aid on the situation. Stress, its causes, and its effect on your horse are discussed at length in Chapter 17 — Stress and Behavior.

Thyroid Function

Earlier in this chapter, I discussed thyroid function in relation to insulin resistance. But it's worth chatting about it some more because many horses are placed on medication that does not necessarily treat thyroid problems.

HYPOTHYROIDISM OR SOMETHING ELSE?

Most horse owners only become familiar with the thyroid gland when they give their horses thyroid medication. Thyro-L may be prescribed to treat obesity related to insulin resistance and/or PPID. The premise for this drug's use is to help your horse lose weight, not to treat an underactive thyroid gland. True hypothyroidism (underactive) is very rare in horses.

If your horse is overweight, suffering from laminitis, or has PPID, his blood tests will often reveal low thyroid hormone (T4). But in the vast majority of cases, this does not indicate an underactive thyroid gland. Instead, it could be due to a number of factors such as pain, stress, and pain relievers. Also, fasting, exercise, high calorie diets, and too much zinc and copper have been shown to increase T4 levels. Furthermore, *low thyroid hormone does not cause laminitis*. It's the other way around — the low reading of a laminitic horse may be due to the pain and fear your horse is experiencing at the time of the test.

Veterinarians use thyroid medication to help a horse gain more insulin sensitivity, and hence lose body fat. And it's true that it can be beneficial for this purpose, but it is only meant for short term use. Do not put your horse on Thyro-L for more than 6 months. I've seen some horses on it for years. This can lead to very serious problems, including bone loss and heart problems. It is so much better for your horse to deal with insulin resistance through diet and exercise; and in the case of PPID, pergolide is safer.

Since it is so common to manipulate horses' thyroid function by adding thyroid hormones, I think it would be helpful to understand a little bit about how this gland works. The thyroid gland sits in the center of the throat and is responsible for controlling thyroid hormone secretion. These hormones are necessary for proper growth, functioning of organ systems, and regulating metabolism (the rate at which your horse burns calories for energy). They are also necessary for building protein and producing body heat.

The hypothalamus and pituitary gland regulate how much thyroid hormone is actually secreted. Thyroid releasing hormone (TRH) from the hypothalamus stimulates the release of thyroid stimulating hormone (TSH) from the pituitary gland. TSH travels to the thyroid gland to stimulate it to secrete thyroid hormones. This cascade of events has to take place for your horse to be healthy. If a defect exists in any one of these areas, the level of thyroid hormones will be disrupted.

Currently, the only practical way to test for thyroid function is by a single measurement of thyroid hormones, typically T4. A much better diagnosis could be made by testing for TSH; however, this test is not, as yet, commercially available for horses. Veterinarians can, however, test for T4 after administering either TRH or TSH, but this is impractical in the field because multiple tests must be done and single dose applications of TRH or TSH are not available. So, the future of thyroid gland testing has a way to go. And perhaps by the time you read this book, the technology will have advanced enough to improve diagnostic tools.

ENLARGED THYROID GLAND

There are circumstances when your horse can have a thyroid gland condition that causes the gland to enlarge. This situation can be benign but it may also cause health problems. Below is a list of thyroid enlargement causes.

Goiter

The thyroid gland is wrapped around the trachea (leading to the lungs) and is close to the voice box (larynx). Since it is also close to the jaw bone, it can be confused with an enlarged salivary gland, so it is best to consult with your veterinarian for an exact diagnosis.

An enlarged thyroid gland is known as hypertrophy or goiter. This can be caused by *too much or too little* thyroid hormone production, or by *too much or too little* iodine in the diet. Foals with low iodine intake can develop a deformed jaw, skull, and also exhibit tendon/ligament problems. Conversely, too much iodine, generally resulting from overfeeding kelp or overlapping supplement sources, can lead to abortions in pregnant mares. Foals born from these mares can develop bone abnormalities. More discussion can be found in Chapters 18 — Breeding, Pregnancy, and Lactation and 19 — Growth and Growing Old.

Age

Older horses are more likely to develop tumors of the thyroid gland. Most of the time, these tumors are completely benign and do not pose a health threat to your horse, unless they become so large as to interfere with normal breathing.

Hyperthyroidism

Hyperthyroidism means that there excess production of thyroid hormones. This condition is quite uncommon. It is caused by a tumor, usually benign, that forms on the thyroid gland. A cancerous tumor is possible, but rare. Treatment usually involves surgery to remove the tumor.

IODINE

Let's talk some more about iodine; you cannot adequately discuss the thyroid gland without a thorough understanding of this mineral. I also provide information in Chapter 5 — Fundamentals of Minerals.

Most of the iodine in your horse's body is found in his thyroid gland. Iodine is necessary for the production of thyroid hormones, thyroxin (T4) and tri-iodothyronine (T3). Within his tissues throughout the body, T4 is converted to the more active form, T3. If iodine is deficient, there will be a reduction in thyroid hormones. If iodine intake is excessive, it can irritate the thyroid gland and block its ability to make hormones. So, in either case, an iodine deficiency or toxicity, the thyroid gland cannot do its job and hypothyroidism results.

Iodine interacts with selenium. High iodine, combined with low selenium intake, leads to thyroid gland damage. If iodine is low, however, even a moderate amount of selenium will bring the T4 concentrations back to normal.

You generally won't find iodine listed in the guaranteed analysis on feed tags. But iodine does naturally exist in most feeds, depending on how much iodine was in the soil where the feedstuff was grown. Don't feed kelp (sea salt) to horses because the iodine concentration is very, very high, nearly 2,000 mg of iodine per kg of dry matter (2000 ppm). Iodized salt or mineralized salt blocks have approximately 70 mg/kg DM (70 ppm), so you can see how much difference there is between the two supplemental sources. Depending on your horse's age and exercise status, an iodine intake of 3 to 5 mg per day is sufficient. Feedstuffs and most grasses are generally low, providing up to 0.2 mg/kg DM. Alfalfa is a bit higher at 0.6 mg/kg DM. So, for example, let's say you are feeding 20 lbs of hay at 0.2 mg/kg of DM. This would provide 1.82 mg of iodine. And let's also assume that your horse is consuming one ounce per day of iodized salt. The salt provides 1.99 mg of iodine. So, in total, your horse is getting 3.81 mg of iodine, which is in the ballpark of a normal requirement. Go to Appendix — Crunching Numbers, to see how this is calculated. But before we leave this example, take a look at what would happen if you were to feed sea salt instead, with 2000 ppm — that same ounce would provide 56 mg of iodine!

The total diet should not contain more than 5 ppm of iodine and because of this, toxicities are much more common than deficiencies. However, an iodine deficiency can occur when minerals are fed free choice and your horse does not consume enough. Iodine, along with other minerals, need to be deliberately included in the overall diet; you truly cannot rely on your horse's ability to discern his need.

Hyperlipemia

This disorder mainly affects minis, ponies, mules, and donkeys. They are especially prone toward extreme insulin resistance; if they become overweight or develop PPID, their cells may not get enough glucose. Oh, they eventually get some, but in the meantime, the body needs energy. So it breaks down (mobilizes) fat at a rapid rate, releasing large amounts of fatty substances called triglycerides into the bloodstream. Elevated fat (also known as lipids) in the blood caused by excess fat mobilization is known as hyperlipemia.

Before triglycerides can be used by the cells for energy, they must first travel to the liver to be "packaged" into molecules known as very low density lipoproteins (VLDL), which are then able to leave the liver and deliver energy-rich triglycerides to cells throughout the body. However, the liver can become overwhelmed, causing VLDLs to accumulate, leading to a fatty liver and potential liver damage.

Do not let your equine friend get too fat. And avoid adding fat to his diet. Additional fat may be reasonable for an insulin resistant horse who requires additional calories, but this is not the best approach for feeding minis, ponies, and donkeys. They have a genetic tendency toward developing hyperlipemia. If your animal starts to develop depression and will not eat, or is colicky, has diarrhea, or exhibits muscle twitching, be sure to contact your veterinarian. A blood sample will be taken to assess triglyceride levels. Give him plenty of grass hay but avoid alfalfa for donkeys and mules since they do better on lower protein diets. And offer him some sugar as a temporary means of providing glucose — sweetened beet pulp is a good choice, as well as apples and carrots.

STARVATION OR STRESS

Hyperlipemia can occur in any equine: horse, pony, mini, donkey, mule, even a zebra if you happen to have one, if the animal is not getting enough to eat, or is experiencing significant stress in addition to the angst caused by starvation. Prolonged food restriction causes excess fat to enter the bloodstream and the hyperlipemia that results can damage the liver as well as the kidneys. Starved horses need special and careful attention.

I know you're wondering why I'm even talking about this when you would never starve your horse. Unfortunately, very unfortunately, there are cases where horses are terribly neglected (and the people responsible are probably not reading this book). But you would be amazed at the question I received recently on my website's forum. The reader asked how long a horse could survive without anything to eat. Even though this was weeks ago, writing about it now still brings up a sick feeling in the pit of my stomach and my eyes fill with tears.

There are many dear people who rescue severely deprived horses and if you're one of them, I've included a special case at the end of Chapter 12 — Weight Management called "The Severely Underweight Rescue Horse." I hope you'll find this helpful.

Nutritional Secondary Hyperparathyroidism (NSH) Also Known as Bran Disease or Big Head Disease

Nutritional secondary hyperparathyroidism (NSH) is associated with a calcium deficiency caused by feeding too much phosphorus or too little calcium. Calcium in relation to phosphorus should always be at least 1:1 and better yet, closer to 2:1.

NSH was more of a problem in the early 1900s than it is today since working horses were fed large amounts of bran from wheat milling plants, hence the name, bran disease. But there are cases nowadays where horses are regularly fed wheat or rice bran and cereal grains without enough forage. These feeds can have calcium to phosphorus ratios as low as 1:6. Commercial bran products are often fortified with calcium to correct this problem — check the label to be certain.

Even pasture and hay should be analyzed for their calcium and phosphorus levels. Orchardgrass, in particular, is apt to have excess phosphorus. Though all forages can vary, most grasses have a calcium to phosphorus ratio of less than 2:1, compared to alfalfa and other legumes with a 4:1 ratio. Higher ratios are fine since most horses can easily tolerate up to six times more calcium than phosphorus.

Calcium and phosphorus compete with each other for absorption sites within the small intestine. If there is more phosphorus in the diet than calcium, not enough calcium will reach the bloodstream. Low calcium levels in the blood stimulate the parathyroid gland (which sits next to the thyroid gland in the throat) to secrete parathyroid hormone (PTH). Its purpose is to replenish calcium by pulling it out of the bones. PTH works with vitamin D to further increase calcium levels by enhancing absorption from the small intestine and reducing urinary calcium losses. Chapters 5 — Fundamentals of Minerals and 6 — Fundamentals of Vitamins offer more information regarding calcium, phosphorus, and vitamin D.

NSH SYMPTOMS

Young horses develop a condition called physitis (also known as epiphysitis) where they become lame in the worst case scenario, or just stiff in milder cases. Growth is abnormal, especially in the legs and head (discussed further in the Chapter 19 — Growth and Growing Old). The large head that results, hence the name big head disease, typically occurs in young horses. Adult horses, however, become unthrifty, stiff, weak, and may have pain when chewing. In severe cases, the teeth can become loose or sudden fractures of long bones may occur.

TREATING NSH

In mild cases, treatment may simply be a change in diet, accompanied by pain relief, and slow, steady exercise. Cereal grains must be eliminated from the diet, since these feeds are very high in phosphorus. Horses that have all the forage they want generally do not have a problem with NSH because grasses and especially legumes (alfalfa and clover) are high in calcium. For this reason, calcium deficiencies are uncommon. But if forage is restricted, combined with feeding large amounts of grain, bran (rice or wheat), and flaxseeds that you grind yourself, a high phosphorus to calcium ratio can be created.

Feeds that are high in oxalates are also a problem because oxalates bind calcium in the digestive tract, making it unabsorbable. Beet pulp, which I often recommend, contains oxalates so its high calcium content is not a true indication of what actually gets absorbed. This is why I like feeding a meal of beet pulp along with an equal amount of alfalfa pellets (and a vitamin/mineral supplement) to allow for enough available calcium.

The calcium level in your horse's diet can also be improved by adding limestone (calcium carbonate) or calcium citrate, both containing no phosphorus. Enough should be added to bring the total calcium to phosphorus ratio up to 3:1. Since limestone does not taste very good and horses may not like its texture, molasses can be added. I prefer, however, calcium citrate because limestone is an antacid (same ingredient that you find in Tums — calcium carbonate), and the subsequent reduction in stomach acid impairs calcium absorption.

Vitamin D is also important because it increases blood calcium levels. Adequate sunlight will allow for vitamin D production; however, insufficient turnout will create a vitamin D deficiency. Even the sun's angle in the upper third of the U.S. may hamper vitamin D synthesis. Fortunately, fresh pasture contains vitamin D; hay has some, but considerably less.

Exercise strengthens bones and is usually helpful in treating NSH. However, if the condition has progressed to osteopathic disorders, exercise should be allowed with caution. Discuss the amount and level of activity with your veterinarian since each case is different.

Endnotes

[1] Modified insulin-to-glucose ratio (MIRG) = [800 – 0.3 X (insulin -50)^2] / (glucose-30)

[2] Adapted from Equi-Analytical Laboratories, Ithaca, NY: www.equi-analytical.com and Safergrass.org: www.safergrass.org

[3] *Nutrient Requirements of Horses*, Sixth Revised Edition, 2007. Washington, D.C.: National Research Council, National Academy Press: 306.

Chapter 14 —
Digestive Problems

If you patiently lead these two legged animals to what you need in order
to perform at your best, they will figure it out in good time.
~ Rita Mae Brown's horse giving advice to a friend

Your horse's digestive system is really quite unique, only shared by other equines and a few zoo animals. Horses are referred to as non-ruminant herbivores. Herbivorous, since they only eat plants, but require assistance from microscopic organisms to digest the fiber found in roughage. Non-ruminant, because unlike ruminants (cows, goats, sheep, etc.), horses do not have a large fermentation vat called a rumen at the beginning of their digestive tract; instead they have a smaller fermentation vat called a cecum toward the end of their digestive tract. The cecum, along with the large and small colon, make up your horse's hindgut. Because his ability to digest fiber exists toward the end of the digestive tract, whereas cows have theirs in the beginning, he does not get as many calories from fibrous forages and therefore has to eat far more than a cow to maintain condition.

This is all discussed in detail in the first chapter — Ground Rules for Feeding a Horse. And throughout this book, I've brought up the importance of providing your horse with a steady supply of forage to keep his digestive tract healthy. Forage is important for proper motility, so the intestinal muscles can keep working. Forage encourages chewing, to neutralize stomach acid. Left without anything to chew on, horses will develop ulcers. And stomach acid will destroy hindgut bacteria, leading to weight loss, gas production, colic, and even laminitis. So what follows are various disorders that can affect your horse's digestive tract. Let's start with a common problem... ulcers.

Gastric Ulcers

An ulcer is an erosion of the tissue that lines the gastrointestinal tract. It can form anywhere along the digestive tract; however, ulcers are more commonly found in the stomach and therefore they're called gastric ulcers. (Colonic ulcers are discussed in the next section.) Cells within the stomach lining produce a very strong acid known as hydrochloric acid (HCl). It is so strong that if you were to spill some on your hand, it would burn a hole in your skin. Fortunately, your horse's stomach is protected by a thick mucous lining (or, rather, part of it is; we'll look at the stomach in a minute).

Your horse produces HCl continuously, unlike our own stomachs where acid is only produced when we eat. *He secretes acid all the time because he is designed to eat all the time.* He is a "trickle feeder," meaning he is supposed to eat small amounts, grazing virtually 24 hours a day, with intermittent stops to rest. Eating requires chewing and chewing produces saliva, a natural antacid that neutralizes acid so it doesn't erode his stomach lining or have a chance to travel down the rest of his digestive tract, causing more trouble.

HCl sounds like a real nuisance, but it is actually quite necessary. Your horse uses it to start the process of protein digestion. Proteins are very long, tightly woven, complex molecules that need to be loosened and cut into more manageable pieces before they can be fully digested. HCl relaxes the protein structure, making the inner portion more accessible to digestive enzymes. And this same acid actually activates an enzyme in the stomach that starts to cleave off shorter strands of amino acids, a process that will be completed later, in the small intestine.

HCl has another important function — it protects your horse from infections. Horses eat off the ground, taking in mouthfuls of bacteria, viruses, and an assortment of organisms. Stomach acid is the first line of defense to kill those microbes. This is why I do not like long term usage of medications that neutralize acid. I'll discuss those medications later.

So far, so good. So what causes an ulcer?

We do. Ulcers are caused by people. Horses rarely develop ulcers in natural settings. Basically there are four things we do to our horses that cause them to develop ulcers: We make them work, we cause them stress, we feed them lovingly but improperly, and we give them pain killers that wreak havoc with their digestive system. I'm here to help you find ways to reduce your horse's risk of experiencing an ulcer, while still being able to work and perform. Let's start by examining each cause separately so you can take steps to prevent this painful condition. And later, I'll tell how you can recognize, diagnose, and treat ulcers.

REASONS ULCERS DEVELOP

Performance

When your horse moves, the acid in his stomach moves with him. To see how this affects his stomach, let's take a closer look.

Your horse's stomach is divided into two main regions: the lower, glandular portion, and the upper, squamous area. An ulcer in one of these locations is referred to as equine gastric ulcer syndrome (EGUS).

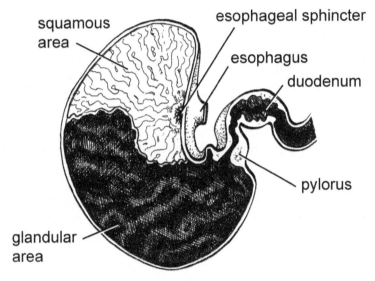

squamous area

esophageal sphincter

esophagus

duodenum

pylorus

glandular area

Anatomy of the stomach

The upper, squamous region does not have a protective mucous lining. Looking at the picture above, it's easy to can see how stomach acid can slosh around to the upper squamous portion when your horse is moving quickly. Events that require speed such as racing, barrels, cutting, or running in general, expose the squamous area to HCl's caustic effect, creating a nasty sore. This is why most performance horses that run extensively will have an ulcer. In fact, 90% of all race horses have ulcers. Dressage, though a slower, more controlled discipline, involves repetitive movements and rigorous training that also leads to ulcers, but to a lesser extent, affecting approximately 40% of dressage horses.

The lower glandular region, unlike the squamous portion, is shielded from HCl by a thick mucous lining, but ulcers can still form in this area; not from running but from constant exposure to acid. That's where stress comes into play.

Stress

Stress can take so many forms, I've devoted an entire chapter to it: Chapter 17 — Stress and Behavior. You know what stresses your horse. Things like an unfamiliar environment, a new barn, loss of a buddy, and introducing a new horse to the herd. But there are other stressors, some of which you may not have much control over, such as stalling, training, performance, and travel. Did you know that ulcers start to show up within three days of your horse's first exposure to a continuing stressful situation? It may also surprise you to learn that a horse that is moved into a stall after being used to pasture turnout will develop an ulcer in less than a week.

Every horse is different; some become stressed over things that other horses barely notice. But one thing all horses share — they like routine. Any time you make a change, whether it is traveling to a strange location, starting a new training method, using an unfamiliar piece of equipment, or even changing his feed, your horse will respond by producing more stomach acid. If the stressor continues for any length of time, as your horse would experience by sudden stall confinement after living outdoors, your horse's stomach, specifically the lower glandular region, will be bathed with a continuous supply of acid. This is why stress that lasts for hours or days leads to an ulcer so quickly. And as I've pointed out earlier, one of the most common and most preventable situations that predisposes your horse to an ulcer, *anywhere along his digestive tract,* is standing for hours without anything to eat. Speaking of which, let's look at the next cause of ulcers.

Improper feeding

The best way to avoid an ulcer is to allow your horse to be a horse. And the best way to do that is to give him pasture turnout — the more time, the better. It not only gives him a steady supply of forage, but it lets him walk around, have a chance to run and buck, and visit with other horses. I realize that it is not always feasible to give your horse all the turnout he wants, but you'll be happy to know that keeping hay in front of him at all times will go a long way toward protecting his digestive system.

Hay is wonderful. It absorbs stomach acid, requires more chewing which results in more saliva, and buffers stomach acid. In fact, ulcers may be completely avoided by giving your horse alfalfa hay; pellets do not offer as much buffering effect.

I know you understand my point, but you may be up against convincing your horse's caregiver who may be stuck in old-school thinking. The best advice I can give you is to give this book to that person! I'm not trying to make anyone feel uncomfortable — well, maybe just a little: enough to sway you to change the way your horse is fed.

> Take the Getty Challenge: Offer your horse all the hay he wants for four weeks and let me know if he's changed.

Do me a favor. You've heard me talk about this so much already, I'd like you to take the "Getty Challenge": Offer your horse all the hay he wants for four weeks and let me know if he's changed. No, I don't mean if he's gotten fatter — I mean his behavior. Is he happier and milder mannered? Does he respond to your commands better and give you his attention? Is he smoother under saddle? Oh, and the weight thing… don't worry — he'll eventually eat only what he needs to maintain a healthy weight.

Starch: You may not realize it but starchy feeds can lead to ulcers. Cereal grains stimulate the release of a hormone known as gastrin which tells the stomach cells to produce more acid; furthermore, they stay in the stomach for a relatively short period of time, leaving an empty stomach behind with all that acid. Hay and other fibrous feeds (such as beet pulp, hay cubes, and bran) take three times as long to leave the stomach.

Starchy feed has an additional impact on ulcer development. The stomach's bacteria (*Lactobacillus* and *Streptococcus*) like to start fermenting starch, resulting in different acids — volatile fatty acids (VFAs). This further increases the acid content of your horse's stomach.

So, in general, 2 lbs of starchy feed at a time is best, but never exceed 4 lbs (weigh your feed!) for an 1100 lb horse. And space your feedings approximately 6 hours apart to prevent accumulation of VFAs. In between those feedings, offer hay — lots of it. And remember the alfalfa; its buffering ability outshines any other hay source.

Pain relievers

Enduring pain is stressful and can have the same effect as mental stressors on your horse's health. But the risk is compounded by overusing non-steroidal anti-inflammatory drugs (NSAIDs). These medications are often necessary, but they are not meant to be used for more than a few days.

NSAIDs such as phenylbutazone (bute) and flunixin meglumine (Banamine) can irritate the stomach lining enough to set up conditions for an ulcer. They inhibit cyclooxygenase (COX) enzymes. These enzymes stimulate prostaglandin production, which causes inflammation. But not all prostaglandins are harmful. Some are beneficial because they help produce mucus that protects the stomach.

I offer a full description of how NSAIDs work along with safe dosing instruction in Chapter 11 — Laminitis.

Summary

Follow these practices as closely as possible, to reduce the chances of your horse developing a painful ulcer:

- Turnout as much as possible
- Offer good quality hay at all times
- Avoid feeding too much grain and always follow up any starchy meal with hay
- Replace cereal grains with feeds lower in starch to reduce VFAs production
- Feed alfalfa to buffer stomach acid (hay or cubes)
- Limit use of NSAID pain relievers
- Watch your horse's stress level

SIGNS OF AN ULCER

Ulcers are tricky. Some horses do not show any overt signs of having them, while others show signs but do not have ulcers. The key is to watch for changes. If your horse starts to eat more slowly, and leaves food left over, this can be your first clue.

Other signs include:

- **Mild and intermittent colic.** He may show sensitivity in his flank, or lie down more than usual. Distress after a meal where he paws the ground and doesn't finish it could also be a sign of pain. But a full-blown colic incident is not likely caused by an ulcer.

- **Loss of condition.** His hair will look dull and his general appearance will not be as good as it once was.

- **Poor attitude.** He may be irritable and nervous.

- **Poor performance.** He may be unwilling to perform as well as he used to, or he may exhibit back and muscle pain.

- **Weight loss.** Lack of appetite can lead to weight loss.

- **Yawning.** Horses seem to yawn excessively when they are experiencing pain, especially mouth and abdominal pain. They do not yawn like we do to increase our oxygen supply, since they do not inhale while yawning.

The problem with these signs is that they are often non-specific. Horses can lose weight, have a poor hair coat, and be unthrifty for a variety of reasons. Some horses with ulcers grind their teeth (bruxism) and yawn excessively, but this can also be a symptom of liver disease, mouth pain, or pain anywhere in the body. Ulcer signs can also include stretching out to urinate, dropping of the penis, and lying on their backs to relieve pain, but these symptoms could also relate to a urinary-tract problem or back pain.

DIAGNOSING AN ULCER

If you suspect an ulcer because your horse lives the lifestyle that would lead to a problem, plus he is exhibiting any of the above signs, it is best to contact your veterinarian. If his symptoms are severe enough, your vet may recommend an endoscopy.

Endoscopy

This procedure is the most accurate diagnostic tool available because a scope is inserted down your horse's esophagus, allowing your vet to see inside the stomach. Colonic ulcers cannot be seen with this method; I will discuss them in the next section.

To perform an endoscopy, your horse has to go without anything to eat for 12 to 18 hours. This can be very stressful. After all, you can't tell your horse that it's only temporary. Isn't that how we get through difficult procedures? We know that it won't last very long so we can get through the discomfort. But your horse thinks his distress will last forever. So before putting him through hours of fasting, make sure he can tolerate the stress. If he is insulin resistant or has equine Cushing's disease, the extra cortisol (stress hormone) can trigger a laminitis attack.

Fecal blood test

An improved fecal blood test is available as another diagnostic tool that shows promise because it can differentiate between blood that comes from the stomach vs the colon. And blood loss can be so slight that you won't see it in the manure. A positive result using this test tells you that there is an ulcer. However, false negatives can be a problem since an ulcer in its early stages may not be bleeding enough to show up on the test.

SmartPill

A high-tech tool that measures stomach emptying time is in the works for horses. It is called the SmartPill Gastrointestinal Monitoring System and has been used in dogs successfully. Basically, it measures how low it takes for the SmartPill to leave the stomach. This is particularly effective in diagnosing pyloric or duodenal ulcers (located in the glandular portion of the stomach and the first part of the small intestine) since an ulcer in one of these areas will delay emptying time.

Blood sucrose

A lower-tech test that is effective in diagnosing severe ulcers is to simply feed sugar and test for sucrose in the bloodstream. Table sugar is sucrose, made up of a glucose and fructose molecule linked together. It is too large to normally be absorbed into the bloodstream and therefore, under normal circumstances it is digested (broken apart) in the small intestine to the individual glucose and fructose units, which can then easily be absorbed. However, if there are severe ulcers in the stomach, sucrose will enter the bloodstream undigested.

TREATMENT

If your horse has an ulcer, or even if you suspect one, see if you can make adjustments your horse's lifestyle that would reduce stress. Even a horse that appears calm can have an ulcer. They're the ones that hold everything inside — perhaps you know some people who do that.

Dietary adjustments

In addition to grass and alfalfa hay, switch from feeding cereal grain to beet pulp. It has as many calories as oats without the propensity for acid production found with starch. And it is high in calcium, which buffers acid. Though not as good as alfalfa, it should be part of your dietary treatment.

Another feeding method, and an easier one, is to simply purchase a low starch commercial feed. But check the ingredients carefully. No oats, no corn, no barley, no wheat middlings, and if there's rice bran, it should be near the end of the list. Look for alfalfa meal, soybean meal, and beet pulp — all low in starch and excellent feeds to help your horse heal.

Fat: For extra calories, feed fat (except to ponies and donkeys). Flaxseed meal is wonderful, not only as a fat source but as an anti-inflammatory food. Rice bran, also high in fat, can be fed in small amounts but do not overdo it because rice bran does have a fair amount of starch.

Oils are not only excellent for calories but they soothe the stomach lining. Just don't feed a large amount of oils that have a pro-inflammatory effect such as soybean or corn oils; choose rice bran oil, canola oil, or a lesser amount of flaxseed oil (if you're not already feeding flaxseed meal). See Chapter 3 — Fundamentals of Fats for a full discussion on these and other fat sources.

High-quality protein: In order to produce new, healthy tissue, your horse needs the ample amino acids that only a high-quality protein can provide. The way to obtain this is simply to add alfalfa or soybean meal to your horse's diet. These legumes will complement the rest of his diet, giving him the protein he needs. If you're feeding a commercial feed, check the list of ingredients for these two legumes; feeds that contain them will generally have between 12% and 15% crude protein.

Prebiotics and probiotics: I like feeding prebiotics to horses that have ulcers because there are literally thousands of microbes living in the hindgut that cannot be replaced by a simple probiotic. Prebiotics offer fermentation products that feed these bacteria, making digestion more efficient and promoting B vitamin synthesis. If your horse is underweight, they are especially helpful.

Probiotics should also be added to replace losses that may have occurred as acid traveled down the gastrointestinal tract.

Medications

Gastric ulcers in humans are generally caused by a bacterial infection (*Helicobacter pylori*) and respond well to antibiotic therapy. However, this organism has not been shown to be the culprit in equine ulcers. So, the drug of choice is omeprazole (same drug found in Prilosec for people). This is a proton-pump inhibitor which turns off the acid-producing enzyme found in the stomach cells. It is marketed under the brand name GastroGard (Merial). This drug is good for short term usage, especially in cases of active training or extensive travel. The more diluted version of omeprazole called UlcerGard (Merial) can be used throughout show season or for chronic conditions.

There are two other less effective medications: H2 blockers and antacids. H2 blockers turn off the H2 receptors on parietal cells (cells that are responsible for producing acid). The four H2 blockers available are cimetidine (Tagamet), famotidine (Pepsid), nizatidine (Axid), and ranitidine (Zantac). They are less expensive than omeprazole, but also less helpful.

Antacids neutralize acid after it has been produced. Saliva, produced by chewing, is a natural antacid. In most commercial antacids, calcium carbonate is the active ingredient. I don't normally suggest antacids because they have to be fed several times each day to have any effect.

Keep in mind that these medications either turn off the acid-making machinery in the stomach or deactivate existing acid; therefore, secondary problems can result. Acid is important. As I mentioned earlier, it helps start protein digestion and it kills microbes that your horse is exposed to every day while eating off the ground; stomach acid is an essential component of your horse's immune system. Its long term reduction can lead to infections.

Herbs: Several herbs are useful in soothing and healing the stomach lining. These include aloe vera juice, ginger, licorice, slippery elm, turmeric, chamomile, goldenseal, and quercetin.

Colonic Ulcers and Right Dorsal Colitis (RDC)

Colitis (inflammation in the colon) and accompanying ulcerations typically affect the right dorsal colon near your horse's right flank. Though not as common as gastric ulcers, they are still a significant problem. More than half of all performance horses experience colonic ulcers but stressors, NSAID usage, and dietary factors can lead to ulcers in non-performance horses as well. If your horse has signs of an ulcer, but an endoscopy does not reveal a problem, it likely is because the ulcer is further down the digestive tract.

SIGNS

At first, your horse may act lethargic. He'll lose interest in eating and have very little energy. He may also experience mild, occasional colic episodes. As the condition progresses, he may develop diarrhea, fever, and completely lose his appetite, leading to weight loss and dehydration.

DIAGNOSIS

If he has diarrhea, it's beneficial to rule out infectious diseases such as salmonellosis and Potomac horse fever, as well as *Clostridium difficile* and *perfringens* toxins. These bacteria are also discussed later in the chapter.

Tests

Blood work results will reveal:

- Elevated fibrinogen
- Low albumin
- Low calcium
- Increased white blood cells
- Low protein (hypoproteinemia)

A fecal blood test will reveal any blood in the manure. It is a good indicator of colonic ulceration, especially when an endoscopy shows no presence of stomach ulcers.

TREATMENT

During this time, allow your horse to rest. Save training and exercise for when he's feeling better, and avoid traveling. The dietary and medical treatments below should help your horse heal within a few months' time.

Diet

Avoid feeding hay: The goal is to decrease gut fill, and hay provides too much bulk. Your horse can graze on fresh grass for 15 minute intervals, four to eight times a day.

Frequent feedings: To decrease the load on the colon and restore normal absorptive function, offer your horse frequents meals of moistened alfalfa pellets, beet pulp, or alfalfa-based complete feeds (no cereal grains) that contain 18-25% fiber. He should not have an empty stomach, so feedings need to be frequent enough to keep him busy throughout the day.

Do this for three to four months and have his protein and albumin levels retested to see if they have returned to normal.

Omega-3 fatty acids: Flaxseed meal or oil is high in omega-3 fatty acids, which will reduce inflammation. Provide 1/2 cup of flaxseed meal or 2 tablespoons of flaxseed oil per 400 lbs of body weight per day.

Water and salt: Clean water and a white salt block should be accessible at all times. If you are already supplying minerals through a commercial, fortified feed, or a vitamin/mineral supplement, this should be sufficient; however if you not supplementing minerals, add a mineralized block.

Vitamins and minerals: Continue feeding whatever vitamin/mineral supplement you have been using; if these nutrients are already coming from a commercial feed, there is no need to add more.

Additional treatments

Medications: Omeprazole, H2 inhibitors, and antacids used to treat stomach ulcers are not effective for RDC and colonic ulcers. Sucralfate, however, if very helpful. It forms a sticky, thick gel that binds to ulcerated areas within the colon, forming a coating to help the area heal. It does, however, reduce absorption of fat soluble vitamins, so if you are adding a vitamin/mineral supplement, do so at least two hours before or after you administer the medicine.

Probiotics: Replenish losses using a potent probiotic, preferably one that contains oligosaccharides to promote healing. It should also contain yeast (*Saccharomyces cerevisiae*), which increases the colon pH by reducing acetate production.

Psyllium: Psyllium seed husks provide soluble fiber that shortens transit time within the digestive tract while increasing water content. It also reduces inflammation. I recommend 1/8 to 1/4 cup at each feeding as an aggressive treatment.

Colic

Colic basically means a "tummy ache." It could simply be a mild disturbance, or severe enough to be life threatening, or varying degrees in between. It is the number two killer of horses; number one being old age!

Colic isn't actually a disease; it's a *symptom* of another problem. Ulcers, intestinal impactions, enteroliths (stones), excess gas production, and alterations in the hindgut pH can lead to colic. Liver problems, urinary infections, abscesses, hot weather, dehydration, and even mental stress or cribbing can also cause intestinal distress. But regardless of the reason, you know your horse is in trouble when he shows signs of abdominal pain. He will lose his appetite, start to sweat, look back at his flank, stretch out to urinate, and lie down and start to roll. This sends any horse owner into crisis mode. This is a *medical emergency* and your veterinarian should be contacted immediately. There are many possible causes of colic, so a wait-and-see attitude can send your horse into a life-threatening situation.

WHILE WAITING FOR YOUR VET TO ARRIVE

It's important to keep your horse as calm as possible. Brushing or even bathing (in hot weather) can be soothing. Remove all hay or feed, but allow access to water. Should you walk him? Maybe. Walking is useful for gas entrapment. Slow walking can relieve pain and may help loosen trapped gas. But know that you won't prevent him from requiring surgery, if it comes to that, by walking him.

We used to think that you should stop your horse from rolling — that it would cause gut displacement — but mild rolling may be your horse's way of getting everything back into place. However, violent rolling can be dangerous and indicates severe pain. If he's rolling violently, get him on his feet. But if he is too weak to stand or cannot remain balanced, it's best to let him be.

You may be tempted to give him a pain reliever, but it's best to wait for your veterinarian to arrive since blocking or lessening pain could interfere with the diagnosis.

Take a look at your horse's gums. They should be pink. If they're bright red or muddy, this indicates poor circulation and dehydration. Learn how to determine the capillary fill time. Press your finger on the gum line by the teeth and then release and note the time it takes for the color to return to normal. This should take no more than two seconds in a healthy horse. A longer time indicates that there are circulation problems.

In addition, it's helpful for your vet to know your horse's pulse, respiratory rate, and temperature. A normal pulse is 32 to 40 beats per minute. The best way to determine this heart rate is by using a stethoscope and every horse owner should have one. If you don't have one, feel for a pulse along the jaw or behind the fetlock. A normal respiratory rate is 12 to 20 breaths per minute. A normal rectal temperature is between 99.5 and 101° F for an adult horse and higher (102°) for a foal. And make a mental note of how much manure he's recently produced and any changes in its condition.

MEDICAL TREATMENTS

Your vet will likely palpate to check for impaction and listen for gut sounds; he/she will also administer short term pain relief. Mineral oil is commonly used and a stomach tube will reveal if fluid is backed up due to an obstruction further along the gastrointestinal tract. These assessments may not tell you the cause of colic, but they can give your vet an idea of its severity and whether or not hospitalization is needed.

Your horse may require surgery. Though details are beyond the scope of this book, surgery is often warranted for situations such as lipoma-related colic (where fatty tumors wrap around the bowel), twists and torsions, telescoping of one bowel segment into another (known as intussusception), sand impactions, and enterolith removal. General feeding guidelines after surgery include gradually increasing bulk, eliminating cereal grains, increasing fat, and like any surgery, providing additional antioxidants (vitamins C and E) to expedite healing and vitamin E to prevent scar tissue and adhesions.

Your vet may pull blood to check your horse's blood sugar level as a diagnostic tool. It has been found[1] that colicky horses will generally exhibit hyperglycemia — high blood glucose levels, exceeding 180 mg/deciliter. This is a dangerously high level and can be life threatening. Once your vet brings it under control, I suggest regularly monitoring your horse's blood glucose concentration to assess his gastrointestinal health.

CAUSES AND PREVENTION

Most colic cases can be prevented by proper turnout, diet, and water consumption. The most common causes are not enough pasture turnout, hay restriction, large concentrated meals, not enough water, poor teeth, and stress. In addition, it is not uncommon for stones (enteroliths) to form around foreign materials such as a horseshoe nail, piece of rope, or plastic. Sand accumulation is also problematic.

Here are some important ways to avoid colic

Keep your horse on full turnout as much as possible: Horses that are allowed to graze on fresh pasture rarely experience colic. I know, I know… when you get to the barn to ride, you want your horse to be ready, so he *has* to be stalled. Convenience for convenience sake, however, can lead to heartache. Take the extra effort necessary and allow your horse to be a horse. He will feel better and be a better performer as a result.

Limit winter stalling: During the winter, colic episodes increase when horses are brought in from pasture. Don't be over anxious to get your horses out of the cold weather. When given a choice, horses would much rather be outside, even in winter.

Having said this, make sure your horse has shelter from a storm. Wind and rain, as well as heavy snow, can make it difficult for him to maintain his normal body temperature. So only in extreme weather conditions is it necessary to stall your horse. I understand that this is not an option for many of you. So, if you must bring your horse inside at the start of winter, slowly ease him into this transition and feed his hindgut by offering a prebiotic.

Prevent heat stress: Hot weather is challenging and horses typically suffer during this time. Shade is a must. If your horse is stalled, fans provide proper air circulation, which is also imperative for respiratory health. Hose down your horse throughout the day to keep him cool. But *be sure to scrape excess water off of him before letting him back out into the sun.* That water can heat up so rapidly that it feels like a heavy blanket in the summer! Colic is a common result.

Provide clean water and salt at all times: A horse will typically drink between 8 and 12 gallons of water each day. So, water needs to be available and close by to where he feeds. Also, water troughs should be cleaned out every few days to make certain that there is no algae scum on the sides of the tank. Bird droppings are especially hazardous since they can carry salmonella bacteria, which can make your horse very ill.

In the winter, be sure the water is heated to approximately 50° F. Any colder than this and your horse will not drink enough to keep his digestive system healthy. In the summer, outdoor water troughs can get very hot. Dump them regularly and refill with cool water.

Always provide a plain, white salt block and add salt to his diet if he's not licking enough. For a full sized horse, you can add 2 tablespoons of table salt per day, divided between meals, to encourage him to drink enough water. Water prevents impactions from forming in his cecum and large colon.

Have your horse's teeth floated annually: Your horse's teeth need to be floated at least once each year; some require floating every six months. Poor dental health leads to partially chewed pasture and hay, which can cause impactions throughout the digestive tract.

Prevent your horse from inhaling his hay: If your horse becomes overly anxious waiting to be fed, he will bolt down his next hay supply, and may colic. Keeping hay in front of him at all times will help him calm down and eat more slowly.

Keep concentrated meals small: Your horse's stomach is small compared to the rest of his gastrointestinal tract (see the illustration in Chapter 1 — Ground Rules for Feeding a Horse). To prevent overloading his stomach, his meal should not weigh more than 4 lbs (that's for an 1100 lb horse). Cereal grains move through the digestive tract very quickly and so can end up in the hindgut; hindgut fermentation of starch is dangerous. The pH is lowered (becomes more acidic) which is asking for a case of colic; it can even cause ulcers and founder (laminitis).

Make changes to the diet very gradually: This will give the bacterial flora in the hindgut a chance to become accustomed to the new feed. Ideally, a three to four week period is necessary to completely switch to a new feed. If you are adding a new supplement to the diet, you don't need to take this much time; however, it's best to add 1/4 of the normal dose the first day, 1/2 the next day, and so on until you reach the normal dosage.

Be consistent in what you feed each day: A warm bran mash once a week in the winter may sound comforting but you are asking for colic. Those hindgut microbes need time to adjust to a new feed. Adding something once every few days is potentially damaging to them and very, very risky.

Keep him well exercised: Your horse's intestines are made of muscles. To keep them in good tone, your horse needs to be exercised. Stall confinement is one of the most common reasons for colic because your horse cannot move much. It can also lead to ulcers, another cause of colic. Pasture turnout offers some exercise as your horse moves from place to place for that next delicious morsel; two to three acres of space per horse is ideal, though I realize not every horse has this much land. So for smaller areas or dry lots, spread hay around in various places to simulate pasture grazing.

Store feedstuffs properly to prevent spoilage and mold: Concentrated feeds should be used within 2 months, especially those that contain corn. Corn can develop mycotoxins which can lead to colic and even death. See Chapter 9 — Fundamentals of Concentrates and By-Products for a discussion on mycotoxins.

Feeds that contain fat can spoil, resulting in free radical formation. Free radicals are volatile, damaging molecules that form inside your horse's body when he is ill or stressed. But you can also end up feeding these harmful substances to your horse if the feedstuff is spoiled. To avoid rancidity, store fatty feeds (flaxseed meal, rice bran, soybean meal, even cereal grains) in a tightly sealed container, preferably in a cool, dry place.

Sun-spoiled and even moldy hay can be fed to cows because the bacterial flora living in the rumen can detoxify materials before they enter the bloodstream. But this is not the case with your horse. Check your hay supply for mold; it may be black, white, or dusty and the leaves will be clumped together. Most horses will not eat moldy hay if they have something better to eat, but there's always one in the bunch that is not as discerning as the rest, who will eat whatever is in front of him and end up with severe indigestion, or worse.

Regularly deworm your horse: If your horse has not been dewormed within the past 6 months, he likely has a heavy infestation. Deworming him at this point could result in colic because of the massive amounts of worms inside his digestive system. So, deworm him gradually, or better yet, with your vet's supervision.

Regular deworming helps prevent colic. A daily dewormer (pyrantel tartrate), along with ivermectin twice each year, is a beneficial plan for most areas of the country. Encysted small strongyle larvae can accumulate in large numbers and need to be eradicated using a five-day, double dose of fenbendazole or a single dose of moxidectin. Large strongyle larvae can migrate through abdominal arteries, leading to aneurisms and circulation blockage. Small strongyles form cysts in the intestinal lining. Tapeworms, in particular, can lead to impactions within the small intestine or cause ileocecal intussusception (where the intestines telescope inside one another). The problem with detecting tapeworms is that they release eggs sporadically, so fecal tests are often inconclusive. A blood test can detect antibodies related to tapeworms, but most veterinarians do not use such tests and prefer to use an appropriate anthelmintic (deworming medication). The only ones that eradicate tapeworms are pyrantel pamoate at a double dose or praziquantel, packaged as a paste deworming combo with ivermectin or moxidectin.

Horses can develop resistance to dewormers which can make them ineffective. So I recommend bringing a fresh manure sample to your vet every 2 to 3 months to make sure your horse is staying healthy. But as I mentioned, tapeworms cannot be detected by a fecal test, so to be sure, it is best to use an anthelmintic that targets them.

Natural dewormers contain diatomaceous earth and are supposedly safer. Diatomaceous earth (DE) consists of fossilized diatoms, a hard-shelled algae. It is basically crystalline silica and the powdered version can be extremely damaging to your lungs as well as your horse's lungs. There are pelleted versions that do not cause lung damage but my concern is that first, DE cannot be wet in order to be effective, and second, it may not have any effect on the larvae that damage abdominal arteries. It is presumed to kill worms through its abrasive, sharp edges, but there are few scientific studies that evaluate its long term effect on the horse's digestive tract lining.

I know some of you have been using natural dewormers that contain DE for years without any problem. My concern is just that — a concern. But until more long term studies confirm its safety, I recommend having your horse's manure regularly tested and using a traditional deworming program.

Prepare your horse for travel two weeks before a long trip: The stress of traveling long distances, combined with changes in water and feed, are tickets for colic. In Chapter 17 — Stress and Behavior, I talk about ways to prepare your horse for travel to keep him healthy. That chapter also discusses other stressors, such as cribbing, which can lead to colic.

Avoid prolonged use of NSAID pain relievers: As I discussed in the earlier section on ulcers, bute and Banamine are often given to horses to relieve pain, but what they do is reduce prostaglandin production. This slows down healing. In fact, prostaglandins themselves, the very thing that causes inflammation, are often given to horses to treat colic to allow the body to repair itself.

CECAL IMPACTION VS DYSFUNCTION

Colic can result when the cecum becomes filled with dry feed, causing an impaction and obstructing intestinal flow. Cecal dysfunction, however, is different. Here the cecum is distended due to fluid accumulation, with solid material found at the base (see how the cecum is situated in Chapter 1 — Ground Rules for Feeding a Horse). In both cases, however, there is extreme abdominal pain and surgery is usually the only remedy.

These disorders can be caused by the following factors:

- Poor dental health, resulting in inadequate chewing
- Coarse, stemmy hay
- Sudden dietary changes
- Overdose or prolonged use of NSAIDS (typically bute and Banamine)
- Tapeworm infestation
- Hospitalization for unrelated reasons, which causes stress
- Extreme stress from other circumstances

Sand Colic

I've decided to discuss this type of colic in its own section because it is different than other forms of colic. It can occur over time, little by little, leading to a deadly compaction.

When your horse eats off the ground, he is bound to eat some dirt, especially if you have loose sandy soils. If his paddock is dry, he'll certainly consume more dirt (sand) than he would from grassy areas. After a while, sand will slowly accumulate to the point where it creates a life threatening compaction within the colon. And the sad part is, you often won't know about this until it is serious, since your horse can go for years without any symptoms, as he steadily builds up more sand.

Sometimes, in relatively early stages, you'll notice bouts of mild colic, accompanied by diarrhea. Your horse may lose weight for no accountable reason. You may even see sand in the manure. If you suspect a problem, do a sand test. Simply place a small amount of manure in a large freezer bag or jar and add water. Shake the mixture to get the manure to dissolve; any sand that's present will sink to the bottom.

To treat sand colic, your veterinarian will likely administer a laxative through a nasogastric tube and may give your horse antibiotics if his colon has been damaged. Unfortunately, if this treatment is not successful, surgery is likely your next option. Remember, any time you give your horse antibiotics, you should provide a potent probiotic to replace the good bacteria that have also been destroyed.

WAYS TO PREVENT SAND COLIC

The most obvious approach toward preventing sand colic is to reduce sand intake. If you feed hay in a dry paddock, consider placing a rubber mat under the hay. Or, you can use elevated hay feeders. But your horse will take a bite of hay and place it on the ground to finish eating so a rubber mat is still helpful.

Psyllium hulls can be helpful in clearing sand on a regular basis. Researchers at Colorado State University[3] revealed that psyllium, combined with a probiotic, helps normalize gut motility, promoting sand removal from the intestinal tract. However, do not rely on these products to do the whole job. *The best way to prevent sand colic is to provide forage — lots of it — all day long.* And make sure your horse drinks plenty of water.

Enteroliths

Enteroliths are intestinal stones that typically develop in the right dorsal colon when a horse eats something foreign: a pebble, piece of wire, a horseshoe nail, cloth, or other non-food item. Crystalline material (often composed of magnesium ammonium phosphate salts) forms around this object and can become as large as 8 inches in diameter! We see a higher incidence of enteroliths in California and this may be due to mineralization of the soil and water supply but it is also likely due to feeding too much alfalfa. Alfalfa is a wonderful hay to feed, but it should never encompass more than 50% of the total hay ration, and somewhat less is even better.

Alfalfa can lead to enteroliths by causing the pH of the hindgut to rise (become more alkaline). A small amount of grain (if your horse is permitted to have starch) will lower the pH. Also adding vinegar to your horse's diet will make his hindgut more acidic. Most horses love apple cider vinegar. Just add approximately one cup to your horse's meal or water bucket.

Magnesium, when combined with high levels of phosphorus and not enough calcium, can also lead to enteroliths. Cereal grains, bran, and flaxseed meal are very high in phosphorus. So your best approach is to never skimp on grass hay because it provides enough calcium. And when feeding bran or flax, choose a commercial product that has added calcium. Also, have your hay analyzed for these three minerals to make sure they're in balance. This is not only important to prevent enteroliths, but also to build healthy bones and joints. See Chapter 5 — Fundamentals of Minerals for more discussion.

Simple pasture grazing, where horses can walk around, seems to prevent enterolith production. This amount of exercise increases gut motility, so stones, when small, are easily passed out through the manure. Even hay, when supplied free choice, will keep your horse's digestive tract moving enough to remove stones before they get too large.

High fiber diets in general are helpful in preventing stones from forming. Beet pulp and hay pellets are good choices as well as commercial feeds that have at least 18% fiber. Psyllium hulls also help clean out the digestive tract of stones — feed 1/2 cup for seven consecutive days out of each month.

In summary, if your horse is prone toward enteroliths, I recommend the following:

- Alfalfa should comprise no more than 50% of the total roughage intake; 30% is safer.

- Eliminate bran, unless it has added calcium.

- Provide pasture grazing, if possible, to provide slow, steady exercise that keeps the gastrointestinal tract in good shape.

- Try to lower the pH of the hindgut either through adding some apple cider vinegar to the diet or, if the horse can tolerate it, a small amount of grain.

- Keep forage levels high to keep the intestines moving.

- Feed a diet high in fiber, and offer psyllium hulls for one week to remove stones early.

- Encourage water drinking to prevent dehydration.

Diarrhea

Loose manure that resembles cow-patties is not considered diarrhea. Diarrhea refers to watery feces and if not controlled, it can be deadly. Its presence means that for one reason or another, your horse may not be digesting his feed. This can cause him to lose weight and the lost fluid can lead to dehydration.

Diarrhea can be acute, meaning it comes about all of a sudden, or it can be chronic, where it lasts for a while, or comes and goes. Let's look at each type separately.

ACUTE DIARRHEA

If one day your horse is fine, and the next he abruptly develops runny diarrhea, accompanied by fever and elevated respiration, or he won't eat, consider this a medical emergency and call your veterinarian immediately.

Acute diarrhea is generally caused by a change in the microflora of the hindgut. Nearly one third of all acute diarrhea (and also colitis) cases result from bacterial toxins produced by either *Clostridium difficile* or *Clostridium perfringens*. Traditionally, diagnosis involves a bacterial culture, which is tedious, time consuming, and expensive. However, the Enzyme-Linked Immunosorbent Assay (ELISA) can test for toxins, rather than the bacteria, providing an easier and more sensitive diagnosis.

Acute diarrhea can also occur in cases of grain overload, peritonitis, stress, and overuse of NSAID pain relievers. Well-meaning horse owners may overdose their horses with drugs such as bute, Banamine, and even aspirin, which can be toxic, resulting in severe diarrhea. Follow your vet's guidelines. The actual dosage limits are shown in Chapter 11 — Laminitis.

CHRONIC DIARRHEA

Chronic diarrhea is differentiated from acute diarrhea by the length of time it lasts. I've seen cases that clear up within a month and other cases that can come and go for years. Your veterinarian will do an overall exam, test a fecal sample for worm infestation, and may draw blood. But once it's been determined that your horse is basically healthy, your vet may give the "shoulder shrug" diagnosis and tell you that the cause is unknown. This can be very frustrating because there must be *something* wrong. But before you get discouraged, there are several routes you can try.

Prevent sand accumulation

Sand accumulation (see sand colic earlier in this chapter) irritates the intestinal lining and is often a cause of chronic diarrhea. Before it gets to the point where surgery is the only cure, try reducing dirt intake by placing a mat on the ground where your horse eats hay. If you're not giving your horse hay free choice, start doing so. And add psyllium to his diet — 1 to 2 ounces per day for 3 to 6 months.

Encourage water drinking

Be sure your horse does not get dehydrated. Add two tablespoons of plain, white table salt (grocery store variety) to your horse's feed each day. Also make sure a white salt block is easily within reach. And clean, temperature controlled water should be always available. As I previously mentioned, when water gets below 50° F, horses will not drink as much. And keep an eye on that big water trough — it should be clean and free of algae accumulation. There also should be no bird droppings in it (they can carry *Salmonella*) or dead insects.

Establish a good deworming program

A proper, consistent deworming program is very important for digestive health. In the case of chronic diarrhea, I recommend giving your horse a five-day, double dose of fenbendazole, or a single dose of moxidectin to remove encysted larvae.

Try changing feeds or hay supplies

There could be something that your horse is sensitive or allergic to in his current feeding program; a different type of hay may just do the trick. Commercial feeds can also contain substances that cause problems. Switch to a low starch, pelleted feed since too much sugar can lead to diarrhea in some horses. But make changes slowly; three to four weeks is best.

Reduce cereal grains

If you are feeding oats, corn, or any other cereal grain, try discontinuing it for a while. Starch that reaches the hindgut is fermented by the bacteria residing there, resulting in lactic acid formation. The lowered pH that results is called hindgut acidosis and can kill these important microbes.

Use a potent probiotic and prebiotic

A potent probiotic, one that has billions (that's 10^9) of colony forming units (CFUs), should be used regularly at a treatment dose until the diarrhea has subsided. Then, a maintenance dose should be continued indefinitely. Look for a product that also contains oligosaccharides to boost immune function and yeast to promote digestion efficiency. In addition to a probiotic, you'll also want to add a prebiotic to feed the literally thousands of different bacteria and protozoa that live in the hindgut. This will make digestion more efficient, since your horse is not absorbing enough nutrients when there is diarrhea.

Give a large amount of vitamin B₁

All of the B vitamins are important for digestive health, but vitamin B_1 (thiamin) in particular, when given at a high dosage, is effective in slowing down intestinal motility and increasing water absorption from the small colon[4]. Give your horse 1 mg per pound of body weight; so a 1000 lb horse will get 1000 mg of thiamin per day. It's best to divide it between meals.

Consider aluminomagnesium silicate

There are commercial products made from aluminomagnesium silicate which may be helpful. This chemical binds to the mucous lining, thereby increasing resistance to bacterial damage, especially from toxins produced by *C. difficile* and *C. perfringens*.

Choking

When a horse chokes, there is something caught in his esophagus (leading to the stomach), not his trachea (going toward the lungs) as you would see with a choking person.

So, the horse can still breathe, which is a good thing since choking would be far more dangerous if that weren't the case. Nevertheless, choking is very frightening and the horse is in deep distress. You can tell if your horse is experiencing this situation if he extends his neck forward and gags. He will drool and food will come out of his mouth and even his nose. But he will not fix this on his own, so don't take a "wait and see" attitude — call your vet immediately. If your horse is not treated, the esophagus can tear or rupture. And material can enter his lungs, leading to life threatening pneumonia.

Your vet will administer a sedative to help him pass the blockage on his own. Or he/she may use a stomach tube with water to push the obstruction down into the stomach. Anti-inflammatory medications will likely be used to help heal his sore esophagus.

Older horses, especially those with poor or missing teeth, are more prone toward choking. But even young horses can experience this problem, especially when they eat very fast. Stress can cause a horse to bolt down his hay too quickly. This often happens in the morning, after a long night of deprivation. If your horse is overly anxious to eat in the morning, he is not getting enough hay to withstand the night.

Fast eating can also occur when horses are fed close to one another, creating competition. Separating your horses or tying them during meals may make each horse feel less threatened. If your horse eats fast even when not stressed, try placing some large rocks in his feed bucket to slow down eating.

Dehydration, which most often occurs during the winter when horses avoid icy water, can create thick saliva, making it difficult to chew and swallow dry feeds. Soaked hay pellets or beet pulp are easy to swallow and provide additional water. Also, encourage water intake by adding salt to the meal.

Finally, eating off the ground is the normal stance for your horse. Most feeders in stalls are close to shoulder height, forcing him to eat in a position that is more likely to cause choking. Switch to ground feeders to help your horse eat more naturally.

Endnotes

[1] Researchers studied horses with acute abdominal pain at the Royal Veterinary College Equine Referral Hospital in the United Kingdom between October 2002 and March 2006.

[2] Morgan, L.M., Coverdale, J.A., Froetschel, M.A., and Yoon, I., 2007. Effect of yeast culture supplementation on digestibility of varying forage quality in mature horses. *Journal of Equine Veterinary Science, 27* (6): 260-265.

[3] Landes, A.D., Hassel, D.M., Funk, J.D., and Hill, A., 2008. Fecal sand clearance is enhanced with a product combining probiotics, prebiotics, and psyllium in clinically normal horses. *Journal of Equine Veterinary Science, 28* (2): 79-84.

[4] I do not have any scientific evidence to substantiate this claim; however, I have witnessed this effect in horses on numerous occasions. In cases of chronic, apparently incurable diarrhea, high amounts of thiamin have been effective. In addition, I have found human use of thiamin to decrease abdominal cramping and solidify the stool.

CHAPTER 15 —
JOINTS, HAIR, HOOVES, AND SKIN

*Nothing could be taken for granted when I was astride her, except
her will to carry me like a strange loving cup of water she was
determined not to spill.*
~ Tess Gallagher

Horses. They're a joy to ride and an even greater joy to watch as they graze
peacefully or kick up their heels and bound across an open field. Strong
and graceful with a willingness to learn and work hard, all for the asking.

Health — that's what we want for our horses. We want their joints to stay
limber, their feet to remain tough, and their hair to glow with a dappled
shine.

Though this book is not a medical guide, I offer a broad perspective on how
to do just that — keep your horse's joints healthy, as well as make him
beautiful on the outside.

As age and experience take their toll on your horse, he may develop arthritis and a full array of joint problems. So let's start there.

Joints

A nutritious diet is meant to provide enough nutrients so every part of your
horse's body benefits and his joints get their fair share. If his diet is lack-
ing, his body will use what's available according to priority. His priority is,
of course, to stay alive, so his life-supporting organs — heart, liver, kidneys, lungs, brain, etc. — will get first dibs on available nutrients. If anything is left over, then and only then, will other less vital tissues (joints,
muscles, hooves, skin and hair) get what they need. So if your horse's joints
are screaming for more support, just leaving him out on pasture won't be
sufficient. An adult horse that is not working *can* thrive on lush, healthy
pasture mixed with grasses and legumes (such as clover and alfalfa), but
aging horses and those that work need additional vitamins and minerals,
amino acids, and omega-3 fatty acids; they may even benefit from a joint
supplement.

Below is a picture of a synovial joint, the most common and most move-able type of joint in your horse's body. His joints have the ability to cushion movement through interacting components. Let's take a look.

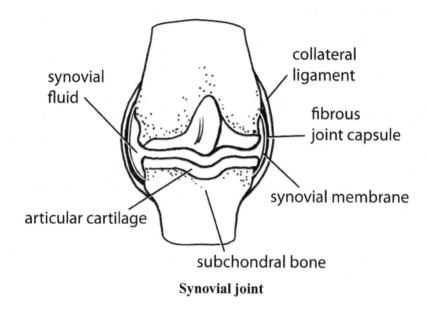

Synovial joint

Cartilage covers and cushions the surfaces of opposing bones. It is made up of a protein known as collagen which serves as a framework for long protein molecules called proteoglycans. Proteoglycans trap synovial fluid within this collagen matrix, which acts as a shock absorber and therefore provides a frictionless surface so the bones don't rub together.

The joint itself is encased by the fibrous joint capsule and the synovial membrane. The joint cavity is filled with synovial fluid, produced by the synovial membrane, which provides lubrication during movement and also delivers nutrients to cartilage. Cartilage does not have a blood supply, so it depends on synovial fluid for nourishment.

Synovial fluid is concentrated with hyaluronic acid and a proteoglycan called glycosaminoglycan, both secreted by the synovial membrane. Fluid is enmeshed within the cartilage, which acts like a sponge — fluid is squeezed out during exertion and reabsorbed during relaxation.

JOINT NUTRACEUTICALS

A nutraceutical refers to any nutrient that is used as a medication. Joint supplements abound, each containing a variety of nutraceuticals — it can get overwhelming trying to choose the right one. Is a joint supplement even necessary? I'm often asked this question. And in cases where your horse has suffered an injury or works and performs hard, the answer is, "Yes." However, if your horse is feeling fine, is not worked consistently, but is just getting up in years, he can probably get by with enough vitamin C and flaxseed meal.

Oral joint products have not been approved by the Food and Drug Administration, making oversight of actual ingredients and purity questionable. So, when choosing a supplement, go with a company you trust, a product that has worked well for you in the past, or one that has the National Animal Supplement Council (NASC) seal of approval for quality assurance.

The ingredients in joint supplements help synthesize cartilage and other joint components, serve as anti-inflammatory agents, or inhibit various enzymes that break down joint tissue. There are many from which to choose; but to help you decide which one is best for your horse, I've listed each ingredient below. I'll start with the ones most popularly found in joint products.

Glucosamine, chondroitin, MSM, and hyaluronic acid

Glucosamine: This is beneficial for horses with osteoarthritis and navicular syndrome. It seems to be best utilized when a horse already has a problem. Whether or not it is effective in preventing an injury has not been determined.

Glucosamine is a sugar (glucose) bound to an amino acid (building block of protein). It reduces inflammation and is a precursor to building blocks found in cartilage. Cartilage cells are able to produce glucosamine from glucose, but supplementation is preferable. If you're giving your horse injections to help his joints, he may do just as well with glucosamine, combined with chondroitin sulfate. It has been shown that long-term supplementation can significantly reduce the number and frequency of glycosaminoglycan injections[1].

Generally, glucosamine is extracted from shellfish and is supplemented in one of two forms: glucosamine HCl or glucosamine sulfate. It doesn't make a difference which one you choose. The sulfate form provides sulfur, which can be used to produce connective tissue. However, many amino acids found in protein contain sulfur, so adding glucosamine sulfate for that purpose is not necessary. There may be some evidence that when the sulfate version is provided, glucosamine levels within the synovial fluid are higher than when the HCl version is used; however, this is not conclusive. So, if I had to make a choice, I'd go with glucosamine HCl because it is more concentrated with glucosamine than the sulfate form and is also more palatable.

One more note... If your horse is insulin resistant, use glucosamine with caution. I discuss its mechanism in Chapter 13 — Metabolic and Endocrine Disorders.

Chondroitin sulfate: Chondroitin sulfate is a glycosaminoglycan, a protein that is enmeshed within cartilage giving it its elasticity. It is usually extracted from animal tissues such as shark cartilage, cow tracheae, or pig snouts (didn't know that, eh?). Because it inhibits the enzymes that degrade cartilage and hyaluronic acid, it is more effective in preventing injuries than glucosamine, but is often combined with glucosamine because they work synergistically to improve joint function. In other words, together they have more benefit than if supplied individually.

MSM (Methylsulfonylmethane): MSM is mainly a source of sulfur, a mineral that is necessary for collagen production. Collagen is a structural protein, not only found in joints, but also in bones, skin, and blood vessels. MSM also has anti-inflammatory properties, and therefore reduces pain.

Hyaluronic acid (HA): Also known as hyaluronan or hyaluronate, HA is another glycosaminoglycan. It is the key component of synovial fluid which provides lubrication. It is also a potent anti-inflammatory agent. Injectable hyaluronate sodium (Legend, made by Bayer) is often preferred over oral supplementation because it places HA directly into the joint or bloodstream. However, oral administration of HA has been shown to be effective in treating joint damage[2]. It can be absorbed from the small intestine into the bloodstream and remain active.

Herbs

Boswellia: This herb comes from the gum resin of an Indian tree called *Boswellia serrata*. The terpenoid portion of the plant inhibits the inflammatory action of damaging prostaglandins.

Devil's claw: Used throughout the years to treat pain, devil's claw is a root extract that also alleviates digestive disorders. It should never be given to a pregnant mare.

Ginger: Also known as a digestive aid, ginger has potent anti-inflammatory properties and may help with joint stiffness.

Grape seed extract: This substance contains antioxidants known as proanthocyanidins which help repair collagen. Proanthocyanidins found in pine bark, commonly called pycnogenols, may have a stronger antioxidant effect.

Rose hips: Derived from the fruit of the rose plant, they are high in vitamin C and bioflavonoids, both potent antioxidants. Rose hips are often times added to human joint supplements. However, research done in Denmark[3] concluded that rose hips are beneficial in treating osteoarthritis pain, inflammation, and decreased motility in horses.

Yucca: The roots of this flowering desert plant contain saponins. Saponins serve as antioxidants and therefore neutralize inflammatory free radicals that cause pain.

Fatty substances

Omega-3 fatty acids: Flaxseeds are highly concentrated in alpha linolenic acid (ALA), and fish oils contain two other omega-3s: eicosapentaenoic acid (EPA) and docosahexaenoic acid (DHA). They significantly reduce joint inflammation, pain, and stiffness. Before giving an aging horse a joint supplement, consider supplementing with flaxseed meal; this may also be sufficient for lightly exercised horses of any age.

The use of fish oils in equine nutrition may have some benefit. However, ALA from flax is converted to the larger fatty acids EPA and DHA, so I usually do not recommend fish oils. Nevertheless, supplementation may be helpful in difficult inflammatory cases or with breeding (see Chapter 18 — Breeding, Pregnancy, and Lactation).

Avocado/soybean unsaponifiables (ASUs): This is the new kid on the block when it comes to equine joint supplementation. Extracts from avocados and soybeans have been shown[4] to increase production of glycosaminoglycans in joint tissue.

Cetyl myristoleate: Concentrated in synovial fluid, cetyl myristoleate is derived from the fatty acid myristoleic acid and cetyl alcohol. It is not found in any foods, only in animal connective tissue. It serves as an anti-inflammatory agent, and hence, relieves pain.

Amino acids

Lysine and methionine: As essential amino acids, they are often added to joint preparations to boost overall protein quality. Collagen is a protein, dependant on an ample supply of essential amino acids for its production. Read more about essential amino acids in Chapter 4 — Fundamentals of Protein and Amino Acids.

Proline: Your horse is able to produce this amino acid, so it is not, by definition, essential. However, it is a necessary component of collagen, making its addition appropriate, though not necessary.

Vitamins

Vitamin B_6 (pyridoxine): Pyridoxine is involved in protein synthesis, thereby adding support and function to joint tissues by promoting the production of collagen. Unlike the other B vitamins, B_6 can cause nerve damage at toxic levels (this is true for humans, too). Until more research is done, it is best to limit its dosage to no more than 200 mg per day.

Vitamin C (ascorbic acid): Vitamin C is a potent antioxidant; therefore it reduces inflammation caused by free radicals. It is added to joint supplements to aid in collagen and connective tissue formation. As horses age, they are less able to produce vitamin C, so supplementation is appropriate to keep their bones and joints healthy. I discuss this further in Chapter 19 — Growth and Growing Old.

Vitamin E: Also a strong antioxidant, vitamin E works with vitamin C to reduce damage from free radicals. Provide at least 1 IU per pound of body weight, more for tougher cases. Vitamin E is available in natural and synthetic forms and while this distinction is not important for other vitamins, natural vitamin E is more active than vitamin E that's produced in a lab. So you'll need to add approximately 10% more of the synthetic version to get the same activity level of the natural source. But whichever version you use, be sure your horse's meal contains some fat for proper absorption, since vitamin E is fat soluble.

Minerals

Manganese: Watch the spelling; this is often confused with magnesium. But manganese is a separate and important mineral for glycosaminoglycan production, found in synovial fluid.

Zinc: You'll often see zinc added to joint supplements. While involved in many body functions, it is needed for maintaining healthy bones and muscles. It should be balanced with copper, since too much zinc can cause a copper deficiency. A 3:1 ratio of zinc to copper is ideal. So pay attention to other sources of zinc in your horse's diet before choosing a joint preparation that adds more.

Copper: Copper is part of enzymatic reactions involved in producing and maintaining connective tissue. Please refer to Chapter 5 — Fundamentals of Minerals for more information about copper's role in protecting bones and joints.

Silicon: You may not be as familiar with this mineral as the others, but it is an important component of connective tissue, hyaluronic acid, and joint cartilage. Adding it to the diet seems to increase tendon and ligament elasticity, helping your horse better withstand performance stress. Silicon in the soil and in feedstuffs occurs in the form of silica, which is not well absorbed. When provided as orthosilicic acid it is well absorbed and beneficial for your horse's hooves, joints, ligament, tendons, and bones.

Others

Microlactin: This is a dried milk protein added to a few commercial joint products. It inhibits the movement of neutrophils (type of white blood cell) to the site of joint pain, thereby reducing inflammation[5] and promoting faster recovery from intense exercise.

Perna canaliculus: A green-lipped mussel (charming thought, no?) that contains glycosaminoglycans and omega-3 fatty acids, it has been shown to reduce joint pain and swelling in dogs[6] because of its anti-inflammatory action. Though found in joint supplements for horses, studies are limited.

Choosing a supplement

When choosing a supplement, it's best to evaluate the stage of your horse's problem. Age-related arthritis, for example, can be slowed down using a joint supplement. Choose one that has both glucosamine and chondroitin, since they seem to work better together. HA also makes a difference in reducing further degeneration.

If your horse is not working, a simple hyaluronic acid preparation may be sufficient. However, if your horse is very active and experiences inflammatory flare ups, it is best to provide a comprehensive joint supplement that contains a large dose of MSM, HA, glucosamine, chondroitin, as well as other anti-inflammatory agents such as boswellia and *Perna canaliculus*. The Horse Journal[7] recommends a maintenance level of 5,000 mg of glucosamine, 3,750 mg of chondroitin sulfate, and 100 mg of hyaluronic acid for a 1000 lb horse. These levels can be doubled for the first 7 to 10 days as a loading dose. And if your horse's diet does not contain a source of omega-3 fatty acids, consider a joint supplement that includes flaxseed meal.

Liquid supplements are initially better absorbed than powders so they act more quickly. But food slows down their absorption, so it really doesn't matter which you choose; go with what is most convenient.

Injectables

Injectable joint medications are classified as pharmaceuticals and are approved by the Food and Drug Administration (FDA). While intra-articular (IA) injections given directly in the joint have benefits, there are some negative aspects to consider. First, they are very expensive. Next, they may not work, especially if the pain is around the joint rather than directly inside. Finally, they may do harm.

A negative reaction called reactive synovitis or "joint flare" can occur, causing severe inflammation which can make your horse lame for several weeks. And the potential for joint infections exists if the joint is exposed to bacteria while being injected.

Having given you the downside, the upside is much more prevalent. The majority of horses receiving these injections experience significant pain relief and increased mobility. And the medication can be administered not only into the joint, but intravenously (IV) or intra-muscularly (IM).

Legend (Bayer): This product is hyaluronic acid (HA) which I described earlier. It is found throughout the body in connective tissue, skin, blood vessels, and joint synovial fluid. It has an anti-inflammatory effect on joints and also protects joint tissue from degeneration. It can be administered IA or IV to allow for total body circulation.

Adequan (Luitpold Animal Health): Typically used to treat osteochondrosis (OCD), this medication is a polysulfated glycosaminoglycan (PSGAG). It can be injected IA or IM. It increases joint flexibility by inhibiting destructive enzymes (proteases) in the joint fluid that break down cartilage. PSGAG also reduces inflammation and increases HA content within the joint, thereby increasing the viscosity of synovial fluid.

Acetyl-d-glucosamine: This is a compounded injectable that is given in conjunction with other medications and/or dietary supplements. It is provided IV or IM.

DISEASES OF THE JOINTS

So far, the purpose of this chapter has been to provide you with information about beneficial nutraceuticals that help prevent joint degeneration, aid in healing, and at the very least, make your horse more comfortable. Now, I'll summarize common joint diseases and include nutritional interventions where appropriate. These descriptions will be brief. Please consult your veterinarian for an accurate diagnosis.

Osteoarthritis (also known as degenerative joint disease)

Osteoarthritis refers to the progressive deterioration of cartilage. When cartilage deteriorates, it becomes less able to protect the joint against friction. And since cartilage does not have a blood supply, it depends on the synovial fluid for nourishment. But unfortunately, when inflammation prevents production of hyaluronic acid, the synovial fluid becomes watery and thin and cannot maintain cartilage integrity.

An injury or strain due to wear and tear can eventually lead to arthritis, where the joints no longer function as well as before. So the goal in treating arthritis is threefold: manage pain, reduce inflammation, and keep deterioration from progressing. Be cautious when using bute for more than a few days. Use of this NSAID and others can actually decrease cartilage production.

Ringbone: This arthritic condition affects the pastern joint and as such, a diet that supports synovial fluid production, along with one that eases pain and inflammation, would be beneficial. The joint enlarges and bone spurs form, reducing joint function. If the joint surface is affected (articular ring-bone) the cartilage and joint lining become enlarged and stiff, causing pain. Ringbone near the joint (periarticular) affects the ligaments and joint capsule, making this type of ringbone more serious. Generally bute is prescribed for short term use, followed by joint injections of HA, Adequan, and/or steroids.

Physitis (epiphysitis)

This is the most common form of developmental orthopedic disease (DOD) which includes other disorders as well: osteochondrosis, subchondral bone cysts, flexural limb deformities, cuboidal bone malformation, acquired angular limb deformities, and juvenile arthritis. With physitis, there is a disturbance within the growth plate of foals.

Nutritional management of physitis is critical. Foals that are overweight or growing too rapidly may develop this disease. In addition, high starch diets can lead to hormonal changes that have been shown to increase the incidence of physitis. Mineral imbalances between copper, zinc, manganese, calcium, and phosphorus can further aggravate this condition.

Copper is especially important because this mineral is needed to produce a strong collagen matrix. Unfortunately, giving your foal more copper will not fix the problem. Foals rely on what they received from their dam during gestation. Therefore a pregnant mare must have enough copper in her system to provide adequate storage within her foal's liver at birth. There is virtually no copper in mare's milk, so the foal born with low reserves will be at high risk for physitis.

When feeding foals at risk for this disease, there are several things to consider (also refer to Chapter 19 — Growth and Growing Old for more on feeding foals):

- **Do not feed a high starch diet.** This means reduce cereal grains or sweet feeds containing cereal grains (oats, corn, barley, etc.).

- **Offer a vitamin/mineral supplement**. Choose a preparation that is specifically designed to provide adequate mineral levels for foals.

- **Provide grass and alfalfa hay.** Offer grass hay free choice along with approximately 30% of the hay ration as alfalfa.

- **Feed enough but do offer grain free choice.** Since excessive growth is a problem, provide a creep feeder for additional calorie needs and to serve as a carrier for any supplementation. See Chapter 19 — Growth and Growing Old for guidelines on creep feeding.

- **Avoid excessive exercise on hard ground.** This will allow growing cartilage to develop normally.

Osteochondrosis dissecans (OCD)

Osteochondrosis is another version of DOD. It can lead to bone cysts or cartilage flaps within the joint, known as osteochondrosis dissecans (OCD). OCD can go unrecognized until the horse starts training. The stifle and hocks are more frequently affected.

As with physitis, mineral imbalances, particularly between zinc and copper, have influenced the incidence of this disease. Excessive starch and too fast a growth rate can also lead to OCD in genetically predisposed horses.

Ligament and tendon damage

Tendons bind muscle to bone; ligaments bind bone to bone. An injury to either of these fibrous tissues is more difficult to heal than a muscle injury since their blood supply is not as good. Researchers at Ohio State University[8] have used a technique where the horse's own blood is condensed and its platelets are stimulated to secrete growth factors that aid healing. This platelet-rich plasma (PRP) is injected into the damaged ligament, leading to dramatic healing where horses were able to return to racing within a year.

Injuries often affect the collateral and suspensory ligaments. From a nutrition perspective, I like to treat ligament and tendon injuries aggressively by providing three key nutrients, in addition to a balanced diet that contains high-quality protein.

Vitamin E should be supplemented at 5 IU per pound of body weight per day. Selenium works with vitamin E, but unless the diet provides less than 1.5 mg of selenium, it should not be added; therefore, choose a vitamin E supplement that does not contain selenium. As I mentioned earlier, since vitamin E is fat soluble, it is best absorbed along with some fat from the meal, so using a powdered version of vitamin E requires the addition of ¼ to ½ cup of oil. Flaxseed, rice bran, or canola oils are best because they do not promote inflammation.

The second nutrient is vitamin B_6 (pyridoxine). All B vitamins (eight of them) work together so a B complex preparation that provides 100 to 150 mg of B_6 is appropriate. Pyridoxine is involved in protein synthesis and therefore aids in production of new tissue.

Finally, omega-3 fatty acids reduce inflammation. Flaxseed meal works well but if the injury is severe, add fish oils instead.

Surgery is sometimes an option to restore soundness. However, before choosing a surgical route, consider one more thing: large amounts of vitamin B_{12}. Vitamin B_{12} is necessary to keep nerve cells healthy. I have been successful in reversing mild forms of nerve damage, which can coincide with tendon and ligament injuries, by administering 5 mg (5,000 mcg) of B_{12} per day (along with folic acid, another B vitamin). Vitamin B_{12} is not found in any plants, so horses must rely on their bacterial flora in the hindgut for its production. It is stored in the liver so your horse can pull it out of storage when needed. However, if the microbial population is compromised in any way (which stress from pain can do) supplementation of B_{12} as well as all the B vitamins is important.

Stringhalt

Stringhalt involves spasms of the joints in the hind limbs, creating a goose-step gait distinguished by the horse pausing with his hind leg elevated and then stomping it to the ground. Nerve degeneration is characteristic of stringhalt, which can be caused by eating various toxic plants such as vetch, false dandelion (*Hypochaeris radicata*), and sweet peas.

Stringhalt may resolve on its own once the horse is removed from the source of toxic plants. Surgery may be an option, but I prefer to start with high dosages of vitamin B_{12} (as I just described) to assist with nerve function. Your veterinarian may prescribe the drug Dilantin (phenytoin).

Stringhalt can occur in any breed and generally affects adult horses. It can be confused with shivers, but shivers may be a result of polysaccharide storage myopathy (PSSM) which is discussed in Chapter 13 — Metabolic and Endocrine Disorders.

Navicular

Navicular syndrome is complex because it involves joints in the feet, but also bones, ligaments, and tendons of the heels. Most horses with this disorder have fluid in the navicular bone region, within the navicular bursa and the coffin joint. This level of inflammation can be helped nutritionally via antioxidant therapy, omega-3 fatty acids, and anti-inflammatory agents such as turmeric, boswellia, MSM, and HA.

An MRI is a valuable tool to diagnose the exact areas of damage. Injury to the sesamoidean ligament is common as well as tears in the deep digital flexor tendon within the hoof capsule. Steroid and HA injections directly into the tendon is a common treatment option.

Equioxx (firocoxib) is a COX-2 inhibitor, so the pain is relieved without inhibiting the COX-1 enzyme, which produces beneficial, healing prostaglandins. Bute and Banamine inhibit both COX enzymes and therefore they reduce the harmful prostaglandins but also remove the helpful ones. Equioxx also has a lower risk of ulcer formation than bute or Banamine. Other treatments are described a little later.

Windpuffs

Hard-working horses, over time, can develop fluid-filled swellings, known as windpuffs, toward the back of the fetlock joint. They generally result from an injured deep digital flexor tendon sheath. They are not painful, just disfiguring. But if the sheath is further stretched or damaged, lameness can result. Hyaluronic injections may be helpful. Fluid accumulation will eventually decrease once work is discontinued; however, if it persists for more than two weeks, have your vet x-ray the joint for possible arthritis.

MEDICAL TREATMENTS

There are many treatments that veterinarians will use for inflammation relief and production of new tissue. Here is a summary of ones I've already mentioned plus a few new ones:

- **NSAID pain relievers.** Consider Equioxx because it specifically targets the COX-2 enzymes rather than all COX enzymes. However, complete suppression of COX-2 enzymes may be counterproductive, so discuss this with your veterinarian before use.

- **Intravenous, intra-muscular, or intra-articular injections.** These include HA (Legend) or PSGAGs (Adequan). A newer injectable, pentosan polysulfate, is derived from beechwood hemicelluloses and shows promise in improving cartilage production without pain relieving action.

- **Corticosteroid injections.** These are often added to Legend or Adequan to further reduce inflammation. However, high doses can damage cartilage, create an increased susceptibility to infections, and even induce laminitis.

- **Interleukin-1 receptor antagonist protein (IRAP).** This inhibits interleukin activity, a mediator of inflammation. The procedure involves harvesting your horse's own serum.

- **Tildren (tiludronate).** A drug that has been helpful for navicular syndrome or bone spavins is Tildren. It may prevent enzymatic degradation of the bone. Though approved in Europe for treating navicular disease and arthritis in the distal hock, as of this writing it is not approved for use in the United States. However, the FDA is permitting experimental use and your veterinarian can request importation of this drug.

- **Others.** Several other treatments are available. Discuss these with your veterinarian:

  - Topical diclofenac cream (Surpass)
  - Magnetic resonance imaging (MRI) joint endoscopy
  - Swimming therapy
  - Shock wave therapy
  - Stem cell injections
  - Articular cartilage cultured cellular transplants

Hair and Hooves

Hair and hoof tissue are very similar; they are both made of the protein keratin. This hard, crusty protein provides an outer protective layer, as well as structural support. Hair and hoof color have nothing to do with strength. Keratinocytes, living cells within your horse's hair and hooves, as well as his skin, produce keratin. These cells rely on a nutrient-rich blood supply in order to produce adequate levels of keratin, to form an outer protective layer.

By the time you see a problem with your horse's hooves and hair coat, there is likely something wrong on the inside. That's because these areas of the body are low on your horse's list of priorities when it comes to survival. Nutrients are typically used first by vital internal organs; if any nutrients remain, they can then be used to feed the hair and hooves. Therefore a glossy coat and strong hooves are good indicators of health. However, one caveat regarding a shiny coat should be mentioned here... When you add fat to the diet, the skin's sebaceous glands will secrete more fat, allowing shiny oils to cover the hair. So your horse's coat will shine, but that will not necessarily be a way to gauge overall health.

Bottom line: Provide your horse with a nutritious diet so he can take care of his entire body, including his hair and hooves.

NUTRIENT OVERVIEW

Here are some key nutrients that promote a healthy hair coat and hooves:

- **Omega-3 fatty acids.** Found in flaxseed and fish oils, these fatty acids support numerous functions in the body. While fresh grass is also an excellent source, there is very little left in hay. This balance is further upset by feeding cereal grains and vegetable oils (especially soybean and corn oils), both high in omega-6 fatty acids. Please review Chapter 3 — Fundamentals of Fats for more discussion on this topic.

- **Lysine and methionine.** These essential amino acids are necessary for producing all body proteins, including sulfur-rich keratin. Methionine serves as a source of sulfur, and is easy to provide as long as the diet contains high-quality protein. Adding a legume such as alfalfa, clover, or soy will complement other feedstuffs, providing your horse with all the essential amino acids he needs.

- **Copper, silicon, and zinc.** These minerals are needed to produce healthy hair, bones, cartilage, hooves, and skin. Zinc should always be balanced with copper with three to four times more zinc. Silicon should be supplemented in the form of orthosilicic acid.

- **Biotin.** All eight B vitamins work together, some to produce protein, others to enhance metabolic functions within cells, but biotin has received the most attention when it comes to hoof health. This B vitamin is part of several enzymes involved in producing fatty acids, as well as promoting tissue growth. Insufficient biotin can result in a soft white line within the hoof structure, as well as hoof crumbling and cracks. By providing at least 20 mg of biotin per day, you can help your horse's hooves strengthen, but be patient — this can take between 6 and 9 months. Biotin, however, is not a "magic bullet"; the diet needs to contain adequate good quality protein and essential fatty acids, and be in mineral balance.

- **Beta carotene and vitamin A:** Vitamin A is necessary for keratin production and healthy skin, and is often added to commercial feeds. Beta carotene, found in plants, is a precursor to vitamin A. It is also a potent antioxidant but is easily destroyed once grass is cut and dried. Therefore, if your horse is on a hay-only diet, vitamin A supplementation is necessary for hair and hoof health.

Selenium toxicity

Hair loss and hoof changes are an indication of an acute selenium toxicity, but in chronic situations where selenium is consistently fed at a high level, alkali disease will result. Alkali disease is characterized by hair loss along the mane and tail, and the hooves will crack around the coronary band. When too much selenium is present, it replaces the naturally existing sulfur found in keratin resulting in tissue breakdown. To be safe, I recommend limiting selenium intake to no more than 0.6 ppm (mg/kg). If you are feeding a commercial feed that is fortified with selenium or you are adding supplements that contain this mineral, it is best to know the selenium level in your hay and pasture so you can add up the total amount given each day. A selenium level between 1 and 3 mg per day is ideal. There is more discussion on this mineral in Chapter 5 — Fundamentals of Minerals.

OVERALL HOOF HEALTH

Young horses

Youngsters need enough room to romp and play in a natural setting to start the process of healthy hoof development. Don't lunge a young horse; the repetitive motions can interfere with normal hoof maturation. The coronary band, in particular, needs to develop properly, since the blood vessels within this structure provide nutrients to the hoof.

Thrush

Protect your horse's feet by keeping him on dry footing. Standing in mud or soiled stall bedding can lead to a variety of bacterial and fungal infections. Every day, if possible, pick your horse's feet to remove manure and debris. The oxygen-deprived condition caused by packed hooves creates an ideal environment for microorganisms to thrive, resulting in thrush. To eradicate this infection you need to disinfect your horse's hooves thoroughly and deeply. If your horse's case is severe, it may require packing the hoof with an antimicrobial agent; simply squirting thrush medication on the hoof will not do the job. And please be very careful with these products — wear rubber gloves to protect your skin and take care to protect your horse's skin, as well. Do not get them on his coronary band. Always consider getting medical help in stubborn cases of thrush, especially if there is any puncture wound or deep cracks in the foot.

Dry hooves

Hoof dressings are often used for dry hooves and those that contain petroleum-based ingredients or pine tar may hold moisture best. However, most hoof dressings get wiped off easily as your horse moves through pasture or stall bedding. Frankly, the best way to alleviate dryness is to create a puddle that your horse will walk through to get to where he's normally going. For example, create a moist area by his water trough that he'll need to stand in while he drinks. This is especially helpful in dry climates that are prone toward drought.

Wet hooves

The opposite problem occurs in areas where the pasture is consistently wet. Hoof hardeners such as those containing acetone, formaldehyde, or formalin-based compounds can be very harsh on the feet because they penetrate into deeper tissues, structurally weakening the hoof wall. Even tiny cracks can lead to infection. If your horse is on wet pasture all day, try leading him to higher ground. If he is stalled at night with dry shavings, the constant expansion and contraction of hoof tissue can be damaging, so proper daily inspection and management are key. Watch for hoof wall cracks and work toward maintaining a relatively even level of moisture in the foot.

Don't use sealants or patches on your horse's hooves. I've heard of folks using car body fillers or even wood putty to patch hooves. This seals up the hoof's ability to breathe and traps bacteria and viruses, leading to infection. And you likely won't notice this problem until the situation is too far along and calls for serious medical treatment.

Hoof supplements

Additional supplementation can be a good idea for any horse that has less than perfect feet. All hoof products contain biotin and some folks simply give their horses pure biotin, but this approach is not the best. Instead, choose a hoof supplement that also offers supporting nutrients, but keep in mind that many hoof supplements are actually complete vitamin/mineral preparations that have additional biotin. So, if you are already feeding another vitamin/mineral supplement or a fortified commercial feed at recommended levels, go for simplicity with only a few ingredients to prevent nutrient overlaps.

HAIR LOSS

Hair growth is complex, involving hormones from the hypothalamus and the pituitary gland that respond to levels of sunlight; colder temperatures influence growth somewhat but are not the main factor in seasonal hair development. As the days get shorter, your horse's winter coat starts to form; as the amount of daylight increases, his winter coat will start to shed. Abnormal retention of the hair coat is indicative of equine Cushing's disease (known as PPID) and is reviewed at length in Chapter 13 — Metabolic and Endocrine Disorders.

Your horse may experience excessive hair loss during the spring as his hair normally starts to shed. This over-reaction leaves him with thin areas before the new spring coat starts to appear. It's a temporary condition and your horse will likely catch up. Be sure to provide a balanced, nutritious diet that includes the key nutrients mentioned earlier, to support a healthy hair growth cycle.

But if there are significant bald areas, other causes need to be examined. Stress, both mental and physical, can cause hair to fall out in clumps. Pregnancy losses, for example, are common because of the demands placed on a mare's body. Nutritional requirements during pregnancy are discussed in Chapter 18 —Breeding, Pregnancy, and Lactation.

Skin problems can also cause hair loss and a biopsy may be necessary to reveal the cause. Conditions such as hair follicle infections, ringworm, or skin mites are possibilities and can be evaluated by your veterinarian.

Skin

Your horse's skin is the largest organ in his body and contains key proteins such as keratin, collagen, and elastin. Though there are many dermatological disorders, those benefitting from nutritional intervention are discussed here. Situations that involve the immune system such as warts, insect bites, hives, allergies, and other forms of dermatitis affected by environmental and food allergens are discussed in Chapter 16 — Immunity Issues.

Worm infestation, in particular pinworms, can cause severe itching and hair loss. Skin conditions such as scratches, ringworm, and rain rot are treatable medical conditions and your veterinarian may need to be consulted. However, any time there is inflammation, itching, pain, or damage to the skin, a balanced diet will aid in healing.

KEY NUTRIENTS FOR SKIN HEALTH

- High-quality protein
- B vitamins
- Beta carotene or vitamin A
- Vitamin D
- Balanced minerals

Some helpful anti-inflammatory agents that reduce pain and itching include:

- Vitamins C and E
- Grape seed extract
- Hyaluronic acid
- Glucosamine
- MSM
- Curcumin (derived from turmeric)
- Omega-3 fatty acids
- Quercetin and other bioflavonoids

COMMON SKIN PROBLEMS

Photosensitivity

A photosensitive horse will become easily sunburned, and crusty, raised scabs may form on his skin, especially on the pink areas. Sunscreen or zinc oxide will offer protection, but photosensitivity involves more than simple sunburn. Consuming photodynamic agents from various plants, in particular St. John's Wort (*Hypericum perforatum*) and buckwheat (*Fagopyrum esculentum*), is the main cause of photosensitivity. Agents found in ragwort, bishop's weed, hound's tongue, horsebrush, alsike clover, and even perennial rye grass (turf type, not forage type) contain alkaloids that can cause liver damage, leading to photosensitivity. Some horses are sensitive to alfalfa and clover. In order for liver problems to become apparent, these plants need to be consumed for several months. The liver dysfunction leads to accumulation of a substance called phylloerythrin (made from chlorophyll) in light-colored skin. Contact your veterinarian for blood work to assess liver function. And if you know what plants are causing the problem, do what you can to remove them from the pasture or the diet.

Seborrhea (dandruff)

Seborrhea is characterized by a dry, flaky, or oily discharge and is one of the easiest conditions to fix, because it indicates that your horse is simply not getting enough fat in his diet. Add flaxseed meal, calcium-fortified rice bran, or oil to his diet (see Chapter 3 — Fundamentals of Fats for a description of different oils).

As far as treatment goes, base it on the type of seborrhea. Dry seborrhea looks like dandruff, and affects the mane or tail. The oily type creates crusts along the elbows and hocks. To control dry seborrhea, use a sulfur-based shampoo once or twice a week; the oily variety does best with a drying shampoo that contains tar or benzoyl peroxide. Soften the crusts with a protective ointment.

Ringworm

Ringworm gets its name from its round appearance, though it is a result of a fungal infection and not a worm. The affected area has a crusty appearance and the hair comes out in clumps. The fungus can remain dormant until conditions are ripe for an outbreak, typically in the fall and winter when there is less sunshine and more moisture.

This condition is contagious (even to humans) and is easily transmitted by anything that carries this fungus. Therefore, it is best to keep tack, blankets, and grooming supplies separate and cleaned with a bleach solution or other disinfectant. Be sure to rinse all the bleach off since it is highly caustic to the skin. Wash your horse with an anti-fungal shampoo and you can try anti-fungal ointments designed for athlete's foot. However, your veterinarian will be best able to give you the proper medication.

But being exposed to ringworm does not necessarily mean that your horse's skin will become infected; a strong immune system will likely counteract exposure. If his immune function is compromised by illness, poor nutrition, or stressful conditions, he will be more likely to succumb to ringworm.

Rain rot (also called rain scald)

Dermatophilus congolensis is the bacterial culprit with rain rot. This organism can normally be found on the skin, but when the skin becomes compromised through minor injury, insect bites, or exposed to rain day after day, the bacterial numbers can increase. The infection looks like a series of small bumps and is usually found along the back, rump, neck and legs. As with ringworm, rain rot is easily transmitted by infected equipment, so proper disinfection is important to prevent spreading.

Rain rot will go away on its own once the weather becomes dry and if your horse is fed properly to keep his immune system healthy. But don't ignore this problem; it is causing your horse pain and discomfort. Your veterinarian may choose to administer penicillin to speed up the healing process.

Scratches

Scratches and its alternative names mud fever, greasy heel, and dew poisoning all basically mean dermatitis. It typically affects the pasterns and heel bulbs, due to constant moisture exposure from a muddy field or wet stall, leading to inflammation, ulcerations of the skin, and infection. The skin will often crack and bleed. So, to begin with, carefully clip the hair from the area and wash gently with an anti-microbial shampoo, being careful not to damage the skin. The goal is to keep the area clean and dry. Avoid heavy ointments because they can seal out oxygen, making the problem worse.

I've recently come across a homemade treatment[9] that I thought I'd share with you. You stir these ingredients together to make a paste and apply it every day until the condition has healed:

    1 tube of 1% hydrocortisone cream
    1 tube triple antibiotic cream

1 tube of clotrimazole cream (such as Lotrimin, used for athlete's foot)
2 Tablespoons of water-based aloe vera cream (do not use an oil based cream, only water based)
One 1,000 IU capsule of Vitamin E — pierce and empty contents
One 10,000 IU capsule of Vitamin A — pierce and empty contents

If after three days, you do not see improvement, try a diluted tea tree oil product (do not use plain tea tree oil since it is very caustic). Also consider applying a concentrated colloidal silver preparation (designed for non-internal use).

Sarcoids

Sarcoids look like flat lesions where the balding skin can have a rippled appearance. The good news is, they are not malignant, they are not painful, and they do not itch. The bad news is, they can be transferred from horse to horse by a virus (typically the bovine papillomaviruses) so good sanitation of grooming equipment is essential. A vaccine is in the works, but a healthy immune system is your horse's best bet against developing this problem.

Allergies

Your horse's skin can respond to allergens from insect bites, feeds, pollen, molds, and other environmental factors, leading to hives. This is an immune system issue and is discussed with other allergies in the next chapter, Chapter 16 — Immunity Issues.

Endnotes

[1] Rodgers, M.R., 2006. Effects of oral glucosamine and chondroitin sulfate supplementation on the frequency of intra-articular therapy of the horse tarsus. *International Journal of Applied Research in Veterinary Medicine,* 4: 155 – 159.

[2] Bergin, B.J., Pierce, S.W., Bramlage, L.R., and Stromberg, A., 2006. Oral hyaluronan gel reduces post operative tarsocrural effusion in the yearling Thoroughbred. *Equine Veterinary Journal,* 38: 375-378.

[3] Winther, K., 2007. A powder made from subspecies of rose-hip may act as structure-modifying in osteoarthritis. *Osteoarthritis and Cartilage, 15,* Supplement 2: B92.

[4] Frisbie, D.D., Kawcak, C.E., and McIlwraith, C.W., 2008. Evaluation of oral avocado/soybean unsaponifiables using an experimental model of equine osteoarthritis. *Osteoarthritis and Cartilage, 16,* Supplement 4: S221-S222.

[5]Bello, T.R., and Allen, T., 2006. The use of MicroLactin for inflammatory conditions in equine veterinary practice. *Journal of Equine Veterinary Science, 25* (9): 380-382.

[6] Bierer, T.L, and Bui, L.M., 2002. Improvement of arthritic signs in dogs fed green-lipped mussel (*Perna canaliculus*). *Journal of Nutrition,* 132: 1634S-1636S.

[7] Kellon, E. M., 2008. *Horse Journal Guide to Equine Supplements and Nutraceuticals*. Guilford, Connecticut: The Lyons Press: 175.

[8] Waselau, M., Sutter, W.W., Genovese, R.L., and Bertone, A.L., 2008. Intralesional injection of platelet-rich plasma followed by controlled exercise for treatment of midbody suspensory ligament desmitis in Standardbred racehorses. *Journal of the American Veterinary Medical Association, 232* (10): 1515-1520.

[9] Homemade remedy is shown in the article, Dew poisoning. *The Horse Journal*, May 2007: 21.

CHAPTER 16 —
IMMUNITY ISSUES

*The time is ours: an early-morning ride, a time to be together and greet
the beginning of a new day. Two of God's creatures, one two-legged, one
four-legged, each with beating heart, throbbing veins, fears, joys and
sorrows. Two beings, separate yet conjoined.*
~ Jacklyn Lee Lindstrom

The environment is brimming with bacteria, viruses, and other microorganisms that can affect your horse's health. Some infections are out of your control. But if your horse does become ill, his ability to heal often depends on the strength of his immune system, which you can influence. He may not even get sick if he is in peak health at the time of exposure. Nutrition and health go hand in hand, so filling in nutritional gaps is key toward keeping your horse hale and hearty.

But what if you already do feed a balanced, nutritious diet and your horse is still suffering? That's when you assert your nutrient muscles and use them in high doses to provide a medicinal effect. At the end of this chapter be sure to take a look at *Dr. Getty's Fighting Formula!*

I discuss individual problems throughout this chapter and conclude with nutrients that are especially effective in protecting your horse against illness. But nothing is better than removing the actual cause of the ailment. For example, one of the best things you can do for your horse is pay attention to his stress level. Stress, whether physical or mental, weakens his immune system. Cortisol, the stress hormone, is the scoundrel; when it becomes elevated, your horse can succumb to illnesses that normally would not faze him. Think about this for a moment... Ever catch a cold? Were you working too hard or not getting enough sleep? Perhaps you weren't eating as well as you should. The cold virus is everywhere, but when does it latch onto you? When you're stressed. And it's the same with your horse. This is a lengthy subject, so if you'd like to learn more, please read Chapter 17 — Stress and Behavior for a full description of stressors and how to handle them (for your horse, not you).

Allergies

Allergens exist in the air and on pasture, and in your horse's feed. Your horse can have an allergic reaction to just about anything — the chemicals we use, the plants we feed, or whatever the wind blows in. Insect bites, too, torment even the most fit horse.

Anything that produces an allergic response stimulates your horse's immune system to combat the problem. Histamines are released, along with inflammatory prostaglandins, leading to respiratory and skin reactions. If your horse has a healthy immune system, he may not be affected by environmental allergens such as grass pollen. But even the best immune function can become exhausted from the constant bombardment of allergy-producing substances. That's where nutrition comes into the picture.

The goal is to bring your horse's over-active immune function back into balance. This is done through proper nutrition. A healthful diet will go a long way toward protecting him against allergies. Check your hay's quality, make sure your horse is getting a complete protein that combines grasses with a legume (such as alfalfa and clover), and fill in gaps with a vitamin/mineral supplement or fortified feed. But *the most important ingredient of all to stabilize the immune system is flaxseed meal or oil.* Its high omega-3 fatty acid content protects your horse against disease by preventing the formation of free radicals. Omega-3s also reduce inflammation and pain, protect his heart and blood vessels, strengthen his bones, joints, and hooves, and give his hair coat a dappled shine. Flaxseeds must be ground for their nutrients to be properly available and absorbed; do not feed whole flaxseeds since most will not be digested. And do not soak them since water promotes oxidation (destruction) of these fatty acids. Instead feed a commercial flaxseed meal that is stabilized against rancidity. You can also use flaxseed oil, but keep it refrigerated and for not more than 6 months. Take a look at Chapter 3 — Fundamentals of Fats for more information about flaxseeds.

Medications such as antihistamines and corticosteroids can be useful. Be careful with dexamethasone because this steroid can induce laminitis in an insulin resistant horse (much the same way a horse with equine Cushing's will develop laminitis). Vitamin C is a natural antihistamine and your horse may not be getting enough if hay is his main forage source or if he is aging.

In many cases, allergy shots are your best answer, especially when the source cannot be controlled. Or a similar approach is homeopathy, so it may be worth contacting an expert in this area.

Insect allergies are especially difficult to control. Physical and chemical barriers are helpful up to a point. Fly predators work nicely but they don't control all types of flies. Feed-through fly preparations are also worth considering. I like feeding extra vitamin B_1 (thiamin) to repel flies. Brewer's yeast is helpful. Apple cider vinegar has not been scientifically shown to reduce insect bites, but there is much anecdotal evidence that indicates it's worth trying. You can add 4 to 8 ounces of apple cider vinegar to a 5 gallon water tub or to your horse's meal. Most horses enjoy the taste and it has the added benefit of reducing the hindgut's pH for horses that are on an all-forage diet.

Garlic is often included in supplements designed to help your horse repel insects. I don't like using these products because first, there is no evidence that garlic reduces insect bites. And second, and more important, garlic can be harmful; it can cause Heinz body anemia. I discuss this problem at the end of the chapter.

Your horse's skin and respiratory system are the most vulnerable to various allergens. Sweet itch, for example, causes an intense itch and is perhaps the most troubling of insect allergies.

SWEET ITCH

Sweet itch is anything but sweet; it is ruthless. Tiny, biting midges — the *Culicoides* gnat, sometimes called "no-see-ums" — relentlessly bombard your horse. Their bites cause an allergic reaction that gives him a horrible itch (pruritus); he'll scratch himself raw. Call your vet — this calls for some serious medicine. He/she will likely prescribe an antihistamine or steroid to control the symptoms. An antihistamine is ok for seasonal situations such as this, but steroids carry risks, including laminitis and secondary infections, because they depress immune function. Nevertheless, they do provide some short-term relief for many horses. And don't forget the flaxseed meal — its anti-inflammatory action will make your horse more comfortable and improve his overall resistance.

That's the key to medication usage — short term. In the meantime, see what you can do about altering your horse's surroundings to keep those nasty gnats away from him. Screens that have small enough openings work well while your horse is in the barn. Outdoors, remove areas of standing water, just as you would to control mosquitoes. And it's helpful to reduce turnout during the early morning and at dusk. A layer of camphor or menthol products are effective barriers. Keep in mind that these insects prefer your horse's abdomen and thigh areas, even though the allergic response occurs along his topline, so fly sheets may not be effective since they offer little protection to the belly. Also, once your horse's skin is affected, fly sheets can be irritating.

But wouldn't it be nice if your horse wasn't troubled by sweet itch? After all, not all horses are bothered by them, so let's allow your horse to join the "no-see-um, no care-um" club. But you have to get aggressive! I'll help you do that — see *Dr. Getty's Fighting Formula* at the end of this chapter.

HIVES

Hives, known as urticaria, are caused by allergens from food, pollen, insects, mold, and other irritants. They appear as swelled areas and are typically found along the neck and chest, but they can be virtually anywhere. Since they can develop from any number of allergens, pinpointing the exact cause can be challenging. It could be something your horse ate, a deworming treatment, antibiotics, or contact with a new type of bedding or cleaning product you used on your tack. Even the weather or exercise can cause this allergic reaction in a sensitive horse.

During an allergy attack, your horse's immune system is heightened. Avoid vaccinations during this time — they can over-stimulate an already hyperactive immune system, leading to an even more extreme allergic response.

Hives should not be ignored since the skin could be damaged with repeated attacks. Your veterinarian may prescribe antihistamines or, in difficult cases, a steroid.

RECURRENT AIRWAY OBSTRUCTION (HEAVES)

Formerly called chronic obstructive pulmonary disease (COPD), this disorder is now referred to as recurrent airway obstruction (RAO) because COPD in horses is not the same as the disease in humans. COPD in humans is most commonly caused by smoking and environmental pollutants, whereas RAO is more like asthma. RAO is normally known as "heaves," which is basically an inflammation of the airways caused by an allergic response.

Symptoms of RAO include:

- Coughing
- Difficulty breathing

- Nasal discharge and flared nostrils, even at rest
- Exercise intolerance
- Lethargy

Muscle wasting is often seen with this condition and lack of exercise was originally thought to be the problem. But these horses have low body condition scores because RAO reduces the amount of oxygen delivered to the muscles, creating muscle damage.

Horses may be genetically predisposed to this disorder. One of the main triggers is mold or mold spores in hay. Hay that is baled while still moist is more prone toward developing mold. You may not have any idea about the conditions under which it was baled, so check it carefully — if you see an area that's clumped together, is black or even white with lots of dust, that's mold, and spores are likely to be dispersed throughout the entire bale. So the ideal situation would be to discard the whole thing. This may not the budget-friendly thing to do, but it is the only way to eliminate risk. However, you could discard the moldy area from that bale and offer the rest of it along with hay from another bale to see which one your horse will eat. If provided with a choice, you may find that he won't eat from the hay bale that had mold.

Dust really aggravates RAO. It irritates the lungs, creating mucus and inflammation. Chronic inflammation of the lungs can lead to scar tissue that reduces the lung's capacity to fill with air. Coughing will result and your horse will be less able to exercise because adequate oxygen is not reaching his blood.

You may not realize it, but your barn is filled with dust hazards that can significantly affect your horse's lungs. Dust particles that are too small to be seen get inhaled deep into the lungs and produce signs of heaves. Here are a few tips for preventing dust[1]:

- Spray a water mist along the aisles before sweeping to minimize dust. Before cleaning stalls or sweeping the barn aisles, move your horse to another location and open all doors and windows. Allow dust to settle for 30 minutes before bringing your horse back into barn after cleaning.

- In the arena, if you can see the dust, there is too much exposure for your horse. Water an arena with a hose or sprinkler before riding to keep dust levels down. This will need to be done several times a day.

- Do not throw hay down from a loft into your horse's stall. Hay contains dust, especially hay that has been stored for several months. Wet it down slightly before your horse digs into it.

- Avoid large barn fans that are placed on the floor at either end of the barn. They blow dust from the ground into the air. Use individual fans for each stall, mounted high enough to be out of your horse's reach.

- Dump pelleted feeds into a bucket outside the stall, rather than while your horse is eating. And if using supplements, add some water or spray your feed with a cooking spray to help powdered products stick to the feed.

- When grooming, spray your brush with water or silicone spray to trap dust.

> Your barn is filled with dust hazards that can significantly affect your horse's lungs.

Infections can also cause RAO. If bacterial, your vet will prescribe an antibiotic. Remember, whenever you give your horse an antibiotic, it kills some beneficial bacteria as well as the damaging ones. So, be sure to give your horse a potent probiotic at the same time, and for a few days following antibiotic usage.

Treatment

Turnout is the best approach for so many reasons, including respiratory health. But if your horse is stalled, make sure the bedding and hay are low in dust and fresh air is circulating throughout the area.

Corticosteroids and bronchodilators are typical medications used to control this disease. However, don't forget nutritional intervention. Check out the end of this chapter for many suggestions. One thing I should mention here, however, is the successes I've had treating RAO with DMG (N,N-dimethylglycine). DMG is produced within each cell but supplementation appears to be helpful in improving respiratory function.

PHOTOSENSITIVITY

Sunburn can occur on any white or pink area of your horse, since the skin isn't protected by pigment (melanin) that gives skin its dark color. But some horses get severely burned and develop scabs and blisters after a relatively short time in the sun. This is referred to as photosensitivity, an allergy to sunlight. Since a true allergy is uncommon, it is likely triggered by liver damage caused by ingesting toxic plants.

Alfalfa and clover are often blamed for photosensitivity because of their high chlorophyll (green pigment) content. But the issue is the liver, not chlorophyll. Chlorophyll is changed to a metabolite called phylloerythrin by the microbes in the hindgut, which under normal conditions is metabolized by the liver. But an impaired liver is unable to get rid of phylloerythrin; therefore, it travels to the capillaries in the skin, reacts with ultraviolet light, and the skin is damaged.

If your horse suffers from photosensitivity, you could try reducing the amount of alfalfa or clover he consumes but your best approach is to find the source of the liver problem. Take a look at Chapter 8 — Fundamentals of Forages for a partial list of toxic plants and ways to identify them.

Equine Protozoal Myeloencephalitis (EPM)

EPM is caused by protozoal organisms known as *Sarcocystis neurona* and *Neospora hughesi* that have the ability to infect a horse's central nervous system. While the exact method of transmission for *N. hughesi* is yet unknown, horses pick up *S. neurona* from an opossum that has completed the life cycle after eating an intermediate host, such as a raccoon, skunk, armadillo, or bird. It sheds the infected sporocysts which are potentially consumed by horses. Most people are not aware that domestic cats can also shed the parasite, but not all cats are infected, and there are as many cases of EPM among horses that do not live alongside barn cats, as there are cases of those that do. So don't remove your barn cat just yet. Bird droppings are also a potential source of infection. Watch for droppings in feed and water supplies, as well as in bedding and tack, not only to reduce risk of EPM but of *Salmonella* poisoning, as well.

A horse can build up antibodies toward *S. neurona* and *N. hughesi* without having the organism invade his central nervous system. But once his nervous system is affected, he'll exhibit balancing difficulty and will not be able to walk normally. Muscles begin to atrophy and depression sets in. It is heartbreaking to see a horse in this condition.

An accurate diagnosis of EPM is the most challenging aspect of the disease because there is no test available that specifically tests for active infection.

Horses with clinical signs will usually be tested using a Western Blot procedure that looks for *S. neurona* antibodies in the cerebrospinal fluid. But many horses will test positive for antibodies and will not necessarily have an affected nervous system. The serum indirect fluorescent antibody test (IFAT) measures antibodies for both organisms; however, a positive result simply means that exposure exists but the nervous system may not be infected. Two other tests are also used, the Enzyme-Linked Immunosorbent Assay (ELISA) and the Polymerase Chain Reaction (PCR), but in both cases their results are not conclusive. However, these tests do provide additional evidence toward a diagnosis. And once other neurological problems are ruled out, your vet will likely want to treat the disorder as EPM.

Drug selections include sulfas along with trimethoprim, sulfadiazine combined with pyrimethamine, ponazuril (Marquis, made by Bayer Animal Health), or nitazoxanide (Navigator, made by IDEXX). Each of these treatments has benefits and drawbacks, so discuss your options with your veterinarian. And be sure to protect the hindgut microbes through a potent probiotic since medications, especially Navigator, can interfere with their growth.

Stress, such as that experienced by intense exercise and performance, increases your horse's risk of developing EPM. Central nervous system proteins produced by stress have been shown to decrease lymphocyte production and function. Microlactin has been used successfully in reducing inflammation[2]. Steroidal drugs, which suppress immune function, can make your horse more likely to become infected but not necessarily develop the disease. Therefore, reducing stress and boosting the immune system is your first step toward safeguarding your horse.

S. neurona doesn't make the horse ill unless it crosses the blood-brain barrier and attacks the nervous system. This is why vitamin E is so important. In proper amounts, it protects this barrier from attack and may prevent the disease from occurring. Give your horse 5 to 10 IU of vitamin E per pound of body weight per day. Be sure to add some fat to the diet to allow for better absorption since vitamin E is fat soluble. If you're already feeding a commercial feed that has added fat, it should be sufficient for adequate vitamin E absorption. If you aren't, then flaxseed meal or oil, rice bran or rice bran oil, canola oil, or some corn oil (though not my first choice) can be added to your horse's meal.

Vitamin B_{12} may protect the nervous system since it is directly involved in producing the myelin sheath that surrounds each nerve cell. I recommend adding 2,000 to 4,000 micrograms per day (that's the same as 2-4 mg).

Chinese herbs such as ginseng and astragalus may offer some protection but how they specifically affect the EPM horse is not proven. Pau d'arco (*Tabebuia avellanedae*), an herb from a South American evergreen tree, can relieve pain and inflammation, but does not eliminate the organism. Stay away from high dosages of garlic, especially if it's raw. It can be damaging in large amounts and lead to Heinz body anemia.

Folic acid supplementation was once thought to be important because pyrimethamine was the drug of choice. This drug inhibits *S. neurona's* ability to produce folic acid, but it also prevents the horse from synthesizing his own folic acid. So we nutritionists would often recommend adding large dosages of folic acid. But in doing so, we were also feeding this B vitamin to the infecting organism, defeating the purpose of the drug. Because of this problem, different drugs are now available that counteract the organism without affecting folic acid production. For example, sulfa drugs, together with trimethoprim, are useful and are more economical than treatment with Marquis. Folic acid is affected somewhat but not severely, and frequent blood tests will help monitor your horse's red blood cells for any folic acid deficiency signs. The goal in using these drugs is to destroy the afflicting organisms but it is a painstakingly slow process and relapses are common.

Viral and Bacterial Infections

There are literally hundreds of viral and bacterial infections that can affect your horse's health. Vaccines, when available, are an appropriate choice for most horses. But they are not perfect and if a horse is already immune-compromised on vaccination day, adverse reactions can occur. Administering several vaccines at the same time can be risky for some horses while others do just fine with this method. Experience is your best guide when it comes to knowing how and when to vaccinate and your veterinarian is your best source of information. However, the bottom line in protecting your horse is to keep his immune system healthy through proper diet and stress management.

In the following sections, I offer some insight into various infections, both viral and bacterial. This book is not intended to be a complete medical guide; instead, it offers practical nutritional and environmental advice to help you work with your veterinarian in managing certain diseases.

VIRAL INFECTIONS

Since antibiotics are not effective against viruses, the best treatment for these infections is time, along with proper nutrition, rest, and reduction of any stress. Horses should be let outside in good weather to enjoy fresh, clean air. They should not be exercised or trailered. Good quality hay needs to be offered at all times, along with additional vitamins, such as vitamins E and C, to provide immune system support. Lysine is also beneficial, especially for herpes virus infections.

Equine herpes virus (rhinopneumonitis)

This respiratory disease is most commonly seen in foals, weanlings, and yearlings, but can affect horses at any age. It is caused by the herpes virus and just like all herpes, it can remain dormant for years and then one day, out of the blue, it can express itself. If a carrier horse becomes stressed, the virus can become active and be shed to other horses, even though the carrier may not show any signs of infection.

Equine influenza

Spread by respiratory secretions, this virus lodges itself within the lining of the respiratory tract. Fever, depression, and anorexia (loss of appetite) are common, along with coughing and nasal discharge. There is a vaccination for this disease which offers protection.

Equine infectious anemia (EIA)

You're familiar with this one if your horse has ever had a Coggins test, generally done before taking him out of state or before a show or sale. In fact, all horses should be tested for EIA. When traveling to horse events, you should only choose those that require proof of Coggins testing. Also, never buy a horse or breed your horse to one without a current Coggins test (within the last 12 months).

The lentivirus that causes EIA is transmitted by blood sucking insects such as horseflies and mosquitoes and affects horses throughout the world. It is transmitted by body fluids, so contaminated needles, dental equipment, and tattooing tools can pass the disease from one horse to another. There is no vaccine, so preventive measures should be taken. Keep flies to a minimum by not only using fly sprays and strips, but also consider a feed-through fly control product or fly predators.

Your horse's immune system at the time of infection significantly affects his response to the disease. If you hear of other cases in your area, have your veterinarian do a blood test, but keep in mind that a false negative can result if the infection is recent. Unfortunately, an infected horse needs to be permanently quarantined and euthanasia may need to be considered.

Warts

Caused by the papilloma virus, warts are often seen on the face and inside the ears. If left alone, they will go away by themselves within two to three months. This virus is contagious so be careful to disinfect your hands, as well as grooming supplies, halters, and other tack used between horses. Flies can transfer the virus from one horse to another, so protect your horse's ears with insect repellent. But there really is no medical treatment that is effective. A strong immune system, through dietary management and stress reduction, is your best defense against warts.

BACTERIAL INFECTIONS

Unlike viruses, bacteria can be killed using antibiotics. Oftentimes a viral infection will set up optimal conditions for a secondary bacterial problem, so even if your horse has a viral infection, antibiotics may still be prescribed. But antibiotic usage has its problems. It does kill the harmful microbes, that's true. But it also kills the beneficial bacteria that live throughout the body, especially within your horse's hindgut, reproductive organs, and skin. Killing his hindgut microbes can lead to colic and even laminitis, so a strong probiotic is essential during antibiotic use and for a few days following. One that contains oligosaccharides will also add immune system protection.

Long term antibiotic treatment is risky and is the main reason there are so many mutated bacterial strains that are resistant to the antibiotics we have available. This is the case with methicillin-resistant *Staphylococcus aureus* (MSRA), a deadly bacterium that affects animals and humans. I'll talk more about this one later. But for now, I want to impress upon you to *use antibiotics only when necessary*, and be sure to use them for at least 5 days so all of the bacteria can be eliminated. Follow your veterinarian's advice when providing this therapy.

Before I get into individual disorders, I'd like to share with you some information on iron. Iron is very commonly added to commercial horse feeds and supplements and it really shouldn't be because your horse gets *plenty* from fresh grass and hay. But the problem with iron is its interference with your horse's ability to fight a bacterial infection. You see, while most iron is stored within specialized blood proteins to prevent bacteria from reaching it, many bacterial strains are nevertheless able to pull it out of storage. Bacteria thrive on iron, so adding more will only delay healing. If you'd like to know more, take a look at Chapter 5 — Fundamentals of Minerals.

Pigeon fever

Pigeon fever is caused by the bacterium *Corynebacterium pseudotuberculosis* and has nothing to do with pigeons. Its name is derived from the appearance the disease causes, creating swelling in the chest (pectoral muscles) that looks similar to a pigeon's breast. The abdomen and groin region can also be affected.

These bacteria live in dry soil (especially during drought conditions) and manure, so manure management is important for its prevention. Flies pick up the organism and transfer it to open wounds and mucous membranes such as the eyes. Chest and abdominal abscesses are the first sign and in severe cases, the abscesses can be internal. Your veterinarian will want to drain mature abscesses so they can be cleaned. Antibiotics are generally not utilized because they may delay the abscesses from maturing.

This infection is extremely contagious to other horses. And it can live in your horse's system for months, making detection impossible until there's an abscess outbreak. Meticulous care needs to be taken to isolate the affected horse and protect healthy horses against fly bites, because it can be transmitted by infected insects. But isolation has its challenges, because your horse will experience stress caused by not being around his buddies, making healing more difficult.

A healthy immune system could prevent this disease. Vitamin E and other antioxidants, as well as flaxseed meal to provide omega-3s, should be part of any healthy horse's feeding regimen.

Strangles

This is another dreaded disease, caused by *Streptococcus equi*, which can infect the lymph nodes in the head and neck. Highly contagious, *S. equi* can remain viable in water for weeks and horses that carry the organism but show no symptoms can shed the bacteria for years.

The first sign of this disease is a fever. 99.0° to 101.5° F is a normal body temperature, so anything above 101.5° should tell you to call your veterinarian. After a few days, a nasal discharge will develop and turn from thin and clear to thick and yellow. Lymph nodes can swell, and the horse will lower his head to relieve the pressure.

Infected or exposed horses should not be allowed to touch noses, and you can carry the disease from place to place with infected hands. So extra sanitation is a must.

One area you might not think of when managing this disease is infected pastures. Manure should be removed and not used as compost. Let a "sick" pasture rest for a month before allowing healthy horses to graze on it.

The good news is, a farm is not contaminated forever. *S. equi* is actually a fragile organism and doesn't live very long, perhaps a maximum of 5 days. It's the constant shedding by infected horses that keeps the organism present. However, a recovered horse should be tested (nasal swabs) every few weeks, at least three times, before being allowed to return to his normal setting and contact with other horses.

Protect a sick horse from the wind and rain and weather extremes. Eating is painful, so feed something soft, such as soaked beet pulp or moistened alfalfa pellets. If necessary, hand feed him. Additional antioxidants, especially vitamins C and E, should be included in the diet. And don't forget water — it should be clean and clear, and at a pleasing temperature.

There are two killed-virus strangles vaccines which can offer some protection but it is not a certainty. An intranasal live-virus vaccine is also available, administered only by your veterinarian for safety, and is your best bet against minimizing this disease. I recommend discussing the options with your veterinarian. Also, before allowing a new horse on your property, ask your vet to test his blood for *S. equi* antibodies because an apparently healthy horse can be a carrier.

MRSA (methicillin-resistant Staphylococcus aureus)

Oh my goodness — this is a scary one because it is resistant to antibiotic treatment and it can take years to get rid of it. This is the one you hear about in hospitals where people go in for one ailment and come out with another. It is easily transmitted by touching an open wound with infected hands. The worst part about it is that it survives on *dry* surfaces. This is not just for your horse's safety (though that's the focus of this book) — it's for *your* safety, too. The best way to prevent transmission of this disease is to wash your hands! Did you hear me? Wash your hands well, with hot water and soap or use an alcohol-based hand gel, often. There are right ways and wrong ways to use disinfectant products, so take the time to educate yourself about the ways this disease is spread.

MRSA has become resistant to most commonly used antibiotics and infected horses need to be isolated from other animals. Only a limited number of people should be allowed to treat an infected horse, and only those who are healthy and without any cuts or sores on their skin. Disinfection is critical, before and after handling the horse.

Lyme disease

This disease is caused by the bacterium *Borrelia burgdorferi*, transmitted by an infected deer tick. Horses that are in close proximity to deer are more susceptible to contracting the disease. Northeastern and central-northern states including Wisconsin and Minnesota have a high incidence of Lyme disease. If the tick is removed within 24 hours, the chances of infection are significantly reduced.

Symptoms of this disease include a sudden lack of energy and depression. Other signs, such as stiffness, painful muscles, and joint swelling are often confused with osteochondritis dissecans (OCD), arthritis, tying up, or even EPM, making an accurate diagnosis difficult. The horse's skin will be hypersensitive, and he will rebel when touched or groomed. Eventually, an infected horse will show neurological signs such as loss of balance or gait abnormalities.

Antibiotics have been successful in treating Lyme disease. It's important to take blood tests, both before and after treatment, to provide a clear assessment of how well your horse is responding.

Nutritional Approaches for Allergies and Other Immune-Related Disorders

Medical intervention certainly has its place, but often there is no cure, just a treatment. Nutritional intervention, however, can not only control symptoms, but may also alleviate the problem at its source by removing borderline nutrient deficiencies that caused it in the first place.

That's why I developed an aggressive approach toward treating stubborn cases. I call it *Dr. Getty's Fighting Formula.*

This approach involves a few key nutrients that, when provided in high dosages, have a pharmacological effect. This means they are used more as drugs than nutrients. Nutrients are meant to keep your horse in a healthy state, free of deficiencies. Drugs are meant to treat and even cure diseases.

Unlike many traditional drugs, however, pharmacological levels of nutrients do not have to be maintained indefinitely. Once your horse is healed, you can slowly reduce the dosage to one that maintains his health while still offering protection against relapses.

Many of my recommendations involve vitamins, and I urge you to read Chapter 6 — Fundamentals of Vitamins to get a better overview of the way they work. You may have to go to your local pharmacy or grocery store to obtain some of these supplements though there are horse antioxidant preparations that may also be suitable. Check the label for exact amounts; you can always supplement the supplement with human products.

Some directions before we start:

- Always build up to these levels slowly, over a period of two weeks.
- Divide them between meals whenever possible.
- Continue this program until symptoms subside.
- Once your horse no longer requires such high amounts, *slowly wean him* down to a normal dosage, taking 3 to 4 weeks to do so. Please refer to Chapter 6 — Fundamentals of Vitamins for information regarding maintenance dosages. Chapter 19 — Growth and Growing Old offers more discussion for young as well as aging horses.
- Do not give this formula to a pregnant mare without your veterinarian's approval.

So here it is...

DR. GETTY'S FIGHTING FORMULA

- **Vitamin C:** 20 mg per lb of body weight (44 mg per kg of body weight). For an 1100 pound (500 kg) horse, that translates into 22,000 mg per day.

- **Bioflavonoids (including quercetin):** 1000 mg for a horse weighing 1000 - 1500 lbs (450 to 680 kg), 1500 mg for over 1500 lbs (680 kg). Reduce accordingly for smaller horses. Bioflavonoids are the antioxidants found naturally in the pulp of fruits and vegetables, and work synergistically with vitamin C.

- **Vitamin E:** 8 IU per lb of body weight (17.6 IU per kg of body weight). An 1100 lb (500 kg) horse would get 8800 IU per day.

- **Selenium:** Provide 3 to 5 mg per day for an 1100 lb (500 kg) horse. Reduce the level accordingly for smaller horses. Selenium is potentially toxic, so before supplementing, be sure to evaluate the entire diet, including hay, for its total selenium content. The total diet should not exceed 0.6 ppm. Please refer to Chapter 5 — Fundamentals of Minerals for more details on selenium.

- **Vitamin A:** 50 IU per lb of body weight (110 IU per kg of body weight). An 1100 lb (500 kg) horse would get 55,000 IU per day.

- **Omega-3 fatty acids:** These can be provided in several ways. Flaxseed meal and oil are excellent in reducing formation of damaging free radicals as well as stabilizing the immune system; however during severe cases, I recommend adding fish oils to offer an even greater anti-inflammatory effect.

  - **Flaxseed meal:** Provide 1/2 cup per 400 lbs of body weight (57 grams per 180 kg of body weight).
  - **Flaxseed oil:** 2 Tablespoons per 400 lbs of body weight (30 ml per 180 kg body weight).
  - **Fish oils:** *These should be added to flax in extreme cases. Reduce flax amount by 1/2.* Provide 2,000 mg fish oils (mixture of omega-3 fatty acids: EPA and DHA) per 400 lbs (180 kg) of body weight. Flaxseed (meal or oil) still needs to be added to provide some omega-6 fatty acids (fish oils do not contain any appreciable amount of omega-6 fatty acids). Please read more about these fatty acids in Chapter 3 — Fundamentals of Fats.

- **Coenzyme Q10:** 50 mg per 100 lbs (45 kg) of body weight. An 1100 lb (500 kg) horse would receive 550 mg per day. Coenzyme Q10 is a potent antioxidant that is just beginning to be recognized as a valuable component in equine nutrition. At relatively high doses, it relieves pain and inflammation by neutralizing free radicals and limiting prostaglandin production.

- **B complex:** Choose a preparation that has all eight B vitamins. For an 1100 lb (500 kg) horse, choose a preparation with the following amounts of all eight B vitamins; adjust up or down by 25% for every 500 lb (225 kg) change in body weight:

  - 100-150 mg of B_1, B_2, B_6, niacin, and pantothenic acid
  - 0.6-1.0 mg of B_{12}
  - 2-5 mg of biotin
  - 5-10 mg of folic acid

- **Spirulina:** This blue-green algae (*Arthrospira platensis*) is a food source that significantly reduces allergy symptoms and improves respiratory function. Provide 2,000 mg per 100 lbs (45 kg) of body weight.

Supporting nutrients

There are a few things your horse should already be getting as part of his overall diet:

- **Vitamin D.** This is especially important if your horse does not get at least 8 hours of direct sunlight each day. Chapter 6 — Fundamentals of Vitamins offers a discussion on vitamin D that you may find helpful.

- **Minerals.** Make certain his diet contains a balance of copper, zinc, manganese, and other minerals. See Chapter 5 — Fundamentals of Minerals for a complete list. Most fortified feeds will provide adequate minerals, as will a comprehensive supplement.

- **High-quality protein.** Add a legume hay (alfalfa or clover) to grass hay to create a 2:1 ratio of grass to legume. If you cannot obtain alfalfa hay, you can add alfalfa pellets or cubes to his meal (they need to be moistened). Or if you're feeding a commercial feed, check for alfalfa or soybean meal (another legume) on the list of ingredients. Take a look at Chapter 4 — Fundamentals of Protein and Amino Acids for a complete discussion on protein quality.

In addition to the above formula, there are many other antioxidants, anti-inflammatory agents, and helpful substances that you can certainly consider adding. Please refer to the section in this chapter where I discuss your horse's ailment — I have mentioned specific supplements that are important to consider. Here are a few more that I have not yet talked about, and are worth considering for your horse:

- **MSM (Methylsulfonylmethane).** Though typically added to joint supplements, its anti-inflammatory properties are beneficial for any source of inflammation.

- **Grapeseed extract.** Also added to joint preparations, grape seed extract contains a potent antioxidant known as proanthocyanidins.

- **Manuka honey.** Honey has been used for centuries because of its antimicrobial properties. It works well as a topical first aid as well as an oral supplement. Collected from the Tea Tree manuka bush native to New Zealand, manuka honey is more potent that other forms; I have found it to be especially effective for seasonal allergies that affect the skin and respiratory system.

- **Probiotics and oligosaccharides.** One of the best ways you can keep your horse's immune system healthy is to protect his digestive tract. A potent probiotic preparation along with oligosaccharides will replace microbes that have been lost due to physical and mental stress, as well as keep his digestive tract healthy.

- **Herbs**. I highly recommend contacting an equine herbalist for suggestions on treating stubborn allergies that have not responded to traditional methods. Herbs can work well with the nutritional supplements I've recommended. However, since herbs can have side effects or interact with medications, be diligent about gathering more information before giving them to your horse.

A Word About Garlic and Heinz Body Anemia...

I bring up this type of anemia, not because it is directly related to immune function, but because it is often a result of feeding garlic to horses in an attempt to repel insects. Garlic (and onions) contain allicin, which is excellent for our health, but is harmful to your horse over the long term. Garlic has antimicrobial properties which can negatively impact your horse's hindgut microbial population. It also lessens the production of a protective enzyme known as phosphate dehydrogenase (PD). Lessened PD levels impair hemoglobin's ability to defend itself against oxidative damage, leading to the production of damaging free radicals. Some oxidative stress is normal but red blood cells can become overwhelmed once their protective enzyme system is altered.

The result is a Heinz body, a tiny growth on the outside of the cell. Damaged cells can be removed from the bloodstream by the spleen, but over time, with consistent feeding of garlic, your horse will develop anemia. He will have a low red blood cell count, jaundice, and dark, reddish urine.

The exact toxic dosage is unclear, but my thinking is, why deliberately feed a known toxin to your horse? Wild onions found in pasture, for example, have been found to create Heinz body anemia. Even household onions, kale, or leeks can induce this type of anemia.

Because garlic's damage creeps up on your horse a little at a time, you won't see any ill effects at first. But after a while, you may notice that your horse has less endurance, his energy level is decreased, and he becomes more susceptible to infections.

There is no scientific evidence that garlic helps as a fly repellent. Yes, there is anecdotal evidence that the smell keeps flies away. And that's likely how garlic-based insect repellents claim to work. The garlic is heated and dried first, which allegedly destroys the damaging allicin, but frankly, I do not trust these products. Furthermore, you'd have to feed an awful lot of garlic to get your 1100 lb horse to stink enough for the bugs to stay away. And I don't know about you, but I love the way horses smell, and I don't think I'd feel that way if they smelled like garlic.

The jury is still out on these supposedly "allicin destroyed" products. I'd be interested in hearing from you about your experience.

Endnotes

[1] Adapted from Barakat, C., 2009, *Equus, 380,* May: 39-49.

[2] Bello, T.R., and Allen, T.M., 2008. An intensive approach in the treatment of clinical equine protozoal myeloencephalitis. *Journal of Equine Veterinary Science, 28* (8): 479-483.

CHAPTER 17 —
STRESS AND BEHAVIOR

In riding a horse, we borrow his freedom. Horses love freedom.
The weariest old work horse will roll on the ground or break into
a lumbering gallop when he is turned loose into the open.
~ Gerald Raferty

Ah, the stress-free life. Free to roam, explore, eat, socialize with friends, and lie down to take a nap. Such a life doesn't exist for most horses. We impose our feeding schedules, our training programs and our housing, and carry them from here to there on long, bumpy trailer rides. Combine these constraints with their inherent nature to flee at a moment's notice, and it's no wonder horses develop stress-related disorders.

Stress depresses the immune system. Horses become less able to combat illness when exposed to viruses, bacteria, parasites, and pollen. Even sunlight can trigger illness in a sensitive horse whose immune system is compromised.

There are numerous causes of stress. You know what they are — weather extremes, intense exercise, trailering, injury, illness, vaccinating, isolation, change in environment, bullying from other herd members, poor nutrition, irregular exercise, and loss of a buddy, to name just a few.

Horses express tension in a variety of ways because they have different personalities. Don't assume that your horse is lazy, defiant, or has a poor work ethic, if he rebels. A stressed horse may buck, kick, bite, and become mouthy. Others start to chew on fences, gates, and even themselves to indicate that they're in pain. Some horses become fearful of new settings or a new object added to a familiar workout. Some horses internalize stress (know some people like that, who hold it all it and then explode?). You know your horse better than anyone, so watch for indications that are not normal for his character.

This is not an equine behavior book, and yet I'm talking about behavior. That's because your horse's mental state affects the rest of his body. This holistic perspective has been my focus throughout this book. Stressed, anxious, nervous, and even depressed horses not only become ill more easily, they have trouble maintaining a normal weight. Some will become underweight and others will actually gain weight from hormonal influences. Muscle development will be abnormal in many cases. And secondary tissues that are not involved in maintaining life — hair, hooves, joints — will show signs of nutrient deficiencies.

In the pages that follow, I offer basic guidelines that will help you prevent or manage stressful circumstances and feed your horse accordingly. Because some nutrients are useful for more than one circumstance, you'll notice that I repeat a number of recommendations. I do this so you won't miss out on information if you decide to read one section of the chapter rather than the whole thing. So no matter how you choose to read this chapter, you'll get the information you need. However, I strongly urge you to read all the "Fundamentals" Chapters (1-10) for a grounding in the nutrition I mention here.

Weather Extremes

Your horse is very uncomfortable during hot weather, especially when it's hot and humid, and every effort should be made to put him at ease. Conversely, he enjoys the winter as long as his coat is thick and able to keep moisture from reaching his skin. Regardless of the temperature extreme, however, your horse's metabolic rate will increase and he will burn more calories to maintain a normal internal body temperature. This is why you'll often see horses lose weight during the summer, as well as during the winter. But winter can be especially harsh for many horses and some preparation is advisable.

ACCOMMODATION FOR WINTER

Horses love it when there's a chill in the air! You can tell they're enjoying the cool, crisp days by the way they start to buck and run. But as the winter temperatures set in, your horse will rely on you to protect him against extreme cold. Some areas of the country have milder winters than others, but no matter when your horse lives, there are adjustments to be made.

First, pasture becomes limited or non-existent and horses must be fed hay. Hay loses many of the nutrients originally found in fresh grass, such as vitamins E and C, beta carotene (for vitamin A production), and omega-3 fatty acids. In addition, exposure to direct sunlight declines during winter, limiting your horse's ability to produce his own vitamin D. It is more important than ever to fill in these nutritional gaps by providing a vitamin/mineral supplement that also includes flaxseed meal for necessary omega-3 fatty acids.

Alfalfa is beneficial for most horses because when combined with grass hay, it boosts the overall protein quality. This helps protect immune function and keep body proteins such as muscles, hair, skin, and hooves, in good condition. Consider offering your horse a 30/70 mixture of alfalfa/grass hay.

Calorie needs and outdoor temperatures

As temperatures fall, energy needs increase. For every 1.8° F below the lower critical temperature (LCT), horses need 2.5% more calories. The LCT ranges from 41° to 5° F, depending on your horse's adaptation to the cold. Calories are expressed on feed labels as digestible energy (DE). An adult horse at maintenance, weighing 1100 lbs, for example, requires 16.7 Mcal per day during mild weather. With each 1.8 ° F below LCT, energy needs increase by 0.42 Mcal. To put this into perspective, one pound of grass hay provides approximately 1.0 Mcal per pound; alfalfa hay provides 1.07 Mcal/lb.

Using this example, let's say this horse is fairly well adapted to the cold and his LCT is 30° F. If the temperature falls to 10° F, his DE requirement will increase an additional 4.7 Mcal, which would be provided by nearly 5 lbs of grass hay. Refer to Appendix — Crunching Numbers to see how this is calculated. But there's no specific way to determine your horse's LCT — it's just your best estimate based on his body condition and how comfortable he appears to be in cold weather.

You could go through these calculations with each temperature drop. But to make things easier, let me give you a quick way to estimate additional hay requirements: For every 4° F below freezing (use wind-chill temperature), add one pound of hay. Or another rule of thumb — for every 10 ° below freezing (wind chill temperature), feed 10% more hay than usual.

Keep in mind that hay DE values vary. I've seen grass hay with DE levels as low as 0.7 Mcal/lb so the only way to know for certain is to have your hay analyzed. Furthermore, the example I used was for an average horse that weighs 1100 lbs and is well adapted to the cold. Your horse, however, may be growing, aging, underweight, ill, have a sparse winter coat, or be unaccustomed to a colder climate. *The best way to overcome all these circumstances is to simply offer hay free choice.* It's the best way to feed for so many reasons, and it removes any doubt regarding how much to feed each day, though some calculations will be necessary to figure how much hay to stock for the winter.

Adding more calories: Wet and windy conditions increase energy needs, making it difficult for your horse to eat enough if hay is his only feed source. If his hair coat becomes wet in frigid temperatures, the DE requirement may increase as much as 50%. Therefore, depending on the condition of your horse, you may need to add concentrates to the diet. You can do this a number of ways. A high fat commercial feed is fine for healthy horses. For the easy keeper, it is best to avoid cereal grains such as oats, corn, barley or sweet feeds. Beet pulp or alfalfa pellets provide calories without much starch and sugar. And don't forget fat sources such as rice bran, flaxseed meal, and oils — they are concentrated sources of calories. All oils provide the same number of calories, but the way the body responds to them can vary. Take a look at Chapter 3 — Fundamentals of Fats for a detailed description of each type of oil.

Heat and calories from microbial fermentation: Your horse derives heat and calories from hay through microbial fermentation in his hindgut. Therefore, the microbial population needs to remain plentiful and healthy. A prebiotic that contains fermentation products will feed these hindgut flora and help your horse digest hay more efficiently. This will not only provide more calories, but also will help him generate heat.

Bran mashes

Many horse owners enjoy occasionally feeding a warm bran mash in winter, with the good intention of offering "comfort food" to their horses. But this practice should be avoided for two reasons. First, consistency in the diet is critical to your horse's digestive health. If you introduce bran once each week, there is a significant risk of colic because the hindgut bacteria haven't had a chance to adjust. The second problem with feeding bran is that it has more phosphorus than calcium. So if you choose to feed bran, be consistent by feeding it daily and choose a commercial product that has added calcium to compensate for high phosphorus levels.

Water

Water consumption is critical during the winter. Do not rely on snow to meet your horse's water requirement. One gallon (128 fluid ounces) of average moisture snow only provides 10 ounces of water. Also, eating snow will force your horse to burn precious calories to keep his body temperature steady.

If at all possible, plan on heating your horse's water. Horses will not drink enough cold water to prevent dehydration and impaction colic, so the water temperature should be maintained at 50° F using heated water buckets or an automatic watering system that is temperature controlled. To encourage your horse to drink enough water (8 to 12 gallons/day) for maintenance, add table salt to his diet — two tablespoons per day, divided between meals. And always keep a clean, plain white salt block nearby. Mineralized or blue (from added iodine and cobalt) salt blocks are only appropriate if hay is the single feed source or if your horse is not receiving minerals from fortified feeds or supplements.

Older horses

Your older horse may need joint protection during the cold months. A good joint supplement is advisable, along with vitamin C for collagen production, since the older a horse gets, the less vitamin C he produces on his own.

If he's a hard keeper, be sure he is not competing with younger, more aggressive horses for his hay. Feed a good quality senior feed, along with added flaxseed meal (use a commercial product that is stabilized and has added calcium to balance for high phosphorus levels). A vitamin/mineral supplement along with added alfalfa for protein (unless his kidneys are compromised) is important to maintain his immune system. Additional fat from rice bran oil can be added. Avoid corn and soybean oils because they are high in omega-6 fatty acids, which promote inflammation.

As your horse ages, he is more inclined to develop a dysfunction of the pituitary gland known as pituitary pars intermedia dysfunction (PPID), commonly referred to as equine Cushing's disease. The main symptoms of this disorder are a long, curly hair coat, increased urination and thirst, reduced muscle mass, and an increased susceptibility to infections. He will be more likely to develop laminitis due to secondary insulin resistance. If your horse is diagnosed with this disease, avoid starchy feeds and do not feed molasses or sugary treats such as apples or carrots. Chapter 13 — Metabolic and Endocrine Disorders offers details on this disease.

Be sure to have your horse's teeth checked before winter sets in. Poor dental health is the number one reason for weight loss in older horses. And consult with your veterinarian about the best deworming program for your area, including tapeworm treatment in the fall.

Feet

If your horse can go without shoes, this is the best time to pull them off to prevent ice and snow accumulation. Be sure to trim his feet in preparation for winter. If your horse is standing in muddy areas, there is an increased likelihood of developing thrush and dermatitis along his lower limbs. Trimming his fetlock feathers and checking his feet each day for infection will help prevent more serious problems.

Blankets

Your horse's winter coat provides him with insulation, provided that his skin doesn't get wet. Therefore, most horses do not need to be blanketed as long as they have access to shelter from the wind, rain, and snow. A winter coat has the remarkable ability to regulate body temperature. Each hair follicle has a small muscle associated with it that can pull the hair to an upright position, increasing air content between hairs, which has an insulating effect.

Don't rush to blanket your horse. If he is healthy, of normal weight, and has a good winter coat, he can do very well in cold weather. Use the wind chill as your guide. If the wind chill temperature goes below 20° F, you should consider blanketing a horse that lives outside. Keep in mind that blankets flatten the hair coat, reducing its natural thermal ability, so only use them when necessary. Watch the blanket weight. Blankets that are too heavy or too tight can diminish hair's natural insulating ability, making it difficult for your horse to maintain a normal body temperature.

If your horse is clipped, however, or if the winter coat growth has been inhibited by artificial light or show blanketing (as can happen with breeding mares and performance horses), then a blanket is necessary. Horses that are thin, ill or recently relocated to a cold climate will also enjoy the added warmth of a blanket. Also, if your horse is sweating after exercise, it is important to blanket him with a sweat sheet until the skin dries. Don't use a hair dryer. It can dry out and damage the skin. Be sure to remove the sweat sheet once the horse dries; damp sheets are not appropriate as winter blankets.

Watch the blanket weight. Blankets that are too heavy or too tight can diminish hair's natural insulating ability, making it difficult for your horse to maintain a normal body temperature.

If you must blanket your horse, use waterproof, breathable materials only, and monitor your horse's coat under the blanket for sweating. When temperatures drop, a wet horse underneath a blanket can be colder than he would be with no blanket at all, and putting on a blanket that has not been properly dried does the horse no favors either. Never put a winter blanket on a horse still sweaty from exercise; cool him out properly and make sure his coat is dry before reblanketing.

Shelter

Turnout is the ideal situation, along with a three-sided shelter or free access to a barn to provide protection against heavy snowfall, rain, and wind. If your horse is stalled, make sure the barn is well ventilated to avoid respiratory problems. If a horse is unaccustomed to stall living, this can be stressful, resulting in ulcers and reduced immune function. So the more turnout you can provide the better.

HEAT STRESS

Keeping your horse comfortable during the summer heat and humidity can be challenging. Turnout, while preferable, should offer access to shade either from trees or a three-sided shelter. Stalled horses should have adequate air circulation. Spray misters, along with fans, are an excellent way to lower the temperature inside the barn.

Exercise should be limited to early morning or late evening when it is less hot. After a workout, your horse will appreciate being sprayed with cool water. This will provide rapid cooling of the skin, and excess heat will evaporate. If the water is cold, introduce it slowly, starting at the feet, and do not be concerned about the common myth that cold causes blood vessel constriction or muscle cramping. *Be sure to scrape the water off of his skin to allow for heat to be released from the body.* If you leave water on his body, it will trap heat and actually cause his internal temperature to rise.

Excessive sweating can bring about dehydration and if ignored, can progress to life threatening heat stroke. Dehydration simply means the loss of body fluids. Sweating is necessary to regulate internal body temperature; required water is first pulled from the bloodstream. As sweating continues, water will be removed from the digestive system and eventually from the spaces between cells. Anxious, erratic, or depressed behavior, or difficulty maintaining balance indicates heat stroke and your veterinarian should be contacted immediately.

Testing for dehydration

The first thing you should do if you suspect dehydration is offer your horse a drink to see if he's thirsty. But the thirst mechanism can fail during dehydration (see Chapter 7 — Fundamentals of Water and Electrolytes). The pinch test is worthwhile: Pinch the skin along the shoulder and release it. The skin should snap back to its original position in less than a second. If it takes longer than this, it is a sign of dehydration. Do this test under ordinary conditions so you know what is normal for your horse. That way you can see if there is a difference during periods of heat and exercise.

Another dehydration test is capillary refill time, assessed by lightly pressing on your horse's gum and then releasing it to see how long it takes for the pink color to return to normal. This should not take longer than two seconds. Any longer, and your horse is dehydrated.

Dark, concentrated urine indicates that your horse is not getting enough water. Your horse will always produce urine to get rid of metabolic waste, but he will conserve as much water as possible if he's becoming dehydrated.

Effects of dehydration

While sweating is natural all year round, your horse can sweat nearly 4 gallons of water (32 pounds of body weight) *per hour* in very hot temperatures. This degree of fluid loss can cause serious illness such as tying up (rhabdomyolysis), colic, thumps (a disorder where the diaphragm flutters), and even death.

Don't work a fatigued horse. Some horses will continue working just to do what you ask, but you will notice that they are breathing very hard, and may even start to pant, though horses cannot breathe through their mouths. At first, panting will be rapid, followed by slower, deeper gulps of air, in an attempt to lower body temperature.

Stressed or exhausted horses that become dehydrated will lose essential electrolytes. Calcium, magnesium, chloride, sodium, and potassium losses increase neuromuscular irritability, causing the diaphragm to flutter each time the heart beats. Colic is also a dangerous possibility. These conditions are considered a medical emergency and should not be ignored.

If fluid is not replaced, perspiration will get very thick, and the skin will feel hot, indicating that body fluids are getting too concentrated. As the horse is less able to sweat, body temperature begins to rise. This leads to heat exhaustion, a more serious situation that affects other areas of the body. Heat exhaustion is apparent when sweating decreases or stops altogether, a condition known as anhydrosis.

Anhydrosis: This situation can affect horses that are sweating excessively for long periods of time. It can come about gradually where only small areas of skin are dry, or it can occur all over the body. Heat is a factor, of course, but its combination with humidity seems to be the main culprit. When it's humid, evaporation cannot occur as efficiently. Body temperature can rise to between 102 and 103 degrees even if your horse is only standing still. Add exercise to the equation and his temperature can reach 105 to 108 degrees, a potentially deadly situation.

It has been postulated[1] that anhydrosis occurs when dopamine, a neurotransmitter, is depleted from the brain. Sweat glands use dopamine, but if it's in short supply, the brain will get priority usage, making the sweat glands shut down. The amino acid L-tyrosine induces dopamine production. There are L-tyrosine supplements available to alleviate anhydrosis.

Treating mild dehydration

As long as your horse is breathing and acting normally, mild dehydration can be remedied by providing a consistent supply of water. To help him recover, give him water after a workout, as much as he wants with short walking breaks in between drinking. Don't worry about the temperature of the water, but if it's ice cold, he may not drink as much as he needs. Cold water will not cause colic or muscle cramping but it may be unpalatable to drink.

Next, restore your horse's electrolytes after exercise. Offer a gallon or two of water with added electrolytes to help bring your horse's levels back to normal. You may need to repeat electrolyte replenishment several times a day if your horse is working especially hard. Follow the recommended directions carefully. Do not add electrolytes to his regular water supply; water needs to be clean and free of additives. *Plenty of fresh water must be available after an electrolyte dosage; otherwise the added electrolytes will concentrate his blood even further.*

Sodium balance: Electrolyte supplementation is designed to replace what has been lost through perspiration. But your horse first needs to have enough sodium before electrolytes can be effective. This is done by providing salt on a daily basis. Plain, white, non-mineralized salt in the form of a salt block, loose salt, or added to meals will keep him in good sodium balance. Stay away from kelp or sea salt; it is far too high in iodine. For more discussion on salt and electrolytes, see Chapter 7 — Fundamentals of Water and Electrolytes.

Know what's normal for your horse!

Horses are individuals. Get familiar with your horse's vital signs — temperature, respiratory rate, and capillary refill time — to better equip you in an emergency. What's more, knowing how much he normally eats and drinks will help you recognize changes and catch problems early.

Transporting

As with any stressor, being hauled for long distances challenges the immune system. Even the best transporting service cannot totally remove the stress factor. Upon arrival it can take a day or two for your horse to recover, making him more susceptible to illness. To lessen the stressful effects of travel, I've provided several nutritional tips below.

PREPARING FOR TRAVEL

Boosting the nutritional value of meals prior to his departure will help prepare your horse for a stressful trip. I am making the assumption that your horse is healthy and fit. He may even be used to traveling long distances. Nevertheless, riding in a trailer for 6 hours or more is difficult for any horse. Therefore, start improving his nutritional status at least 2 weeks prior to the trip.

As a side note… A horse that is in poor shape, aging, or ill should have his health needs attended to long before the trip. In addition, if your horse is not accustomed to riding in a trailer, practice traveling with frequent short trips to ease the anxiety for the longer jaunt.

There are basic feeding tips that apply to all horses to keep them in good condition. So first make sure you're doing the following:

- Provide all the good quality grass hay and/or pasture that he wants. This will keep the digestive system moving and functioning normally.

- Meet additional calorie needs by adding an appropriate commercial feed, concentrates, beet pulp, or alfalfa pellets.

- Do not switch feeds before travelling. New feeds should be introduced slowly, allowing three to four weeks of gradual change.

- Fill in nutrient gaps with a comprehensive vitamin/mineral supplement. This is especially important if your horse is strictly on hay and/or pasture, or if a commercially fortified feed is fed in small quantities, but not at the recommended feeding amount.

- Water needs to be clean, free from algae, insects, and bird droppings. It should be available at all times. In cold weather, water should be temperature-controlled to promote enough consumption and prevent dehydration.

- Pay attention to salt intake. If your horse is not getting enough salt from a salt block, add two tablespoons (one ounce) of salt per day, divided between meals. Choose plain, white, table salt that you buy in your local grocery store. Whether or not to get the iodized version depends on iodine supplementation from other sources. In the summer when horses sweat more profusely, increase salt supplementation to 4 tablespoons per day. For a complete discussion refer to Chapter 7 — Fundamentals of Water and Electrolytes. I also bring up this subject in the Chapter 1 — Ground Rules for Feeding a Horse.

In addition to the basics above, adding the following nutrients (starting two weeks before travel) will protect your horse's immune function throughout the trip and afterwards. Regardless of whether the travel is for a short time away from home or to a new permanent destination, keep him on these added nutrients for a week or two after travel to help his system recover from the stress and/or acclimate to the new location. Then gradually wean him off of the extra supplements over a week's time (with the exception of vitamin C — take 3 to 4 weeks to wean the horse off of this vitamin). Afterwards, you can return your horse to his previous, regular diet or make adjustments appropriate to his new situation (i.e., heavier or lighter exercise load, change in pasture, etc.).

Stress diet

- **Vitamin E.** Provide 1.5 to 3.0 IU per pound of body weight (commercial feeds are not typically fortified with this much vitamin E). Since vitamin E is fat soluble, there needs to be some fat in your horse's meal. A word of caution… When adding vitamin E, most supplements contain the mineral selenium. Too much selenium can be toxic. So before using a vitamin E/selenium supplement, check the selenium level in the overall diet. For an 1100 lb horse, it should ideally be between 1 and 3 mg per day, or as much as 5 mg/day for an athletic horse. However, the entire diet should not contain more than 0.6 mg/kg (ppm) of selenium. To assist you with the calculations, see Appendix — Crunching Numbers: Chapter 5 calculations. If the diet already has enough selenium and you want to add vitamin E, use a pure vitamin E supplement. Since horses require more vitamin E than we once thought, you may want to continue providing at least 1 IU per pound of body weight, even after your trip is completed. Take a look at Chapter 6 — Fundamentals of Vitamins.

- **Flaxseed meal.** Flax is high in omega-3 fatty acids which regulate immunity, reduce inflammation of joints and muscles, and aid in keeping the coat and hooves healthy. Use a commercial flaxseed meal product that is pure (no added grain), stabilized (to protect against rancidity), and has added calcium to balance out its naturally high phosphorus content. (Grinding your own flaxseeds is inadvisable for two reasons: it starts to go rancid within hours and it contains too much phosphorus.) Feed 1/2 cup (4 fluid ounces, but 2 ounces by weight) per 400 lbs of body weight each day. Divide this amount among meals and if your horse has never had flaxseed meal before, build up to this level over a week's time. Consider continuing feeding flaxseed meal once your trip is completed because of its excellent health benefits.

- **Magnesium.** This mineral is poorly supplied by most horse diets, making marginal deficiencies commonplace. Because it is necessary for nervous system health, even a slight deficiency can result in poor performance, lack of energy, and changes in demeanor. Head shaking may also occur and responds well to supplementation. Add magnesium at a rate of 5,000 mg per 500 lbs of body weight. Build up to this level over a few days since magnesium has a laxative effect and loose manure may result. This is normal and will stabilize itself.

- **Prebiotics.** These are not the same as probiotics which contain live microbes. Instead, prebiotics contain fermentation products that feed the existing bacterial flora living in the hindgut. These bacteria are vital to a horse's health because without them your horse will not be able to digest fiber (from hay, pasture, or any other fiber source). Stress can reduce microbial levels, so prebiotics offer protection against losses. Prebiotics can be discontinued once the source of stress is removed.

- **Oligosaccharides.** These are substances that improve immune function within the gastrointestinal tract. They are often packaged with probiotics (live microbes) and significantly improve your horse's health. Look for a probiotic product that offers oligosaccharides and use it during periods of stress and following your trip.

- **B vitamins.** There are eight B vitamins and they work together to keep your horse healthy in a variety of ways. One of the main functions of B vitamins is to keep the nervous system calm. A B complex supplement is beneficial at a double dose. Be careful when choosing a B complex preparation since most of them are marketed as "blood builders" that contain iron. Avoid such products because horses already get plenty of iron from their forage. Too much iron can interfere with immune function.

- **Vitamin C.** This vitamin is an antioxidant, meaning it neutralizes damaging free radicals that are produced during stress. Young horses manufacture enough vitamin C on their own. As horses age, however, they are less able to produce enough of this vitamin. But even a young horse that is preparing to travel can benefit from additional vitamin C each day to combat stress. I recommend 10 mg of vitamin C per pound of body weight. Build up to this level over a two-week period and do not abruptly stop feeding vitamin C after the trip since your horse's body will have become accustomed to the higher dosage. Instead, take 3 to 4 weeks to wean him off of this vitamin. If your horse is over 16 years of age, you may want to continue supplementation. See Chapters 6 — Fundamentals of Vitamins and 19 — Growth and Growing Old for more information.

- **Water.** It is very difficult to carry enough water for an entire trip and many horses will not drink unfamiliar water. Therefore, help your horse become accustomed to flavored water before the trip so you can carry the flavoring agent with you. It is best to start two weeks before travel. Apple juice is a favorite — add 1/4 cup of juice per 5 gallons of water. If your horse needs to avoid sugar, artificially sweetened fruit punch or Kool Aid can be used.

GUIDELINES WHILE TRAVELING

While on the road it may not be feasible to add all of these supplements. But allow your horse to consume hay throughout the trip to maintain his gut motility and reduce boredom. It is important to provide the same hay with which your horse is familiar, not only to encourage eating but to protect his digestive tract against sudden changes in diet.

Every effort should be made to make your horse comfortable. Do not cross-tie your horse. This is a common and unfortunate practice. Your horse needs to have an unrestricted head so he can easily eat hay. Furthermore, when the head is elevated above the withers for any period of time, the respiratory tract cannot drain properly, leading to infections. The physical stress of head confinement further reduces immune function, making your horse more vulnerable to unfamiliar pathogens that he will likely encounter at your new destination.

Water consumption is critically important while on the road. Since it is difficult to provide water in a moving trailer, stop every 1 1/2 hours to offer your horse water. Stopping not only gives you a chance to water your horse, but it also allows his legs to rest from the strain of balancing during movement. One way to offer water is to lower a feed bucket full of fresh water into the trailer window. Add 1/4 cup of the flavoring agent to which he's become accustomed. Carry a 5-gallon container of clean water (without juice) with you on the trip and refill it as necessary.

If the trip is going to be made in one day, simply offer hay. If the trip entails stopping overnight and your horse is boarded, concentrated meals can be provided. The number of meals depends upon the length of time off the trailer. The goal when boarding is to be as consistent as possible with the at-home schedule with regard to the number of meals and the times that they are offered. However, while traveling in the trailer (even if stopped), it is best to avoid feeding concentrated meals that will overwork the digestive system.

SIGNS OF DISTRESS

I do not recommend using tranquilizers for nervousness; horses need to balance themselves during the ride, and dopey, drugged horses are more likely to injure themselves. You're already giving him magnesium as part of his stress diet, but if additional calming is necessary, you can try vitamin B_1 in large dosages (1 mg per pound of body weight), or small amounts of tryptophan (an amino acid). Before using tryptophan, experiment with its effect on your horse so you know how much to use to get the desired effect. Later in this chapter, I'll discuss these and other calming agents.

If your horse won't eat while being transported, he may be experiencing physical distress. Each time you stop, check him for elevated respiration, reluctance to eat hay or drink water, stocking up (swelling of legs), diarrhea, or restlessness. Stocking up indicates that your horse is retaining fluid and the blood is too concentrated. Encouraging him to drink more water will dilute the blood, allowing for natural electrolytes to be removed in the urine. Do not give him salt or additional electrolytes — his blood is already too concentrated.

Diarrhea, depending on the severity, may simply be a sign of mild mental stress and will likely right itself once your horse has settled in to his new location. While stopped, give him a very small meal of moistened alfalfa pellets along with a probiotic and some salt.

If your horse has not eaten for several hours, the potential for colic is high. Also, he needs the calcium that hay provides to prevent stress tetany, associated with calcium losses from excessive sweating. This condition is indicated by twitching, muscle spasms, and stiff, rigid limbs. Excessive sweating is alleviated by giving him an electrolyte supplement (which usually contains calcium) in one gallon of water, followed by all the clean, fresh water he wants. Colic and stress tetany are serious conditions and warrant immediate medical care. Your veterinarian should be aware that you are traveling. Keep his/her number handy as well as the names of equine veterinarians in the cities through which you are traveling.

UPON REACHING YOUR DESTINATION

At your destination continue to provide all the hay your horse wants and make certain that he is drinking at least 8 gallons of water each day. Salt is important and a white salt block should be within easy reach. Give him hay immediately, but it is best to wait 4 to 8 hours after arriving to serve him his usual meal. As I mentioned earlier, continue feeding the stress diet for one to two weeks at his new location or after you get back home. This will keep your horse's immune system in top shape.

Training and Boarding

Performance does not necessarily mean stress. I've seen many performance horses that are relaxed and healthy. These horses are treated like horses, not performance cars. They are fed high amounts of forage while cereal grains/sweet feeds are kept to a minimum, if fed at all. Meal sizes are small, in tune with the horse's relatively small stomach size. And they get turned out on pasture most of the time. Changes in routine are made very gradually — repetitive activities provide a level of security for horses, so for these relaxed horses, a new training method or performance maneuver is introduced slowly.

Take your time, be patient, and never train while you're having a bad day. Horses sense your tension. Instead, take a day off, groom your horse, talk to him, and just "hang out." You'll be better tomorrow, and so will he.

If you must stall your horse, do it in baby-steps. Horses that are accustomed to turnout will develop ulcers within one week of barn stalling. If at all possible, bring your horse's pasture buddy inside, too, for familiar social contact.

Reducing boredom should be your goal when making your stalled horse more comfortable. A barn filled with constant activity and interaction with people and other horses, combined with a riding/training routine, will keep your horse mentally and physically stimulated so his barn home will be a reassuring place to be. Conversely, being held in an isolated stall can be devastating, resulting in repetitive habits such as weaving, kicking, chewing, and cribbing. Horses become depressed and may stop eating.

Stall design, cleanliness, ventilation, insect control, floor coverings, and proper maintenance are all essential factors. My goal in writing about this subject is to emphasize how stress reduction improves your horse's health. You can offer the best diet possible, but if your horse is too stressed to eat it, fine nutrition won't do him much good. It's a balance between proper diet and environment that makes the horse whole.

AGITATED HORSE, BORDERLINE DEFICIENCY?

Agitated, nervous horses that are normally well behaved may be suffering from borderline nutrient deficiencies that are not obvious or considered "text book" in their appearance. Nutrients such as magnesium and the B vitamins protect the nervous system and ease tension. Below is a list of some helpful nutrients and herbs that have a calming effect:

Calming agents

- **Magnesium.** This mineral is included in the stress diet mentioned earlier. It is also useful in alleviating anxious behavior during training and boarding. If your horse has a short attention span, is jittery, spooks more easily than he used to, and seems unusually stressed, a magnesium deficiency may be to blame. Magnesium is quite effective in calming the nervous system in horses that are suffering from this kind of deficiency, even a minor one; try it first in your attempt to ease tension. Magnesium works together with calcium to promote muscle contraction and relaxation — so the two minerals need to be in the proper proportions, preferably in a 2:1 ratio of calcium to magnesium. The ratio can be as high as 1:1, but magnesium should never exceed calcium. Most grass and alfalfa hay provides some magnesium but it is not readily absorbed, so supplementation is helpful. I recommend adding 5,000 mg of magnesium per 500 lbs of body weight.

- **Vitamin B$_1$ (thiamin).** This is one of eight B vitamins that work together to keep various bodily systems in good health. Thiamin in relatively large dosages of 1 mg per pound of body weight per day eases depression, anxiety, and jumpiness in many horses. If magnesium is not helpful, try thiamin next.

- **Vitamin B$_6$ (pyridoxine).** Serotonin production in the brain depends on vitamin B$_6$. Serotonin is a neurotransmitter that may be out of balance in stressed or depressed horses. Therefore, this B vitamin is useful in lessening depression and creating a sense of calm. The dosage needs to be monitored because unlike the other B vitamins that are excreted in the urine when given in excess, vitamin B_6 can have toxic effects on the nervous system. To be safe, do not exceed 200 mg per day.

- **Vitamin B_{12} (cobalamin).** The nervous system is protected by vitamin B_{12}. Horses that have muscle spasms, startle easily and are difficult to handle may have a mild deficiency of this vitamin. Since vitamin B_{12} is not found in plants, your horse relies on the microbes in the hindgut for its production. Anything that compromises their numbers will affect the vitamin B_{12} status.

- **L-tryptophan.** This is an essential amino acid (building block of protein); it must be in the diet because a horse is not able to produce it. When fed alone, without any other amino acids, it is capable of crossing the blood-brain barrier and promoting serotonin production. There are many supplements available that contain L-tryptophan. But the label usually omits the fact that it should not be added to a meal. Doing so will reduce its ability to get into the brain because it will be used instead with other amino acids to build body tissues. For best results, offer L-tryptophan in between meals. An empty stomach offers maximum effect for this amino acid, but as you know, I do not recommend allowing your horse to have an empty stomach. But as long as L-tryptophan is not added to a concentrated meal, it will be better utilized. Experiment with the amount since its effect varies between horses. Some horses become dopey and appear drugged, which is not the effect you want. Start with 500 mg and build up to as much as 2,000 mg. You can offer it three to four times per day, depending on your circumstances.

- **Chamomile.** This herb binds to brain receptors to ease mild cases of anxiety and fretfulness. It is safe to use with no known side effects or interactions. Give it 7 to 10 days to see an effect.

- **Valerian.** On the list of prohibited substances, this herb should not be used when competing. Its long-term safety has not been determined, so use it with caution and for not more than a month. Valerian has a sedative effect and may over-tranquilize your horse. It is useful, however, for situations where a horse is adjusting to a new environment. As with all herbs, it takes a few days for blood levels to become elevated, so do not expect instant results.

- **Black cohosh, passion flower, ginger root, hops, and wood betony.** I clump these herbs together because they are often included in calming supplements. In general, they have been shown to lessen stress-related symptoms. Though safe to use, keep in mind that herbs contain diluted (natural) drugs and can interact with other medications and exhibit long term effects. If you have a pregnant mare, or your horse suffers from liver or kidney problems, do not use herbal preparations without your veterinarian's approval.

Weight Changes

Just like you, your horse's weight is affected by mental stress. Some stressed horses cannot eat, their metabolic rate surges making them burn more calories, and the motility of the digestive tract slows down, making digestion a challenge. On the other hand, some horses gain weight when stressed. They overeat, they store more fat, their metabolic rate slows down due to hormonal changes, and they seek relief through eating.

Unlike people, however, once the stressor is removed, horses are able to let go of the emotional garbage that we often carry around with us. Horses are still able to tap into their survival instincts and eat what they need to regulate their weight, no more and no less, when fed forage free choice, just as they'd experience in the wild.

WEIGHT LOSS

Physical stress, such as pain, illness, and weather extremes cause more calories to be burned. Ample grass and alfalfa provide the foundation for your horse's diet, but adding fat sources, such as flaxseed meal and rice bran, will offer more calories and increase digestion efficiency. Avoid excess grain (starchy feeds) since this can create more acid production and may lead to laminitis. Specific guidelines on how to boost calories for the underweight horse are offered in Chapter 12 — Weight Management.

Cold weather leads to weight loss if not enough calories are offered to maintain internal body temperature. Hot, humid weather also leads to increased calorie needs for the same reason. These weather extremes and how to handle them are discussed at the beginning of this chapter. In summary, keep hay in front of your horse all the time — especially in the winter — to encourage heat production. During the summer make every effort to cool your horse down. Frequent bathing (don't forget to scrape the excess water off), fans, shade, and relaxation during the hottest part of the day will make a difference in his ability to sustain a normal body temperature.

Mentally demanding situations can also lead to weight loss. Hard training, for example, not only burns more calories, but can lower immune function due to secretion of stress hormones, cortisol and epinephrine (also called adrenalin). Other psychological stressors, discussed throughout this chapter, have the same hormonal effect. Changes in body composition, particularly muscle, can also occur when these hormones are consistently elevated.

Weight gain

A stressed horse can hold on to too much body fat. Ironically, restricting feed, especially hay and pasture, can make your overweight horse stay fat. This is because of cortisol secretion. Cortisol is released during stress; not having something to graze on continually is very stressful for your horse. It goes against the horse's natural design that dictates eating small amounts continuously throughout the day. Cortisol creates insulin resistance and insulin resistance causes body fat to be stored. This is why I make such a big deal out of letting your horse self-regulate his hay/pasture intake — to help his body maintain a normal weight. An overweight horse will lose weight when you take away the stress of forage deprivation.

Ulcers

We used to think that most ulcers in humans were caused by excess acid production resulting from stress. But we've known for years that only a very small percentage of human ulcers are due to stress. Most are either caused by excessive NSAID pain reliever use or by a bacterial infection known as *H. pylori*.

But such is not the case with horses. Stress does cause ulcers. Well, actually it's the *cause* of the stress that causes ulcers. Not making sense? Read on.

Intense training, for example, is a stressor that can lead to ulcers. Exercise, especially running, causes stomach acid to slosh around to the unprotected upper squamous region. Ninety percent of race horses and more than two-thirds of performance horses that are involved in speed events have ulcers.

Dressage horses are not immune, though the incidence is lower at thirty to forty percent.

Another cause of stress is not being able to graze continuously. Stalled horses are notorious for ulcer development. Horses that stand for hours in a dry paddock without any hay will develop ulcers. The reason is physical — their stomachs release acid all the time and they need small amounts of forage to absorb this acid.

If you've read Chapter 14 — Digestive Problems, then you already know about ulcers. But it is worth repeating here because physical and mental demands are the most common causes and therefore the most preventable causes of ulcers. I won't go into how to recognize or treat an ulcer here, so please refer to Chapter 14 for plenty of information.

Laminitis

Most cases of laminitis are due to elevated insulin levels. Diet has a significant role in regulating this hormone. But the stress hormone cortisol also elevates insulin. For example, putting your overweight horse on a reduced-hay "diet" because his excess fat led to laminitis will often trigger another laminitis attack. Please take a close look at three chapters: Chapter 11 — Laminitis, Chapter 12 — Weight Management, and Chapter 13 — Metabolic and Endocrine Disorders. You'll get a firm understanding of how weight, insulin, and stress all interact and can lead to this disabling condition.

Hyperlipemia

Hyperlipemia (sometimes referred to as hyperlipidemia, a similar but less severe condition), means "elevated fat levels in the blood." During stressful situations, fat is likely to be mobilized from fat cells into the blood to provide energy to muscles and other tissues. Though some fat mobilization is normal and healthy, excessive amounts resulting from prolonged stress, can lead to liver damage.

This condition is not only caused by stress; it is also a result of insulin resistance. Ponies, donkeys, and miniature horses are particularly prone to hyperlipemia syndrome. Take a look at Chapters 1 — Ground Rules for Feeding a Horse, 11 — Laminitis, and 13 — Metabolic and Endocrine Disorders for more information on preventing this situation.

Behavior

It makes sense that physical pain, intense exercise, isolation, boredom, discomfort, and other stressors will make your horse behave abnormally. A stressed horse is not centered — is out of balance. Time and time again, I see horses change and behave like their natural selves when allowed to graze freely, socialize with friends, and romp around. Some folks have expressed concern that their horses are more spirited now that they are no longer stalled and have free access to forage. Yes, you read that correctly… concern. They are surprised by the new horse that has emerged. Let this be an indication instead, that your horse is finally able to show his true, healthy personality. Express joy on his behalf.

HOT HORSES

Agitated, nervous horses can be helped nutritionally. First, though, you should make every attempt to determine the cause of your horse's distress, because even the most healthful diet cannot completely counteract the effects of past or ongoing fear, pain, loneliness, or stress. Such stressors (as well as past abuse) can take their toll over time and create nutrient deficiencies, depress immune function, and lead to secondary illnesses. Once stressors are removed or remediated, however, diet can make an enormous difference in the nervous horse's behavior.

There are several calming agents that you can use and they're listed earlier in this chapter. But I'd like to emphasize three main approaches that are designed to regulate hormonal levels and address underlying deficiencies, rather than just calm the behavior.

- **Avoid high amounts of starch and sugar.** These cause blood glucose (sugar) levels to rise dramatically. The hormone insulin is released in large amounts to allow glucose to leave the blood and enter the tissues. This pronounced sugar high, followed by drastic plummeting of blood glucose, may affect your horse's behavior. It doesn't trouble all horses, just some. If your horse is sensitive to this hormonal change, simply switch his diet to one that does not contain cereal grains or molasses. Sugary treats such as carrots and apples, as well as cookies made from grain, should also be avoided.

- **Add magnesium.** As I've mentioned before, magnesium works with calcium to allow for proper muscle contraction and relaxation. Tense, tight muscles are helped by adding magnesium to the diet. There is no need to add calcium if your horse is getting enough forage, since grass and hay contain ample calcium. But magnesium is often in low concentration and is not readily absorbed. Therefore, most horses do not get enough magnesium.

Magnesium oxide and citrate forms are absorbed best. Start by adding 5 grams (5,000 mg) of elemental magnesium per 500 lbs of body weight. Take into account any magnesium found in fortified commercial feeds. You should see an improvement in his skittish behavior within three weeks. If not, magnesium is not the issue. Your next step would be to add B vitamins.

- **Increase B vitamins.** Four of the eight B vitamins are involved in deriving calories from carbohydrates, protein, and fats in the diet. They are thiamin (B_1), riboflavin (B_2), niacin, and pantothenic acid. Thiamin has been given a lot of press lately because of its ability to calm an edgy horse. It does, in fact, help. But it is much better to provide all four of the B vitamins involved in energy metabolism.

The other four are pyridoxine (B_6), cobalamin (B_{12}), folic acid, and biotin. These support your horse by promoting healthy red blood cells, synthesizing body proteins, and protecting the nervous system. The bottom line is — they all work together. So do your horse a favor and supplement all eight using a B complex preparation.

CRIBBING

Your horse presses his top teeth against a solid object, arches his neck, and swallows air in a rocking motion. A grunting or gulping noise emerges. This is cribbing. Its true cause is unknown but genetics along with stressful circumstances appear to be the underlying problems. Cribbing is such a seriously addictive habit that many horses will actually prefer it to eating, and will slowly waste away.

Early weaning can lead to this negative behavior later in adult horses and while there's nothing you can do to change the past, you can take measures to reduce physical discomfort and mental strains that contribute to cribbing. Cribbing collars may discourage the behavior but they do not relieve the urge, causing more stress for your horse. Drugs and even surgery may be something to consider in extreme situations. In many cases however, managing his conditions will lessen the behavior. Here are some suggestions:

Turnout as much as possible

Freedom to graze and roam will have a remarkable effect on stopping this habit. If this is not feasible, give him as much outdoor space as possible.

Keep hay in front of your horse

You will be amazed at what this one simple change will do for your horse's demeanor. He will calm down, respond to commands more easily, have a better attention span, and be a much happier horse. That's because you're feeding him like nature intended — grazing on forage as much as he wants. And it is fascinating to see how health improves — weight normalizes, hormones are balanced, and the immune system is stabilized, making for a much better horse.

Do not isolate your horse

Non-cribbers will not "catch" the cribbing habit by seeing another horse do it. This is a common myth and there is absolutely no evidence that this behavior is contagious. Furthermore, isolation is one of the most stressful things you can do to a horse. He needs to have companionship to feel secure.

Consider ulcers

The pain and discomfort of ulcers can lead to cribbing. Basic nutritional management to cure ulcers includes free choice hay, water consumption, removing starchy feeds (grains such as oats, corn, barley, wheat, rice, etc.) and sweet feeds, and restoring microbial populations through probiotic use. Chapter 14 — Digestive Problems provides more details.

HEAD SHAKING

Chronic side-to-side tossing of the head appears to be caused by many issues. Allergies (discussed in Chapter 16 — Immunity Issues), sensitivity to sunlight, nerve dysfunction, mouth pain, stress, and even a herpes virus infection are a few postulated reasons for this behavior. Eye drops of sodium cromoglycate have shown promise in reducing head shaking caused by seasonal allergies[2].

Magnesium (discussed earlier in this chapter) and spirulina are other nutrients that may be helpful. Spirulina (blue-green algae) has been shown to decrease nerve stimulation. I discuss more about this nutritious supplement in Chapter 16 — Immunity issues.

Lysine supplementation is effective in treating viral infections, especially those caused by the herpes virus. This amino acid is safe at high doses so if other treatments have failed, give it a try. An appropriate dosage would be 5 to 10 grams per day.

EATING MANURE

Eating one's own manure is referred to as coprophagy. It is very common, and even important, for a foal to exhibit this behavior. As he starts to eat grass and hay, he needs the bacteria found in manure to build up his own hindgut's levels.

Adult horses who eat manure, however, have other things going on. If your horse has this habit, consider the following possible reasons:

- The microbial population in his hindgut may be diminished due to antibiotics, stress, excess acid from not grazing continuously, or too much starch and sugar in the diet.

- He may be bored.

- Chewing produces saliva, a natural antacid. If he has nothing to eat for a few hours, he'll look for something to chew on in order to relieve his discomfort.

- He may have an ulcer.

- Not enough magnesium, iron, or the B vitamins will prompt him to seek these nutrients in manure.

- Salt is in short supply. Check to make sure he's not competing with other horses for the salt block.

This behavior can become a habit, so do what you can to alter his situation. Change his routine, offer hay at all times, make sure his diet is balanced and complete, and reduce stressors.

WEANING

Weaning is rough on a little guy or gal. I'm not sure where the idea of weaning at 4 to 6 months of age came about. Perhaps it was simply a matter of convenience. But this is far too young to take a foal away from his mother. A mare in the wild will wean her young once she gives birth to a new foal. If the mare is impregnated shortly after foaling, 11 months will pass before the new foal is born. Eleven months. (Did you hear me? Eleven months!) So wait a little while. The closer we can reflect this natural schedule, the healthier your foal will be during growth and as an adult. And don't worry about your mare; she's fine with this approach.

Once you do start weaning it should be done slowly. Allow your foal to become accustomed to the change by experiencing it in small doses. Never isolate your foal abruptly. Help him to adjust gradually, very gradually, to the idea that there is another way of doing things.

Not only is your foal suffering from separation anxiety, he is also having to get used to eating a diet made entirely of cold, dry, hard stuff instead of warm, wet, soft milk. Eventually, of course, this will be the correct change in diet, but little by little, step by step.

Early weaning leads to negative behaviors as an adult. This statement should not surprise anyone. And yet the mentality remains that the more quickly we get the foal away from his mother's teat, the better off it will be for all involved. Sorry… it doesn't work that way.

So, delay a little longer. Eleven months may not be practical, I understand that, but give your foal 6 to 8 months before you start the process. He'll be a better horse in the long run.

How and what to feed your foal during this time, and throughout his growth period, is discussed in Chapter 19 — Growth and Growing Old.

SLEEP

Sleep — a basic need of survival. Among the other benefits of sleep, adequate rest enables a horse's system to process nutrients for growth, cell repair, and nervous system protection. Mature horses will sleep up to two hours per day, broken into short periods; foals and young horses need more sleep than adults.

Contrary to popular misconception, horses do in fact sleep deeply while standing. Being on their feet makes it easier to flee from predators. And they are not just dozing; they can actually go into a deep sleep for roughly 20 minutes while standing. However, lying down periodically is still necessary for obtaining total rest.

Being prey animals, horses' sleep must be taken in frequent breaks of short duration, ideally in a group situation where some take turns resting while others remain alert for dangers. Ever see two horses together in a pasture where one is lying down and the other is standing? They rely on each other.

Horses that are alone often do not sleep adequately and may not attempt to lie down for fear that they will be too vulnerable. And a solitary horse will attempt to rest but will startle out of sleep at the slightest disturbance.

Your horse can sleep just about anywhere as long as he feels secure, and that includes a good sleeping surface that is dry and not muddy. Slippery conditions make it difficult to stand up, especially for an older horse, so he may choose not to lie down, which can ultimately rob him of a complete rest.

Make certain your horse's circumstances allow him to get enough good-quality sleep. His health and behavior depend on it.

Endnotes

[1] Raymond LeRoy, a biochemist from Phoenix, AZ developed the supplement One AC to combat anhydrosis. It has been tested at the University of Florida.

[2] Based on research from the Animal Medical Centre in England.

Chapter 18 —
Breeding, Pregnancy, and Lactation

Her fine gaze seemed to flow out from her with mysterious shadowy
sweepings like lantern light in a field.
~ Tess Gallagher

Pregnancy is a time of change. Day by day the growing fetus will quietly pull nutrients away from your mare's muscles and bones at an ever increasing rate. By the time the mare reaches her last three months of gestation, her nutritional needs will have compounded dramatically in order to support the rapidly growing life inside her.

I cannot overemphasize the importance of nutrition for optimizing the breeding experience for your mare. Stallions also need to be in good condition; a healthy stallion produces healthy sperm. Therefore, proper nutrition will increase the likelihood of conception.

Once pregnant, your mare's nutrient intake needs to be managed not only to produce a healthy foal, but also to have her finish as healthy as when she started. Pregnancy depletes nutrient reserves; and once her foal is born, she'll need even more nutrients to produce ample and nutritious milk. Careful attention to her diet will replenish her losses and keep her healthy for years to come.

In addition to meeting her nutrition needs, you'll want to become very familiar with the entire process. Research on line or get a good book well in advance of the happy occasion to help you know what to expect and how to manage potential problems. One of my favorite books is *The Complete Foaling Manual*[1] because it has thorough explanations of how to care for your mare prior and during delivery, as well as immediate guidelines for the newborn foal.

I'm often asked how long a normal pregnancy should take. Because each mare is an individual, it can vary within a certain range. Normal gestation lasts between 320 and 360 days — 11 months on average. Your mare will develop a pattern and follow her own gestation length year after year. Maiden mares, of course, are difficult to predict. However, there are several factors that can influence gestation length:

- **Season**. The longer days of April, May and June make gestation time shorter. Mares that are put under artificial lights during the winter months will respond as though it were spring, and give birth sooner.

- **Age.** The older your mare, the longer she'll take to deliver.

- **Genetics.** Draft breeds and stockier horses tend to have shorter gestations than lighter breeds; donkeys tend to carry a fetus longer than mares.

- **Nutrition.** Nutritionally deprived mares have longer pregnancies. This is mainly a result of inadequate attachment of the placenta within the uterus, increasing gestation length simply because the fetus takes longer to get the nutrients it needs.

Preparation for Breeding — Mares

WEIGHT

Before being bred, your mare's body condition score should ideally be between 5 and 7 on the Henneke[2] body condition scale (see Chapter 12 — Weight Management). Breeding her at the right weight will increase the likelihood of her having a smooth pregnancy and a healthy foal. And she'll have enough reserves for lactation, which is far more demanding on her body than pregnancy.

If she is too thin, help her reach this weight. She'll get through the pregnancy in much better shape if she starts out in a fleshy condition. It will be virtually impossible to help her gain weight while she's in foal, especially during the last third of her pregnancy when her energy needs are very high.

If she is too heavy, help her lose weight by reducing or even eliminating her grain or other concentrated feed. You can provide a small, carrier meal for supplements, but her energy needs can easily be met by grazing on pasture and/or hay. But do not ever restrict her forage intake. This can actually prevent her from losing weight (see Chapter 12 — Weight Management for an explanation).

Before being bred, your mare's body condition score should ideally be between 5 and 7 on the Henneke body condition scale.

Exercise your mare. Stay within her comfort level; if she hasn't been worked in a while, build up slowly. This will get her muscles in good shape for a healthy delivery and help her burn calories if she has too much weight on her bones.

OVERALL HEALTH

Pregnancy takes its toll on your mare's body so it makes good sense for her to be healthy before breeding. If she wasn't in the best of health during a previous pregnancy, give her a break before breeding her again. Use this time to boost her nutrient reserves, test her blood for deficiencies, and give her plenty of turnout and exercise.

An older broodmare may start to exhibit signs of aging — poor teeth, creaky joints, and inefficient digestion. Before she is bred, get her teeth floated, make sure she has vitamin C added to her diet to build joint tissue (vitamin C synthesis declines with age), and give her a daily prebiotic to promote microbial health in the hindgut.

Don't breed her if she is suffering from chronic laminitis or has equine Cushing's disease. If she has a cresty neck or fat deposits along her back and rump, she is insulin resistant and should not be bred while in this state. Having her blood tested before a pregnancy is also a wise decision, to rule out any unapparent health problems.

PLAN FOR VACCINATIONS AND DEWORMING

Vaccinations

To help prevent diseases in your mare and protect the nursing foal against microorganisms that can appear in the milk, it is important to have your pregnant mare vaccinated. There are standard protocols regarding the types and timing of vaccinations; however, always consult with your vet for the best approach for your mare. Here are the guidelines[3]:

- **Equine rhinopneumonitis (killed virus).** This virus is also known as equine herpes virus and is responsible for infectious abortions.

Vaccinate at the beginning of the third, fifth, seventh, and nine month of pregnancy.

- **Tetanus, rabies.** Give these vaccinations four to six weeks before foaling.

- **Equine influenza.** If your mare is exposed to unfamiliar locations, vaccinate every two to three months during gestation; otherwise, wait until four to six weeks before foaling.

- **Equine encephalomyelitis (eastern and western).** Administer in late spring or early summer, before insect season. If foaling in late season, this vaccine should be given again four to six weeks before foaling.

- **Botulism (toxoid).** The initial vaccination involves three injections at one-month intervals, followed by a booster four to six weeks before foaling.

- **Strangles.** Only use this vaccine if warranted, based on your mare's specific situation; it is not routinely administered.

- **West Nile virus.** Obtain your veterinarian's approval before administering this vaccination; recommendations for pregnant mares have not been standardized.

- **Equine viral arteritis (modified live virus).** Pregnant mares are not normally vaccinated for this disease. Prior to breeding, check the stallion for possible shedding of this virus, and vaccinate your mare if the stallion is a carrier. Mares must be isolated from other horses for three weeks after vaccination and annual boosters are recommended.

Deworming

Use the following guidelines when deworming your mare while pregnant:

- **Deworming preparations (anthelmintics).** These should not be used during the first two months of pregnancy, or the last few weeks before foaling.

- **Remainder of gestational period.** Throughout the remaining time, deworm your mare every six to eight weeks using ivermectin to prevent roundworm (ascarid) larvae from being transmitted to your foal. Or a daily dewormer (pyrantel tartrate) can be safely used to kill ascarid larvae, along with a twice-yearly ivermectin dose (spring and fall) to protect your mare against bots.

Preparation for Breeding — Stallions

I suppose I should say a word about the guys! Not that I mean to neglect them, but you really don't need to do much out of the ordinary to meet their reproductive needs besides feeding them a nutritious diet. This entails giving them more than just hay or putting them out to pasture until their services are needed — they should be in top condition to optimize sperm production. Therefore, it's important to do the following:

- Keep his body condition score between 4 and 6.

- Add a legume, such as alfalfa, to his overall forage ration.

- Feed concentrates if he has additional caloric needs.

- Fill in nutritional gaps with a comprehensive vitamin/mineral supplement.

- Give him flaxseed meal to provide omega-3 fatty acids.

- Make sure he is getting at least 1 IU of vitamin E per pound of body weight each day.

- Balance vitamin E with selenium: up to 3 mg of selenium per day for an 1100 lb horse if he is not working and no more than 5 mg if he's being exercised intensively. Heavier horses can tolerate slightly more, where the total diet does not exceed 0.6 ppm of selenium.

- Make sure he is consuming the salt block you've provided. If not, add salt to his meals to meet his sodium requirement.

- Keep him hydrated by providing fresh, clean water nearby at all times.

Fatty acids for sperm health

Actually, there *is* something special you can do for your stallion during breeding season that will further improve sperm quality. You can improve the ratio of two fatty acids, docosahexaenoic acid (DHA) — an omega-3 fatty acid, and docosapentaenoic acid (DPA) — an omega-6 fatty acid. The higher the DHA to DPA ratio, the more motility and speed his sperm will have.

There are two ways to increase this ratio. First, lower the DPA level by decreasing his vegetable oil intake. Most feeds are fortified with soybean or corn oils, which are very high in the omega-6 fatty acid called linoleic acid (if you need to brush up on your terminology, review Chapter 3 — Fundamentals of Fats). Linoleic acid gets converted to DPA and that's where the problem lies — a diet that contains too much omega-6 has a negative impact on stallion fertility.

The second approach is to replace vegetable oil with fish oil. I know horses don't eat fish if they can help it, but just don't tell your sweet fellow and he'll be fine. Seriously though, fish oils are high in the omega-3 fatty acid DHA. The higher the DHA, the higher the DHA to DPA ratio. And you've accomplished your goal.

Flaxseed meal is high in the omega-3 fatty acid known as ALA, which gets converted to DHA, but the amount is not sufficient to have a marked effect. Give him flaxseed meal, by all means, to keep his immune system healthy and his joints flexible, but also add fish oils.

The Pregnant Mare

Throughout her pregnancy, your mare should be fed a nutritious, balanced diet that is forage-based, contains high-quality protein, and includes appropriate supplementation to fill in any vitamin/mineral gaps. For the first eight months, in fact, her diet will look pretty similar to her pre-pregnancy program. In the last three months, this will change — we'll get to that later.

The key to normal fetal development is proper nutrition and hormonal balance. Nutrients are needed to produce hormones such as insulin, thyroxin, and cortisol, which are then used to regulate nutrient uptake and metabolism within the growing fetus.

A NUTRITIOUS, BALANCED DIET

Proper nutrition certainly makes sense, but what, exactly, is a good diet for your pregnant mare? Easy — for the first eight months there are just a few basic ingredients:

- Fresh pasture and/or good quality hay
- Alfalfa
- Vitamin E and selenium
- Comprehensive vitamin/mineral supplement
- Flaxseed meal, if on hay-only
- Salt
- Concentrates if extra calories are needed

Fresh pasture

Pasture grazing is the best foundation for your broodmare. It provides some exercise, and keeps her stress level down. But just as important, fresh grass provides vitamin E and beta carotene (which is converted to vitamin A inside her tissues). It is also an excellent source of omega-3 fatty acids. However, overgrazed, unhealthy pasture can have toxic weeds, so walk the land to check for potential problems. I offer some things to look for in Chapter 8 — Fundamentals of Forages.

Good quality hay

Whenever your mare is not grazing on fresh grass, she should have free choice hay. Hay should be less than a year old and correctly stored, look and smell fresh, and be free of mold. Have your hay analyzed by a laboratory. Your sample should be taken from the center of several bales. Bring it to your local county extension service, nearby vet school, or send it to Equi-Analytical Laboratories — www.equi-analytical.com.

Alfalfa

Alfalfa's protein content complements that of most grasses to create a complete, high-quality protein source. Your mare needs at least 10% protein, but it should come from a combination of grasses and legumes. Alfalfa is also high in calcium, which will protect her bones from calcium losses during fetal development and lactation.

Vitamin E and selenium

Fresh, lush grass contains vitamin E, but levels diminish as the grass gets taller and especially when it is cut, dried, and stored as hay. A pregnant mare requires 1 to 1.5 IU of vitamin E per pound of body weight each day, and as she gets further along in her pregnancy her vitamin E intake should increase to 2 IU per pound of body weight. Most feeds and supplements do not add enough vitamin E, so read the label carefully to see how much vitamin E she's getting and supplement the difference. Before I talk about other supplements, let's get to selenium.

Selenium works with vitamin E and your mare needs at least 1 mg per day. But do not exceed 3 mg per day for an 1100 lb mare because selenium has a narrow range of safety. Heavier mares can have more, up to 0.6 ppm of the total diet. I offer an extensive discussion on selenium in Chapter 5 — Fundamentals of Minerals. Briefly, I'll emphasize here that the only true way to know the selenium level in your pasture and hay is to have them analyzed. Then you know what you're dealing with, and won't have to wonder about whether or not to add a supplement. Before considering a supplement, don't forget to add together selenium levels from all sources including any fortified feed or supplements you're currently using.

Once you know the total selenium content in your mare's diet, you can decide between adding a supplement that contains vitamin E plus selenium or one that has only vitamin E. Vitamin E is available in natural and synthetic versions; they're discussed in Chapter 6 — Fundamentals of Vitamins.

Comprehensive vitamin/mineral supplement

Even if your mare is on pasture most of the day, but especially if she is getting only hay, you'll want to make sure all the nutritional gaps are met by using a product designed for pregnant mares. The main reason for a supplement, even at this early stage, is for her to have enough nutrients for fetal growth while keeping her own tissues healthy. For example, beta carotene is lost in hay. It is needed to produce vitamin A inside your mare's body for her own health, but is also secreted in her colostrum and milk. Or consider a diet low in calcium; this will result in calcium removal from your mare's bones, leaving her in a nutritionally compromised state, though her fetus will get all that he needs. So your best approach is to keep your mare on this supplement throughout her pregnancy and while she is lactating.

Flaxseed meal

Omega-3 fatty acids are found in abundant supply in fresh grass. However, they are destroyed during hay production and storage. If your mare is fortunate enough to have access to pasture throughout the day, you do not need to add flaxseed meal. But if hay is her predominant forage source, give her 1/2 cup of flaxseed meal per 400 lbs of body weight. Don't grind your own — it starts to spoil within hours and has too much phosphorus in it. Purchase a commercially-prepared flaxseed meal that is stabilized and has added calcium to balance the phosphorus.

Salt

A salt block should always be available. Keep it clean so your mare will enjoy licking it. A mineralized salt block is only appropriate for an all-forage diet. *Do not feed kelp (sea salt).* Its high iodine content is potentially toxic, causing damage to her foal's muscles and bones or even a miscarriage.

Concentrates

If your mare has been exercising or performing prior to becoming pregnant, by all means, keep up the physical activity. She'll likely need more calories than what forage can provide, so continue feeding concentrates but consider switching your feed to one that supports broodmares. If you feed it according to directions, you do not need to add a vitamin/mineral supplement. If it contains flax, additional flaxseed meal may not be necessary. But if you are feeding less than what is recommended, add a multiple vitamin/mineral product, just at a comparably reduced level.

FORAGE TROUBLES

Fescue toxicity

It's best to keep your mare away from fescue, but this is especially critical during her last three months of pregnancy. Fescue can be infested with the endophyte fungus called *Neotyphodium coenophialum* which may lengthen gestation and lead to a thickened placenta that can detach during delivery, causing dummy foal syndrome. She may not produce milk, a condition called agalactia. And worst of all, the fetus may not survive. If your mare is exposed to this fungus, contact your veterinarian; there are medications that can counteract its adverse effects.

Glycoside, blister beetles, round bales

Johnson grass, sorghum, and sudan, as well as sorghum-sudan hybrids, can induce miscarriage due to their toxic glycoside content. Please refer to Chapter 8 — Fundamentals of Forages for more details about these grasses as well as the potential for blister beetles in alfalfa. Potential problems with round bales are also discussed.

THE LAST THREE MONTHS

Your mare's nutritional needs will dramatically increase during the last three months. She requires more calories and more protein, and there are specific minerals that need to be balanced, not only for the unborn foal who will double in size during this time, but also to prepare for milk production. Let's take a closer look…

Calories

During this time, the mare's energy requirement progressively increases by 10 to 20%. Mares that do not get enough calories will lose weight, resulting in decreased colostrum and milk production. Conversely, obesity can also result in limited milk production.

She'll gain nearly a pound per day during this period. As the fetus gets larger, it takes up more and more space, making the mare's gut capacity smaller. If left to graze on nothing but grass and hay, she won't be able to eat enough to meet her high caloric need. Concentrated feeds are the answer. But watch her weight — keep her body condition score between 5 and 7 where she is fleshy but not fat.

Allow her to self-regulate by giving her free choice pasture or grass hay. If given the chance, she'll only eat what she needs to maintain her pregnancy and store energy for later lactation. She will likely consume the equivalent of 2 to 2.5% of her body weight. Limiting the hay supply will cause her to eat her forage hurriedly and increase stress hormone secretion, leading to weight gain. Never let her stand without something to graze on — she can develop an ulcer, and the stress can potentially cause colic or laminitis.

Table 18-1 shows the recommended energy needs during this stage of pregnancy.

Table 18-1 Digestible Energy (Mcal/day) Requirements During the Last Three Months of Gestation[4]

Month	Mature Body Weight (Pre-Pregnancy)				
	200 kg (440 lbs)	400 kg (880 lbs)	500 kg (1100 lbs)	600 kg (1320 lbs)	900 kg (1980 lbs)
9	7.7	15.4	19.2	23.1	34.6
10	8.1	16.2	20.2	24.2	36.4
11	8.6	17.1	21.4	25.7	38.5

To fulfill her increasing energy needs, Table 18-2 offers some suggestions.

Table 18-2 Mcal/lb of Common Feedstuffs[5]

Feedstuff	Average Mcal/lb
Warm-season grass hay	0.95 to 1.07
Cool-season grass hay	0.99 to 1.07
Alfalfa hay	1.00 to 1.19
Grain hay (oat, rye, wheat)	0.95 to 0.98
Beet pulp (unsweetened)	1.27
Beet pulp (2% molasses)	1.29
Flaxseed meal	1.30
Oats	1.50
Rice bran	1.52
Soybean meal	1.63
Wheat bran	1.46
Oil	4.19 per lb or 0.27 per fluid ounce
Grain-based commercial feeds	1.20 to 1.70 depending on fat level

Keep in mind that your hay can have far different energy values than those shown in Table 18-2. I've seen timothy hay, for example, that has only 0.6 Mcal/lb. On the other hand, I've seen alfalfa hay with 1.4 Mcal/lb. So use this table only as a guide and test your hay for its exact digestible energy (DE) content.

Prevent hyperlipemia: A very thin mare will mobilize large amounts of fat within her body in an attempt to meet her energy need. This results in a condition called hyperlipemia. All horses can develop this disorder, but donkeys and mules are more susceptible. Your mare or jenny will have an unthrifty appearance, be lethargic, may not drink or eat, and suffer liver damage. Donkeys and mules are discussed further in Chapter 1 — Ground Rules for Feeding a Horse.

Protein

Dietary protein sources should be balanced to provide all of the amino acids the mare needs to synthesize body proteins. At this time she will require more than just forage, though forage should still be the basis of her diet. Mix grasses with alfalfa to make certain her protein quality is high. I like feeding a 40/60 mixture of alfalfa/grass during this period.

If she has adequate calories but not enough protein, I recommend adding 1 lb of a 30% protein supplement for every 500 lbs of body weight. To ensure complementary amino acids look for ingredients such as soybean meal, alfalfa meal, beet pulp, and rice bran. (Review Chapter 4 — Fundamentals of Protein and Amino Acids.)

Lysine: Your mare cannot produce this amino acid, therefore it is called *essential*. There are nine other essential amino acids, most of which are easily provided in the average horse's diet. However, lysine is often in low supply. It is necessary for growth, and therefore important for the development of the fetus.

During the first two trimesters of pregnancy, a diet that contains at least 0.3% lysine is adequate. Most commercial feeds contain at least 0.6%. But during the last three months, lysine requirements increase by 50%, to approximately 40 grams of lysine each day for an 1100 lb mare.

Once you calculate the total lysine content in your forage and feed, you can correct any shortfall by using a lysine supplement. Most grasses and legumes have adequate lysine, but it's always best to know the specific amount in your forage. If you do not have access to that information, you can estimate lysine content — grasses have roughly 0.5% lysine; legumes have approximately 0.9% lysine. If your mare ate 20 lbs of grass hay and 10 lbs of alfalfa, for example, her lysine intake would be more than 86 grams, far exceeding her 40 gram minimum requirement (see Appendix — Crunching Numbers for a detailed computation). Therefore, lysine needs are generally met through adequate grass and alfalfa intake.

Minerals

Commercial feeds are usually fortified with minerals but their levels typically run only 40 to 70% of the NRC table values[6]. Forages can vary dramatically based on the mineral concentration of the soil, the stage of maturity of the plant, and seasonal condition. Therefore, I recommend adding minerals to your mare's diet — not individually, but combined into a comprehensive supplement to meet all mineral (as well as vitamin) requirements.

Calcium, phosphorus, and magnesium: These three minerals need to be in balance. The best way to do this is to mix grasses with a legume, and rely on your broodmare vitamin/mineral supplement to provide additional amounts of these three minerals. There should always be more calcium in the diet than phosphorus or magnesium. Your mare can safely tolerate up to six times more calcium than phosphorus, though a 2:1 ratio is ideal. Magnesium should also be 1/2 that of calcium. In terms of concentration, the diet should contain at least 1.0% calcium, 0.5% phosphorus, and 0.5% magnesium.

Copper and physitis prevention: During the last 3 months of pregnancy, your mare's diet should contain at least 50 ppm of copper to prevent her foal from developing physitis (sometimes called epiphysitis). It is important that your mare have enough copper to ensure adequate transfer to the growing fetus *before* birth. There's virtually no copper in her milk. And giving copper to a foal is not effective in preventing physitis. Copper is required by the growing fetus for proper collagen synthesis and when deficient, the cartilage matrix within the bone and joints weakens.

Iron, zinc, and manganese: These three minerals, along with copper, should be balanced to prevent detrimental interactions. Chapter 5 — Fundamentals of Minerals offers details on each of these, but during these last three months of gestation, the minimum concentrations should be increased to 150 ppm iron, 150 ppm zinc, and 120 ppm manganese.

Selenium: As I mentioned earlier in the chapter, selenium has a small range of safety. Because of this fear, it's easy to under-dose selenium. Your mare needs at least 1 mg per day to support antioxidant function within the cells, along with vitamin E.

Iodine: Adequate iodine allows for normal fetal growth. A deficient newborn may not thrive. Too much iodine, on the other hand, can be just as devastating. Iodine normally crosses the placental barrier and enters the fetus; it also ends up in the milk. Therefore the fetus or nursing foal can easily develop an iodine toxicity, while the mare herself may go unaffected. To maintain a normal iodine level, your mare should receive between 3 and 5 mg per day throughout pregnancy and lactation. This translates into between 0.3 and 0.5 ppm for 22 lbs of feed. The maximum tolerable level of iodine is 5 mg/kg (ppm) but your mare's diet should never reach that amount. Earlier in this chapter, I mentioned the danger of feeding kelp (sea salt). It is extremely high in iodine — can contain as much as 2000 ppm — and should never be fed to a pregnant mare, or any other horse for that matter.

Simplifying the diet

There are so many possible feed combinations that to show you one or two would help only a very few people, leaving most folks in the dark. If you're like the majority of horse owners, you want to simplify your feeding plan, not sit down with your pen and calculator, adding up every gram. I'd be pleased to help you with the calculations for your specific hay and feed, but suffice it to say that your mare's needs are best met by balancing a forage-based diet with added concentrates and one of the many suitable broodmare supplements available.

Example: If your mare is consuming 25 lbs of 8% protein hay during her first 8 months of pregnancy, it will provide her with 908 grams of protein. During her last three months of gestation, if you add 3 lbs of a legume that contains 15% protein, this will give her an additional 204 grams of protein, and will supply adequate high-quality protein to take her through foaling. Take a look at Chapter 4 — Fundamentals of Protein and Amino Acids for a full discussion on protein quality. Furthermore, her energy needs may not be met, so give her at least two meals per day of a commercial feed or, if you mix a special feed yourself, add a comprehensive supplement.

The Lactating Mare

Milk production is more demanding than pregnancy. While lactating, your mare's energy and protein needs markedly increase. She also needs more minerals. That's because she is producing nearly 4% of her body weight in milk during the first two months of lactation. For an 1100 lb mare, that translates into 5.5 gallons of milk per day (one gallon weighs 8 lbs). Milk production declines to about half that over the next four months to accommodate her foal's decreasing demands as his diet changes to include more forage and solid feed. Nevertheless, as long as she is producing milk, she needs additional nutrients to maintain good condition. An undernourished, lactating mare will develop porous bones, lose muscle mass, have depressed immune function, and suffer from a variety of deficiencies affecting her vital organs as well as her skin, hair, and hooves.

COLOSTRUM

Milk production doesn't actually occur until 24 to 48 hours following birth. Prior to that time your mare will produce colostrum. This milky substance contains antibodies that your foal needs to survive. It should be consumed within three hours and no more than 12 hours after birth. More details on colostrum are provided in Chapter 19 — Growth and Growing Old.

Dripping milk in advance of foaling

This is not a good sign. Valuable colostrum, vital to the foal's survival, is being lost. If your mare is leaking colostrum before foaling, start planning now on getting colostrum from another source. Frozen colostrum is fine as long as it has been stored at -4° F, and for not more than one year.

I once had a veterinarian tell me to use super-glue on my mare's udder to prevent colostrum loss! Let's just say this… he was better at legs than teats! Moral of that story is that vets often have areas of specialization, so find one who feels comfortable helping you with your pregnant mare.

More on colostrum is provided in the next chapter — Growth and Growing Old.

ENERGY REQUIREMENTS

First two months

During her first two months of lactation your nursing mare needs around 3% of her body weight in total feed. Her exact energy requirement will increase from her non-pregnant state by 0.8 Mcal for every kg of milk produced. For illustration purposes, let's assume your mare's pre-pregnancy weight was 1100 lbs. According to the National Research Council (NRC)[7], her energy need was 16.7 Mcal/day if she was not exercising. Now that she has begun to produce milk, you will need to feed her an additional 16 Mcal each day to address her increased needs. See Appendix — Crunching Numbers for this calculation. Table 18-2 provides information on the number of Mcal found in common feedstuffs.

Subsequent months

Her caloric needs will gradually decrease after the first 2 months as the foal's decreasing needs demand gradually less milk production. By her sixth month of lactation she'll require 15% fewer calories. And once her foal is weaned, her energy needs will return to pre-pregnancy levels.

OTHER REQUIREMENTS

Protein and lysine

Protein and lysine requirements nearly double during the first two months of lactation. By the time she reaches her sixth month, her requirement will lessen but still be 40% more than she needed while pregnant.

Minerals

Calcium, phosphorus, and magnesium: Calcium levels increase nearly two-fold during the first two months of lactation, slowly declining after that to slightly more than she needed during her last month of pregnancy. Therefore, keep feeding at least 30% of her forage as alfalfa until her foal is weaned. You can then decrease alfalfa intake to 10 to 20% of her forage ration to maintain normal health.

Phosphorus should remain balanced with calcium, preferably at 1/2 the calcium amount, though levels can be as low as 1/6th of the calcium's content. Check your hay analysis report for adequate phosphorus; low-phosphorus hay is more common that you think.

Magnesium requirements are not as high as phosphorus needs; however they do increase during lactation. According to the NRC, magnesium should be 1/2 to 1/3 the level of phosphorus. However, this is a minimum requirement and since it is not well absorbed from forages, I prefer to increase magnesium up to the same concentration as phosphorus as long as calcium is at least double the level of phosphorus.

Copper, iron, manganese, and zinc: Requirements remain constant throughout lactation and increase only slightly from pregnancy needs. Continue feeding the same vitamin/mineral supplement fed during pregnancy, for as long as your mare is producing milk.

Endnotes

[1] Jones, T., 2002. *The Complete Foaling Manual.* Stallside Books.

[2] Henneke, et. al., 1983. *Equine Veterinary Journal, 15* (4): 371-372.

[3] *The Merck Veterinary Manual*, 2008. Whitehouse Station, NJ: Merck & Co.: Table 04: Example of vaccination schedule for broodmares, www.merckvetmanual.com.

[4] Adapted from: *Nutrient Requirements of Horses,* Sixth Revised Edition, 2007. Washington, D.C.: National Research Council, National Academy Press: 294-302.

[5] *Nutrient Requirements of Horses,* Sixth Revised Edition, 2007. Washington, D.C.: National Research Council, National Academy Press: 304-306.

[6] Berger, L.L., 1997. Variation in the trace mineral content of feedstuffs. *The Professional Animal Scientist, 12*: 1-5.

[7] *Nutrient Requirements of Horses,* Sixth Revised Edition, 2007. Washington, D.C.: National Research Council, National Academy Press: 298.

CHAPTER 19 —
GROWTH AND GROWING OLD

*It wasn't long before I saw light come on in her eyes. And then one day
she put her head against my chest as I stood next to her, and I could feel
her give her heart to me.*
~ Audrey Pavia

Preparing for Delivery

The more familiar you are with the foaling process ahead of time, the
calmer you'll be when the grand event occurs. You'll be able to tell the difference between what is normal and what requires medical attention. Read
all you can on the subject and get yourself a good foaling manual, such as
the one I mentioned in the previous chapter, that is easy to understand and
has lots of photographs to help you visualize the process.

At this point, I'll move on to the newborn foal. But before I leave the topic
of preparation, I have a very important suggestion: Contact a reliable
breeding farm that keeps colostrum on hand, for the possibility that your
mare rejects her foal, or becomes too ill to nurse. This is one the best preparations you can make; once your foal is born there won't be any time to
start searching for colostrum. A special section, The Orphaned Foal, is at
the end of this chapter, just in case.

The Newborn Foal

Congratulations! Your foal's birth is a time for celebration. But before you
bring out the champagne, you have some work to do.

UMBILICAL CORD

The umbilical cord will naturally break during delivery when your foal
kicks or when his dam stands up. Never manually cut or break the umbilical cord. If it breaks prematurely on its own, causing blood loss, apply pressure to the end of the cord until the bleeding stops. Do not tie it.

Disinfect the stump as soon as it breaks apart, or once the bleeding sub-
sides. Have a diluted (4:1) solution of chlorhexadine or Betadine ready in

a small squirt bottle. Saturate the navel to prevent bacteria from entering this highly vulnerable area. Continue applying the solution a few times each day for at least three days. If at any time the navel becomes hot, painful, infected, or starts dripping urine, consult your veterinarian immediately.

PREVENTING CONSTIPATION

Shortly after your foal starts to nurse, he will experience his first bowel movement, eliminating meconium — the manure that accumulated in his bowels during gestation. It is very dark and hard, and is sometimes difficult to pass, leading to bloating and colic. Nursing helps stimulates bowel activity, but he may not suckle because of the discomfort. He may try to nurse, but may only end up with a milk mustache; be certain that he's successful and actually drinking.

If your foal appears to be struggling to have a bowel movement, administer an enema. An enema is easy to give and will soften the fecal balls so they pass easily. Use a dilute soapy solution (2 ounces of mild dish soap added to 16 ounces of water) or an adult-sized enema that you buy at the drugstore. Choose the sodium phosphate, not the mineral oil version. Keep it outside if the weather is warm or place it in a bowl of warm water — your foal will not appreciate a cold enema and you'd like your relationship to get off to a good start.

Stand behind your foal while another person restrains him by holding his shoulders so he cannot move forward. Avoid grabbing him under the rib cage since his ribs are soft and can easily break. Lift his tail and gently, very gently insert the tip of the enema into his rectum. To make it easier to insert, you can use sterile lubricating jelly, but not petroleum jelly (e.g., Vaseline) on the tip. Slowly squeeze the fluid into his rectum. If any bulging occurs, his rectum is full and you should withdraw the enema. Meconium should pass within 15 minutes. It will be dark and hard. Some foals have a large amount and may require a second enema. However, *do not use more than two enemas*; repeated use can cause an overdose of phosphate. If a second enema does not provide relief, call your veterinarian.

NURSING

Your newborn foal may decide to take a nap before he nurses. When he does decide it's time, he first has to figure out how to untangle his legs, stand up, and find his mother's udder.

Don't fret if it takes a little while, as long as your foal starts to nurse within three hours after birth. It's during this period that his digestive system is best able to absorb antibodies from colostrum. His survival depends on the immunity this provides since foals are born without antibodies. A foal that does not receive any colostrum within 18 hours of birth can die.

Colostrum

Colostrum is defined as the first secretion from the mammary gland after delivery. This thick, creamy "first milk" contains concentrated immunoglobulins, specialized antibodies that provide immunity to your foal against bacterial infections. Your veterinarian should check your foal's IgG level (immunoglobulin G, the main immunoglobulin in mare's colostrum) within 18 to 24 hours after your foal is born, providing an opportunity for medical attention to correct the situation if the level is too low.

Potential Problems Shortly After Birth

RUPTURED BLADDER

Keep a close eye on your foal's urine output. His bladder could have rup-tured during the birthing process and urine can build up inside the abdomen. Even a small rupture can create a severe electrolyte imbalance, making him feel ill, and he will stop drinking. His urine should be pale and very dilute. If it is dark and concentrated, it means that he is not nursing enough. Contact your veterinarian if you suspect a problem. When caught early, this condition can be surgically corrected.

DUMMY FOAL

Dummy foal syndrome, medically known as hypoxic ischemic encephalopathy, is not immediately apparent upon birth. Your foal may act normally for the first few days and then quit suckling and act peculiarly — leaning against the fence, wandering about aimlessly, and having trouble finding his dam.

During a normal delivery, the amniotic membrane is torn open allowing your foal to breathe. If this does not happen soon enough, or if the placenta detaches from the uterus (a red bag delivery) the brain will initially be deprived of oxygen, causing it to shut down. Eventually, oxygen levels rise and that's where the trouble starts — fluid leaves the bloodstream and enters the brain, causing cerebral swelling and eventual brain damage. But the brain is not the only organ that suffers; his kidneys can fail, the gastrointestinal tract motility will slow down, and the heart will develop arrhythmia.

In addition, nursing behavior will become erratic and may stop completely. As a result, the blood glucose level will plummet, leaving the brain without any source of nourishment since it relies on glucose for energy. To prevent seizures, your veterinarian will administer glucose intravenously (IV).

Vitamin C and magnesium are used to block toxic injury to nerve cells. Vitamin E and dimethyl sulfoxide — DMSO (a sulfur-containing substance) may also be administered to reduce existing nerve damage. These and other nutritious supplements (e.g., protein, fat, vitamins, and minerals) can be provided through a stomach feeding tube.

Unfortunately, by the time treatment is in place, the destruction may be too advanced. Nevertheless, you should do all you can to reduce further nerve damage. Antibiotic usage may be called for if your veterinarian suspects an infection. Another treatment, typically used in human medicine, is hyperbaric oxygen therapy (HBOT). HBOT is used to treat decompression in deep-water divers, as well as various neurologic and autoimmune disorders. In horses, it works the same way — it forces oxygen under pressure into the brain and tissues throughout the body, thereby reducing edema (swelling) in the brain and repairing damaged cells in the kidney, heart, and intestines. Though not considered mainstream, HBOT may be worth discussing with your veterinarian.

If your foal has not experienced seizures, the prognosis for recovery is good. He likely received an adequate amount of colostrum since symptoms don't start until days after delivery. And once your foal can go back to nursing normally, parenteral feeding (IV or stomach tube) can be discontinued.

FOAL HEAT DIARRHEA

During days 5 to 14 of life, your foal may develop mild diarrhea. This condition is called foal heat diarrhea because the timing coincides with his dam's first post-foaling estrus, and it is seemingly due to hormonal changes affecting the composition of her milk. But foals raised without a dam also develop diarrhea around this time, so there is no connection. The most likely reason is due to bacterial changes in the cecum and large colon.

Every foal is born with a sterile hindgut and ingests bacteria by suckling off his dam's teat and mimicking her grazing from the ground. He also will eat her manure, a practice called coprophagy. Though it looks nasty, it is normal and necessary.

To further assist with microbial levels, consider feeding a probiotic until the diarrhea clears up. These commercial preparations contain yeast (*Saccharomyces cerevisiae)*, and bacteria such as *Enterococcus faecium* and various strains of *Lactobaccillus*. Be sure to check the concentration level; foals need at least 100 *billion* colony forming units (CFUs). This is denoted by 10^9. If the label says 10^6, that indicates millions; this concentration is not nearly high enough to have a beneficial effect. Some preparations also contain oligosaccharides, which I recommend for added immune system support.

Your foal's system should stabilize within a week. If diarrhea continues or gets worse, or if he shows signs of depression, have your veterinarian look at him. Blood tests can be taken to rule out sepsis or renal (kidney) dysfunction. A fecal culture can test for pathogens such as *Salmonella* or *Clostridium*.

JAUNDICE

Jaundice, known as neonatal isoerythrolysis, can occasionally occur when the foal's blood type is different that his dam's, resulting in the mare producing antibodies against her fetus. This does not affect the foal until after he is born and he drinks these antibodies from her colostrum. The antibodies attack the foal's red blood cells, making it difficult to carry oxygen to his cells, including his brain. This situation can be fatal and an affected foal will require a blood transfusion to survive. The mare should be completely milked out until her colostrum is gone. Then is it safe for the foal to return to normal nursing.

The Growing Foal

Every foal is an individual and will develop somewhat differently. Genetics, breed, and your broodmare's nutritional status all play a role in how healthy your foal will be. All foals, however, have basic dietary needs. Before looking at those, let's determine his weight.

ESTIMATING FOAL WEIGHT

At birth, your foal will weigh approximately 10% of his dam's pre-pregnancy weight. A healthy foal will gain weight rapidly — as much as 3 lbs per day — depending on the breed. Heavier breeds will gain weight more quickly than lighter breeds or ponies.

When your foal is between 7 to 90 days old, to calculate his weight wrap a soft tape measure around his girth — just behind the wither and elbows. You'll find a picture showing how to place the tape in Chapter 12 — Weight Management. Use the following formulas:

7 to 28 days:
[Girth (inches) – 25] divided by 0.07 = Weight in lbs

28 to 90 days:
Add 10% to the above calculation.

Example: A three-month old foal, with a girth circumference of 43 inches, will weigh 283 lbs. See Appendix — Crunching Numbers for an illustration of this calculation.

CREEP FEEDING

Nutrient needs during the first two months of your foal's life are met through his dam's milk and some pasture or hay. He will also nibble on whatever you're feeding your mare. Though he will still nurse beyond two months, her milk is not nutritious enough to meet his growth needs — that's when a creep feeding setup can be beneficial.

You can start creep feeding as early as 4 weeks of age. He won't eat very much at first, but it will introduce him to a new way of eating. The idea behind creep feeding is to offer a place where your foal can eat without competition from adult horses. Blocking an area with a low horizontal bar, high enough for him to move under but which blocks larger horses, is one way to do this. Place his feeding area where he can at least see his dam and even touch noses. You could tie your mare while your foal is eating, but that forces him to eat his entire meal at once. Foals eat more slowly and will nibble a little at a time. It's much better to allow him to go back and forth over the course of a few hours; this will promote better digestion. Uneaten feed should be discarded and his feed bucket should be cleaned before his next meal.

What to feed

Your foal should eat the equivalent of 1.0 % of his body weight, divided into two or three feedings each day. Use the calculation shown earlier to figure his weight. Foals typically grow approximately 100 lbs per month during the first 6 months; after that, the growth rate tapers off until they reach their adult weight.

Hay: Grass hay should be offered free choice. Add alfalfa to the mix to provide a 2:1 ratio of grass to alfalfa.

Feed a low starch diet: Too much starch has been implicated in causing osteopathic disorders in growing foals (discussed later in this chapter). Yet feeding a low starch diet during this age is particularly challenging because your foal needs extra energy that forage alone cannot provide. A commercial feed is your best choice. However, most feeds designed for growing horses are grain-based; therefore I advise you to search for a formula that supplies most of its calories from non-starchy sources such as rice bran, flax, soy, and beet pulp.

If you prefer, you can mix your own ingredients and add a vitamin/mineral supplement. A handful of oats can be included for flavoring, but the majority of the meal should be from soaked beet pulp, flaxseed and soybean meals, and perhaps some rice bran. Do not feed corn or barley — they are poorly digested. Alfalfa pellets are also a good addition, but keep them to a minimum until he's at least three months old. The high-fiber content of hay pellets cannot be fermented for energy until there are enough microbes in his hindgut.

Protein: The total protein concentration in his diet needs to be high — at least 16% to support synthesis of new tissue as he grows. If you feed a commercial product designed for growth, check the crude protein percentage. Don't be afraid if it's higher than 16% — it will be diluted by his forage intake, bringing the total concentration in line.

Probiotics: Some companies add probiotics to their growth formulas and there is no harm in giving these to your foal. His hindgut microbial population will naturally increase on its own, of course, but feeding extra will help his digestive tract mature more quickly, allowing for better forage digestion.

WEANING

It's in your foal's best interest to start offering solid feedstuffs before weaning to avoid post-weaning development problems. Foals that are abruptly switched from milk to solid feed will experience a sudden growth spurt that can interfere with normal skeletal maturation. In addition, creep feeding during the weaning process significantly reduces stress.

Weaning stress

The longer you can wait to start the weaning process, the better. Foals are typically weaned between 4 and 6 months of age, mainly for convenience or business-related reasons. Weaning is very stressful for a foal and can result in injury, weight loss, ulcers, and depressed immune function. Early weaning often leads to behavioral problems in adult horses.

If your situation permits, wait until he's at least six and preferably eight months old to start gradually moving him away from his dam. The ideal situation is to have other foals around to keep each other company. But if this is your only foal, try putting him over the fence for 30 minutes with something tasty to eat, where he can still see and even touch his mother. Steadily increase this time, paying close attention to your mare's behavior when you reunite them. She may start to wean him herself, making the time away from mom not so bad.

A mare in the wild will naturally wean her foal once the next newborn arrives 11 months later. This does not harm her and while her milk isn't particularly nutritious during these later months, it allows the foal to progress normally toward adulthood.

Once weaned

Continue to give him all the hay he wants, including half as much alfalfa, along with 1 to 1.5% of his body weight from concentrates. As he gets closer to a year old, you can reduce the amount of concentrate since he'll be better able to sustain his weight on forage. His nutrient needs, however, cannot be met by an all-grass diet — he'll require additional energy along with vitamins and minerals. I'll discuss specific needs later in this chapter, but for now, let me elaborate on two disorders potentially caused by the diet — developmental orthopedic disease and bran disease.

Preventing Developmental Orthopedic Disease

Developmental orthopedic disease (DOD) describes a group of musculoskeletal conditions affecting bone and cartilage formation in growing horses. They include physitis/epiphysitis, osteochondritis dissecans (OCD), Wobbler's syndrome, cervical vertebral malformation (CVM), subchondral bone cysts, and contracted tendons (discussed further in Chapter 15 — Joints, Hair, Hooves, and Skin).

DOD is typically seen in rapidly-growing horses; however not all horses that grow quickly will develop DOD. Genetics plays a significant role in how fast your foal will grow, but the key is to manage proper growth, whether genetically predetermined or not, by offering a diet with adequate protein, proper levels of the trace minerals copper, manganese and zinc, and enough energy, best provided by fat and forage. Non-structural carbohydrate (sugar and starch) intake should be limited.

Foals that are sold at an early age are typically weaned as early as three months old, and then fed high-concentrate diets that contain large amounts of starch and very little water, in order to show a "well-grown" foal at market. These foals look good because of their size, but it is unlikely that they will grow into healthy adults. This practice is immoral in my opinion and should be discouraged by first, not purchasing a foal younger than six months old, and second, demanding accurate feeding records.

SWEET AND STARCHY FEEDS

I mentioned earlier that I discourage horse owners from feeding cereal grains to growing foals, yet I have seen many foals grow up on oats without any problem. That's because diet isn't the only factor leading to DOD; genetics likely plays a significant role. However, sweet or starchy feeds *can* lead to DOD, initiating a cascade of hormonal changes. Scientists[1] have shown that the high glycemic value (resulting from starch and sugar intake) of these feeds leads to elevated insulin levels, and subsequent changes in growth hormone production that influences cartilage development.

PROTEIN

Protein does not cause DOD[2], contrary to popular belief. If low-quality protein is fed, it will be used for energy instead of body protein production, so over-feeding anything that supplies energy is not advisable. But when a mixture of protein sources are fed, the overall quality will be high, allow-ing for synthesis of body tissues.

MINERALS

Calcium and phosphorus are the predominant minerals found in bones and should be in proper balance. Your first step toward evaluating the calcium and phosphorus content of your foal's diet is to have his forage tested. Next, look at the levels provided by his feed or supplements. Once you've determined the total amounts of these minerals, make certain that there is more calcium in his diet than phosphorus.

Copper-deficient foals have a higher incidence of DOD but it will not help to give your foal extra copper. His dam needs to have enough in her diet so her foal can be born with adequate storage levels (see Chapter 18 — Breeding, Pregnancy, and Lactation).

SKELETAL GROWTH VS WEIGHT

As we move forward in our understanding of DOD it's beneficial to pay attention to your foal's skeletal growth rather than his weight. Weight has more to do with fat and muscle than bone structure. To monitor your foal, keep tabs on his wither height. This will give you a better idea how fast he's growing. Never deprive your rapidly-growing foal of enough to eat in an attempt to reduce his chances of developing DOD. Fortunately not many people do this anymore; the goal is to moderate growth with a nutritious diet so his developmental rate will coincide with his genetics.

Preventing Nutritional Secondary Hyperpara-thyroidism (NSH)

NSH is commonly called bran disease because feeding too much bran, which is very high in phosphorus, without enough calcium leads to bone demineralization, disruption of joint cartilage synthesis, possible detach-ment of tendons and ligaments, and even bone fractures. The facial bones become thickened, distorting the head, hence the name "big head disease" that's often used to describe this disorder. Eating can be impaired as well as normal breathing due to changes in jaw structure and loosened teeth.

Your growing horse will have stiffness in one or more legs, joint tender-ness, and a stilted gait. In more extreme cases he can become lame due a disturbance in growth plate development known as physitis (also called epiphysitis). Other dietary factors can also cause physitis; please refer to Chapter 15 — Joints, Hair, Hooves, and Skin for more information.

Treatment of NSH simply involves adding calcium-rich feeds such as alfalfa and beet pulp, or a calcium supplement. Recovery is likely — most bony changes can be reversed when enough calcium is added to produce a calcium to phosphorus ratio of 3:1 to 6:1. Be careful when adding calcium supplements — calcium carbonate, calcium citrate, or calcium oxide are sources that only add calcium but calcium phosphate or bone meal also contain phosphorus.

NSH involves parathyroid hormone, produced by the parathyroid gland (located next to the thyroid gland in the throat). Since it is an endocrine disorder, you'll find more discussion in Chapter 13 — Metabolic and Endocrine Disorders.

Deworming and Vaccinations

DEWORMING

Overuse of anthelmintics to counteract worms, combined with seasonal variations and level of exposure, have made deworming especially controversial. A one-size-fits-all deworming regimen is no longer effective and each case needs to be discussed with your veterinarian.

Of particular concern are ascarids larvae, *Parascaris equorum,* that can migrate to your youngster's lungs. Adult worms in the intestine can cause blockages and colic. While your foal is still young, he can shed eggs in his manure, putting other young horses at risk. By the time he reaches 2 years, however, he will likely have developed immunity and eggs will no longer appear in his manure.

VACCINATIONS

Colostrum is your foal's first source of immunity protection. Maternal antibodies gradually diminish as he gets older, making him rely on his own antibodies. Therefore, it is a common practice to vaccinate foals between four and six months of age, and as early as three months when the broodmare's vaccination status is not known[3]. The optimal age for vaccinations continues to be researched; therefore, I recommend consulting with your veterinarian.

Pneumonia

The most common cause of pneumonia in foals is the bacteria *Rhodococcus equi*. Most infections occur early — between two to three months of age. It's during this time that a foal starts losing the immunity he received from his dam.

The initial stages of the disease are difficult to detect. Your foal may have a low grade fever, but there is rarely any nasal discharge. But eventually your foal will have difficulty breathing and he will develop diarrhea.

R. equi lives in infected manure and infects the soil, making management very difficult. The key to prevention is a healthy immune system. Overcrowding and stress can suppress your foal's ability to counteract infection.

Unfortunately there is no vaccine for *R. equi*, but experimental treatments with immunostimulants[4] and the metal gallium have been shown to decrease its proliferation. Other respiratory diseases such as equine herpes virus and influenza can be prevented by vaccinating your pregnant mare (see Chapter 18 — Breeding, Pregnancy, and Lactation). By boosting your broodmare's immunity, the colostrum will be concentrated in protective antibodies for your foal.

Six to Twenty-Four Months

As your youngster continues to grow, you'll notice a weight gain of approximately 0.75 to 1.25 lbs per day for the first year. By the time he reaches 1 1/2 years old, he will have reached 90% of his mature height and nearly that level in weight. Growth will slow down to approximately 100 lbs per year until he has fully matured. But all this depends on his breed and other genetic influences. It's best for him to have a moderate body condition score, between 4 and 6 on the Henneke system. See Table 12-2 in Chapter 12 — Weight Management for a description of each score.

Your yearling's appetite will be less than when he was younger, but more than what it will be as an adult. Colts tend to grow at a slightly faster rate than fillies and therefore need to eat more. Fillies fed the same as colts are inclined to become obese.

The combined forage and concentrate intake should amount to approximately 3% of his body weight. Complete pasture grazing, along with 30%

alfalfa and a vitamin/mineral supplement, may be sufficient as long as the grass is lush. If your pasture is not healthy enough, you can supplement his diet with good quality grass hay, alfalfa, and enough concentrate to maintain a normal body weight. Fresh grass can provide all the vitamin E and omega-3 fatty acids he needs, but if he's grazing on stressed pasture or gets only hay, you'll want to include additional vitamins and omega-3 fatty acids.

NUTRIENT REQUIREMENTS

The following nutrients need to be included in your growing horse's diet:

- High-quality protein
- Lysine
- Fat for additional energy
- Omega-3 fatty acids
- Fiber
- Vitamin A or beta carotene
- Vitamin D
- Vitamin E and selenium
- B vitamins
- Minerals

High-quality protein and lysine

By offering a variety of feedstuffs, the amino acid content of the entire diet is enhanced. Legumes in particular, especially soybean meal and, to a lesser extent, alfalfa, will provide additional lysine, an essential amino acid. Soybean meal typically has 3% lysine, whereas alfalfa hay has 0.9%. Other feeds such as beet pulp, oats, and rice bran have 0.5%, 0.6%, and 0.7%, respectively. When the lysine content of the diet is suitable, the other nine essential amino acids are likely present in correct amounts. Lysine content in forages is highly variable, so it is worth having your pasture and/or hay analyzed. You'll find 0.6 to 0.8% lysine added to many feeds and supplements because it is the amino acid that is most likely to be deficient. The minimum lysine requirement steadily increases from 29 to 47 grams per day as your horse ages and his exercise level increases (based on a mature weight of 1100 lbs). Methionine and tyrosine are also added to further boost protein quality and should be in relative proportion to lysine. For more information on protein, review Chapter 4 — Fundamentals of Protein and Amino Acids.

A reasonable amount of protein for weanlings is 170 grams per 100 lbs of body weight (slightly less for yearlings). To put this in perspective, let's look at an example... A 600 lb weanling needs to consume at least 18 lbs (3% of body weight) per day of concentrates and hay combined. His protein requirement is 1020 grams (600 X 170 g/100 lbs body weight). If you were to feed 6 lbs of a 14% crude protein commercial feed, you'd provide 381 grams of protein, leaving the rest to be supplied by grass and alfalfa hay.

8 lbs of grass hay (at 10% protein) and 4 lbs of alfalfa (at 18% protein) will do the trick — 363 grams of protein from the grass hay and 327 grams from the alfalfa. His total protein intake from concentrated feed, grass hay, and alfalfa is 1071 grams. This is a little more than his requirement but within a safe amount. Plus the protein content of your hay and alfalfa may vary. I show how these numbers were calculated in Appendix — Crunching Numbers.

But as you know from reading this book, I prefer offering hay free choice to allow your horse to self-regulate his intake. This is the best way for him to maintain a normal weight. If given the opportunity, a 600 lb weanling will likely consume 2% of his body weight in forage, which is exactly what we found to be appropriate in the above example to meet his protein needs. I find a 2:1 mix of grass hay to alfalfa (half as much alfalfa as grass hay) to be ideal for foal growth.

Fat and omega-3 fatty acids

Your young horse needs more energy while growing than he will at maturity. Carbohydrates from grain provide calories, but as I mentioned earlier, starchy diets can lead to osteopathic disorders. Protein also provides calories, but shouldn't be used for work and exercise; protein should be used to build and repair tissue. That leaves fat — more concentrated in calories and safe to feed.

Rice bran: To offer additional calories, this is the best source of fat. Rice bran oil contains some essential omega-6 fatty acids but not nearly as much as soybean oil, the most commonly added fat source in horse feeds. Read more about this in Chapter 3 — Fundamentals of Fats.

Omega-3 fatty acids: These are best supplied by flaxseed meal. Give your horse 1/2 cup per 400 lbs of body weight. Flaxseed meal not only has extra calories, as all fat sources would, but its high omega-3 fatty acid content keeps the immune system healthy and promotes development of strong bones and joints.

Fiber

Now that your horse's hindgut is becoming more mature, the foundation of his diet should be from fibrous sources — hay and pasture. He still needs some concentrates to provide energy for growth, but the microbes in his hindgut are now in sufficient numbers to ferment fiber to supply him with calories. Give him all the grass hay and/or pasture he wants, with a controlled amount of alfalfa.

Beta carotene or vitamin A

Here again, fresh grass will provide all the beta carotene your horse needs. Hay, of course, does not. Since beta carotene is converted to vitamin A once inside your horse's tissues, commercial feeds will likely be fortified with Vitamin A. A safe amount of vitamin A supplementation is 15 IU per pound of body weight. Chapter 6 — Fundamentals of Vitamins offers more explanation about this nutrient's role.

Vitamin D

Vitamin D is necessary for proper calcium metabolism and bone growth. If your growing horse gets plenty of sunshine, he likely produces enough on his own. If, however, he is stalled or lives in a part of the country that has more cloudy days than sunny ones, make sure he obtains 3 IU per pound of body weight per day from his feed or supplements.

Vitamin E and selenium

Fresh pasture is your best source of Vitamin E as long as the grass is not stressed from drought, heat, or over-grazing. As you've heard me say many times throughout this book, hay has virtually no vitamin E left because it is easily destroyed by oxygen and heat.

Vitamin E and selenium serve together as antioxidants; therefore they protect your growing horse against damage caused by free radical formation due to stress, infection, or injury. Selenium works with vitamin E, but I urge you to evaluate his entire diet for the total selenium content before considering a selenium supplement.

Growing horses should have *at least* 0.5 IU of vitamin E per lb of body weight for maintenance and preferably closer to 1 IU per lb of body weight. For example, an 800 lb yearling would require a minimum of 400 IU per day. Exercise, performance, training, and stress increase the requirement. At least 1 mg of selenium should be included, but no more than 0.6 ppm of the entire diet per day. Chapters 5 — Fundamentals of Minerals and 6 — Fundamentals of Vitamins have full discussions on both of these nutrients.

B vitamins

Fresh pasture, and to a lesser extent, hay, along with normal microbial production will ensure that your horse has enough B vitamins. However, horses have individual needs and illness or stress can increase the B vitamin requirement. There are several B vitamins and they are discussed individually in Chapter 6.

Minerals

Trace minerals such as zinc, manganese, copper, cobalt, and iodine are usually included in commercial feeds for this age group. The zinc to copper ratio should be approximately 3:1, and a 2:1 ratio of zinc to manganese is adequate. Major minerals — calcium, phosphorus, and to a lesser extent, magnesium — are also added. Iron is plentiful in pasture and hay so additional supplementation is not necessary. Excess iodine can alter bone development so avoid mineralized salt blocks if you're already providing minerals from a fortified feed; avoid using sea salt because it can be very high in iodine. See Chapter 5 — Fundamentals of Minerals for a complete synopsis of these and other minerals.

EXERCISE

Growing horses need the space to run and play that only turnout can provide — the more the better. They'll develop healthy hooves, strengthen their bones, and muscles will become stronger. To compensate for a small area, I've seen folks, all with good intentions, longe their horses or walk them on a mechanical walker. But these types of repetitive movements can damage developing tissues, doing more harm than good. If space is limited, consider pasture-boarding your horse elsewhere where he and his buddies can tear across large areas of land.

Putting a young horse in training where he's taken from total freedom and housed in a stall, will cause minerals to leach from his bones and joints. He needs to have bursts of galloping and racing, where he can run up and down hills, and interact with other horses to prevent bone loss. Without the opportunity to sprint and romp around at least five days a week, your horse will not be prepared for any rigorous activity. Taking him out for a walk or for his daily exercise cannot take the place of turnout for preventing bone loss. The good news is that even a couple of hours a day of turnout in a good environment will help your youngster grow into a healthier horse.

REACHING MATURITY

Most horses obtain their mature height and weight by the time they reach 4 years of age. Some large breeds, however, including drafts and warm-bloods, will continue growing for four more years. Lighter breeds such as Thoroughbreds and Arabians, as well as donkeys, ponies and minis reach adult height by age 3 in most cases.

Your goal in feeding beyond your horse's second year will depend on how much energy he needs to maintain a healthy weight, while meeting his nutritional needs. I find an all-forage diet, including some alfalfa (reduced to 20% by this time), plus a comprehensive vitamin/mineral supplement to be adequate. Vitamin E and omega-3 fatty acids are still needed as well as adequate lysine. Past two years old his minimum lysine requirement decreases to a maintenance level of 27 grams per day[5] (for a mature weight of 1100 lbs). However, horses that are working or performing have additional need of virtually all nutrients. The next chapter, Athletes, provides a clear overview to keep your active horse in peak condition.

Growing Old

Advances in veterinary medicine and greater attention to nutrition have made it possible, and even probable, that your horse will live well into his 30s. A 20 year old is no longer considered an old horse — he's middle-aged, yes, but may still be as active as ever. I have a client whose horse lay down and died peacefully one day after 46 years of fruitful living. Perhaps you've seen one even older. But it's apparent that individuality plays as much a role in the way horses age as it does for us. There are changes, however, that go along with growing old, no matter at what age they become noticeable. Some horses have trouble gaining weight, others become too fat. Teeth wear down, making chewing difficult; some may even lose teeth. Most horses experience a decline in immune function and get sick more easily or develop allergies. Muscle mass may diminish and joints can become stiff. Digestion and absorption efficiency declines.

All these changes come about gradually, but as your horse starts to show signs of aging, the diet you've been feeding all along may now be obsolete and it's time to tweak it a bit to meet your horse's needs.

DIETARY GUIDELINES FOR SENIOR HORSES

A senior-friendly diet takes into account your horse's reduced saliva production. Dry food is difficult to chew and nearly impossible to swallow when there is not enough saliva. This natural aspect of aging is easy to manage by simply moistening your horse's feed; he'll appreciate having his meal a little on the mushy side. Also, consider spraying your hay with water before feeding (this doesn't work well in winter, of course!) to make it easier to chew; most horses enjoy wet hay. I found this out one day when my old fellow preferred to stand out in the rain to eat his hay, instead of choosing the dry supply in the barn.

Digestion efficiency is not what it once was, leading to diarrhea, electrolyte imbalances, and weight loss. It starts in the small intestine where your horse produces digestive enzymes that break down carbohydrates, protein, and fat into small pieces that can be absorbed into the blood stream. As your horse ages, however, he produces fewer and fewer of these enzymes, leaving undigested food to enter the hindgut where it is either fermented (which can lead to colic or laminitis) or ends up in the feces. Malnutrition results simply because his tissues never receive the nutrients from his meal. Senior feeds are designed to prevent this problem. They are pre-cooked and extruded (formed into kibbles) that are easy to digest. Many senior feeds add digestive enzymes to their formulas to further assist with digestion.

> A senior-friendly diet takes into account your horse's reduced saliva production. Dry food is difficult to chew and nearly impossible to swallow when there is not enough saliva.

The fibrous portion of your horse's diet passes through the small intestine to the cecum and large colon, to be digested by billions of microbes. Trouble arises when these microorganisms die. Possible causes include: stomach acid reaching the hindgut because of inadequate saliva production (saliva neutralizes acid), pain and mental stress, illness, or administering antibiotics. The hindgut floras are necessary to protect your horse against diarrhea, weight loss, colic, and even laminitis. For this reason, probiotics are often added to senior feeds or supplements designed for aging horses. Prebiotics also support the hindgut but rather than adding living microbes, they contain fermentation products that feed existing bacteria, making digestion more efficient.

The importance of flax

Flaxseed meal or oil is really a must for all horses, but especially for seniors. Its high omega-3 fatty acid content supports immune function, keeps joints and muscles healthy, regulates blood insulin levels, promotes healthy skin and hooves, and makes your horse shine.

I recommend feeding 1/2 cup of flaxseed meal or 1 ounce of oil per 400 lbs of body weight. Freshly ground flaxseeds start to spoil within hours so they need to be ground daily. Also, since they are very high in phosphorus, I prefer using a commercial product that adds calcium, unless the diet is already very high in calcium.

Supplementing vitamin C

When young, your horse was capable of producing his own vitamin C. Now that he's getting older, he's losing that ability. He'll get ample vitamin C from fresh pasture, as long as it is lush; but hay has virtually no vitamin C.

I routinely recommend vitamin C supplementation for all horses starting between 16 and 18 years of age (unless they are grazing on healthy pasture). Your horse's joints will improve and you may even find that a joint supplement isn't needed. That's because vitamin C is used to repair collagen found in joints and bones, as well as tendons, ligaments, and other connective tissue throughout his body. It also prevents your horse's teeth from falling out.

Depending on your horse's age, add between 3 to 5 mg per pound of body weight per day. Once your horse is over 20, give him 10 mg for every pound of body weight.

Vitamin C also acts as an important component of your horse's immune system. Its antioxidant capability neutralizes damaging free radicals, thereby protecting cells from disease. Take a look at Chapter 6 — Fundamentals of Vitamins for a complete discussion about vitamin C.

Complete senior feeds

Commercially produced senior feeds are designed to be complete. But
don't let the word "complete" confuse you. It means that the feed is fortified with enough nutrients to meet your horse's complete nutritional needs.
It does not mean that your horse can do without a steady supply of pasture
or hay. Your horse needs to have something to graze on at all times to maintain intestinal motility and keep his bacterial flora in good shape. If your
horse has trouble chewing hay, there are alternative approaches toward supplying fiber; I discuss these a bit later under dental issues.

Here are some guidelines when feeding a commercial senior product:

- Feed according to directions to provide enough vitamins and minerals; if your horse is fed less than the recommended amount, add a
  comprehensive vitamin/mineral supplement.

- Always weigh your feed; scoop size refers to volume, not weight.

- Feed frequent, small meals; no more than 4 lbs at a time and preferably three to four times a day to avoid overloading his digestive system.

- Avoid sweet and starchy feeds; many horses can no longer metabolize
  high levels of sugar. Feeds that contain a large amount of oats should
  be avoided, and do not feed corn because of its poor digestibility.

- Look for 12-14% protein, 5-10% fat (depending on your horse's
  weight), and at least 15% fiber.

- Check the ingredient list for high-quality protein sources such as soybean meal and alfalfa. Alfalfa is fine for horses with normal kidney
  function.

- Look for added B vitamins.

- Vitamin E concentration should be at least 200 IU/lb; selenium concentration should not exceed 0.6 ppm.

- Calcium should not exceed 1.1% and phosphorus should be approximately 0.7%.

Making your own feed

If you prefer, you can combine basic ingredients to make your own feed. Mix them together with warm water to make chewing easier and prevent choke. Here is a good formula:

- 2 lbs of alfalfa pellets
- 1 lb beet pulp
- 1/2 lb rice bran
- 1/2 lb wheat bran
- 1 lb steamed oats (optional — horses with insulin resistance or equine Cushing's should not have added starch)

The added bran (both rice and wheat) provides additional phosphorus to compensate for your aged horse's reduced absorption ability. It must, however, be balanced with calcium which is supplied by the alfalfa pellets and beet pulp. Rice bran adds needed fat in addition to phosphorus.

You'll need to add a comprehensive vitamin/mineral supplement and one ounce (two tablespoons) of salt. If your supplement contains approximately 1000 IU of vitamin E and 1 mg of selenium, you won't need to add more. If, however, he needs more vitamin E and his selenium needs are already met, choose a plain vitamin E supplement. Do not add selenium beyond his requirement; it has a narrow range of safety, so please refer to Chapter 5 — Fundamentals of Minerals to make sure your horse is supplemented correctly.

The overweight horse may not need added concentrated meals

As your horse gets older, his metabolic rate becomes more sluggish, increasing his tendency to gain weight on the same amount of feed. If he has weight to lose, he doesn't really need anything other than pasture and hay except for a small meal each day to serve as a carrier for supplements such as flaxseed meal, vitamin C, and a comprehensive vitamin/mineral supplement.

Never restrict forage — he needs to be able to graze all the time. Going for hours without eating will, ironically, prevent him from burning fat and he'll remain heavy. This is described in Chapters 12 — Weight Management and 14 — Digestive Problems.

You'll also want to increase his activity — even pasture turnout will encourage him to move more. Exercise not only burns calories but increases muscle mass. The more muscle he has, the more calories he'll burn even while resting.

While getting your horse to lose weight can be a problem, the underweight horse can be even more challenging. There are several reasons for weight loss, which I discuss next.

TROUBLE GAINING WEIGHT

Sometimes it's difficult to notice if your horse is losing weight. Weight change is gradual and by the time you realize it, he may have taken off a hundred pounds. I have found it helpful to take a picture of your horse every week or so to give you an objective view. Or, getting a baseline weight and measuring him regularly can also give you a basis for comparison.

Before giving him more to eat, try to determine the reason for weight loss. Worm infestation, ulcers, infections, liver or kidney disease, even cancer can cause weight loss. Pain and mental stress can also make it difficult for your horse to hold a normal weight. The most common reason for weight loss in older horses, however, is poor dental health.

Poor teeth and mouth pain

Horses' teeth continually push out from below the surface, where the enamel is deeply embedded in the jaw bones. The supply is limited and tooth material will eventually run out, but it is intended to last a horse's lifetime.

To protect your horse's teeth, have them examined more often than the typical once-a-year protocol for younger horses. A qualified veterinarian or equine dentist should look at your horse's mouth at least every six months. Crooked teeth or normal wear along the tops of molars will inhibit his ability to chew, making mature or stemmy hay impossible to eat. His teeth need to be floated regularly to remove sharp points that develop. Otherwise they will dig into his soft mouth tissue, making eating an extremely painful experience. If his mouth is neglected his teeth and gums can become diseased, leading to tooth loss.

Don't be fooled into thinking his teeth are fine as long as he's eating. Sometimes horses will look as if they are eating normally even though they are suffering; their nature is to appear strong against predators and avoid rejection from their herd. Of course, your horse doesn't have to worry about these things but his instincts may tell him to be stoic about his pain.

Keep an eye on him as he eats and watch for these signs of dental problems:

- Dropping clumps of partially chewed feed out of his mouth (quidding)
- Tendency to choke (large pieces of food blocking the esophagus)
- Undigested feed in his manure
- Loose manure (cow-patties)

Forage: Even though he cannot chew as well as before, he still needs forage. Start by soaking soft hay or hay cubes. These can be fed free choice. Choose either grass hay cubes (timothy is the most common variety) or timothy-alfalfa cubes (unless he has liver or kidney problems).

Hay replacers also work well — they come in pellets or as chopped hay. You can moisten them but many products cannot be offered free choice because they are often fortified with vitamins and minerals.

Mushy feed: Adding water to your horse's meal to make a mush is the most comfortable way to feed and will prevent choke. Some horses like mushy feed and others are picky about it. Adding alfalfa pellets or something yummy such as apple sauce or mashed carrots (baby food works well) will likely appease the persnickety horse.

Fast metabolic rate

If your horse burns energy quickly, he needs more calories than forage can provide. Cereal grains offer extra calories but I tend to avoid feeding them. Their high starch content aggravates ulcers, can lead to colic, and can induce laminitis (founder) in an insulin-resistant or cushingoid horse. Instead, feed fat; it is very well tolerated and can be fed up to 10% of his diet. Depending on how much weight he needs to gain, you can add up to 1 cup of oil per 500 lbs of body weight per day. Start off with smaller amounts until he gets used to it, since most horses do not like oily feed. And choose oil that is relatively low in omega-6 fatty acids, such as canola or rice bran oil, since high omega-6 intake causes inflammation. You can use flaxseed oil, but no more than 1/3 cup per day. See Table 3-1 in Chapter 3 — Fundamentals of Fats for a list of fats and their fatty acid composition.

Fat can also be provided by adding a high fat feedstuff such as rice bran or flaxseed meal. As I mentioned earlier, when feeding rice bran, make sure your horse is also being fed something that is high in calcium such as alfalfa or beet pulp to balance out rice bran's high phosphorus content. He needs more phosphorus at his age but you don't want it to exceed calcium levels. Or you can purchase a commercial rice bran product that has a little extra calcium added to correct for this naturally inverted calcium to phosphorus ratio.

Commercial flaxseed meal products also have added calcium to balance flaxseed's high phosphorus content. So the same guidelines apply: feed it along with a high calcium feed. Never feed flaxseeds whole, even if you soak them — you're wasting your money and not benefitting your horse because they will pass through his system undigested.

Competition

During mealtimes consider separating your old fellow from bullying horses. Also offer hay in several piles so if he is pushed away from one he can easily go to another.

Some old horses literally get tired while eating and will stop for a while to rest; when they come back, the other horses may have finished his meal. So do what you can to prevent this from happening.

Reduced hindgut microbial population

You can feed the lushest of pastures, or the finest hay available but your horse won't receive enough calories if his hindgut is not heavily populated with fiber-digesting microbes. Without these microorganisms, all that beautiful forage will end up in your horse's manure. There really isn't any way to accurately diagnose this problem but if your horse is having trouble gaining weight and you've ruled out any medical issues, try giving him a prebiotic. As I mentioned earlier, prebiotics do not contain live microbes like probiotics do; instead they feed the existing bacteria, making them better able to digest forage. Better digestion means more available calories and hence, weight gain.

OTHER AGE-RELATED PROBLEMS

An aging body does not work as efficiently and can succumb to any number of disorders. There are some health situations where I cannot recommend a specific nutrient for prevention or treatment. Nevertheless, an overall nutritious diet will help your horse delay or even prevent the chance of developing problems such as:

- Cancer of the salivary gland, lymph, perineum, and eyes
- Melanoma, especially prevalent in white and gray horses
- Uterine infection
- Moon blindness (anterior uveitis)
- Cataracts

Many age-related problems, however, like the ones that follow, do respond well to nutritional intervention.

Joint and muscle deterioration

Most, if not all, horses over the age of 20 will develop arthritis to some degree. Your horse's knees seem to be the main site of deterioration, though other joints can be affected. Joint supplements are helpful for the vast majority of horses; more serious cases may benefit from injections. Please refer to Chapter 15 — Joints, Hair, Hooves, and Skin for more discussion on joint health and treatment.

Stall confinement makes arthritis worse and makes muscles tight. You know what that feels like if you've ever sat in one place for several hours. Mild exercise helps lubricate stiff joints and builds up surrounding muscles. Even if you don't ride your horse, the more pasture turnout he gets the better off he'll be. Since his ability to move with any degree of speed may be hampered, be careful not to place him with rambunctious youngsters.

Tendons and ligaments lose elasticity over time, reducing your horse's agility and speed. Muscle mass starts to decline, giving your horse's top line a swayed appearance. In addition to exercise and preventing your horse from becoming overweight, there are several nutrients that I find helpful in boosting joint and connective tissue strength and lean body mass:

- Gamma oryzanol (found in rice bran extract)
- Branched chain amino acids (appropriate building blocks of protein)
- Vitamin B_6 (involved in protein synthesis)

- Vitamin C (for collagen production)
- Vitamin E (prevents tissue damage)

Insulin resistance and equine Cushing's disease

Insulin resistance can occur at any age, but the older your horse, the more likely he'll develop this hormonal disorder. Obesity, especially as fat deposits along the crest of his neck, down the crease of his back, or on his rump or chest, indicates that he is insulin resistant, significantly increasing his risk of laminitis (founder).

An insulin resistant horse produces too much insulin in response to sugar and starch, making it necessary to stop feeding sweet feeds, cereal grains, and sugary treats (including carrots and apples). Pasture grazing may also need to be restricted to safer times of the day or may need to be completely eliminated depending on the severity of the case. To help you make the best decision, have your pasture and hay analyzed for sugar, fructan, and starch levels.

Equine Cushing's disease, referred to as pituitary pars intermedia dysfunction (PPID), requires the same dietary changes. PPID is more likely to occur in older horses and is characterized by excess production of the hormone cortisol. Symptoms include a curly hair coat that does not shed in the spring, increased urination and thirst, muscle wasting, and a ferocious appetite. Cortisol creates secondary insulin resistance, so a low starch diet will help tame insulin levels. However, medication may also be necessary.

There are plenty of low starch feeds available for insulin resistant and cushingoid horses but overweight horses should not be fed more than the amount necessary as a carrier for supplements.

If your horse is used to having a treat, he will feel deprived if you greet him empty-handed. You can offer alfalfa cubes but they're very dry, so be sure to break them into small pieces. You can also obtain cookies and trail mixes from Skode's Horse Treats — this is the only company I've found that produces treats that are low in sugar and starch.

Magnesium is very helpful in reducing circulating insulin levels and I generally recommend giving your horse 5,000 mg per 250 lbs of body weight. However, before supplementing magnesium, it's important to have your horse's blood tested to reveal possible kidney problems.

There are three chapters that provide more information on these topics: Chapter 1 — Ground Rules for Feeding a Horse, Chapter 11 — Laminitis, and Chapter 13 — Metabolic and Endocrine Disorders.

Reduction in immune function: Insulin resistance and PPID depress immune function, which is why you'll often see abscesses form in the feet and elsewhere. Protecting the hindgut microbial population is crucial during this time since microbes provide significant immune protection. If your horse is suffering from abscesses or any other bacterial infection, your veterinarian will likely administer an antibiotic, which further compromises the bacterial flora in the hindgut.

Antibiotics are important, don't get me wrong. But you should give your horse a potent probiotic to replace losses. Choose a product that *also contains oligosaccharides*. These long-chain sugar molecules benefit the immune system. Look at the label to for this substance, sometimes written as mannooligosaccharides. A yeast known as *Saccharomyces cerevisiae* is also beneficial since it produces oligosaccharides.

RESPIRATORY CONDITIONS

Recurrent airway obstruction (formerly known as COPD) and respiratory allergies are more likely to occur in senior horses as immune function wanes. The most effective treatment involves managing his environment for dust by soaking his hay and providing turnout. Nutritional support is provided by adding flax, antioxidants including vitamins C and vitamin E, and specialized herbs. Refer to Chapter 16 — Immunity Issues for more details.

LIVER AND KIDNEY DISEASE

The only way to know if your horse's liver or kidney function is impaired is to have his blood tested. The *only* way.

Liver disease

If your horse's liver is not functioning properly, it cannot produce glucose (blood sugar), necessitating higher carbohydrate levels in the diet. Protein and fat, however, need to be reduced to compensate for a less efficient metabolism. Use the following guidelines:

- Commercial feeds should have no more than 10-12% protein and less than 5% fat. Many senior feeds contain protein and fat above these levels, so read the labels carefully.
- Avoid alfalfa, clover, soybean meal or flaxseed meal because they are too high in protein.
- Eliminate feeding fatty feedstuffs such as rice bran or sunflower seeds.
- Avoid adding oil to the diet.
- Add a moderate amount of oats to boost blood glucose levels.
- Consider adding the herb milk thistle to help the liver eliminate toxins.
- Supplement vitamins and minerals, along with extra B vitamins to support liver function.

Kidney disease

The kidneys are responsible for getting rid of excess calcium; when their function is impaired, calcium remains in the kidney and forms stones which are very painful to pass. Calcium levels also build up in the bloodstream, which can be fatal.

The kidneys are responsible for excreting nitrogenous wastes, so protein intake needs to be lowered. Fat, however, can remain at normal levels. Attention should be given to the following:

- Reduce total protein intake to 8% by avoiding high protein feeds.
- Have your hay and pasture tested for protein and mineral concentrations.
- Avoid high calcium feeds. Therefore, do not feed alfalfa or beet pulp. Dietary calcium levels should be less than 1%.
- Phosphorus should remain in balance with calcium, but too much phosphorus should be avoided; therefore do not feed rice or wheat bran, or flaxseed meal.
- Oil can be added to the diet for extra calories.
- Flaxseed oil can be added to provide omega-3 fatty acids.
- Vitamin E supplementation is worthwhile.
- Avoid supplementing water-soluble vitamins — B vitamins and vitamin C — since the kidney is responsible for removing excesses.
- Do not add mineral supplements and mineralized salt blocks due to their calcium content.

Bottom line

Your horse's genetic background combined with his health status throughout his growing and adult years will influence how well he ages. If he was fed well all his life, with attention paid toward filling in nutritional gaps, he will likely live longer and with fewer ailments.

Throughout his later years he still needs to have regular deworming treatments, vaccinations, and hoof care. Maintain regular and more frequent visits from your equine dentist — healthy teeth are a priority. If he's missing teeth, he'll need softer meals but attention to fiber intake is still the foundation of his diet, as it is with any horse.

You are the best judge of how well your senior horse is aging. By keeping track of his weight, his eating habits, and his overall condition, you can make appropriate adjustments to his diet that will impact his health and overall quality of life.

The Orphaned Foal

Your foal requires 72 ounces (2 1/4 quarts) of colostrum during his first 18 hours of life. But this need is not always met. Your mare may not produce enough colostrum, she may be ill, or inattentive and refuse to nurse. Or in the worst case scenario, she may be either at risk of dying or actually dead.

If you are left in the unfortunate situation of having an orphaned foal, it is a manageable situation, with a little patience and knowhow.

Timing is critical. To build up proper immunity, your foal needs colostrum replacement immediately — within the first 3 to 12 hours of life. Remember, beyond 18 hours, your foal completely loses his ability to absorb antibodies from the gastrointestinal tract.

Colostrum replacement

Colostrum can be supplied from another mare or from a frozen supply. When frozen, it can be safely used within one year. If stored for longer than that, its antibodies may not be active enough to protect your foal's immune system. *Do not thaw frozen colostrum in the microwave* — microwaves will kill the very antibodies your foal needs. Thaw it in the refrigerator or in a bowl of warm water. Keep it in warm water until it reaches body temperature (99° to 101° F) in order to simulate mother's milk.

Call your friends and family to help — you'll need to feed 4 ounces every hour for the first 18 hours.

MILK REPLACEMENT

After 18 hours of colostrum feeding or if your foal was fortunate enough to have nursed for the first day of his life before losing his dam, you can start feeding him milk. There are two ways to accomplish this — a nurse mare or a milk replacer. A milk replacer will meet his nutritional needs but he will not receive the socialization that a nurse mare provides.

Nurse mare

To coax a nurse mare into accepting your foal, physical restraint or tranquilizers are often used but I prefer trying a more positive approach. Since a mare will use her senses — sight, smell, and sound — to identify her foal, you can at least camouflage her sense of smell by changing your foal's scent (mentholated petroleum jelly works well) or help him smell more like her own by rubbing her milk or sweat on his body.

A lactating dairy goat can serve as an alternative to a nurse mare. Place her on a bale of hay so your foal won't have to go through contortions to reach her udder.

Weaning and creep feeding will follow a normal schedule (discussed elsewhere in this chapter). However, if your foal is given a milk replacer, weaning will take place much earlier.

Milk replacer

It is often difficult to find a nurse mare, which is why there are so many milk replacement products available on the market. Choose a commercial product designed for foals. Do not use cow's milk because it does not have the correct nutrient proportions for a horse; calf milk replacers are also inappropriate because they do not contain enough protein for normal foal growth and may contain antibiotics. Choose a product that contains between 20% and 24% crude protein, 15-16% fat, and not more than 0.5% fiber.

If your foal develops diarrhea or bloating, the milk replacer may need to be diluted. If he becomes lethargic or starts to colic, it is a medical emergency and your veterinarian should be contacted immediately.

For the first few days, you'll need to use a bottle. The best nipple size is one that is designed for lambs. After about a week, you can help your foal become accustomed to drinking from a bucket. For the first two weeks, he'll require 8 feedings per day, once every 3 hours. Table 19-1 offers an orphaned foal feeding program provided by Colorado State University Extension[6].

Table 19-1 Orphaned Foal Milk Replacer Program

Day/Week	Amount	Feedings per Day
19 hours through Week 2	6 quarts daily	8
Week 3	7-9 quarts	6
Week 4	4-6 quarts	6

By the end of week 4, you can start weaning him off of milk replacer and introduce a creep feed (discussed earlier); also let him nibble on hay. Wean him slowly so by the time he's two to three months old, he'll be completely off of milk replacer.

Since your foal is not familiar with other mares he may not develop normal bacterial flora in his hindgut. Foals typically eat their dam's manure to build up their own microbial population. Bacteria found on pasture will provide some exposure, but in this case, I recommend giving him a probiotic to help him digest forage.

Endnotes

[1] Many studies how shown how diets that produce high glycemic peaks (diets high in sugar and starch) increase the risk of developing DOD:

Glade, M.J., and Belling, T.H., 1986. A dietary etiology for osteochondroitic cartilage. *Equine Veterinary Science, 6:* 175-187.

Pagan, J.D., 2001. The relationship between glycaemic response and the incidence of OCD in Thoroughbred weanlings: A field study. *Proceedings of the American Association of Equine Practitioners, 47*: 322-325.

Ralston, S.L., 1995. Postprandial hyperglycemia/hyperinsulinema in young horses with osteochondritis dissecans lesions. *Journal of Animal Science, 73*: 184.

[2] Protein intake has no effect on the incidence of DOD as exhibited by the following studies:

Harris, P.A., Staniar, W., and Ellis A., 2005. Effect of exercise and diet on the incidence of DOD in the growing horse: Nutrition and prevention of growth disorders. Julliand, V. and Martin-Rosset, W. (eds). *EEAP Publication No. 114*: 273-291.

Savage, C.J., McCarthy, R.N., and Jeffcott, L.B., 1993. Effects of dietary energy and protein on induction of dyschondroplasia in foals. *Equine Veterinary Journal, Supplement 16*: 74-79.

Schryver, H.F., Meakim, D.W., Lowe, J.E., Williams, J., Soderholm, L.V., and Hintz, H.F., 1987. Growth and calcium metabolism in horses fed varying levels of protein. *Equine Veterinary Journal, Supplement 16*: 280-287.

[3] Source: Study done by Tracy Sturgill, DVM from the University of Kentucky's Gluck Equine Research Center in Lexington, described in: Sellnow, L., 2009. Building immunity. *The Horse, May*: 26 – 30.

[4] Source: Study done by Steeve Giguere, DVM, Ph.D., Dipl. ADVIM, of the University of Florida, described in: Sellnow, L., 2009. Building immunity. *The Horse, May*: 26 – 30.

[5] *Nutrient Requirements of Horses,* Sixth Revised Edition, 2007. Washington, D.C.: National Research Council, National Academy Press: 298.

[6] Adapted from: Colorado State University Extension. http://www.extension.org/pages/Feeding_Orphan_Foals/print

CHAPTER 20 —
ATHLETES

Deeply I sat, fixed to the slap, slap, slap, slap of her trot,
and the counterpoint thud-plod, thud-plod of her heart,
enchanted by a soft percussion I felt a part of, floating
above the syncopated rhythm like a melody.
~ Diane Ackerman

An athletic horse brings to mind one with speed, control, endurance, and the ability to focus, who is in top shape, muscular, and healthy, where every cell in his body works together to bring about the perfect form. His performance may be before the crowds or just between the two of you as you ride the trail, practice in the arena, or work on the farm. Whatever purpose you've given him, he relies on you to give him the best food, sufficient rest, and the care he needs to be your devoted partner.

Your athletic horse's nutritional needs are enhanced, though they're not especially different from other horses'. But the more work we ask of him, the more nutrients he needs to do the job and recover so he's fit enough to do it again and again. This chapter examines how the diet should change when we ask him to work harder, to keep him sound and prevent injury. The goal is to optimize his ability and performance so you — and he — can take pride in your shared accomplishments.

Defining Levels of Activity

It is difficult to generalize the amount of energy your horse expends for activities because there is so much variation. You have the weight of the horse to consider, but you also have the weight of the rider, the ground conditions, climate, and exercise intensity. The complex calculations that address each factor are beyond the scope of this book, but we can categorize activity according to its type and duration to help with diet planning.

Let's standardize our terms so we can all be on the same page. The National Research Council (NRC) provides definitions of four levels of exercise: light, moderate, heavy, and very heavy[1]. These are general descriptions, and times and intensity levels can vary, but they give you an idea of what each category entails.

- **Light exercise.** 1-3 hours per week; 40% walk, 50% trot, 10% canter. Includes recreational riding, beginning of training programs, or occasional showing.

- **Moderate exercise**. 3-5 hours per week; 30% walk, 55% trot, 10% canter, 5% low jumping, cutting, or other skill work. Includes giving lessons, recreational riding, beginning of training/breaking, more frequent showing, polo, and ranch work.

- **Heavy exercise.** 4-5 hours per week; 20% walk, 50% trot, 15% canter, 15% gallop, jumping, other skill work. Includes ranch work, polo, frequent and strenuous show events, low to medium level eventing, race training (middle stages).

- **Very heavy exercise.** Various; ranges from 1 hour per week speed work to 6-12 hours per week slow work. Includes racing, endurance, and elite 3-day eventing.

Nutrient Requirements

VARIATIONS BETWEEN ACTIVITY LEVELS

Before we discuss individual nutrients, I'd like you to see how your horse's requirements change the more exercise he does. Using the nutrient requirements of an 1100 lb (500 kg) horse as an example, take a look at the trends rather than the exact amounts, since your horse's weight may be considerably different. Table 20-1 shows you the requirements for six key nutrients.

Keep in mind that these are *minimum* requirements and your horse may be getting more than the table indicates. In most cases, that is perfectly fine; certainly it is for the nutrients shown in Table 20-1. However, some minerals, such as iron, zinc, and copper, need to be in proper proportion to one another to prevent competition for absorption sites within the digestive tract. And others, like selenium and iodine, are toxic in high doses. I'll discuss these later in the chapter as I go through each nutrient classification. For the most part, I'll be speaking in generalities rather than giving you exact amounts to feed. There are as many combinations of ingredients as there are horses, so my goal is to arm you with information so you can create the best diet for your horse's particular circumstance.

Table 20-1 Daily Nutrient Requirements for Varying Exercise Levels: 1100 lb (500 kg) Mature Weight[2]

Exercise Level	DE (Mcal)	Crude Protein (g)	Lysine (g)	Ca (g)	P (g)	B₁ (mg)
Maintenance	16.7	630	27.1	20.0	14.0	30.0
Light	20.0	699	30.1	30.0	18.0	30.0
Moderate	23.3	768	33.0	35.0	21.0	46.3
Heavy	26.6	862	37.1	40.0	29.0	62.5
Very heavy	34.5	1004	43.2	40.0	29.0	62.5

DIGESTIBLE ENERGY

The term energy is synonymous with calories. It's called digestible energy (DE) because it doesn't account for fecal losses, but only for what actually gets absorbed into the blood stream. Your horse uses DE to do work, but it is also needed to sustain internal organs, secretions, digestion, and a multitude of bodily functions. Some of it is even given off as heat. But the bottom line is… the more your horse exercises the more DE he needs to maintain a normal body condition, inside and out.

If DE is insufficient, your horse will use his available stores for exercise, and actually mobilize (remove) nutrients from his own body tissues to meet the additional demands placed upon him. He'll lose body fat and muscle mass, and his bones will thin. So it is critical for his health that his maintenance requirements be met first, followed up by additional calories for exercise.

For those of you who like to crunch numbers, the digestible energy calculations that follow[3] can help you decide if your horse is getting enough calories to meet his work requirements. To use these formulas, you'll have to convert your horse's weight from pounds to kilograms; simply divide lbs by 2.2. For example, an 1100 lb horse weighs 500 kg (1000 divided by 2.2 = 500).

- **Light exercise.** DE (Mcal/day) = (0.0333 X body weight) X 1.20
- **Moderate exercise.** DE (Mcal/day) = (0.0333 X body weight) X 1.40
- **Heavy exercise.** DE (Mcal/day) = (0.0333 X body weight) X 1.60
- **Very heavy exercise.** DE (Mcal/day) = (0.0333 X body weight) X 1.90

Notice in Table 20-1 that the number of Mcal required increases steadily as work becomes more intense. But what this table doesn't tell you is how energy is metabolized — either aerobically (with oxygen) or anaerobically (without oxygen) or a combination of both. Your horse's diet should be designed for the specific way calories are burned. Some disciplines are relatively light in intensity where the heart rates rarely goes above 150 beats per minute and your horse's breathing remains constant. This type of aerobic activity uses fat or carbohydrates to fuel your horse's muscles. Exercise that increases the heart rate and calls for short bursts of energy shifts your horse's metabolism into an anaerobic mode. Carbohydrates, unlike fat, can be burned without oxygen and are therefore the predominant energy source needed for racing and other speed events. However, when carbohydrates are relied on as the main energy source, your horse will produce lactic acid, which slows him down as he waits for his muscles to recover. Fat takes the place of carbohydrates during aerobic activity and is burned gradually, thereby sparing carbohydrates from being used up too quickly. For that reason, it is beneficial to include more fat in your horse's diet; you can safely add 10 to 15% of the diet as fat.

Any runners out there? You know that when you're jogging at a slow enough pace to be able to talk to your running partner, your breathing is normal and steady, supplying your tissues with oxygen. You'll burn carbohydrates for a short time to get the flames going to begin burning fat and fat will sustain you for the majority of your run. But if you shift into a sprint, your breathing becomes faster, your heart rate increases, and you can't possibly hold a conversation because there is not enough oxygen to talk; your cells are in anaerobic mode and they're relying on the carbohydrates in your cells to give you enough energy.

The same is true for your horse. He needs carbohydrates as his main energy source to either start aerobic fat burning or fuel short bursts of anaerobic activity. Feeding enough carbohydrates is easy to do, so easy in fact, that it often crowds out fat and protein in the diet. We'll get to those nutrients in a minute, but let's talk carbs...

Carbohydrates

Carbohydrates exist in structural (fibrous) and non-structural (starch, sugar, and fructan) forms. Hay and pasture supply both of these and therefore should be offered to your horse free choice to provide an amount equal to 2 to 3 % of your horse's body weight. How can you give him a set percentage if he has all the hay he wants, you ask? You don't; you let him decide. Horses are capable of eating only what their bodies need and will self-regulate their intake when forage is consistently available. What makes them overeat is the physical discomfort and mental stress that they endure when deprived of anything to chew for several hours.

Any horse that is out on the job for long hours, whether he's covering ground on the trail, packing equipment into the wilderness, doing a 50-mile endurance race or gathering range cattle, needs to rest and replenish himself. This involves more than letting him take a breather to relax his heart and legs; it means allowing him to stop and eat from time to time. Good horsemanship entails respecting your horse's innate physical need to have something in his stomach all the time.

Please read Chapters 1 — Ground Rules for Feeding a Horse and 14 — Digestive Problems. You'll get a clearer picture of how your horse's digestive system was meant to function and how disregarding his biological needs can lead to all sorts of trouble.

Oats, corn, barley, and other cereal grains, as well as their by-products and beet pulp, offer concentrated amounts of non-structural carbohydrates and digestible fiber. As I discuss at length in Chapters 2 — Fundamentals of Carbohydrates and 9 — Fundamentals of Concentrates and By-Products, these feed sources produce the bulk of your horse's energy needs. The key is to feed small amounts, often. At least four meals a day are necessary to feed enough concentrates without overloading the digestive tract. The stomach has a relatively small capacity compared to the rest of the gastrointestinal tract and a meal that is too large can lead to colic. Too much starch at one time in the small intestine not only can cause colic but also may bring about laminitis once the hindgut bacteria get hold of it. So limit the amount of grain fed at one time to no more than 2 lbs (weigh your feed to be accurate) and combine the grain with other feedstuffs that are safer, such as hay pellets, beet pulp, and fatty feeds, to create a meal that doesn't exceed 4 lbs in weight.

One more note… if your horse is still growing he runs the risk developing osteopathic disorders when fed high amounts of starch. Please refer to Chapter 19 — Growth and Growing Old for more information on this important topic.

Fat

Fat is a significant contributor to your horse's overall energy requirement. It has more than double the calories of carbohydrates and is safe to feed. But most important, it burns slowly, sustaining your horse through periods of endurance. And since fat can be metabolized in place of carbohydrates during slow, steady, aerobic exercise, it saves the carbohydrates for those moments when your horse needs a gust of sudden energy.

There are many ways to add fat to the diet. You could simply add oil (and we'll talk amounts in a minute) or you can feed rice bran or flaxseed meal. Sunflower meal is also high in fat but is not as popular. But not all fat is created equally; each has its own fatty acid profile, making some better for your horse than others. To brush up on your fat lingo, review Chapter 3 — Fundamentals of Fats.

A few guidelines on feeding rice bran or flaxseed meal… Rice bran (and any bran, for that matter) is far too high in phosphorus to be fed safely by itself; you run the risk of upsetting the calcium to phosphorus balance. But a commercial product that has added calcium to correct this ratio is an excellent source of fat and calories. One pound of rice bran provides 1.5 Mcal and contains 15-20% fat.

The fat in rice bran contains something known as gamma oryzanol, which you may be interested in — it's a fatty substance that has a steroid-hormone like effect that appears to promote muscle development, reduce inflammation, and improve behavior. Rice bran and rice bran oil are not very concentrated, so you would need to use a rice bran extract that offers a more condensed version of gamma oryzanol. My experience with giving it to horses to optimize their performance has been very favorable.

Flaxseed meal is a must for all horses, but especially athletes because it provides high amounts of omega-3 fatty acids that protect his heart, lungs, and immune function, as well as his joints and feet. Limit the amount you feed to no more than 1/2 pound per day (that's equivalent to two 8 ounce cups in volume). This amount will give your horse 1.2 Mcal (flaxseed meal has 2.4 Mcal/lb) and with nearly 40% fat, it will make a dent in his DE needs while making him feel and look spectacular. Like rice bran, it is high in phosphorus, so never grind your own; purchase a commercial product that adds calcium and is also stabilized to prevent early spoilage.

Fat provides 9.2 Mcal per kg. That's a lot; carbohydrates have only 4.0 Mcal/kg. You can safely give a full-sized horse up to 2 cups of oil per day, which would provide 4.4 Mcal. (To see how this was calculated, go to Appendix — Crunching Numbers.) Now look at Table 20-1. You can see that by providing 2 cups of oil, you'll meet nearly 13% of a heavily exercised horse's DE need and more than 20% of the requirement for a lightly exercised horse. So fat makes a significant contribution to the overall DE content, without the bulk of grain.

One thing you should know before increasing fat — it takes a few weeks for your horse to start using fat instead of carbohydrates. To kick start fat burning, you must make him do strenuous exercise. Mild, slow training will not force his cells to choose fat for energy and he'll continue to burn up his carbohydrate supply. So, before you enter that race, run barrels, or take him on the polo field, give him at least a month of hard training with extra fat in his diet. You'll notice that he'll have more endurance and won't fatigue as easily. Plus, he'll have a smoother temperament because extra fat creates an even blood sugar and insulin response.

PROTEIN

Protein has calories, but it should never be used to meet your horse's DE requirement. Leave that to the carbohydrates and fat in his diet. Instead, protein should serve as a source of amino acids that your horse can use to build the proteins that his body needs. When we add protein to our horse's diet, we generally think of building muscle mass, but that's only one of hundreds of proteins in his body. Each tissue, whether it is muscle, bone, blood, liver, heart, arteries, skin, hair, hooves — the list goes on and on — has its own specific proteins which are made up of long, branched chains of amino acids. So the goal in feeding protein is to make sure that your horse has all the building blocks (amino acids) he requires to build and replace body tissues.

A protein source that has all the essential amino acids in proper proportion is considered complete and referred to as a high-quality protein. Chapter 4 — Fundamentals of Protein and Amino Acids discusses this in detail. But I'm not suggesting that you evaluate each feed for its amino acid content.

Instead, you need to know just one simple rule: *add a legume to cereal grains or grass to create a high-quality protein.*

There are two commonly fed legumes — alfalfa and soybean meal. Soybean meal is actually much better because it comes very close to being a perfect protein source, with all the amino acids in their right proportion. Alfalfa is not as good, but still worthwhile, and boosts the overall protein quality of your horse's forage intake.

If a legume is not added to your horse's meal, the overall diet will likely be low in several amino acids. The one that tends to be the most limiting (low) is lysine. That's why you'll often see it added to horse feeds and supplements. But there are others that should be added and most commercial performance feeds will include methionine and tyrosine, as well as the branched-chain amino acids leucine, isoleucine, and valine. Your horse cannot produce these on his own; therefore they must be in his diet. If you mix your own ingredients, be sure to add a complete protein supplement to ensure that your horse is getting what he needs.

> Soybean meal comes very close to being a perfect protein source, with all the amino acids in their right proportion.

Take a look again at Table 20-1. Look at the crude protein and lysine requirements. As expected, they both rise as exercise gets more intense. But you need to be aware that crude protein is really just a measure of how many amino acids are in the feed; it tells you nothing about the specific ones or whether or not they're in the right amounts. Lysine requirements are shown to help you boost overall protein quality, but instead of adding a lysine supplement, add a legume to provide not only lysine but other essential amino acids. The overall protein intake should be 12-14% of the diet, and even more if your horse is still growing (see Chapter 19 — Growth and Growing Old).

VITAMINS

Fresh, healthy pasture provides the highest levels of vitamins, but turnout is not always feasible, making hay the source of forage for most performance horses. Unfortunately, hay starts losing vitamins the moment grass is cut; the longer hay is stored, the more vitamins are lost. Hay that is more than a year old has virtually no vitamins left. So, supplementation is critical. I recommend a comprehensive vitamin/mineral supplement to fill in the gaps. Individual vitamins are discussed in Chapter 6 — Fundamentals of Vitamins.

However, if you feed a commercial product, it is likely fortified with nutrients. But you'll want to make sure you're feeding it according to directions, and that it contains the following key vitamins that are principally involved in meeting athletic needs:

B vitamins

There are eight B vitamins (discussed in detail in Chapter 6 — Fundamentals of Vitamins) but four of them are needed for the body to derive calories from carbohydrates and fats: thiamin (B_1), riboflavin (B_2), niacin, and pantothenic acid. The NRC only provides requirements for thiamin and riboflavin and Table 20-1 shows thiamin needs increasing as your horse requires more energy. Instead of just feeding extra thiamin and riboflavin, add a B complex preparation that offers these four B vitamins as well as the others. Many of them are marketed, however, as "blood builders" which contain iron; I do not recommend adding iron to your horse's diet unless he has a bleeding ulcer (which as a performance horse he may be inclined to develop). But hay is high in iron and too much iron can be problematic. I discuss iron in detail in Chapter 5 — Fundamentals of Minerals.

Biotin is a B vitamin that is often supplemented to enhance hoof growth. While important for hoof (and hair) health, it is part of a larger equation — healthy hoof tissue development requires high-quality protein and trace minerals. Adding 20-30 mg of biotin to a balanced diet offers hoof protection, but be patient — it typically takes 6 months to see results.

Vitamin A

Horses get plenty of beta carotene, a precursor to vitamin A, from fresh grass. But this antioxidant, by its very nature, is destroyed by the oxygen in the air. And since we cannot store hay in air-tight containers, it's bound to lose its beta carotene content. One nice way to add beta carotene to your horse's diet is to give him carrots. One to two pounds, spread out over the course of the day, will satisfy his need as well as his sweet tooth.

Vitamin D

Vitamin D, the sunshine vitamin. That is, unless your horse doesn't get much sunshine — then you need to add it to his diet. And even if he is out in the sun, the natural oils in the skin, necessary for vitamin D production, can be washed away by excessive bathing or coated with fly sprays or coat conditioners. Your horse needs vitamin D to protect his bones and joints, and maintain muscle function.

Vitamin C

This vitamin protects your horse in a variety of ways. As an antioxidant, it neutralizes damaging free radicals caused by the stress of intense exercise. As work demands increase, your horse's need for antioxidants goes up. This is especially critical for race horses to help promote healthy respiratory function, reduce inflammation, and prevent lung hemorrhages.

Vitamin C's antioxidant capability boosts your horse's immune system. It has been shown that strenuous exercise has a deleterious effect on immune function in humans, and it now appears to be true for horses[4]. While some exercise makes the immune system stronger, overworked horses are more susceptible toward developing infections.

Vitamin C is also necessary for production of collagen, the structural protein that gives bones and joints strength and maintains blood vessel integrity. During periods of vigorous training and performance, give your horse 3 to 10 mg of vitamin C per pound of body weight per day depending on his age and condition. As horses get older (above 16 years old) they produce less vitamin C on their own. Please be aware that your horse will develop a dependency on extra vitamin C, so if he's off training for a season, slowly wean him down from this high dosage.

Vitamin E and selenium

Like vitamin C, vitamin E is a potent antioxidant. During maintenance, I advise a daily dosage of 1 IU per pound of body weight but as your horse's workload increases, build up to as much as 5 IU per pound of body weight. Since vitamin E is fat-soluble, be sure the meal contains some fat to promote adequate absorption. Read about selenium in Chapter 5 — Fundamentals of Minerals because vitamin E works with selenium to protect your horse against free radical damage. But selenium can be over-supplemented with toxic results. A maintenance level between 1-3 mg per day for an 1100 lb horse is ideal; increase this amount up to 5 mg per day for the athletic horse. Heavier horses will require more, up to 0.6 ppm of the entire diet. Therefore, remember to account for all selenium sources when calculating how much, if any, to add. Please refer to Chapter 5 — Fundamentals of Minerals for more details on selenium.

MINERALS

Minerals interact, some synergistically, some blocking the action of others. That's why minerals need to be properly balanced. Most commercial feeds and supplements do this for you. Where you can run into trouble is if you feed cereal grains or bran (rice or wheat) that do not include balanced minerals. These feedstuffs, as I mentioned earlier, have considerably higher levels of phosphorus than calcium; excessive phosphorus can affect the strength of your horse's muscles and bones, potentially contributing to lameness.

Iodine, like selenium, is potentially toxic. And if selenium levels are too low, the damaging effect of iodine is enhanced, producing changes to the thyroid gland. Have your hay analyzed to determine its iodine concentration and add up iodine levels from all feedstuffs and supplements to make certain that the entire diet does not contain more than 0.6 ppm. One of the most common sources of iodine is a mineralized or blue salt block, so evaluate use of these based on how much iodine already exists in your horse's feed. Sea salt can be excessively high and I suggest avoiding it.

Trace minerals such as copper and zinc work together to produce healthy bones, cartilage, and connective tissue. They improve stress tolerance and physical endurance. Too much zinc depresses copper absorption, so keep ratios to no more than 4:1 zinc to copper to provide approximately 48 mg of zinc and 12 mg of copper per 100 lbs of body weight each day.

Avoid free choice mineral preparations. The premise behind feeding these is that your horse will take what he needs. And while I promote this idea when feeding hay, I do not recommend it for minerals. These preparations may not only be ineffective, they can be harmful. Horses are not able to discern their need for minerals (with the exception of a few electrolytes) so free choice mineral consumption can result in imbalances, deficiencies, and potentially toxic doses. Therefore, *the only way to know if your horse's mineral requirements are being met is to make sure they are added in measured amounts to his feed.*

Sodium, chloride, and other electrolytes need to be replenished after strenuous activity. And water consumption should be encouraged; even a slight level of dehydration can negatively impact performance. Please refer to

Chapter 7 — Fundamentals of Water and Electrolytes for a complete discussion on the importance of salt, water needs, and how to administer electrolyte supplements.

Calcium, phosphorus, and electrolytes

I want to spend more time on calcium, phosphorus, and other electrolytes because of their importance to your athlete.

As long as the foundation of your horse's diet is from forage, he will likely get enough calcium. It's always best, however, to have your hay supply tested to make certain that the phosphorus content is less than its calcium level. If phosphorus exceeds calcium it not only leads to developmental orthopedic disease (DOD) in growing horses, but also causes bones to demineralize as a result of excess parathyroid hormone secretion (see Chapter 13 — Metabolic and Endocrine Disorders).

It's not uncommon for performance horses to receive very little hay and copious amounts of grain. This can have many negative consequences, including ulcers, colic, and laminitis, but in terms of calcium, it is often poorly supplied. Grain, grain by-products, and other concentrates have very little calcium and an abundance of phosphorus. The resulting imbalance can lead to:

.

- Tying up (poor muscle contraction and relaxation)
- Heart arrhythmia
- Colic (reduced intestinal motility)
- Inability to regulate body temperature
- Joint stress and poor joint development in growing horses
- Porous, weak bones than can easily fracture
- Impaired bone development in young horses

One of the most common ways that athletic horses become calcium deficient is through excessive sweating. Low blood calcium, known as hypocalcemia, can lead to stress tetany, thumps, and exhausted horse syndrome.

Stress tetany is typically seen in horses that are transported long distances in hot trailers. Their muscles will spasm and become stiff.

Thumps, known as synchronous diaphragmatic flutter, is a neuromuscular problem combined with a hypersensitive phrenic nerve (the nerve that regulates movement of the diaphragm). It occurs when there are electrolyte losses, which include not only deficient calcium but also sodium, chloride, potassium, and magnesium.

Exhausted horse syndrome is just like that: Horses that exert themselves beyond their level of conditioning literally become exhausted and perspire profusely. Electrolyte imbalances lead to colic and/or tying up, and the horse shuts down.

Adequate hay will prevent these calcium-related problems and will also provide critical amounts of chloride, an electrolyte that is often undersupplied; salt does not provide enough. Your horse should have an amount of good quality hay equal to at least 2% of his body weight. If he develops a "hay belly" as a result, that is not fat — it's gas. And it is a normal by-product of microbial forage digestion in the hindgut. It indicates that his digestive tract is working and it should not be discouraged.

Exercise Induced Pulmonary Hemorrhage (EIPH)

Any fast or intense exercise can cause the lungs to bleed. In mild cases you may not even notice it, and attribute your horse's erratic behavior to nervousness. In more extreme cases, however, there's no missing the trail of blood coming from his nostrils. But no matter the severity, any blood in the lungs is a source of inflammation and potential infection. The more irritated and inflamed the horse's lungs, the smaller the airways become, setting off a continuous cycle of bleeding with each subsequent performance.

There are many theories about the exact cause of EIPH, but there's no doubt that poor nutrition can cause weakened capillaries. Add high blood pressure to the situation, which naturally occurs as heart rate increases, and it's easy to see how these tiny blood vessels can rupture.

The way to prevent EIPH is to first take care of the lungs by providing clean air for your horse to breathe. Barns are notorious for fumes and dust. See Chapter 16 — Immunity Issues for ways to help your horse's respiratory system stay healthy. Besides managing his physical surroundings, attention to his nutritional needs will make a difference. Ever know anyone who bruises easily — where just a slight bump causes a discoloration of the skin? That's a sign of a vitamin C deficiency along with not enough protein. And it's the same with your horses. Vitamin C produces the glue, collagen, that holds capillary cells together. If collagen production is diminished, capillaries rupture, plain and simple. Collagen is a protein; to make more your horse needs amino acids, building blocks of protein. If your horse's diet contains low-quality protein, he will use what few amino acids he has to take care of more life threatening concerns — collagen production will be low on his list of priorities.

Please refer to Chapter 6 — Fundamentals of Vitamins for more information on vitamin C. Please pay attention to this vitamin. It is felt that supplementation is not necessary because horses produce their own vitamin C (whereas we cannot). And it's true — they can produce vitamin C but their need may exceed their supply when stressed, both physically and mentally.

Nutrients to heal a broken bone

Bones need building blocks to heal. Check your horse's current diet and add enough of the following nutrients to bring them up to these therapeutic levels:

- Soybean meal or protein supplement — 200 g protein per 100 lbs of body weight
- Vitamin C — 20 mg per pound of body weight
- Vitamin B_6 — 0.15 mg per pound of body weight
- Silica (orthosilicic acid) — 0.4 mg per pound of body weight
- Vitamin A — 50 IU per pound of body weight
- Vitamin E — 5 IU per pound of body weight
- Alfalfa — 2:1 grass to alfalfa for calcium and phosphorus
- Magnesium — 5,000 mg per 500 lbs of body weight
- Copper — 12 mg per 100 lbs of body weight
- Zinc and manganese — 48 mg per 100 lbs body weight
- Hyaluronic acid — 10 mg per 100 lbs of body weight

Ergogenic Aids

Any unconventional nutrient that is used to enhance performance or support your horse's body against damage from strenuous exercise is called an ergogenic aid. Most of the time, however, they don't work. Any time a claim seems too good to be true, it probably is. However, there are some worth noting, even if the evidence is anecdotal, and those are the ones I'll list here.

GAMMA ORYZANOL

I've already mentioned gamma oryzanol, but let me add a little more to my previous discussion.

Gamma oryzanol's popularity is based on human use to build muscle and while there is no current method to measure changes in muscle mass in horses, there is reliable anecdotal evidence that suggests that the horse's muscle tone and condition improves when gamma oryzanol (at least 700 mg/day) is supplemented.

CREATINE

Creatine has been around for a long time in the human athletic arena. And it appears to have promise with horses as well. Though not a part of your horse's diet, since it is mainly found in meat and fish, his body is able to produce creatine. In the muscles, it is phosphorylated (phosphorus is attached) to create phosphocreatine, which plays an important role in maintaining an instant energy resource known as ATP. Without ATP, muscles would not be able to respond quickly. So the theory goes, that adding more creatine to the diet provides the muscles with extra "energy currency," giving your horse more power. It appears to be effective, especially when provided in high dosages, but much research remains.

L-CARNITINE

L-carnitine is an amino acid metabolite made from lysine and methionine inside your horse's body that is necessary in order for fat to enter the cells, so it can be burned for energy. Therefore, muscles require L-carnitine to burn fat. As I mentioned earlier, fat is a better source of energy for slow, endurance types of activities, making L-carnitine supplementation worthwhile when high amounts of fat are added to your horse's diet.

LIPOIC ACID

Lipoic acid, in the DL-alpha form, shows promise as an effective ergogenic aid. It is an antioxidant, and therefore has the ability to neutralize damaging free radicals formed during intense exercise. When fed at 10 mg per kg of body weight to Thoroughbreds, no adverse effects were found and the level of oxidative stress during activity was reduced[5]. In another study[6], higher levels of lipoic acid were given to Standardbreds with the same results. They received 25 mg per kg of body weight before exercising. Not only was there a significant reduction in free radical formation, but their muscles recovered more quickly.

Summary

Expression of athletic prowess requires the support of added nutrition. This chapter highlights important dietary changes you can make to help your horse excel at his discipline. Attention to mineral balance, antioxidants, omega-3 fatty acids, high-quality protein, and enough forage to keep the digestive system functioning normally, are all crucial elements to keep our equine athletes sound and healthy.

A working horse can develop the same health issues as any other horse and that is why I urge you to look over the other chapters in this book. They will give you a fundamental understanding of each nutrient and type of feed as well as help you deal with health conditions and changing life stages.

Endnotes

[1] *Nutrient Requirements of Horses*, Sixth Revised Edition, 2007. Washington, D.C.: National Research Council, National Academy Press: 26.

[2] Ibid., p. 298

[3] Ibid., p. 26

[4] Cappelli, K., Verini-Supplizi, A., Capomaccio, S., and Silvestrelli, M., 2007. Analysis of peripheral blood mononuclear gene expression in endurance horses by cDNA-AFLP technique. *Research in Veterinary Science 82* (3): 335-343.

[5] Williams, C.A., Hoffman, R.M, Kronfeld, D.S., Hess, T.M, Saker, K.E., and Harris, P.A., 2002. Lipoic acid as an antioxidant in mature thoroughbred geldings: a preliminary study. *Journal of Nutrition 132* (Supplement 2): 1628S-1631S.

[6] Kinnunen, S., Oksala, N., Hyyppä, S., Sen, C.K., Radak., Z, Laaksonen, D.E., Szabo, B., Jakus, J., and Atalay, M., 2009. Alpha-Lipoic acid modulates thiol antioxidant defenses and attenuates exercise-induced oxidative stress in Standardbred trotters. *Free Radical Research, June* (22): 1-9.

APPENDIX —
CRUNCHING NUMBERS

This chapter offers step by step instructions on the calculations found throughout this book. If you need further assistance with these or any other calculations, please let me know. My contact information is provided in the introduction.

Before turning to specific examples, you may find it useful to review some metric terms and common conversion factors used between the U.S. and metric systems.

U.S. and Metric System Measurements and Conversions

MEASUREMENT TERMS

Appendix Table 1 Common Measurements of the U.S. and Metric Systems		
	U.S. System	**Metric System**
Weight	Ounce (oz) Pound (lb): 16 ounces	Milligram (mg) Gram (1000 mg) Kilogram (1000 g)
Volume	Teaspoon (tsp) Tablespoon (T): 3 teaspoons Ounce (oz): 2 tablespoons Cup (C): 8 ounces Pint (pt): 16 ounces Quart (qt): 32 ounces Gallon (gal): 128 ounces	Milliliter (ml): also called cubic centimeter (cc) Deciliter (dl): 100 ml or 1/10 of a liter Liter (L): 1000 ml
Length	Inch (in) Foot (ft): 12 inches Yard (yd): 36 inches	Millimeter (mm) Centimeter (cm): 10 mm Meter (m): 1000 mm
Energy	Calorie (cal) Kilocalorie (kcal): 1000 calories Megacalorie (Mcal): 1000 kcal	Joule (J) Kilojoule (kJ): 1000 joules Megajoule (MJ): 1000 KJ

CONVERSIONS

Appendix Table 2 Weight Conversions Between U.S. and Metric Systems		
	Measure	**Conversion**
Weight		
kg and lbs	One kg equals 2.2 lbs	Multiply kg by 2.2 to get lbs Divide lbs by 2.2 to get kg
lbs, grams, and kg	One lb equals 454 grams One lb equals 0.454 kg	Multiply lbs by 454 to get grams Divide grams by 454 to get lbs Multiply lbs by 0.454 to get kg Divide kg by 0.454 to get lbs
ounces and grams	One ounce (of weight) equals 28.375 grams	Multiply ounces by 28.375 to get grams Divide grams by 28.375 to get ounces (weight)

Appendix Table 3 Concentration Conversions Between U.S. and Metric Systems		
	Measure	**Conversion**
Concentration		
Percent	Percent means one hundredth: 1/100	Convert percent to a decimal by moving the decimal to the left two places.
ppm (mg/kg)	ppm means one millionth: 1/1,000,000	Divide mg by kg. See ppm calculation.
Mcal/lb and Mcal/kg	One kg is equal to 2.2 lbs	Multiply Mcal/lb by 2.2 to get Mcal/kg Divide Mcal/kg by 2.2 to get Mcal/lb
Mcal/kg to MJ/kg	1 Mcal equals 4.184 MJ (megajoules)	Multiply Mcal/kg by 4.184 to get MJ/kg Divide MJ/kg by 4.184 to get Mcal/kg

Parts per million (ppm):

- In terms of feed concentration, ppm refers to mg/kg (since a mg is one millionth of a kg).
- To use ppm to obtain mg of a particular nutrient, convert feed weight (in lbs) to kg and then multiply by ppm to get mg.

Example: A feed contains 300 ppm of iron. That's the same as 300 mg/kg. If you feed 4 lbs of that feed, multiply 4 lbs by 0.454 to get kg. Then multiply kg by 300 mg/kg to get the iron mg.

$$4 \text{ lbs X } 0.454 \text{ kg/lb} = 1.816 \text{ kg of this feed}$$
$$1.816 \text{ kg X } 300 \text{ mg/kg} = 544.8 \text{ mg of iron}$$

- To convert mg to ppm, go in the opposite direction. Remember, ppm is the same as mg/kg. If you know that 4 lbs of a certain feed contains 545 mg of iron, first convert 4 lbs to kg: 4 lbs X 0.454 kg/lb = 1.82 kg. Next, to get mg/kg, divide 545 mg (the amount of iron in your feed) by 1.82 kg, which equals nearly 300 mg/kg (or ppm).

Appendix Table 4   Volume Conversions Between U.S. and Metric Systems

	Measure	**Conversion**
Volume		
quarts and liters	One quart equals 0.95 liters	Multiply quarts by 0.95 to get liters Divide liters by 0.95 to get quarts or
	One liter equals 1.055 quarts	Multiply liters by 1.055 to get quarts Divide quarts by 1.055 to get liters
ounces and ml	One teaspoon equals 5 ml	Multiply teaspoons by 5 to get ml Divide ml by 5 to get teaspoons
	One tablespoon equals 15 ml	Multiply tablespoons by 15 to get ml Divide ml by 15 to get tablespoons
	One ounce equals 30 ml	Multiply ounces by 30 to get ml Divide ml by 30 to get ounces

Appendix Table 5 Energy Conversions		
	Measure	**Conversion**
Energy		
MJ and Mcal	1 MJ equals 0.239 Mcal One Mcal equals 4.185 MJ	Multiply MJ by 0.239 to get Mcal Divide Mcal by 0.239 to get MJ Multiply Mcal by 4.185 to get MJ Divide MJ by 4.185 to get Mcal
MJ and kcal	1 MJ equals 239 kcal One kcal equals 0.004185 MJ	Multiply MJ by 239 to get kcal Divide kcal by 239 to get MJ Multiply kcal by 0.004185 to get MJ Divide MJ by 0.004185 to get kcal

Calculation Instructions for Specific Examples

CHAPTER 1 — GROUND RULES FOR FEEDING A HORSE

Calculating selenium content in the diet:

Using the feed in Table 1-3 Generic Feed Label, here is how you would calculate the number of grams of selenium:

The selenium content is listed as 0.20 ppm. If you were to feed 2 lbs of this feed:

Step 1: Convert pounds to kg:
            2 lb X 0.454 kg/lb = 0.908 kg of this feed

Step 2: Calculate mg of selenium:
            0.908 kg X 0.20 ppm = 0.18 mg selenium

CHAPTER 4 — FUNDAMENTALS OF PROTEIN AND AMINO ACIDS

Calculating lysine and methionine content in a feed

The National Research Council (NRC) publishes lysine requirements based on adult weight and activity level. A 500 kg horse weighs 1100 lbs. To convert kilograms to pounds, simply multiply kg by 2.2:
$$500 \text{ kg X } 2.2 = 1100 \text{ lbs}$$

The NRC publishes the lysine requirement for this horse (who is at maintenance) to be 27 grams per day.

The first scenario takes a look at 30 lbs of warm weather grass (on a dry matter basis, so this would be equivalent to approximately 33 lbs of hay, since most hays average 90% dry matter):

Step 1: To calculate the lysine level, you must first convert 30 lbs of hay to grams, since we want our lysine level to be in grams:
$$30 \text{ lbs X } 454 \text{ g/lb} = 13620 \text{ grams of hay}$$

Step 2: Looking at Table 4-2, the percent lysine in warm weather grass is 0.04%. Multiply the hay grams by this percentage, to give you grams of lysine:
$$13620 \text{ grams X } 0.0004 = 5.45 \text{ grams lysine}$$

Step 3: Table 4-2 states that there is 0.01% methionine in this hay. Multiply the hay grams by this percentage to give you grams of methionine:
$$13620 \text{ grams X } 0.0001 = 1.36 \text{ grams methionine}$$

The second scenario replaces 8 lbs (dry matter) of warm weather grass with alfalfa hay:

Step 1: Calculate the total grams of lysine in this mixed hay: 22 lbs warm weather grass and 8 lbs of alfalfa hay:

Grass Hay:
$$22 \text{ lbs X } 454 \text{ g/lb} = 9900 \text{ grams of hay}$$
$$9900 \text{ grams X } 0.0004 = 3.96 \text{ grams lysine}$$

Alfalfa Hay: Table 4-2 states that there is 0.21% lysine in alfalfa hay:

8 lbs alfalfa hay X 454 g/lb = 3632 grams of hay
3632 grams X 0.0021 = 7.63 grams lysine

Total grams of lysine in 30 lbs of this mixed hay = 3.96 + 7.63 = 11.6 grams of lysine

Step 2: Do the same for methionine.

Grass Hay:
9900 grams X 0.0001 = 1.0 grams methionine

Alfalfa Hay: Table 4-2 states that there is 0.06% methionine in alfalfa hay:
3632 grams X 0.0006 = 2.18 grams methionine

Total grams of methionine in 30 lbs of this mixed hay = 1.0 + 2.18 = 3.18 grams of methionine

Calculating grams of protein in an 8% crude protein hay

Example: How many grams of protein are provided by 18 lbs of 8% protein hay? To calculate this:

Step 1: Convert lbs of hay to grams:
18 lbs X 454 grams/lb = 8172 grams of hay

Step 2: Multiply the grams of hay by the protein percentage:
8172 grams X 0.08 = 654 grams protein

Example: How many grams of protein are provided by 16 lbs of this same hay? And does it meet the 630 gram/day requirement?

Step 1: 16 X 454 grams/lb = 7264 grams of hay

Step 2: 7264 grams X 0.08 = 581 grams protein

This amount is short by 49 grams if the horse requires 630 grams of protein per day. You would need either to feed more of this hay or supplement protein with meals.

CHAPTER 5 — FUNDAMENTALS OF MINERALS

Macromineral content

Macrominerals refer to calcium, magnesium, phosphorus and others. Refer to Chapter 5 for a complete list. They are expressed as g/lb or a percentage.

Example: Calcium level in your hay is 0.10% or 0.46 g/lb. How many grams is your horse getting in 20 lbs of hay?

1)   Percentage method:

Step 1: Convert 20 lbs of hay to grams:
20 lbs X 454 g/lb = 9080 grams of hay

Step 2: Multiply grams by the percentage:
9080 grams X 0.0010 = 9.08 grams of calcium in 20 lbs of hay

2)   Concentration method:

Since the concentration is in grams per pound, there is no need to convert lbs of hay to grams.

Simply multiply lbs of hay by the concentration:
20 lbs X 0.46 g/lb = 9.2 grams of calcium in 20 lbs of hay

The amounts are close using both formulas, but not exact due to round off variation in the analysis.

Micromineral content

Macrominerals include iron, zinc, copper, and others. Refer to Chapter 5 for a complete list. These are expressed as mg/kg or ppm. Sometimes they are referred to as mg/lb.

Example: Iron content in your hay is 107 ppm (same as mg/kg) or 48 mg/lb. How many mg of iron are in 20 lbs of hay?

1)   PPM method (same as mg/kg):

Step 1: Convert lbs of hay to grams:
20 lbs X 454 g/lb = 9080 grams of hay

Step 2: Divide grams by 1000 to convert grams to kg:
9080 ÷ 1000 = 9.080 kg of hay

Step 3: Multiply kg of hay by concentration:
9.080 kg X 107 ppm (mg/kg) = 971.56 mg of iron
in 20 lbs of hay

2)   Mg/lb concentration method:

Since this concentration is already in lbs, there is no need
to convert lbs of hay to grams. Simply multiply lbs of hay
by the provided concentration to get mg of iron:
20 lbs X 48 mg/lb = 960 mg of iron in 20 lbs of
hay

The difference in results between the two methods is due to the
measurement variation from the analysis procedure.

Determining the calcium to phosphorus ratio of your feeding plan

Example: You feed the following diet:
12 lbs of grass hay (Ca 0.47%; P 0.26%)
8 lbs of alfalfa hay (Ca 1.22%; P 0.28%)
3 lbs of a commercial feed (Ca average 1.00%; P 0.60%)

Calcium calculations:

1) Grass hay:
12 lbs X 454 g/lb = 5448 grams of grass hay
5448 grams X 0.0047 = 25.61 grams calcium

2) Alfalfa hay:
8 lbs X 454 g/lb = 3632 grams of alfalfa hay
3632 grams X 0.0122 = 44.31 grams calcium

3) Commercial feed:
> 3 lbs X 454 g/lb = 1362 grams commercial feed
> 1362 X 0.01 = 13.62 grams calcium

4) Total calcium in diet:
> 25.61 + 44.31 + 13.62 = 83.54 grams calcium

Phosphorus calculations:

1) Grass hay:
> 12 lbs X 454 g/lb = 5448 grams grass hay
> 5448 X 0.0026 = 14.16 grams phosphorus

2) Alfalfa hay:
> 8 lbs X 454 g/lb = 3632 grams of alfalfa hay
> 3632 grams X 0.0028 = 10.17 grams phosphorus

3) Commercial feed:
> 3 lbs X 454 g/lb = 1362 grams commercial feed
> 1362 X 0.0060 = 8.17 grams phosphorus

4) Total phosphorus in diet:
> 14.16 + 10.17 + 8.17 = 32.50 grams phosphorus

Calcium to phosphorus ratio:

Calcium grams divided by phosphorus grams:
> $83.54 \div 32.50 = 2.57$
> Expressed as a Ca:P ratio: 2.57:1

Calculating iron concentration (ppm)

Example: 30 lbs of forage contains 2000 mg of iron. Here is how the ppm was calculated:

Step 1: Convert lbs of hay to grams:
> 30 lbs X 454 g/lb = 13620 grams of forage

Step 2: Convert grams to kg:
13620 grams divided by 1000 will give you kg. So, 13620 grams is equivalent to 13.620 kg. We are converting grams to kg because ppm is the same as mg/kg.

Step 3: Calculate ppm (mg/kg) in the hay:
Since we know there are 2000 mg of iron in the diet and the total diet weighs 13.620 kg, we simply divide 2000 by 13.620 to get mg of iron per kg of hay:

$$2000 \text{ mg} \div 13.260 \text{ kg} = 146.8 \text{ mg/kg or 147 ppm}$$

Calculating selenium content

First example: The example used was a diet that contained 30 lbs of dry matter. If the diet contains 5 ppm, there would be 68 mg of selenium in that diet. This, of course, is way too high, but here is how the 68 mg is calculated:

Method 1: Parts per million is the same as mg per kg of feed. 30 lbs of feed can be converted to kg by simply dividing by a conversion factor of 2.2 lbs per kg:

$$30 \text{ lbs} \div 2.2 \text{ lb/kg} = 13.64 \text{ kg of feed}$$

Since the diet contains 5 mg of selenium for every kg, multiply 13.64 by 5:

$$13.64 \text{ kg X 5 mg/kg} = 68.2 \text{ mg selenium}$$

Method 2: Another way to look at parts per million (ppm) is the number of millionths there are in a feed. 5 ppm is the same as 5/1,000,000 or 5 millionths. Using our 30 lbs of feed, first convert 30 lbs to mg, since we want our selenium value to be in mg:

Step 1: There are 454,000 mg in one lb, so multiply 30 by 454,000:

$$30 \text{ lbs X 454,000 mg/lb} = 13,620,000 \text{ mg of feed}$$

Step 2: Multiply by the fraction 5/1,000,000 (5 millionths):

$$13,620,000 \text{ X } 5/1,000,000 = 68.2 \text{ mg selenium}$$

Second example: The next example was a diet that contains 0.1 ppm of selenium. How many mg of selenium does it contain? Using our 30 lbs of feed, we can do this one of two ways:

Method 1: Using the 0.1 mg/kg route:

$$30 \text{ lbs} \div 2.2 \text{ lb/kg} = 13.64 \text{ kg of feed}$$
$$13.64 \text{ kg X 0.1 mg/kg} = 1.36 \text{ mg selenium}$$

Method 2: Using the 0.1 ppm route, we'll get the same result:
30 lbs X 454,000 mg/lb = 13,620,000 mg of feed
13,620,000 mg X 0.1/1,000,000 = 1.36 mg selenium

CHAPTER 6 — FUNDAMENTALS OF VITAMINS

Calculating vitamin C supplementation amount

The maximum amount of vitamin C to supplement is suggested at 44 mg per kg of body weight. So, let's say you have a horse that weighs 1000 lbs.

Step 1: Convert pounds to kg by dividing pounds by 2.2 lb/kg:
1000 lbs ÷ 2.2 lb/kg = 454.5 kg of body weight

Step 2: Multiply the number of kg that your horse weighs by 44 mg/kg:
454.5 kg X 44 mg/kg = 19,998 mg vitamin C

To covert mg to grams, simply move the decimal over three places, or divide by 1000:
19,998 mg is equivalent to 19.998 grams, which can logically be rounded up to 20 grams vitamin C per day.

Calculating vitamin A intake

Our example used a horse weighing 400 kg, and a maintenance requirement of 30 IU/kg of body weight:
Multiply the weight (that's already in kg in this example) by 30:
400 kg X 30 IU/kg = 12,000 IU of vitamin A per day

CHAPTER 13 — METABOLIC AND ENDOCRINE DISORDERS

Thyroid gland

In this section, the iodine intake was calculated for 20 lbs of grass hay and 1 ounce of salt (both iodized plain salt and sea salt). Here is how it was calculated:

20 pounds of grass hay with an iodine concentration of 0.2 mg/kg dry matter (which is the same as ppm):

> **Step 1:** Convert lbs to kg:
> 20 lbs X 0.454 kg/lb = 9.08 kg of hay

> **Step 2**: Multiply kg by ppm to get mg:
> 9.08 kg X 0.2 mg/kg = 1.82 mg iodine in the hay

1 ounce of iodized table salt with an iodine content of 70 mg/kg:

> **Step 1:** Convert one ounce of table salt to kg:
> 0.454 kg/lb ÷ 16 ounces/lb = 0.028 kg table salt

> **Step 2:** Calculate mg of iodine:
> 0.028 kg X 70 mg/kg = 1.99 mg iodine in 1 ounce of table salt

1 ounce of sea salt with an iodine content of 2000 mg/kg:

> **Step 1:** Convert one ounce of sea salt to kg:
> 0.454 kg/lb ÷ 16 ounces/lb = 0.028 kg sea salt

> **Step 2:** Calculate mg of iodine:
> 0.028 kg X 2000 mg/kg = 56 mg of iodine in 1 ounce of sea salt

CHAPTER 17 — STRESS AND BEHAVIOR

Calculating additional hay requirements during cold weather

For every 1.8° F below the lower critical temperature (LCT), horses need 2.5% more calories. The LCT ranges from 5° C to -15° C[1] or 41° to 5° F, depending on the horse's adaptation to the cold. So, for this example, LCT is 30° F and the temperature falls to 10° F.

To do this calculation, you need to know two things[2]:

1) Your horse's total energy needs (Mcal) in mild weather based on weight and exercise level: In this example, the horse weighs 1100 lbs and is not doing any work, and his energy requirement is 16.7 Mcal per day.

2) Your hay's digestible energy (DE): In this example, one pound of hay provides 1.0 Mcal/lb.

Step 1: Since the energy needs increase by 2.5% for each 1.8° F increment, the additional energy needs equal:
16.7 Mcal/day X 0.025 = 0.42 Mcal/day of additional energy needed for each 1.8° F increment

Step 2: The temperature fell 20° F below the LCT, so calculate the total additional energy requirement:

First, there are 11.1 increments that the temperature dropped: 20° ÷ 1.8° = 11.1
Next, multiply 11.1 by the amount of energy needed per 1.8° increment:
11.1 X 0.42 Mcal/day = 4.67 Mcal/day needed for this temperature drop

Step 3: The hay in this example has 1.0 Mcal/lb. Calculate the number of pounds needed to provide 4.67 Mcal:
4.67 Mcal/day ÷ 1.0 Mcal/lb = 4.67 lbs/day of hay, rounded up to 5 pounds.

CHAPTER 18 — BREEDING, PREGNANCY, AND LACTATION

Calculating lysine content in 20 lbs of grass hay plus 10 lbs of alfalfa

- Grass hay offers approximately 0.5% lysine
- Alfalfa hay offers approximately 0.9% lysine

Step 1: Convert pounds of hay to grams since lysine is fed in grams:
Grass: 20 lbs X 454 g/lb = 9080 grams of grass hay
Alfalfa: 10 lbs X 454 g/lb = 4540 grams of alfalfa hay

Step 2: Multiply grams of hay by the lysine concentration:
Grass: 9080 grams X .005 = 45.4 grams lysine in grass hay
Alfalfa: 4540 grams X .009 = 40.9 grams lysine in alfalfa hay

Step 3: Add lysine concentrations together:
$$45.4 + 40.9 = 86.3 \text{ total grams of lysine}$$

Energy needs of an 1100 lb lactating mare during first two months

In this example, we know that for every kg of milk produced, a mare needs to have 0.8 Mcal more per day.

Step 1: Determine the number of lbs of milk produced. On average, a mare will produce 4% of her body weight during the first two months.
$$1100 \text{ lbs X } 0.04 = 44 \text{ lbs of milk produced}$$

Step 2: Convert lbs of milk to kg:
$$44 \text{ lbs} \div 2.2 \text{ lb/kg} = 20 \text{ kg of milk}$$

Step 3: Determine her increased energy need:
$$20 \text{ kg X } 0.8 \text{ Mcal/kg} = 16 \text{ Mcal}$$

CHAPTER 19 — GROWTH AND GROWING OLD

Calculating foal weight

The example used is a three-month old foal with a girth circumference of 43 inches.

Step 1: Calculate his weight at 7 to 28 days using this formula:
[Girth (inches) – 25] divided by 0.07 = weight in lbs
$$[43 \text{ inches} – 25] \div 0.07 = 257.1 \text{ lbs}$$

Step 2: For 28 to 90 days (which our example fits in), add 10% to the above calculation:
$$257.1 \text{ X } 0.10 = 25.7$$
$$257.1 + 25.7 = 282.8, \text{ which was rounded up to 283 lbs}$$

Weanling's protein needs met by sample diet

Weanlings should have 170 grams of protein per 100 lbs of body weight. In this example, we have a 600 lb weanling. He's fed:
- 6 lbs concentrate (14% CP)
- 8 lbs grass hay (10 % CP)
- 4 lbs alfalfa (18% CP)

Step 1: Calculate his protein requirement based on his weight:

170 grams X 6 = 1020 grams/day of protein required

(We multiply by 6 because he weighs 600 lbs and he needs 170 grams of protein for every 100 lbs of body weight.)

Step 2: Calculate the grams of protein for each food source remembering to first convert lbs to grams:

6 lbs concentrate (14% CP) provides: 6 lbs X 454 g/lb X 0.14 = 381 grams protein

8 lbs grass hay (10% CP) provides: 8 lbs X 454 g/lb X 0.10 = 363 grams protein

4 lbs alfalfa hay (18% CP) provides: 4 lbs X 454 g/lb X 0.18 = 327 grams protein

Step 3: Add the three amounts together and compare to his protein requirement:

381 + 363 + 327 = 1071 grams protein in diet

Compared to his requirement (1020 grams of protein), this hay mixture is slightly more than adequate and would be appropriate to feed.

CHAPTER 20 — ATHLETES

Since fat provides 9.2 Mcal/kg, how many Mcal are in 2 cups of oil?

To do this, you must first change ounces of oil into kg. You'll need to have the following bits of information:
- Two cups equals 16 fluid ounces
- Each fluid ounce of oil weighs 30 grams
- There are 1000 grams in a kg

Step 1: Convert fluid ounces of oil to grams of oil:

16 oz X 30 g/oz = 480 grams of oil

Step 2: Convert grams to kg:

480 g X 1 kg/1000 g = 0.480 kg of oil

Step 3: Calculate Mcal in the oil:

0.480 kg X 9.2 Mcal/kg = 4.4 Mcal in 2 cups of oil

Endnotes

[1] Smith, B.P., 2009. *Large Animal Internal Medicine, Fourth Edition*. St. Louis, Missouri: Mosby Elsevier: 160.

[2] *Nutrient Requirements of Horses, Sixth Revised Edition*. 2006. Washington, DC: National Academies Press.

INDEX OF TERMS

CPSIA information can be obtained
at www.ICGtesting.com
Printed in the USA
BVOW06*0026190117
473816BV00011B/147/P